SYNTHESE LIBRARY

STUDIES IN EPISTEMOLOGY,

LOGIC, METHODOLOGY, AND PHILOSOPHY OF SCIENCE

Managing Editor:

JAAKKO HINTIKKA, *Florida State University, Tallahassee*

Editors:

DONALD DAVIDSON, *University of California, Berkeley*
GABRIËL NUCHELMANS, *University of Leyden*
WESLEY C. SALMON, *University of Pittsburgh*

VOLUME 155

R. J. NELSON

Truman P. Handy Professor of Philosophy
Case Western Reserve University

THE LOGIC
OF MIND

KLUWER ACADEMIC PUBLISHERS

DORDRECHT / BOSTON / LONDON

Library of Congress Cataloging in Publication Data

Nelson, R. J. (Raymond John), 1917-
    The logic of mind.

    (Synthese library ; 155)
    Bibliography: p.
    Includes index.
    1. Mechanism (Philosophy) 2. Mind and body.
3. Intellect. I. Title. II. Series: Synthese
library ; v. 155.
BD435.N44 1989   128'.2   88-8219

ISBN 90-277-2819-4
ISBN 90-277-2822-4 (Pbk.)

Published by Kluwer Academic Publishers,
P.O. Box 17, 3300 AA Dordrecht, The Netherlands.

Kluwer Academic Publishers incorporates
the publishing programmes of
D. Reidel, Martinus Nijhoff, Dr W. Junk and MTP Press.

Sold and distributed in the U.S.A. and Canada
by Kluwer Academic Publishers,
101 Philip Drive, Norwell, MA 02061, U.S.A.

In all other countries, sold and distributed
by Kluwer Academic Publishers Group,
P.O. Box 322, 3300 AH Dordrecht, The Netherlands.

printed on acid free paper

The proper study of mankind is
man — Pope

The proper study of mankind is
invertebrate neurobiology —
Society for Neuroscience, 1975.

If God intended me to understand my
mind, he wouldn't have given me one —
Vernon Rowland

The proper study of mankind is the
science of design — Herbert Simon

TO MY CHILDREN
  Susan
  Steven
  Peter

TABLE OF CONTENTS

PREFACE   xiii

CHAPTER I / INTRODUCTION   1

1. The Revival of Mental Philosophy   1
2. Mechanism   2
3. Naturalism   6
4. Two Problems of Mind   12

CHAPTER II / WHAT IS A RULE OF MIND?   15

1. Signals and Control   15
2. Turing Machines   18
3. Logic and Logic of Mind   24
4. Nerve Networks and Finite Automata   37
5. Computer Logic   45
6. Glimpses from Psychology   53
7. Summary on Rules   56

CHAPTER III / BEHAVIOR AND STRUCTURE   59

1. Some Varieties of Automata   59
2. Fitting and Guiding   75
3. Empirical Realism   83

CHAPTER IV / MECHANISM – ARGUMENTS PRO AND CON   89

1. Thinking Machines   89
2. The Argument from Analogy   92
3. Psychological Explanation and Church's Thesis   100
4. On the Dissimilarity of Behaviors   101
5. Computers, Determinism, and Action   108
6. Summary to the Main Argument from Analogy   116

CHAPTER V / FUNCTIONALISM, RATIONALISM, AND COGNI-
TIVISM   119

1. Psychological and Automaton States   120
2. Behaviorism   131
3. Neorationalism   142
4. Cognitivism   157

CHAPTER VI / THE LOGIC OF ACCEPTANCE   162

1. Universals, Gestalten, and Taking   164
2. Acceptance   171
3. Expectation   186
4. Family Resemblances   195

CHAPTER VII / PERCEPTION   199

1. Perceptual Objects   199
2. Perception Perspectives   208

CHAPTER VIII / BELIEF AND DESIRE   212

1. Perceptual Belief   213
2. Desire   218
3. A Model of Desire   225
4. Standing Belief – Representation   232

CHAPTER IX / REFERENCE AND TRUTH   251

1. Pure Semantics versus User Semantics   251
2. Belief Sentences   253
3. Denotation   263
4. A Theory of Truth   270
5. Adequacy   273

CHAPTER X / TOWARD MEANING   280

1. Linguistic Meaning   280
2. Propositions   282
3. Intensions of Names and Predicates   292

CHAPTER XI / PSYCHOLOGICAL THEORY AND THE MIND-
BRAIN PROBLEM   304

    1. Realism and Reduction   305
    2. Explanation   311
    3. Free Will   319
    4. Mental Occurrents   322

TABLE OF FIGURES, FORMULAS, AND TABLES   337

NOTES   339

BIBLIOGRAPHY   369

INDEX   381

PREFACE

This book presents a mechanist philosophy of mind. I hold that the human mind is a system of *computational* or *recursive* rules that are embodied in the nervous system; that the material presence of these rules accounts for perception, conception, speech, belief, desire, intentional acts, and other forms of intelligence.

In this edition I have retained the whole of the first edition except for discussion of issues which no longer are relevant in philosophy of mind and cognitive psychology. Earlier reference to disputes of the 1960's and 70's between hard-line empiricists and neorationalists over the psychological status of grammars and language acquisition, for instance, has simply been dropped.

In place of such material I have entered some timely or new topics and a few changes. There are brief references to the question of computer *versus* distributed processing (connectionist) theories. Many of these questions dissolve if one distinguishes as I now do in Chapter II between free and embodied algorithms. I have also added to my comments on artifical intelligence some reflections on Searle's Chinese Translator.

The irreducibility of machine functionalist psychology in my version or any other has been exaggerated. Input, output, and state entities are token identical to physical or biological things of some sort, while a machine system as a collection of recursive rules is type identical to representatives of equivalence classes. This mild technicality emerges in Chapter XI. It entails that so-called "anomalous monism" is right in one sense and wrong in another.

Cognitivism, notably Fodor's, is based on machine functionalism but the differences with my mechanism are too deep to pass over lightly, especially as regards mental representations. So cognitivism comes in for discussion in several places, mainly in Chapter V. For cognitivism representations are laden with meaning, and the intentionality of beliefs comes down to the semantics of an internal language of thought. For mechanism preceptual beliefs have intentionality independent of any language and the semantics of natural language is derived from perception. Cognitivism aims to map out foundations of cognitive science proceeding from quite general philosophical intuitions. Mechanism aims at philosophical justification of the computer hypothesis, which others generally assume, by trying to show that a few detailed, piecemeal models satisfy conditions recommended by our "folk" intuitions.

I am irritated by holism. Hill (1987) thinks that any definition of 'perceptual belief' must necessarily allude to past belief, and hence only implicit definition is possible. Mine is explicit, so he thinks my theory is flawed. For him a theory of belief and other attitudes is attained by canvassing principles of Folk Psychology everyone knows, and explaining their logical and semantical properties. These principles are *ascriptive*; so for him there is no question of individuation as there is for all functionalists. Since I am a materialist in matters of mind, I am driven to reductive definition (via machine theory). Holistic principles of belief, desire, action, etc. interaction are something else, and my task is to show the reduced idea satisfies them.

The book falls into two parts: Chapters I through V plus XI deal with philosophical matters and VI through X with development of a theory using abstract turing machine and automaton models.

Chapter I lays the scene and distinguishes two kinds of mental philosophy: one focuses on intelligence, the nature of language, cognition, and belief; the other on the classical mind-body problem – consciousness, sentience, pains, qualia, and the like. Except for the end of Chapter XI the book is about cognition and perception, not pains and raw feels.

Chapter II introduces from a historical point of view the fundamental ideas of automaton and turing machine and their use in logics, primitive nerve net theory, generative grammar, computer circuit theory, and early forms of machine theories of mind.

Chapter III goes into considerable detail about function and structure: behavioral equivalence, homomorphisms, realization and embodiment of structures, and introduces a realistic thesis based on a Quinean notion of descriptions that guide versus descriptions that fit, behavior.

Chapter IV presents Turing-type arguments in support of mechanism and defends it once more against what I regard as misapplications of Gödel's Theorems, and against behavorist accounts of intentionality.

Chapter V contains a refutation of Rylean and Skinnerian behaviorism, a criticism of machine functionalism, an analysis of Chomsky's theories of acquisition and knowledge of grammars, and a review of cognitivism. All this by way of providing contrasting background for mechanism.

Chapters VI and VII initiate plausibility arguments for mechanism starting with perception. I give conditions (among them Wittgensteinian strictures

against common defining properties for perceived types) an explication
should satisfy and construct a sequence of explicit definitions (explications)
in automata-theoretic terms that satisfy the conditions. Along the way I
give explications of *taking* as an intentional act, and of *expectation* using
an application of an idea of self-reference going back to Gödel and the
recursion theorem.

Chapter VIII introduces perceptual belief, desire, and action in automaton
terms and shows they collectively satisfy certain holistic folk principles. I
mean this to be a threat to Quine's version of Brentano's Thesis, which says
that there is no getting out of the circle of intentional concepts definitionally.

Chapters IX and X introduce in a rather tentative way the semantics of
a core language — one that is first order, tenseless, and contains only predicates that apply in direct percetual experience (sensible predicates, expressed
in occasion sentences). This includes a theory of reference and truth which is
meant to satisfy both Hartry Field's demands for reference and Michael
Dummett's demands for a truth theory. The central idea is that reference
derives from the intentionality. Intentions are introduced in terms of *ways*
of computing — based on the idea of partial recursive function —, which
is a kind of naturalization of Fregean *sense.*

Chapter XI discusses explanation and prediction in psychology when
construed mechanistically; reducibility; Searle's arguments against computer
explanations; and varied topics about the will and morality — all in a pretty
loosely—connected way. It ends with a reintroduction of type identity for
mental occurrents (qualia and feelings) and speculates about causal properties
of sentient states.

There are many cross-references in a book such as this. The conventions
used are as follows. References to sections of chapters are as in 'Section II.2'
which means Section 2 of Chapter II; for figures, 'Figure III.1' means Figure
1 of Chapter III; tables, 'Table IV.II' which means Table II of Chapter IV;
labelled formulas, 'VI(6)' which means expression (6) in Chapter VI; and for
notes, 'Note VII.18.' Notes appear at the end of the book before Bibliography.
For the reader's convenience I have included a Table of Figures, Formulas,
and Tables before Notes. All symbolic conventions are explained in the text.

I am indebted to so many over so long a period of time that is is hard to
track down the influences on my thought. My earliest serious reading was
of the writings of Dewey and Peirce. The idea of mind in all aspects as inferential is certainly Peircean. But still I learned most from Carnap, especially
his way of looking at philosophical problems, although of course I long ago
dropped the unrelieved positivism, as did Carnap himself. The idea of a rule

of mind is similar to a Chomskian rule of grammar but it is Chomsky extended beyond concerns of language, is less rationalistic, and mechanized. My borrowing of the thought of Putnam and Quine reveals itself throughout the book. I do not, however, have any reason to believe that either of these men would advocate everything in or even much of, this book. The key to the mind, I am convinced, is Gödel's work and Post's anticipation of what today we call a 'mechanist' or 'computationalist' theory of mind. Although neither man was a professional philosopher or psychologist, the work of both makes possible a revolution in our study of the human being.

During the writing of this book I have had many fruitful, enlightening, and oftentimes chastening interchanges with Noam Chomsky, Leon Harmon, Rick Herder, Christopher Hill, Mortimer Kadish, Vernon Rowland, and quite especially, Hendrieka Nelson. Over a period of many years I have been philosophically stimulated and encouraged by my good friends Mortimer Kadish and Jack Kaminsky.

While planning the present edition I have gratefully taken advantage of numerous suggestions and criticisms from (in addition to those friends mentioned above) Jerry Aronson, David Helman, Robert Rynasiewicz, Stuart Shanker, and Tak Yagasawa.

June, 1988   R. J. NELSON

CHAPTER I

INTRODUCTION

1. THE REVIVAL OF MENTAL PHILOSOPHY

Mental philosophy sank to a low ebb in Western thought in the second quarter of this century. During that dry period, psychology was dominated by behaviorism, and philosophy by a somewhat attenuated form of positivism. The rule of the day was to look outward: the nature of mind, thought, perception, and emotion was to be discovered in external animal and human behavior, not in the inward probings of consciousness. The practice was to rule out not only the private images, passing thoughts and pains, which were generally held to be accessible to introspection alone, but physiological processes of the brain as well. Internal states, physical as well as mental, were banished: these states, maintained one of the leading proponents of the movement, are not relevant in a causal analysis of the behavior of living systems (Skinner, 1953, p. 35). Thus mental entities of all kinds together with the brain and its operations were segregated from mental science, which did not leave much for the theoretical psychologist or the philosopher to do except defend the narrow methodology.

The recent revival of cognitive psychology and mental philosophy can be attributed to two independent developments. The first was a chain of successive relaxations of the positivist theory of meaning. The second was the invention of the stored-program digital computer. The net effect of changes in the theory of meaning has been to liberalize construction of psychological theories. What counts as scientific sense today no longer has to be restricted to directly observable actions and reactions of the organism but might include both conscious and unconscious mental states and perceptual, linguistic, and cognitive processes inside the head. Roughly speaking, psychology is now allowed to employ concepts having approximately the same methodological status as those admitted in physics. Any concept that fits coherently into a theory otherwise having operational significance is legitimate. In particular, when the theoretician talks about data that are open to public inspection, he does not necessarily exclude subjective images, feelings, hopes, and memories — all of which at an earlier day were considered to be strictly private. Internal mental entities, then, have regained their credentials as data fit for psychological and philosophical study. Those very things which had been banished under logical positivism quickly became central concerns of neuroscientists as well as of psychologists and computer and systems engineers.

The digital computer brought in its train a host of ideas relevant to the study of mind. First, 'artificial intelligence', if not quite a household expression, nevertheless identifies a lively and controversial field of research, especially in the United States. Most informed persons are aware by now that computers have been programmed to play chess, prove mathematical theorems, compose music, and draw pictures. Many of us have engaged in more than one dispute over whether or not machines can think. Computer simulation of natural language processes is a significant research area in psychology and psychiatry. Second, the mainstream of research in psycholinguistics springs from the same source as computer logic. This is especially true of the present and near past work in transformational grammars. Third, mental philosophy itself, in particular functionalism, cognitivism and mechanism, quite explicitly draws on computer concepts and analogies. I shall trace the steps leading from the early days of computer science to current forms of mechanistic philosophy in the next chapter, so there is no need to dwell on more of the details here.

The logic of mind that is developed in this book is a child of these developments. In fact as I see it language, thought, belief, perception, and expectation, indeed all human cognitive abilities and traits, are proper targets for logical analysis and theorizing; and the style of the approach has been influenced by computer logic and programming concepts more than anything else. Thus many of the mental phenomena that had been legislated out of scientific practice by an overly restrictive empiricism are now the subject of a philosophical theory that is grounded in computer logic. This unites the two historical developments.

2. MECHANISM

The logic of mind guides all of our cognitive processes and activities. This logic is not the logic of the textbooks, and having it does not imply that we think or act correctly all of the time. However it does imply that the mind follows a system of rules which operate below the level of consciousness for the most part.[1] According to the theory I shall advance, the logic of mind is similar to the system of rules that governs the operations of a digital computer and hence it is correct to say that a mind is 'machine-like'.

Traditional mechanism teaches that the mind is the brain and that the brain functions under the ordinary laws of physics and chemistry. In this tradition mechanism is first and foremost *materialism*: the mind and brain are identical and there is no hovering spiritual stuff or covert homunculi guiding cognition. Just as a computer circuit has or is guided by an inbuilt logic, so a brain has its inner logic; but the brain is all there is, and its logic is determined by its purely physical make-up. This theory is traceable to Democritus and Lucretius and in somewhat different form in modern times to Hobbes and La Mettrie.

But this theory is not mine. The ontology is essentially the same: there is no separable, ghost-like mind in my version of mechanism either. But the conception of a rule in the logic of mind is quite different than that of a law of physics of biochemistry. The logic of mind is relatively *independent* of this or that brain stuff and its physical laws. Conceivably, the same logic could govern *substantial* minds, a view which is quite close to Leibniz' pluralistic idealism. As others before me have argued, the theory of the logic of mind is perfectly compatible with materialism, dualism, idealism, or any other mind-body philosophy (cf. Burks, 1972/73; Putnam, 1960). So in advocating this theory, I am not bound to classical materialism. The version I accept is closer to naturalism, a realistic naturalism which has certain affinities to Aristotle. The rules constituting a logic of mind are *formally distinct* from the material (or possibly other) medium they are embodied in, and in this respect, the theory resembles classical 'moderate' realism rather than nominalism in any of its forms, materialistic or idealistic. Hence the historical similarity is to Aristotle and Scotus, not Lucretius. In contemporary terms, the body *realizes* the logic of mind much as physical space realizes formal geometry or the arithmetic of numbers realizes formal number theory.

One should not, however, stake too much on the likeness to realism. What is informed by the logic of mind is not undifferentiated matter, but ordinary physical objects such as brains or assemblages of hardware. Further, the logic of mind could be the same in a possible world of silicon-based 'organic' compounds that provide the basic ingredients of living things. Or, pushing further into the world of science fiction, men in such a world might be conscious robots guided by exactly the same logic as ours. Moreover your logic and mine are probably not identical although they are essentially the same. The rules that guide A are the same as those that guide B in the sense that a Nägeli edition of Bach is like a Bach-Gesellschaft edition, not in the sense that two copies of a Nägeli are alike. So the analogy to Aristotelian realism is pretty weak; two individuals composed of radically different matters could have identical logics (form), while two individuals composed of the very same species-specific stuff could have different guiding logics.

A curious thing about the logic of mind is that its theory is an application of certain parts of logical theory, as is the logic of computers. It would not be amiss to call this theory 'the logic of the logic of mind' except for the pleonastic ring. For the mind *has* a logic by which it indeed operates while at the same time logic is used to *describe* these operations. To avoid the slightly pretentious 'logic of logic' I used 'theory of the logic of mind' above, but in the remainder of the book I will use 'logic of mind' ambiguously, sometimes referring to the theory and at others to the subject.

I hope that the brief comparisons with other thought suggest that the logic of mind is a *metaphysical doctrine*. Human cognitive activity is not merely amenable to computer simulation or to modeling by certain logical formulas. The logic of mind is literally in the mind and guides it, as should of course be quite plain from my tagging the theory 'realistic'.[2] For the time being it will perhaps suffice to say that these rules are *recursive* and are represented in the theory by *nondeterministic finite automata* (NFA). The concept NFA will be explained in the next chapter. Quite a bit hinges on 'represented,' which we cannot dwell on yet except to say that the logic of mind is essentially equivalent to that of some finite automaton without being exactly the same. Here, again, there is considerable play on 'same' and 'different' that will require careful attention. For the moment, given the provisos mentioned, the logic of mind is that of a nondeterministic, finite automaton.

Not all philosophers who would endorse a similar type of mechanism also accept the qualifier 'nondeterministic'.[3] Briefly, a nondeterministic system is one in which an application of a rule of the system can be followed by application of some other (or the same) rule at one time and an entirely different one at another. The situation is exactly the same as that of a proof context in formal logic: rules may be applied in any order. The principal difference is that in formal logic the application is consciously determined while in mental logic application is for the most part unconscious. Both cases, the conscious and unconscious, I will show, are entirely compatible with underlying *deterministic* bodily processes. This somewhat counterintuitive theory marks another way in which I part company with traditional mechanistic materialism, which makes no room for nondeterministic phenomena.

The term 'mechanism' has so many connotations from which I should like to insulate the reader's mind that it is tempting not to use it. To most persons the term connotes cogs, wheels, and levers, and perhaps electronic devices, and to philosophers it connotes determinism and conformity to the laws of physics. As just explained, I reject both connotations of the term. Further, classical mechanism is nonteleological while mine is not. I take a necessary character of mind to be its intentionality, but unlike Brentano, believe that in principle this essential trait can be *explained*. Thus the logic of mind accommodates purpose in a way quite different than classical mechanism, which denies purpose altogether of all events in the universe. In view of these deviations from the traditional usage, why use the term? There is not that much in a word. There are three reasons.

The first is that the newer meaning of 'mechanism' which I am using is common in science. Mathematicians have talked about mechanical and effective methods for a long time, and in this century — following Hilbert — of mechanical proof and decision procedures in logic. Moreover, computers are *machines*, and the rules they follow are like the rules of mind. The theory of Turing machines and other automata is sometimes called 'mathematical machine theory'. Also, systems and control engineers use 'machine' in about the same sense but extend it to include so-called analogue machines. Under these usages the term does *not* entail cogs, determinism, materialism, or nonpurposiveness.

The second reason is that it is precisely the 'mechanical' notion of formal logic as pursued in the Hilbert programme that led to Gödel's work on the incompleteness of formal systems. From that work there ultimately emerged by way of John von Neuman and the recursion theorem of mathematical logic the idea of self-describing automaton systems. The latter is at the heart of my approach to intentional aspects of mind, indeed to mindedness itself.[4]

The third reason for clinging to the term is to mark off plainly my position from functionalism, cognitivism, and rationalism. All four appeal to computer or automaton ideas. Many functionalists explain psychological states as role-playing, which states may play independently of the stuff they happen to be made of, in computation, and tend to take role playing as covering the notion of intencionality. Cognitivists picture the mind as more or less literally "instruction driven", in analogy to programmed computer, and as manipulating symbols in a manner quite like that governed by program instructions. These symbols are often regarded as semantically endowed mental representations. Mechanism, however, considers mind more nearly as embodied in neural hardware, not as an abstract program. I am opposed to both functionalist and cognitivist attempts to account for the intentional as they appear to presuppose what a mechanist believes calls for analysis.

Finally, the rationalist version of functionalism embraces a doctrine of innate ideas in its theories of language acquisition, but I find the reasons for this to be inadequate and the historical affiliations with continental rationalism to be quite dubitable.

3. NATURALISM

The logic of mind is a variant of naturalism. Following Dewey and in present times Quine, I place man in a biosocial setting. Like other animals he lives under an imperative to adapt or die; but unlike other organisms he is a member of a social complex organized under various moral, political, economic, etc. institutions controlled by elaborate language mechanisms. In such a situation the rules of mind change — they evolve in the natural selection process, and they also change when certain types of learning take place.

This naturalist position is worth stressing, for it is not entailed by mechanism as such.[5] The latter is perfectly compatible with almost any ontology of mind and, moreover, with a contemporary form of rationalism that almost totally ignores the bio-social setting of the individual mind. Learning, and in particular learning to speak a language, is largely a social phenomenon. Many contemporary rationalists overlook this fact, although perhaps would not deny it if pressed. They think of learning as an individual question; indeed learning is explicitly said to be a function solely of the individual and data (see Chomsky, 1975b, pp. 14 ff.). This somewhat isolationist picture of the person leads rationalists to the doctrine of innate ideas. At the same time they do insist, as I do, on the mental reality of guiding rules and historically are among the first to advocate the logic of mind along the lines I have been describing.

Other scientists who would no doubt accept a computer logic analysis of many mental or neurological processes — perhaps short of mechanism as a comprehensive philosophy — explicitly reject naturalism in favor of dualism. I do not propose to discuss their views until the final chapter.

The logic of mind attempts to fill in certain sections of naturalist philosophy which up to this time have remained on a sketchy, programmatic level. There are three main topics I want to introduce here in order to give the reader the flavor of the logic: the intentional; language and meaning; and dispositions.

One can find in John Dewey a considerable emphasis on the intentional character of mind. For him, mental states are symbols, and the role of symbols provide a "directive force for operations that when performed lead us to non-symbolic objects" (Dewey, 1916, p. 226). Similarly, today's functionalist holds that mental states are functional or role-playing and thus essentially representational. But although it is true that these thinkers stress the intentional character of mind, their treatment of it remains on a schematic, promissory level. Functionalism postulates a mechanism which a logic of mind seeks to analyze. Fairly detailed suggestions of ways to approach expectation, perception, belief and other 'propositional attitudes' are made in later chapters using the concept of self-describing automata.

There is also a way of coping with problems of meaning and intension within the logic of mind. I can best review the situation by alluding once again to the mental entities we debited positivism with excluding from philosophy and psychology. For some naturalists, in particular Quine, some of these entities are still to be excluded as we have no means of individuating them. The paradigmatic cases are sensa, images, ideas, and concepts — in short conscious or awareness states of various kinds. Now if these mental things are eliminated there do not seem to be any entities left to be meanings of linguistic expressions. Unless meanings of terms can be identified with physical attributes the only place to put them is inside the head, in a special Platonic realm, or in relation to use in the speech act. It turns out that very probably none of these (except some version of Platonism or of possible world theory) will do. Quine banishes these 'creatures of darkness' wherever they are and attributes meaning to entire theories rather than to shorter expressions where meaning is anchored in what he calls 'patterns of stimulation' (Quine, 1960, pp. 31 f.; also, 1969a, pp. 154–157). But there is a way of treating meanings as nonmysterious mental *processes* that enables one to say what they are in nature and to individuate them. Terms which have the same reference but different meanings are semantically distinguishable via *computations*. Roughly, a term applies to an individual or a collection (including the null individual and null set) in virtue of a computation which is governed by rules of mind. Different rules that govern the same extensional application are associated to different terms, and it is to this difference in rules that we trace unlikeness in intension. Terms have the same meaning if the rules of application are the same. This captures 'synonymy'; and the meaning or intension of a term can be taken as a synonymy class, just as cardinal number is a class of equipollent sets.

Some naturalists still lean toward behaviorism and believe that many mental features and traits are dispositions, a concept which everyone uses but few understand. The idea, which was brought to prominence in *The Concept of Mind*, is to 'unpack' mental dispositions in behavioral terms.

A person is indolent, for instance, if he would shirk doing the difficult thing if he were presented the option between doing something difficult and not doing it. In general, sentences expressing dispositions are replaceable by subjunctive conditionals that say what such and such a person would do if such and such circumstances were to obtain. This view of mental traits is an improvement over philosophies that posit mysterious powers or virtues; but as every student knows, subjunctive conditionals are not all that clear either. To understand the mental – if the Rylean approach is right in principle – requires an analysis of dispositions less foggy than dispositions themselves. I myself advocate the 'place-holder' view, but not the version maintaining that dispositional terms are placeholders for eventual explanations in physical science. Mental dispositions are *automata*. To say that X is vain is to say that she has a certain kind of automaton in her. To the reader this might sound strange, but will sound less so when he understands that having an automaton structure (vanity) is, in effect, having internal bodily states that mediate X's responses to certain situations where she makes herself prominent. The motivation is the same as Ryle's: account for mental traits without invoking ghost-like agents. But, as we shall see, it is impossible to account for mental features in terms of overt behavior alone, which is essentially the same as saying that the insides count. Mechanism, my version of it anyway, is like behaviorism; it eschews indwellers which can not be coaxed into clear light. But there is such a thing as *internal* behavior, and the outer can not be understood without it.

A fourth distinctive mark of naturalism, of a piece with its unwavering insistence on the bio-social nature of man, is its refusal to disjoin philosophy from natural science, and in particular to place mental philosophy and epistemology apart from and prior to psychology. Naturalism contains no first philosophy. This point of view does not seem to present any problems for mental philosophy except for those who see paradox in man studying his own nature. For some philosophers this paradox seems to show itself in an especially distressing form in the old puzzle about sense data and physical bodies. There seems to be a circularity in appealing to the physical sense organs in just the *statement* of the problem of how to claim knowledge of an external world if all we have to go on ultimately are sense data. Quine's way of handling the situation, which I accept, is as follows. If knowledge based on sense impressions is held to be illusory, it is because natural science itself tells us of deviations between sense and reality. Hence knowledge is not wholly illusory (Quine, 1973, pp. 2–3). I grant that the argument is good only so far as it goes. There are other arguments in favor of solipsism, for instance, which do not depend upon the concept of illusion but which I do not intend to discuss here.

All I really ask is that mental philosophy be accorded the same status as any other empirical theory. Acceptance of this principle is crucial in a theory of perception. Perception is a relation between a person and objects of some sort. It is possible to consider that relation from the perspective of an observer such as a psychologist conducting experiments in perception on subjects, or from that of the perceiver himself. Since Descartes, philosophers have taken the second point of view. Presumably, many or most nonnaturalist epistemologists would maintain that the second is the only relevant philosophical stance to take, given the *epistemological* problem of perception, while the first is all right for the empirical psychologist who is not concerned with the ultimate grounds of knowledge. Contrarywise, the naturalist claims that it is just by taking the perception relation as an empirical one that we can hope to resolve the sense datum-object paradox. A consequence is that the epistemologist "can appeal to physical receptors or sense stimulation and . . . drop the talk of sense data and talk rather of sensory stimulation" (Quine, 1973, pp. 2–3). Epistemology thus becomes a part of psychology, and is liberated from the old tangles of sensa and external objects.

Turning to the metaphysical side, taking this policy toward a theory of perception and knowledge by no means disposes of the *ontological* problem of sense data, or, for that matter, of any of the classical problems of consciousness and mind. Can we deny conscious mind and its states entirely? This question directs us back to a reconsideration of the nature of mind which we dropped at the end of Section 2.

'Logic of Mind' connotes mind, although I previously said that I agree with materialism on the score that there is nothing but the body, which is governed by formally distinct rules. It is tempting to identify mind with these rules, although I prefer not to encourage the tendency to hypostatize which is often aroused by use of names such as 'the mind.' Instead, I will say that a necessary condition for a being *to have a mind* or *to be minded* is that its behavior be guided by rules of a certain sort. But this condition is too broad as it admits worms. For the minded body is not only the brain, but includes any body parts animal or otherwise that are guided by such rules. The behavior of *annelida*, for example, can be explained by representing automata and is guided by a simple set of rules; so if worms satisfy whatever other conditions we later impose, then they are minded. Not all minded things, if this account is correct, are capable of intentional behaviors — witness the worm; yet a central part of the philosophical tradition is the view that mind is intentional. If we preserve this tradition and if intentional properties are analyzable in the logic (as proposed above), then to have a mind is to have rules of a complexity sufficient to account for the intentional. We might later wish to add the further requirement that the organism have a command of language, although this will require an analysis of the connections between language and intentionality. This quite safely rules out the worm.

The brain of *annelida* amounts to very little. However, this is not the reason it fails to qualify as being minded. The reason as just suggested is that its behavior is not intentional and its 'mental states' are not symbolic. For all I know a being could have intentional attitudes without having a brain, and this might be true even in this world, witness the computer. So mind (so far) is body guided by formally distinct rules of a certain order of complexity, a complexity sufficient to attribute intentionality to its behavior.

It is quite possible that sufficiently elaborate digital machines or robots satisfy this condition, but they lack another, which is *feeling*. I mean by 'feeling' the real thing, *raw* feeling, not feeling in the metaphorical sense of the computer engineer when he says that a computer senses or feels something. There is no distinction to be made in the computer world between dreamless sleep and being awake or between anesthetized and nonanesthetized states. As far as I know only living things feel; and as computers do not feel they are not minded. Further, I regard it as a mistake – principally because of the confusion that is generated – to apply such concepts as thought, cognition, cleverness, etc. to computers, because they are not aware of anything, although they well might have nonconscious intentions. All of this sounds rather dogmatic and arbitrary and has to be defended.

My version of mechanism, in summary, holds that a being has a mind if and only if its body or certain body parts are guided by formally distinct rules (essentially of a nondeterministic finite automaton) of a complexity sufficient to account for intentionality, and it is capable of conscious feeling. The setting of the theory is naturalistic, the significance of the setting being that mind has evolved in a bio-social matrix in terms of which certain aspects of intelligence and learning must be understood.

The strictly physicalist policy toward perception and knowledge which I am borrowing from Quine thus by no means disposes of sensations, feelings, and in general of conscious events. These mental things are still with us on the metaphysical side of the theory. We may be free of one sort of bondage in our attempts to understand perception and conceptions. But we still have to untie Schopenhauer's 'world knot'. It is, in other words, one thing to insist that our understanding of human knowledge proceed as an empirical enterprise, and quite another to deny our own inner states of awareness.

So far as I can see, mechanism as such has nothing whatever to say about the relationship between physical states and states of awareness such as pains or ideas, although it does specifically address itself to the understanding of cognition, intelligence, and other such attributes of mind. The two conditions of mindedness thus seem to be quite separate. It is easy to picture a very simple automaton — at the level of a mouse — that would be sentient, and by contrast a very complex one that could do anything we can do but be completely unfeeling. The functionalist view of mind does frequently argue that a sufficiently complex computer could feel. But I will argue in Chapter XI that it is a mistake to identify states of awareness with either 'functional' or logical states as not all of the latter are conscious nor do they all correlate with brain complexes, while neuroanatomy does tell us that feeling states do have some kind of material correlation with cortical processes. I regard the tendency toward a kind of emergence theory which is detectable in earlier functionalists such as Dewey and Mead as very unsatisfactory (Dewey, 1925, p. 267; Mead, 1938, pp. 77–78). Nor am I willing to follow Quine or Feyerabend into the barrens of eliminative materialism. The emergence theory is too vague for philosophical comfort and materialism is ambiguous. Pain no doubt plays a role in the behavior of organisms and qua 'functional' can be explained in principle, without assuming a mental entity on the proximal side of an unbridgeable chasm separating it from the physical. In this sense one can explicate (or, equivalently, eliminate) 'pain.' But this does not touch the ontological question of what pain *is* (Nagel, 1972, pp. 220–224), any more than construing consciousness as the faculty of responding to one's own responses explicates 'consciousness' (Quine, 1966, p. 214). A computer can respond to its own responses yet almost certainly lacks consciousness in the ordinary sense of the word as applied to your and my feelings. There is a categorical confusion here, pure and simple. It is a mistake to think that the concept of pain *qua* functional explicates quality.[6]

The naturalist position of the logic of mind, then, while emphasizing the inclusion of philosophy in science and the strictly empirical (i.e. psychology-based) theory of knowledge, does not go on to exclude phenomena which are all too obviously a part of the natural world. This suggests that there are two quite different problems of mind, a topic which must be explored in somewhat greater depth.

4. TWO PROBLEMS OF MIND

A strange thing about the mind-body problem is that the paradigmatic cases of purely mental entities are 'raw feels', i.e. stabbing pains, sensa, after-images, and qualia, all of which are instances of sensation or feeling but not of conception or thought, although at times of course one does have conscious thoughts. Other mental things and processes which we are not consciously aware of, such as our deeper beliefs, some of our hatreds, our discovery of proofs of theorems in mathematics, or our thoughts about transcendental numbers or infinity do not show so prominently in current discussions of mental phenomena. We speak of scientific knowledge or of talent in writing poetry as *intellectual* and of the mind. On the other hand in ordinary discourse, we speak of pains and vivid pleasures as *bodily*, not mental. But philosophers, since Descartes, who denied feelings of animals, put pains in the toe in the same category with thoughts of π, whence philosophy of mind comes to be study of the identity or lack thereof of toe pain and nerve fiber stimulations!

I am, however, less interested in the locus of the world knot than in the distinction between sorts of entities as intimated at the end of the last section, and consequently in the definition of two rather separate types of problems. The logic of mind, we have seen, being a kind of theory of logical rules, is independent of matters concerning the *stuff* of mind. If this be true, then it is at least plausible that intelligent behavior could be understood quite independently of questions about the status of raw feels, pains and the rest. This is just another way of expressing Quine's claim about the dispensability of sense data in theory of perception, only now I am proposing to banish these things from the whole field of the *logic* of mind, but not from mental philosophy altogether.

There are many ways of classifying mental entities, but for our purpose it will suffice initially to divide them into two classes in a way which has been proposed by Richard Rorty (1970).

Following him, I will call entities such as pains, ideas (sense impressions) and datable thoughts 'mental occurrents'. I will call beliefs, expectations, hopes, knowings, ideas (qua 'plans of action') 'mental features.' Occurrents are events, some of which we are directly aware of in our conscious moments, and hence are *particulars* of a certain sort. Features are *generals*: they are of Peirce's category of *thirds* or representations. Similar distinctions have been made by many philosophers.[7] Not all events are mental occurrents since some events are purely physical and *prima facie* do not have any quality of 'raw feel'. Features on the other hand could all be physical, that is to say, be present in a completely physical system.

Both Rorty and Herbert Feigl depend on this distinction in order to isolate the source of the mind-body problem. Rorty maintains that only occurrents

... generate the opposition between the mental and the physical, when this opposition is considered an opposition between two incompatible types of entity. ... [They] are the paradigm illustrations of what is meant by the Cartesian notion of the mental as a separate realm. The latter class [features] of entities are entities which, *if we had never heard of thoughts and sensations*, would never have generated the notion of a separate 'realm' at all. If we had no notion of a mental *event*, but merely the notion of men having beliefs and desires and, therefore acting in such and such ways, we would not have had a mind-body problem at all, and Ryle would have had no motive for writing. Believing and desiring would have appeared simply as distinctive *human* activities, and our only dualism would have been one between human beings qua agents (i.e., qua moving in ways to be explained by reference to beliefs and desires) and as mere bodies (i.e., qua moving in ways that can be explained without reference to beliefs and desires). This dualism would have been a dualism not between mind and body nor between the mental and the physical as distinct realms, but simply between ways of explaining the doings of human beings – psychological explanations and nonpsychological explanations (Rorty, 1970, p. 408).

Similarly, Feigl makes up a list of opposites which might be held to generate the mind-body problem and rejects them one-by-one. For example, he rejects the nonspatial versus spatial distinction, holding that what we are now calling 'occurrents' obviously have locations and even sizes, while to ask for the location or size of a feature (a universal or general) is a crude category mistake. Further, he rejects the purposive-mechanical opposition on the ground that the distinction can be drawn within the animal realm and even within technology – as between regulative and nonregulative devices (Feigl, 1958, pp. 409 ff.).

The upshot for both thinkers is, as Feigl puts it, that "the central puzzle of the mind-body problem is the logical nature of the correlation laws connecting raw feels [occurrents] with neurophysiological processes" (Feigl, 1958, p. 406). I prefer to call this problem the 'life-body' problem because, contrary to the Cartesian tradition, it appears wherever there is sentience. Again quoting Feigl, "it becomes clear that ... the scope of the two criteria (*sentient* and *sapient*) is not necessarily the same. The two concepts are not coextensive" (Feigl, 1958, p. 412). Mental occurrents (or perhaps better *conscious* occurrents) are events in the lives of higher animals, as I think most biologists who experiment with animals (and perhaps most philosophers) would hold on rather strong analogical grounds. Such animals, I want to argue, although certainly subject to rule-governed behavior are not *minded*, that is, are presumably automata but not complex enough to use language as we do, to think, etc. My point in this reference to animals is that Rorty's and Feigl's attempts to isolate mind in opposition to body seem only to isolate life or at least animal life, and that problems of mind proper are ones concerning belief, intentions, perceptions, language, and so forth – in short, concerning mental features. Here again there is a much closer resemblance to classical philosophy than to modern: animals have "feelings of pleasure and pain" but no power of "thinking or calculation" (Aristotle, 434^a2 and 433^a10). And this departs both from Descartes in placing feeling in the body and from much current philosophy which identifies the truly 'mental' with pains.

There is a host of problems here, not all of them verbal. Although pains are bodily, not mental from my point of view, I still count sentience as a necessary condition for mindedness, which rules computers and robots out. For the mind does have a kind of unity, and the distinction among mental entities, whence of problem areas too, is only a formal working one. But heeding Descartes' advice, which unfortunately for the metaphysical tradition he himself did not always follow, a way to advance is to break a problem up into conceptually workable parts and to let synthesis come later. When the time comes we shall see that our working distinction itself lacks clarity, for occurrents such as events in which there is *awareness of* in distinction to mere *awareness*, are clearly intentional and hence feature-like, although they are not universals in themselves. Thus it must be recognized that the concept of mental feature is quite vague. Intentional traits such as beliefs are clear-cut cases; but what about emotions? A lasting adoration of Venus is no doubt intentional. But what about a momentary lusting? How lasting does lusting have to be to count as a feature, not an event, and how intense does feeling have to be to count as conscious?

However, eschewing further refinement for the while, the principal justification for the separation of the two problems of mind, besides the methodological one, is categorical. It is simply a mistake to ask for a functional or behavioral (i.e., featural) characterization of pain *qua* pain or to ask for an account of perception (a feature) in terms solely of passive admission of impressions, which are prime cases of conscious occurrents.[8] But this observation as well as others which could be made in justification of the distinction are better left aside in favor of the argument of the book as a whole.

CHAPTER II

WHAT IS A RULE OF MIND?

There are rules of thumb, rules of law, rules of games, rules of habit (he does this as a rule) and rules of strategy at least, and they differ one from the other. What is a rule of mind? Well, it is similar to a rule of logic, but not the same in its governing. A good way to introduce and elaborate the idea is to trace its history. What I shall have to say is incomplete. Attributions I make as to the origin of the idea are subject to correction by historical scholars — if and when they decide to turn to the subject.

1. SIGNALS AND CONTROL

As far as I have been able to determine the explicitly stated hypothesis that persons are machines, put in the form 'men are finite automata' was set forth by the Soviet mathematician A. N. Kolmogoroff.[1] What I have said so far in the previous chapter should have dispelled any thought that Kolmogoroff was reviving Lucretius or La Mettrie. Nor are his automata the blindly operating, clocklike artifacts of antiquity and early modern times or the animal-automata of Descartes. This much is clear. But it is less clear whether this new form of mechanism should be *attributed* to him. The idea was certainly intimated by Emil Post as early as 1921 and then later by A. M. Turing and John von Neumann, as we shall now relate.

In order to understand the idea, it is worthwhile to compare the old with new examples of automata. Many are essentially clocklike in that the operations they perform are strictly predetermined by the structure of the mechanism. The famous clock at Strassburg announces the hours by a sequence of elaborate scenes, including a procession of the apostles and crowing roosters — all represented by ingenious mechanical figures. Albert the Great had an android butler that opened the door to visitors and saluted them. The story has it that St. Thomas Aquinas smashed it to bits. If he did, all he found inside was some kind of crude gadget considerably simpler than a present day automatic dishwasher. All of these automata (including the dishwasher) are clocklike and should be distinguished from systems which are influenced by *stimuli*, such as animals, computers, or home furnaces. The

Strassburg clock and Albert's butler go their own way and are imperturbable, while this is not true of animals or computers. Also, the clocklike automata lack *internal control*, which animals and computers do not. Most artificial automata considered until quite recently ran autonomously (their 'own way', without being subject to stimuli or inputs) except for *external control*.

To get the right understanding of the concepts of autonomy and control as they are used in modern theory, one must distinguish between *energy inputs* and *signal inputs* to a system. A heating system with thermostatic control is the standard example. The energy input to the system is coal or gas, while the signal input is the difference between the room temperature of the room to be heated and the thermostat setting. If the difference is zero or positive the energy input is *off* and the furnace does not produce heat. If the difference is negative, the energy input is *on* and gas or other fuel is burned and heat produced. The thermostat is the *control* of the system. Here the operation, burning fuel, depends on what signal ('stimulus') is present, and the control is internal to the system, meaning that the system controls itself without intervention from the outside.

The concept of control and the distinction between energy and signal inputs were first clearly developed in control engineering and became key theoretical concepts in cybernetics. *Cybernetics* is a form of mechanism which goes back to World War II, and is frequently confused with the kind of philosophy discussed in this book. It is worth a short digression to discuss the difference. What has been termed the 'Cybernetical Hypothesis' (by Williams, 1951) is the theory that the principle mechanism of the central system is negative feedback; feedback was exemplified in the discussion above of a signal input to a heating system. However the subject includes much more, and applies to a wide variety of systems, both analog and digital. Norbert Wiener (1948) who introduced the term cybernetics', included among its concepts automatic control theory, the logical nerve net theory of Pitts and McCulloch, information theory, and digital computer design and programming concepts among others. These do not form a conceptually homogeneous whole but rather a family of loosely related ideas in which input and control are central. Only nerve networks and digital computers are automata in the strict sense we are introducing. The Pitts-McCulloch theory will be described later.

Let us return from this digression to clocks. A clock has only energy input and no internal control (this is not true of many newer clocks and watches). Energy for a spring-wound pendulum clock is put into the system by winding, and control, if any, is exercised by an external agent who adjusts the pendulum to regulate time intervals. Clocks are therefore autonomous as they are not available to signal inputs. Autonomous systems can be quite complex; for example, automatic dishwashers and record changers. Outside control can be exercized to select various modes of operation of a record changer. However one could convert it to a nonautonomous system by adding some kind of device for determining the correct running speed for a given record. The changer thus equipped could exercise its own control to govern different modes of operation in adaptation to the nature of the input or stimulus, that is, some signal standing for 33, 45, or 78 rpm.

Of the three foregoing examples only the clock is an automaton, and is in particular an *autonomous automaton*, a locution which I will avoid from now on. The meaning, as is apparent from the discussion, is almost the opposite of the ordinary sense of 'autonomous' in political or moral discussions. Henceforth where there is occasion to make the distinctions, I shall use 'input free automata' for the autonomous case and simply 'automata' for the nonautonomous. A finite nondeterministic automaton has input, and as already explained is governed by rules which are open to any sequence of application. The automata of Descartes, which we shall have occasion to refer to more than once, are presumably input-free, and whatever input Descartes and his contemporaries might have recognized as applicable to animals were energy inputs and had a strictly causal efficacy. Indeed speech, which Descartes believed to be limited to human beings, is a prime example of a system of *signal* inputs. So the logic of mind in contrast to input free automata has signal inputs and internal control.

What counts as input to a system and what counts as internal rather than external control is somewhat arbitrary and depends on the boundaries and level of description of the system. If you consider a home furnace system apart from thermostatic control, then it is input free and controlled from the outside — you shall have drawn a boundary in such a way that the control device is now an external agent that turns the furnace on or off. Oppositely, if you consider a system including a clock and its user as component interacting parts of a whole, it has to be reckoned as one having internal control inputs, namely signals emitted from a subsystem including the user, his eye, comparative information from a phone call, and so forth. In these examples the level of description is determined by what is taken to be a part or subsystem, and what a whole. These concepts figure heavily in some of the current objections to mechanism and will be discussed at some length in later sections. In the logic of mind we generally place the boundary of an organism at the skin, but this posit will vary depending on the context of a particular inquiry.

2. TURING MACHINES

In the real world many sorts of things, both natural and artificial, are open to perturbing signals and thus embody control, but not all are automata. We have isolated the important idea of a signal input in order to avoid confusion with clocklike things, but we have yet to explain what an automaton system of rules is. It is the nature of the rules that distinguishes an automaton from other signal input and control systems. The earliest formulation of automaton-type rules is due jointly to A. M. Turing and Emil Post. I shall introduce the idea by way of example.

Suppose that a resourceful clerk, Ernest, is given the task of converting strings of symbols given to him on slips of paper into reverse strings. For example if he is given a string

    abab

of *a*'s and *b*'s, his task is to write the string backwards yielding

    baba

on the same piece of paper. To simplify the example, we will suppose that all the strings given to Ernest to work on are composed of *a*'s and *b*'s only, and to make the example complex enough to be barely interesting, we will suppose that the presented strings can be of any finite length, so that the clerk must be immortal — you can not put an age limit on his life: if you did there would be strings so long he could not work through them.

Now Ernest decides to build a machine to perform this extremely dull task so that he has time for better things such as keeping accounts. He notes that the machine must be able to tell an *a* from a *b*, and that it must be able to write *a* and *b*. It must be able to erase; and it must be able to move back and forth over the strings of symbols. This much is quite obvious to Ernest when he examines what he himself does when he reverses strings. He also knows that the machine he is designing will be far more complex than Albert's android butler (that could not tell one thing from another — except for the opening of the door, which simply set off its energy transactions) because it is going to have to be able to remember, at least for a short while, whether it has just detected an *a* or a *b*. So in addition to organs for *sensing* (*cum* discriminating) *a* and *b*, *rewriting* (erasing *cum* writing) and *moving* right and left over the *input* string, it must have means for remembering symbols it has sensed. We shall refer to these means as *memory* or *internal states*.

Having noted all of these requirements his device must fulfill, Ernest faces the nontrivial task of invention. By some poorly understood mental process that puts him in a class with A. M. Turing, who was the inventor of what he is about to rediscover,[2] Ernest hit upon the idea that (1) the rules which *direct* the symbol manipulation could be used to *design* the device, that is to say, the rules could be made to *guide* the device; and (2) these rules need be of just *two* kinds: (a) *a rule to do something*, here either rewrite a symbol or move along the string being reversed; and (b) *a rule to change a memory state*. Both of these rules will depend (he saw) on the symbol sensed at a given them and the *present* memory state. Thus a rule of kind (a) will say, in effect: "when in state so and so, if you see a symbol *s, do* such and such . . . "; and one of kind (b) will say under exactly the same antecendent conditions: "*change to* memory state such and such. . . . "

These rules are represented by special strings of symbols called *quadruples*. To see how they are written, let us use symbols q_0, q_1, q_2, etc. as names of memory states (in an animal, q_0 might be a state of the whole body or a state of excitation of certain neurons, for example); let us use s_0, s_1, s_2, etc. for *input symbols* the machine is able to read or sense; and finally R and L for movement one symbol to the right or left. It is convenient to think of a string of symbols-to-be processed as occupying consecutive squares on a tape, so that R and L have the meaning "move right (left) one square."

A *quadruple* is a string of one of the following three forms:

(i) $q_i s_j s_k q_l$

(ii) $q_i s_j R q_l$

(iii) $q_i s_j L q_l$.

Each quadruple embodies *two* rules, one of kind (a) and one of kind (b). Thus, (i) means *both* (a'): when in state q_i if you see the symbol s_j *print* s_k (do something); and (b'): when in state q_i, if you see the symbol s_j, go to memory state q_l (remember something). These distinguishable operations can be combined so that (i) can be read straight out:

When in state q_i sensing s_j, print s_k and go to state q_l.   (1a)

Similarly (ii) [(iii)] reads:

When in state q_i sensing s_j, move $R(L)$ one square and go to state q_l.   (1b)

Although quadruple rules may be read in the style just displayed, it is extremely important to keep in mind that each quadruple expresses two rules, one to do something, and one to assume a new memory state. In the following discussion, we will proceed abstractly and not exploit Ernest's insight above that quadruple rules provide a design (a kind of blueprint) for an actual reversing device. (We will pursue the 'guiding' property of rules in Section III.2). For the time being (until we examine computer diagrams and neuron networks), we shall just concentrate on the rules *in abstracto* to see how they work with the string reversal problem.

Now that Ernest has decided on the form of rules he will use, he must discover precisely the right ones for the reversal task. His finding these is somewhat less miraculous than hitting on the right general forms (i)–(iii), and is of the order of difficulty in writing computer programs, although Ernest never heard of such (nor did Turing at the time his machines were invented). He decides that the machine will begin its operations in an initial state q_0 at the left of any string presented; it will then seek and find the right-most symbol and copy it in the next square to the right of the initially given string. Next, it will find the next-to-the-right-most symbol and copy it at the extreme right; and so on. The rules are quite elaborate, but probably cannot be simplified. There are twenty:

TABLE I
Symbol-reversing Turing machine.

(i)	q_0aRq_0		(xi)	q_2Baq_3
(ii)	q_0bRq_0		(xii)	q_3aLq_3
(iii)	q_0BLq_1		(xiii)	q_3bLq_3
(iv)	q_1acq_2		(xiv)	q_3cLq_1
(v)	q_1bcq_4		(xv)	q_4aRq_4
(vi)	q_1cLq_1		(xvi)	q_4bRq_4
(vii)	q_1BRq_5		(xvii)	q_4cRq_4
(viii)	q_2aRq_2		(xviii)	q_4Bbq_3
(ix)	q_2bRq_2		(xix)	q_5cBq_6
(x)	q_2cRq_2		(xx)	q_6BRq_5

This is a system of *Turing machine* rules, not rules of a finite automata, but they are similar; we shall get to the latter type rules later in our history.

The reader should go over in his mind the 'straight-out' version of a few of these rules — that is, the full sentence in the style of (1a) or (1b) of which the quadruple is a kind of abbreviation. Note that these rules contain new symbols c and B which are not in the set of symbols $\{a, b\}$ that are components of the input strings to be reversed. Their presence will be explained in due course.

Now to see how this machine works, suppose Ernest to have been given a string

$babbb$

Then the machine begins at the left in state q_0, as already stipulated, scanning the left-most symbol b. Let us depict this initial situation in the following manner:

$q_0 babbb.$

Quadruple (ii) of Table I applies; it directs the machine to move right (R) one square and to change (in this case to stay in) state q_0. The result of this *operation* is an unchanged string, but a new total situation has arisen in which the machine is now scanning a while in state q_0, thus:

$bq_0 abbb.$

Such notations are called *instantaneous descriptions*. The reader should take care to note that instantaneous descriptions are not input strings or strings in process, but are strings indicating both the result of application of a rule and conditions for application of a rule. Strings as such (in which no q-symbols occur) will be called simply 'strings'. In the current example above there are *two* instantaneous descriptions, but only *one* string common to both (occupying the *same* squares) obtained by deleting q's.

With these conventions in mind let us begin anew, indicating to the right of an instantaneous description (*i.d.*) its source or justification.

(1) $q_0 babbb$ initial *i.d.*
(2) $bq_0 abbb$ from (1) by rule (ii)
(3) $baq_0 bbb$ from (2) by (i)
(4) $babq_0 bb$ from (3) by (ii)
(5) $babbq_0 b$ from (4) by (ii)
(6) $babbbq_0$ from (5) by (ii).

At this stage of the computation the *i.d.* indicates that the machine in state q_0 is scanning a blank square. It will be helpful to represent blank squares by the letter 'B', so that line 6 can be rewritten

(6) $babbbq_0 B$ from (5) by (ii).

This convention says precisely that any string ... B ... is the *same string* as . . . .

So far the machine has found the right-most end of the string. According to the plan Ernest has in mind, it must rewrite the right-most symbol b in the blank space; it accomplishes this task by moving left, scanning the right-most symbol, overwriting a c, moving right a space, and rewriting the right-most symbol. The c serves to help the machine keep track of its operations. These moves are established in the next four steps:

(7)	$babbq_1b$	from (6) by (iii)
(8)	$babbq_4cB$	from (7) by (v)
(9)	$babbcq_4B$	from (8) by (xvii)
(10)	$babbcq_3b$	from (9) by (xviii).

The machine now seeks (and if the rules of Table I are correct, *finds*) the next-to-right-most symbol of the original string (in this case, again a b), and rewrites it to the right of the b that was just written at the end of step (10). This next cycle takes seven steps:

(11)	$babbq_3cb$	from (10) by (xiii)
(12)	$babq_1bcb$	from (11) by (xiv)
(13)	$babq_4ccb$	from (12) by (v)
(14)	$babcq_4cb$	from (13) by (xvii)
(15)	$babccq_4b$	from (14) by (xvii)
(16)	$babccbq_4B$	from (15) by (xvi)
(17)	$babccbq_3b$	from (16) by (xviii).

At (17), two of the symbols have been rewritten. The rules are then applied step-by-step until eventually the string $babbb$ is completely reversed. Note that two key states are q_2 and q_4. q_2 has the significance that the machine has just sensed an a (steps k, $k+1$ below), and q_4 that it has just sensed a b (steps (12)–(13)). The last fifty steps are as follows:

.
.
.

(k)	$bq_1acccbbb$	from (k−1) by (vi)
(k+1)	$bq_2ccccbbb$	from (k) by (iv)
(k+2)	$bcq_2cccbbb$	from (k+1) by (x)

.   .
.   .
.   .

(k+8) $bccccbbbq_2B$
(k+9) $bccccbbbq_3a$ from (k+9) by (xi)

.
.
.

(k+17) $q_1bccccbbba$
(k+18) $q_4cccccbbba$ from (k+17) by (v)

.
.
.

(k+27) $ccccbbbaq_4B$
(k+28) $ccccbbbaq_3b$ from (k+27) by (xviii)

.
.
.

(k+37) $q_1ccccbbbab$
(k+38) $q_1Bccccbbbab$ from (k+37) by (vi).

At (k+38) it uses rule (vii) and enters a routine of erasing c's, using (xix) and (xx), achieving

.
.
.

(k+49) q_5bbbab

There is no quadruple in Table I with q_5b as left-most pair of symbols, so the machine halts, having completed its task. It is recommended that the reader fill in the steps (17)–(k) as well as the other indicated omissions as an exercise, tedious and dull though it be.

Table I is an example of a *Turing machine*, albeit a rather limited one, and as such is a kind of *automaton*. It is an automaton in virtue of the character of rules, (i)–(xx) that constitute it. These are examples of *recursive* rules, and it is rules of this type (roughly) that provide the logic for the logic of mind.

Now to relate the idea of an automaton to our earlier discussions of mechanical systems having signal inputs and internal control is very simple and straightforward. The symbols s_0, s_1, s_2, . . . (a, b in the example) are *signal* inputs, and *internal control* is represented by that part of our rules that specifies a *next state* q_1, given an input s_j and a *present state* q_i. And further to relate the idea to our preliminary characterization of mind in Chapter I, a necessary condition for mindedness is being (or having, or embodying) an automaton of a certain complexity sufficient for accounting for the intentional (we are a long way from this).

3. LOGIC AND LOGIC OF MIND

This summary statement of what we have discussed so far leaves a lot unsaid. What does the logic of mind have to do with logic? What does it mean to say that a rule is 'recursive'? What does it mean to be or to embody rules? *How* are rules embodied? Where does nondeterminism enter in (Ernest's machine is deterministic, as each step in its operation is functionally dependent on the previous one)? In order to approach these latter questions we shall return to our history. So far we have explored but the *first* stage, which goes back to 1936, and in a dim way which we shall attempt to brighten later, to 1921.

Taking up first the question of the relevance of logic to a logic of mind, we recall that a logic consists of sentences made up of symbols from a given list, a subset, perhaps empty, of sentences called 'axioms', and a collection of relations of sentences called 'rules of inference'. A proof for a logic is a sequence of sentences governed by rules of inference which terminates in a sentence called a 'theorem.' We are particularly interested, for analogical purposes, in the *generation* of proofs, and in the *embodiment* of the logic, which is a rather ill-defined complex including a person (the logician, who 'knows' the axioms and rules or looks them up), his books, pencil and paper, blackboard, etc. We think of the logician finding or creating and writing down a proof as proof generation. This trio of ideas is analogous to a musical composition (logic); the performer, piano, read or memorized score (embodiment of the logic); and the performance (generation of proofs); or, say, to a list of grammatical rules of English, an embodiment (internalization in a person's mind) and speech events (generating meaningful phonemic sequences).

A *formal* logic, as the reader already knows, is one in which the proofs are *effective* − i.e., one can tell by a purely routine procedure based on inspection of sequences of sentence tokens whether a given sequence is indeed a proof.[3] To say that a logic is 'formal', then, is tantamount to saying that the logician (the 'embodiment') could generate any old sequences of sentences and effectively pick out the proofs. This fact is the basis of proof procedures in logic, which are prototypes of recipe-like or algorithmic procedures in computing.

Now in order to answer some of the questions we asked a few paragraphs back about relevance of logic, recursiveness, embodiments, etc., it will be necessary to discuss (1) how the foregoing notion of effectiveness or of a recipe-like procedure can be made precise — this leads to the idea of the Turing machine which we already have an example of; (2) how the idea of a proof is generalizable to one of rule-generated sequences where not truth or validity but other properties of sequences are of moment; (3) how automata concepts come to be applicable outside of logic to more general kinds of information than sentences of logic. In Table I we have already seen an example of an automaton that manipulates strings which do not look anything like sentences of a school logic; but we want to go beyond to cases where symbols of an automaton might be pebbles, electronic circuit pulses, firings of neurons, or stimulus patterns on the surface of organisms.

(I) In the 1930's the relatively vague notion of an effective or algorithmic process was cleared up in terms of the technical concept of *Turing computability* or *recursiveness*. Some mathematical operations such as addition can be performed in a strictly canned, mechanical process that could be carried out by an unimaginative clerk. Similarly, some procedures in logic, like determining tautologies by truth table, are algorithmic — just follow the rules. Other operations, both in mathematics and logic, are not. The problem thus emerged to distinguish in an exact way between algorithmic problems and those requiring imaginative powers. This is done in terms of Turing computable functions or more generally, for applications to logic and elsewhere in computer and cognitive science, in terms of Turing machine symbol processing.

A Turing machine *computation* is a finite sequence of instantaneous descriptions. The sequence of descriptions of Ernest's string reverser, beginning with $q_0 babbb$ and ending with $q_5 bbbab$, is already an example of a computation. To see how this applies to numerical functions we think of the arguments of the function being coded in some appropriate notation — ordinary decimal notation will do, but for various technical reasons it is easier to deal with numbers in binary notation — and then being inscribed on a Turing machine tape. Now if there exists a Turing machine that starts from an instantaneous description made up of the machine initial state and the coded arguments of the function and that computes the value of the function for those arguments, then we say that the function is 'recursive'. A good way to guarantee that a Turing machine exists is to *construct* or design one, which is usually a more or less intuitive, hit-or-miss process similar to Ernest's in designing a machine for reversing strings. Let us consider an example. We want to know whether addition is recursive. What we do is invent a Turing machine such that if any two positive integers are encoded and inscribed on the machine's tape, the machine will run through a computation that ends with the sum of the two integers printed on that tape. If this project is possible, then addition is recursive. If it is not (no matter how clever one is he cannot design the right machine), then addition is not recursive, and the sum of two numbers could be determined only by the use of mental powers that transcend effective processes. The collection of all those functions that can be computed in this way by some Turing machine are *Turing computable functions.*

The proposition that all effective (or algorithmic) arithmetical functions are Turing computable is known as *Turing's Thesis.* Another historically coincident way of characterizing Turing computable functions leads to the labelling "recursive function", and to a companion, completely equivalent thesis, that says that all effectively calculable arithmetical functions are recursive. This is known as *Church's Thesis.*[4] For reasons discussed in Section II.7 I shall avoid terminological problems by consistently using 'recursive' instead of 'Turing computable', and 'recursive rule' for Turing quadruples and more generally still, as explained after we have seen enough examples to get the hang of the notion. I shall also refer to the joint thesis as the *Church-Turing Thesis,* and more simply yet as CT. Finally, as explained later, I shall construe CT broadly to apply not only to arithmetic but to all data processes that are generally regarded as algorithmic.

CT is used in logic to establish that some process or operation is recursive; then by (the converse of) CT it follows that it is algorithmic. A logic is formal if its proofs are recursive. A formal mathematical system such as number theory is *complete* if every closed sentence or its negation can be generated by a Turing computation. And a logic has a solvable decision problem if its theorems constitute a recursive set, or alternatively stated, if each formula of the logic can be determined to be a theorem or not by a Turing machine computation.

These facts are familiar to everyone who has been exposed to an adequate symbolic logic course. What may seem strange is the proposal that these rather arid if not formidable concepts be expanded to a theory of mind! For the logic of mind accounts for mental features as effective processes, and if we accept Church's Thesis this suggests that persons are Turing machines! This is not *quite* our proposal, but before going on to further refinements let us note that as logicians working within a formal logic, we *are* (or do not need to assume we are any more than) machines.

Simple as these machines are in point of the sparse set of operations in their repertoires, they are sufficient for computing all of the mathematical functions which, on intuitive grounds, one would believe are calculable by an algorithm. A remarkable consequence of Turing's thought is that there must be a *universal* machine, namely one that can do anything any other Turing machine can do. Turing's universal machine can thus calculate *any* function which, by CT, one would consider to be strictly calculable by mechanical means. These machines have exactly the same elementary capabilities as our string reverser, namely they are characterizable by the three basic types of rule, the quadruples (i)–(iii) of p. 19. The only difference is that a universal machine begins calculation from a tape containing not only the input string, but another string which is a coded representation of the machine that it is to simulate. A universal machine is essentially equivalent to Leibniz' idea of a universal reasoning calculus or *calculus ratiocinator,* assuming that his ideas of a precise, universal language finds adequate expression in strings of Turing machine symbols.

Notice that when we ran through a computation on Ernest's machine *we* played the role of a universal machine. Following an algorithm represented by quadruple rules of the sort that appears in Table I we could compute *any* recursive function, in principle, given enough time and paper. A digital computer, provided that it has access to unlimited amounts of tape or other bulk data medium is equivalent to a universal Turing machine. It too computes just the recursive functions and it computes any such function according to a program, which is analogous to the simulated machine a universal machine imitates.

If one were to examine the design of a universal machine she would discern two sets of quadruple (recursive) rules: (a) those that inform the machine; and (b) the coded quadruples of the machine to be simulated. Analogously in a computer she would be able to distinguish (a') the machine itself which is designed to embody recursive rules (as we shall see), and (b') the program, which incorporates rules for a given process. The quadruples (a) are *embodied* in the universal machine design. I will also say the algorithm, which by CT the rules represent is *embodied.* On the other hand the rules (b) are *free* as they can be removed from tape and replaced by those of some other machine; and the represented algorithm is also *free.* Similarly for computers.[5]

This is an extremely important distinction as it marks a major difference between mechanism, which holds that at least some rules of mind are not free, and cognitivism which tends to think of perception and cognition as symbol manipulation via free algorithms (See Section II.6).

Although John von Neumann is generally credited with the idea of a stored program machine which *can perform calculations on its own program,* the idea already appears in Turing's work as we have just seen.[6] It is not clear whether either Turing or von Neumann saw that an actual computer is a Turing machine until sometime in the mid 1940s, although von Neumann knew of Turing's paper in 1938 when he invited him to come from England to the Institute for Advanced Study at Princeton (see Goldstein, 1972, pp. 274–275). At any rate by the early 1950s, design engineers referred to electronic computers being developed under their hands as "universal Turing machines".

(2) Although historically speaking the purpose of Turing's theory of machines was to provide a precise notion of an effectively calculable function,[7] the theory is applicable to any kind of symbol manipulation operations, or more generally still, to any digital or discrete entities. For instance we have already seen that the machine theory can be used to characterize the capabilities of an actual digital computer. I wish to sketch now some of the implications of the concept of the Turing machine as a formal system beyond the conventional concerns of deductive logic. In particular I should like to emphasize that a Turing machine is itself a formal system, as perhaps was noticed by the reader when I explained a computation on the string reversing machine. For a computation, which you will recall is a sequence of strings beginning with the initial instantaneous description, is recursive: *another* Turing machine could be specified whose task would be to tell whether a given sequence of the reverser was indeed a computation. Further, the initial instantaneous description plays exactly the same role as an axiom and each of the quadruple rules of Table I as a rule of inference in a logic, as we shall argue in some detail in a moment, and are themselves recursive rules. This phenomenon of systems which can talk about systems like themselves is perhaps the most essential property of Turing machine theory and the theory of recursive functions. In symbolic logic it is manifested in the practice of formalizing the metalanguage of a language, perhaps in the *language itself*, as in Gödel's famous incompleteness theorem. We will exploit this phenomenon in the development of the beginnings of the theory of intentionality in Chapters VI–X.

However, what is of most interest to us at this point about the self-reference of formal systems and in particular of Turing machines is the intimation that these systems are more general than formal logics, in other words that computational processes form a subject matter in their own right. This observation certainly did not escape Turing. But the development of the fundamental insight should really be credited to the American mathematician Emil Post, as should contemporary mechanism. There is not space here to review the contributions of this remarkable man, except in rather brief outline.[8]

Post taught that not only theorems of formal logics but strings of characters in other very general symbolic systems, called 'combinatory systems', can be generated by effective processes. He also was able to show that all rules of inference of any kind of a system that today we would characterize as a 'formal' system can be boiled down to 'productions', that is to say, essentially to rewriting rules of the kind discussed in linguistics and computer science (but not, strangely enough, in elementary logic courses in philosophy departments). A few paragraphs on we shall render Turing machine quadruples as Post-type production rules (Post, 1947). His third contribution, which was of as great importance for a mechanist theory as his generalization of formal systems and treatment of rules of inference, were his thoughts – which were quite sketchy – about the possibilities of a mechanical theory of mind. When one reduces logics to very general symbolic systems it becomes fairly reasonable to think of all mental processes as falling within their scope, namely as being effective processes within such systems. A stumbling block, however, was Post's anticipation of Gödel; for, if formal systems (later, Turing generable systems) no matter how general are incomplete, then it seems that our minds must transcend any such congeries of rules. However Post argued that the incompleteness properties of formal systems *did not imply that man is not a machine*, "but only that man cannot construct a machine which can do all the thinking he can".[9] Mechanism, as I wish to defend it in this book, is not necessarily implied by this enigmatic statement because Post's use of "machine" here is not sufficiently unambiguous. In an odd way he apparently meant to be invoking incompleteness as an argument to distinguish man *qua* machine of some kind from whatever he can construct in the way of an ideal mathematical machine. If he had in mind here the machines of his 1936 paper (see Note 8) then he seemed to be opposed to mechanism in the form being presented here. I will defend the thesis that man is a machine in precisely that form in the later chapters. Nevertheless, we find in his insights all of the basic ingredients of the mechanist hypothesis: symbolic (cognitive) processes are formal in the new extended sense and follow rules which are generalizations of the recursive rules of inference in ordinary logic.

After Post's own application of his generalized approach to formal technical problems in mathematics in the mid 1940s, the next major step in the expansion of the idea of a formal system outside of the domain of deductive logic was Chomsky's revolutionary work in linguistics beginning in the mid 1950s. The key idea is that the grammar of a natural language such as English can be described in part by a formal system including a finite number of productions or rewriting rules of the same kind Post introduced as generalized rules of inference.[10] Strictly speaking there is doubt as to whether English, for example, can be described by means of production rules alone. According to Chomsky and his followers the so-called 'surface structure' of sentences in vernacular languages can only be accounted for in terms of certain other rules, called transformations, which map 'deep structures' — generated by the formal systems we are about to describe — onto the sentences we actually use. As we shall see, however, the need for such rules, if it finally turns out that the ordinary phrase-structure type rewriting rules are insufficient, does not imply that language usage is not an effective process.

To the professional linguist perhaps the main importance of this key idea lies in its accounting for the *infinite character* of the language and for *grammatical structure*. As an example of a *phrase structure language* which illustrates these two points consider the following fragment of English. Its grammar consists of a *vocabulary*, an *initial symbol* S which means 'sentence', and twenty-one *rewriting rules*, which are Post-type substitution rules (our example, like any example of a Chomsky-type phrase structure language, is an instance of a Post formal system). The vocabulary has two parts, a *nonterminal* and a *terminal*. For our example the terminal vocabulary is the set

{ is, was, a, the, pretty, little, blond, girl, or, but, and, she }

while the nonterminal is the set

{ NP, VP, C, Pr, Adj, Adv, Art, N, V }.[11]

The force of the distinction between terminal and nonterminal is that substitutions under the rewriting rules may be made for the nonterminals but not for the terminals, as the construction of a few sentences of the language will show in a moment. The twenty-one rules of the grammar are the following:

TABLE II
A simple phrase-structure grammar.

R_1	S	→	NP + VP	R_{11}	Adj → pretty
R_2	S	→	S + C + S	R_{12}	Adj → little
R_3	S	→	Pr + VP	R_{13}	Adj → blond
R_4	NP	→	Art + Adj + N	R_{14}	Adv → pretty
R_5	N	→	Adj + N	R_{15}	N → girl
R_6	Adj	→	Adv + Adj	R_{16}	N → child
R_7	VP	→	V + NP	R_{17}	V → is
R_8	Pr	→	she	R_{18}	V → was
R_9	Art	→	a	R_{19}	C → and
R_{10}	Art	→	the	R_{20}	C → or
			R_{21} C → but		

Each sentence of this language is the last line of a finite sequence of strings starting with S such that each line after S follows from an earlier line by application of one of the rules. Consider 'the little girl is a pretty child'. We begin with S:

1. ·   S.

From 1 we obtain

2.   NP + VP

by use of rule R_1: NP + VP is substituted for S in 1. Next, we use R_4 and obtain

3.   Art + Adj + N + VP

and then R_7

4.   Art + Adj + N + V + NP

Imitating the usual display procedure in elementary logic we continue:

5.   Art + Adj + N + V + Art + Adj + N, by R_4
6.   the + Adj + N + V + Art + Adj + N, by R_{10}
7.   the + little + N + V + Art + Adj + N, by R_{12}

.

.

.

etc.

the + little + girl + is + a + pretty + child.

One can see that the sentences generated by this kind of derivation process will add up to an infinite set because of rule R_2 which is a 'self-embedding' rule. What this means is simply that the symbol S occurs to the right of the arrow as well as to the left, hence the rule can be applied over and over again *ad infinitum* constructing ever longer sentences connected by the junctives 'and', 'or', and 'but' (rules $R_{19}-R_{21}$).

We may picture the grammatical structure of this rather dull example in a *derivation tree*, as drawn below. Note that this tree has an S at the root which corresponds to the first step S in the earlier derivation, and then the structure of the tree pretty much follows steps of the conventional derivation.

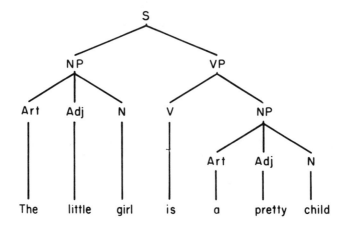

Fig. 1. Derivation tree.

The diagram shows that the sentence consists of two main phrases, a left and a right; the left has three constituent parts and the right two. Again, the right of the right has three parts.

A better example is 'she is a pretty little girl', which can be read in two ways, that is to say, which has two different grammatical structures. In Chomsky's theory the two structures reflect two distinct derivations, one which expresses that a certain girl is pretty little and another that a certain little girl is pretty. Here they are, given directly in tree form. The reader should be able to supply his own formal derivations (Figure 2).

The tree analyses are informal adjuncts to the basic theory which, un-adorned, goes a long ways toward accounting for the human competence to manage an infinite supply of sentences with the constituent structure of each informing its generation.

Before returning to the main line of the discussion it is of some importance in order to emphasize the unity of the main ideas underlying mechanism to see that a Turing machine computation is the same sort of process as a sentential derivation à la Chomsky. Each of the quadruple rules of Table I can be written as a Post-type production rule: Rules of form (i) can be written

$$q_i s_j \rightarrow q_l s_k;$$

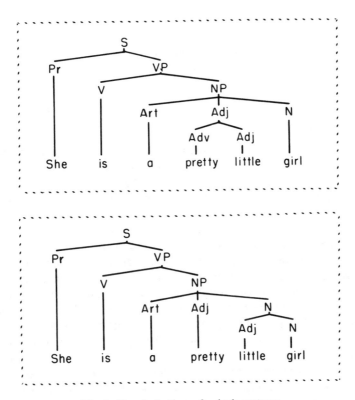

Fig. 2. Two derivations of a single sentence.

those of form (ii),

$$q_i s_j s_k \rightarrow s_j q_l s_k;$$

and those of form (iii),

$$s_k q_i s_j \rightarrow q_l s_k s_j.$$

And in the machine for computing the reversing transformations the rule (ii) of Table I becomes

$$q_0 b s_k \rightarrow b q_0 s_k$$

so that the first step of the computation from

$$q_0 babbb$$

yields

$$bq_0abbb$$

by rewriting q_0ba by bq_0a. Likewise rule (i) becomes

$$q_0as_k \rightarrow aq_0s_k.$$

This applied to the above line yields

$$baq_0bbb.$$

(In both of these new rules s_k is used as a variable in order to avoid writing a separate rule for each letter in the vocabulary of the Turing machine.) Thus Turing machines, too (as well as the usual logics, as was shown by Post) can be thought of as embodying just rewriting or production-type rules. This fact is of modest theoretical importance, for it gives us a kind of exemplar for the systems we want to term 'automata'.

Pre-Chomskian linguistics for the most part aimed primarily at classifying elements of human language, and not at explaining grammatical structure or at accounting for human linguistic usage. Chomsky's seminal discovery is that an approach in the style of modern logic can advance linguistics beyond taxonomy to the level of explanatory science. His discoveries stand to linguistics (and to some thinkers, to psycholinguistics and even psychology itself) as Darwin did to biology (Searle, 1972). The impact of Chomsky's work on philosophy of language and philosophy of mind has been no less great. However in the context of our present discussion the most significant aspect of his contributions to computer science, psychology and philosophy is the suggestion that basic linguistic and thought processes are mechanical in the sense we are here elaborating. One significant if not most typically human mental feature is brought within the pale of a strictly mechanistic theory.

I must caution the reader that the last statement is one with which Chomsky may not or does not on all occasions seem to agree. A transformational grammar, in the first place, represents the human being's syntactical *competence* in language, and not necessarily his actual *performance* — for example no man will ever utter more than a finite number of sentences, few of which will be perfectly grammatical — and yet he is *capable*, given an indefinitely long life and absence of supervening environmental and cultural influences, to generate perfectly grammatical sentences without limit. As a linguistic performer, perhaps man is not a machine, but something quite different, or if a machine something considerably less than a full universal

Turing machine. Second, as already intimated, transformation rules, if needed, may not be recursive rules. And third, although both speech and syntactical understanding be mechanical processes, the same might not be true of language acquisition or of semantical phenomena. Both the generation of sentences (speech), and recognition and understanding of sentences could be purely mechanical processes, being representable at least in principle by systems of recursive rewriting rules, while the learning of language might not be. There appears to be good reason to say that the learning of language is a *much* more complex phenomenon than the use of language once learned. We will have more to say about these topics in later chapters.

(3) Turing machines, Post systems and Chomsky grammars all operate on strings of *symbols*. But of course any digital, discrete objects will do — entities one can count, roughly. The example just discussed illustrates this fact, because one can conceive of a Turing machine wherein the symbols *a* and *b* are replaced by pebbles, people, stimulations of an organism's receptors (with the organism performing the reversing transformation), and so forth.

The remainder of our account, which historically overlaps that already delivered, concerns attempts of varying degrees of scientific usefulness or of philosophical significance to model a range of phenomena using essentially logical methods. I shall not attempt to assess the importance of any of these enterprises beyond stating that they all played a part in bringing the mechanist and, more generally, the contemporary functionalist hypothesis to a position of philosophical standing. All of these models or schemes turn out to be variations on the same basic Post-Turing theme, although superficially they appeared for a while to involve quite separate ideas.

Our version of mechanism claims that human beings are nondeterministic finite automata. It is now time to trace the development of this idea and to relate it to Turing machines and grammars of the Chomsky variety. The idea probably had its source in the mathematical theory of discrete Markov processes. This theory considers a finite number of states $q_0, q_1, \ldots, q_n$ of some system together with a set of transition probabilities $p_i(l)$ which specifies the probability of the system going from state q_i to q_l. Claude Shannon, in developing his theory of discrete state sources for information channels, assumed that for each such state-to-state transition there is a symbol from a finite alphabet which is emitted (Shannon and Weaver, 1949).[12] These symbols may be chosen from languages such as English, from continuous sources of information such as modulated carrier waves made discrete by a quantizing process, and so forth — a good example is the quantized television signal. Although Shannon did not look at the matter in quite this way, it is clear that such a Markovian information source consists of a collection of rules of the form

$$q_i \rightarrow s_j q_l$$

where, as in Turing machine logic, the q's are the states of the system and the symbols s_j are elements of the vocabulary. In addition, there is an initial state q_0 and each rule or transition has an associated probability $p_i(l)$. Now a Markov process of this kind generates a string of symbols as follows: the system in state q_0 goes to some state q_j and emits s provided that $q_0 \rightarrow sq_j$ is a rule of the system and that an appropriately random device picks q_j with its assigned probability $p_0(j)$. Then the system goes to q_k and emits s' provided there is a rule $q_j \rightarrow s'q_k$ with appropriate probabilities, and so forth.

Note that what we have on our hands is again simply a system of Post-type rewriting rules — with associated transition probabilities. If one *drops* the probabilities and adds rules of the form $q_i \rightarrow s$ the resulting system is precisely a Chomsky-type *finite state grammar*, which is by definition a system wherein the q's and s's are the nonterminal and terminal symbols of the vocabulary respectively, and the expressions $q_i \rightarrow s_j q_k$ are the rewriting rules.[13]

If the reader will compare such a grammar (see Note 13) with the fragment of English which we used as an illustration several pages back he cannot fail to note that both systems contain *more than one rule* with a fixed nonterminal to the left. For example, the English fragment of Table II has three rules with a nonterminal S to the left of the arrow, while the language of the last footnote has two rules with S on the left and four with V. As in any familiar logical system such as the propositional calculus, if there were no possibility of more than one line following from others in a proof there could be no more than *one* derived sentence. Systems having more than one rule which applies to a line in a derivation are said to be *polygenic*, and lead to the concept of *nondeterministic* automata and Turing machines.

Finite state grammars are not finite automata in the technical sense, but they are very closely related. In effect, a finite automaton is a finite state grammar in which the rewriting rules of the former are kind of inverse of the latter: if $q \rightarrow sq'$ is a rule of one, then $sq \rightarrow q'$ is a rule of the other. The essential similarity of the two concepts is so striking it is a wonder their basic equivalence was not precisely proved until 1960!

4. NERVE NETWORKS AND FINITE AUTOMATA

We have already traced half of the story behind the relation of finite automata to finite state grammars to the theory of stochastic processes and to the work of Shannon and Chomsky. The other half begins with the discovery by Pitts and McCulloch (see McCulloch and Pitts, 1943) that the activities of neurons in the brain considered under some not too implausible idealizations are *propositional functions of time*. This is no place to attempt a detailed exposition of the theory and we shall have to be satisfied with a few remarks which I hope will be at least suggestive. A neuron is considered to have a finite number of inputs (or for inner neurons, synaptic inputs) each capable of two states (electrical potential levels) which we call 'T' and 'F', and one output, the axon, which also has two states. At any time t each of these input and output entities are T or F. If x is an input, we may write $x(t)$ to express the value of x at t. If z is an output, we likewise may write $z(t)$ for the value of z at t. Under Pitts and McCulloch's assumptions all neurons have a certain response or *lag* time, which may be taken to be a standard unit of time designated by 1. It turns out that the output is always some *truth function $\mathscr{F}$ of the several inp*uts to a neuron, so that the operation can be represented by an expression of the following form:

$$\mathscr{F}(x_1(t), \ldots, x_n(t)) \equiv z(t+1).$$

This expression represents the axon state in terms of the inputs, as does the following diagram

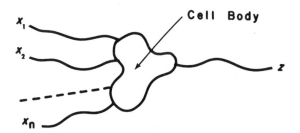

where the cell body of the neuron as schematically depicted realizes the function $\mathscr{F}$. Here '$\equiv$' is the familiar material biconditional, $\mathscr{F}$ is a truth function of the inputs x at time t as just explained, and $z(t+1)$ indicates the output state at a time of lag 1 beyond the neuronal input stimulation.

Owing to the anatomy of nerve cells, $\mathscr{F}$ can always be directly written as a disjunction of conjunctions of the propositional functions x, some of which may be negated.[14] Negated inputs are so-called *inhibitory* inputs and the unnegative ones are *excitatory*, but I have not indicated this in the schematic figure.

Axonal outputs of neurons might be inputs via synaptic couplings to other neurons, including themselves, and so on to yet other neurons, and by this proliferation produce nerve networks of arbitrary complexity. In the following diagram there are three neurons interconnected in various ways.

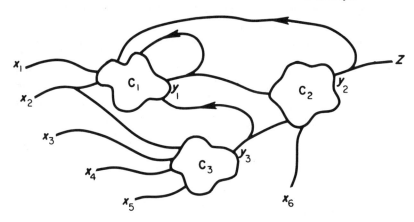

Fig. 3. Nerve network

The inputs $x_1, \ldots, x_6$ may be outputs of other neurons or *external* inputs (stemming from external receptors of various kinds). The axonal outputs of the cells are y_1, y_2, and y_3 for c_1, c_2, and c_3, and the ultimate output of this network is $z (\equiv y_2)$. In the diagram we think of the signals at $x_1, \ldots, x_6$ as passing from left to right, except for the feedback fibers from cell c_1 to itself and from c_2 and c_3 to c_1. In the general case the axon of each neuron of the net might be an input through a synaptic connection to every neuron including itself, so the axon state of each cell is a truth function of all the inputs and outputs. For this particular net, we have four expressions — one for each cell and one for the ultimate output z. The function corresponding to each c_i are $\mathscr{F}_i$, $i = 1, 2, 3$:

$$\mathscr{F}_1(x_1(t), x_2(t), y_1(t), y_2(t), y_3(t)) \equiv y_1(t+1)$$
$$\mathscr{F}_2(x_6(t), y_1(t), y_3(t)) \equiv y_2(t+1)$$
$$\mathscr{F}_3(x_2(t), x_3(t), x_4(t), x_5(t)) \equiv y_3(t+1)$$
$$z(t) \equiv y_2(t).$$

If we think of the net as operating starting at some conventional time $t = 0$, then we must also (as a little thought will show) assign some *initial value* to each cell axon y, say, $y_i(t) \equiv$ F for all i, or whatever other value the facts of the net supply. Thus we also have, say,

$$y_1(0) \equiv y_2(0) \equiv y_3(0) \equiv \text{F}.$$

In general any neuron network of this idealized kind can be represented by a pair of sets of equivalence formulas

$$y_i(0) \equiv \text{F (or T)} \tag{2a}$$
$$y_i(t + 1) \equiv \mathscr{F}_i(x_1(t), \ldots, x_n(t), y_1(t), \ldots, y_m(t)) \tag{2b}$$

where $i = 1, \ldots, m$ is the number of neurons, y_i is the axon of the ith neuron, $x_j, j = 1, \ldots, n$, is the jth of n synaptic inputs or inputs from external sense organs, and $\mathscr{F}_i$ is the truth functional (of propositional functions) realized by cell c_i. The ultimate outputs of the network (axons that excite muscular or other extra-neuronal processes) can be represented by equivalences

$$z(t) \equiv y_k(t) \tag{2c}$$

where k ranges over the indices of the output neurons.[15]

Pitts-McCulloch nerve networks are our first examples of finite automata, as sought. Since these networks have just been described in terms of the (idealized) anatomical details, it is not crystal clear that they have much to do with a system of Post production rules $qs \rightarrow q'$ as asserted a page or so back. To see that nets do embody such rules (just as the logician with his papers, or a Turing machine embodies a logic) we take a side excursion through a way of treating automata as abstract *mathematical systems*. The idea, in precise formulation, is due to Kleene (1951) although it certainly was in the air before 1951.[16]

First we rechristen inputs x_j and axons y_i *input elements* and *state elements* respectively. Now we form the n-tuple $(x_1(t), \ldots, x_n(t))$ of input elements; the value of this n-tuple at any designated time t is an *input*. In Figure 3 there are six input *elements* $x_1, \ldots, x_6$ and since at any t each element can be either T or F (or as we now prefer to write, '1' or '0') there will be 2^6 *inputs*. One of them for instance, is $(0, 1, 0, 1, 1, 1)$, which is the 6-tuple of values of input elements $x_1(t) \equiv 0, x_2(t) \equiv 1, x_3(t) \equiv 0, \ldots$ for some t. Finally, we assign an arbitrary abstract symbol to each input. For definiteness let us suppose we correlate s_0 to $(0, 0, 0, \ldots, 0)$, s_1 to $(0, 0, 0, \ldots, 1)$ s_2 to $(0, 0, 0, \ldots, 1, 0)$, etc. Using this assignment, the set $\{s_0, s_1, \ldots, s_{63}\}$ is the set of possible inputs to Figure 3.

Similarly we collect the ambiguous values $y_i(t)$ of state elements in ar m-tuple $(y_1(t), \ldots, y_m(t))$ a value of which for some t, is a *state* of the net In Figure 3 a possible state is $(1, 0, 1)$ which is the 3-tuple of values of the axons of the cells for some t. There are 2^3 possible states. Again, we effect an assignment of arbitrary abstract symbols (which must be distinct from the s's) to the states, say q_0 to $(0, 0, 0, \ldots, 0)$, q_1 to $(0, 0, 0, \ldots 1)$, and so forth.

There is nothing sacred about these assignments. s_0 could just as well be correlated to $(0, 0, 1, \ldots, 1)$, s_1 to $(1, 1, 1, \ldots, 1)$ etc. All that is needed is that the assignment be one-one and onto. Any such assignment is a *binary code* or *coding*, and the inverse is a *decoding*. What we have just done is *decode* the binary entities to an *abstract automaton*. Returning to states, we let $\{q_0, q_1, \ldots, q_7\}$ be the set of states for the example.

Let us generalize this abstract treatment of nerve networks so that for a cell c_i there might be a finite number of values other than 2, as in the conventional binary case. A certain system might have, for instance, two cells, one with 3 axon values and one with, say, 7, and a possible state might be $(2, 4)$ − assuming the values are labelled 0, 1, 2 and 0, 1, $\ldots$, 6 respectively.[17] If there are α cells, then the total number of states of the network will be the product $a_1 \cdot a_2 \ldots a_\alpha$ where a_i is the number of distinct values of the axonal output of c_i.

Similarly consider the inputs. Each net input will have its own number, say b, of values that cause a reaction across the synapse of a cell it impinges on (for interior cells of course the axon of one impinges through a synapse on the cell body of others so input values in the interior will also be axon values − see (2b)). If there are β ultimate input fibers x to the net, then the number of input states will be $b_1 \cdot b_2 \ldots b_\beta$.

Finally we can associate abstract symbols $s_0, s_1, \ldots$ to the separate β-tuples of values of the ultimate input fibers x and $q_0, q_1, \ldots$ to the internal states (α-tuples of values of axons) as in the binary case. Focusing on just the properties that the s's and q's are distinct and comprise finite sets, we now see that a finite automaton consists of these two sets of abstract symbols (indeed, any arbitrary objects) and a function M from the cartesian product of $\{q_0, q_1, \ldots, q_n\}$ and $\{s_0, s_1, \ldots, s_m\}$ to $\{q_0, q_1, \ldots, q_n\}$. In mathematical notation this is written

$$M: Q \times S \to Q.$$

In some more detail: (2b) tells us that $y_i(t + 1)$ depends on all the x and y values at t, so abstracting again from explicit reference to time and supposing

q_i is the symbol assigned to $(y_1(t), \ldots, y_m(t))$, s_j to $(x_1(t), \ldots, x_n(t))$ and q_k to $(y_1(t+1), \ldots, y_m(t+1))$, we have derived that (q_i, s_j) is mapped by M to q_k if and only if (2b) holds. So, again, a *finite automaton* is essentially a pair of finite, non-empty disjoint sets Q and S together with a map $M: Q \times S \rightarrow Q$. Some of a net's axonal outputs, we saw, were ultimate in that they split into fibers not feeding back via synaptic connections to inner cells. To incorporate these into our generalized picture we use (2c). If there are k of these then we assign, in a way harking back to our earlier assignments of s's and q's, symbols o to k-tuples of O's and 1's, in the binary case, or of other values in the general case. Then (2c) serves to define another function from a subset (ultimate axons only) Q' of Q to the set O of all the o's. We term this function 'N', and write '$N: Q' \rightarrow O$' in the usual mathematical style. So the complete formulation is that a *finite automaton* comprises now *three* sets Q, S, O and the two abstract finite functions M and N.[18]

In our example of Figure 3, the network itself or the corresponding formulas (2a, b, and c) (which we did not specify in detail, but could) completely determine M and N; so in this case we say that $M: Q \times S \rightarrow Q$ and $N: Q' \rightarrow O$ are such that the values (written now in the customary notation) $M(q, s) = q'$ and $N(q) = o$ are given by the net. This completely defines the two functions. In general, without going through the coding procedure that assigns s's to m-tuples, q's to n-tuples and o's to k-tuples as above, these functions are given by or simply *are* tables. The following Table III is a finite automaton:

TABLE III
Finite automaton table.

q \ s	M		N
	s_0	s_1	
q_0	q_1	q_0	
q_1	q_0	q_2	
q_2	q_2	q_2	o

Here, $Q = \{q_0, q_1, q_2\}$, $S = \{s_0, s_1\}$, $O = \{o\}$ and the M part of the table shows that (q_0, s_0) maps into q_1, (q_0, s_1) to q_0 (or $M(q_0, s_0) = q_1$, $M(q_0, s_1) = q_0$), and so forth. Only q_2 has an output o (written to the right of q_2 under N) associated to it, i.e., $N(q_2) = o$.

It does not take much imagination to see that (a) a finite automaton table can be written as a list of productions of the Post type, $qs \to q$, and $q \to c$ (the reader is invited to do so for the example just given); and (b) a Turing machine, in either the quadruple (p. 19) or production-type (p. 32) formulation can be written as a pair of function tables with M being the map from $q_i s_j$ to s_k and N from $q_i s_j$ to $\{R, L, s_k\}$. Table I turns out to be Table IV when written in this new way.

TABLE IV
Tabular form of Turing machine.

q $\backslash$ s	M				N			
	a	b	c	B	a	b	c	B
q_0	q_0	q_0	$-$	q_1	R	R	$-$	L
q_1	q_2	q_4	q_1	q_5	c	c	L	R
q_2	q_2	q_2	q_2	q_3	R	R	R	a
q_3	q_3	q_3	q_1	$-$	L	L	L	$-$
q_4	q_4	q_4	q_4	q_3	R	R	R	b
q_5	$-$	$-$	q_6	$-$	$-$	$-$	B	$-$
q_6	$-$	$-$	$-$	q_5	$-$	$-$	$-$	R

Facts (a) and (b) suggest that a Turing machine might be realized by a nerve network: if one could work backwards from a table to a construction of an idealized net (one *can*, even by an algorithm, i.e., by use of *another* Turing machine!) and associate operations move R or L and print a, b, c or a Blank (which can be done) the resulting system would be a Turing machine, except for the tape, which makes all the difference in the world. At the moment let us be satisfied to observe that an idealized neuron system embodies recursive rules and by CT, realizes an *embodied* algorithm.

The computational or information-processing power of a Turing machine resides in its having an infinite external memory on tape. One can imagine a machine to be supplied with a factory that adds tape on either end whenever the machine is about to run off. A nerve net, on the other hand, 'takes in' input in one direction only, which can be shown to be equivalent to having a finite tape of some definite bounded length. Hence nerve nets can perform much less complex processing than full Turing machines, and as we shall now see are in a certain sense equivalent to finite state grammars.

Kleene studied the question of what strings of inputs will cause a finite automaton starting off in an *initial internal state* q_0 to end up in a designated *final* state q_F. An answer to this question would tell us in exact mathematical terms what tasks a finite size nerve network can perform. We may regard all such tasks for finite automata as species of detection or recognition of sets of strings.

The automaton of Table III can be shown to 'recognize' all and only the elements of a certain set as follows. To avoid notational clutter let's rewrite 0 for s_0 and 1 for s_1 in Table III:

TABLE IIIa

q \ s	M		N
	0	1	
q_0	q_1	q_0	
q_1	q_0	q_2	
q_2	q_2	q_2	o

Then IIIa accepts any string having a block of 1's of any length followed by a block of any length of 0's following by a single 1, followed by any mixture of 1's and 0's. This is an infinite set of strings 111 ... 000 ... 1*xxx*. IIIa accepts such strings in the exact sense that when a sequence of inputs of this kind are sent into the corresponding nerve network that realizes IIIa it goes into a final state q_2 and emits an output o (cf. Section VI.2).

Kleene proved that the family of sets of strings for which there are accepting finite automata is a certain rather restricted subfamila of the recursive sets of logic, namely of those sets whose elements can be decided by Turing machines. But the details are not particularly interesting for our purposes: our main concern is to relate finite automata to grammars of the Chomsky type. Later we shall use them as models of perception.

In tracing the development of the automaton idea from Pitts and McCulloch to Kleene we have almost completed the second half of the story about finite state grammars and finite automata. Recall I promised to show that they were governed by similar rules, specifically the type of one being kinds of inverses of the other; and this is so: finite state grammars have rules of the forms $q \rightarrow sq'$ and $q \rightarrow s$, while finite automata have rules of the forms $qs \rightarrow q'$ and $q \rightarrow o$. Thus except for a certain radical difference, a simple grammar and a simple automaton appear to be very similar: one *generates* a set, a Chomsky language of strings, via a set of rules which are a kind of inverse of those of a finite automaton, which *recognizes* certain sets of strings. The radical difference is that the automata are *deterministic* − i.e., the relation of qs to the next state q' as just noted above, is a mathematical function −, while the relation of q to qs in grammar is polygenic or *nondeterministic* − i.e., a nonfunctional relation. This circumstance suggests to us that there might be such a thing as a *nondeterministic* finite automaton which would be of some theoretical interest. (A deterministic grammar would be of no interest as it would generate but *one* sentence. We have already mentioned this once above.) Indeed, just this idea was caught by Rabin and Scott (1959).

Simply stated, a *nondeterministic finite automaton* is one in which the next state from an input and a present state is not unique. Such a system might, therefore, contain rules such as

$$qs \rightarrow q'$$
$$qs \rightarrow q'' \tag{3}$$

where $q' \neq q''$. We might imagine that such a machine recognizes strings by moving from state to state aided by a little demon that chooses the next state from among the possibilities allowed by the rules. For these automata we say that a set of strings is *accepted* if and only if for every string in the set there exists a sequence of states (constructed, if you please, by the demon) leading to an ultimate output. Quite clearly, the event of injecting a sequence into such a machine would not in every case lead to acceptance. But despite the looseness of a nondeterministic machine it was shown by Rabin and Scott that the recognized sets are precisely the same as those recognized by deterministic automata; in other words every ordinary deterministic finite state automaton is equivalent to some nondeterministic finite automaton and *vice versa*. In due course we will make as much philosophical hay of this as we possibly can.

It did not take long to notice that nondeterministic automata and finite state grammars are the same − as we have said − one having rules which are a kind of inverses of the other's, and both nondeterministic. From this fact it was easy to show, using the above stated equivalence, that the sets of strings Kleene characterized as being recognized by finite automata comprise exactly the same family of sets as the finite state language of Chomsky.[19] Thus at bottom nerve networks and grammatical rules, which no doubt the mind some how internalizes, turn out in simple, idealized cases to be essentially the same theoretical items. The languages one can recognize are exactly the same as those that can be generated by a speaker. This circumstance already suggests that a theory of perception (visual, auditory, etc.) for an organism having a finite brain will be not unlike a theory of linguistic recognition. This has been noticed by many workers in the field, and I will develop my own connections in later chapters.[20]

This completes that part of the historical sketch up through the discovery of finite automata.

5. COMPUTER LOGIC

At the same time the concepts from logic just reviewed were being explored as models of grammars and nerve networks, they were also being applied to switching and computing networks. It occurred to a number of people at roughly the same time that sequential switching circuits, either electromagnetic, electronic, or later solid state, as used in telephone networks and in the then newly developing digital computers, are finite automata *with output*. These automata have also been referred to as *sequential machines* or *finite transducers.*[21] The automaton models these writers used turn out to be essentially the same as those we squeezed out of Pitts-McCulloch nerve networks, with the exception that the output map N has as its domain the entire set of symbols Q, and not some subset as we determined from expression (2c). Hence, these automata viewed as mathematical systems consist of three finite sets Q, S, O and a *next state* or *transition function M* and an *output function N*. Just as before, the M function is defined on the cartesian product of Q and S and as just explained, N is defined on Q. Automata in this form were studied by Moore, whose results we will use heavily below in discussing behaviorism in contrast to mechanism. Another formulation (this time due to Mealy and Huffman more or less jointly) takes the N function to be defined again on the cartesian product of Q and S; but these two formulations of finite automata with output can be shown to be completely equivalent. Kleene's accepting automata are quite special as the recognition behavior of his machines is signaled by a single positive output, o of O.[22]

Throughout the rest of this book I shall always use the expression 'finite automaton' or 'nondeterministic finite automaton' for machines with full output, whereas I shall use 'accepting' for automata that recognize strings in the sense of Kleene's version of the theory of nerve nets.

In 1957 Burks and Copi showed that a stored program digital computer, including its (finite) tape or other external store as part of the automaton internal states is a finite automaton under certain idealizations, especially

that the circuitry thereof be error-free and perfectly synchronous in operation (Burks and Copi, 1957). They accomplished this task by proving that all
functions of standard computers, such as those of the arithmetic and control
units, can be realized by idealized logic components which are quite similar
to neurons in significant respects. The logic components include organs
that realize the truth functions of two variables and another organ called a
delay which simply displaces a 0 or 1 signal one *clock* time of a machine.
Some electrical or electronic devices naturally embody, with appropriate
pulse-shaping, certain functions — for example a vacuum triode realizes
negation, and an NPN transistor embodies the Peirce stroke ($\downarrow$) function
of elementary logic. Microminature or monolithic semiconductor circuitry
has still other logical properties. However it is quite convenient and completely sufficient to use 'and-or-not' logic; and besides for most people it is
easier to follow. So the basic ingredients of computer (or any other logical
switching circuit systems or binary (two-valued) discrete state *signal* systems)
includes the following componentry: the *and, or*, and *not* functions, and
the *delay*. In logic diagrams these are represented as shown in the next
figure.

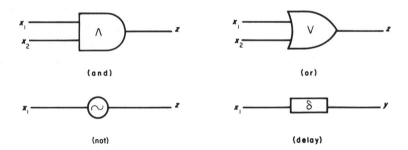

(and)   (or)

(not)   (delay)

Fig. 4. Logic components.

The *and* component has the function $z(t) \equiv x_1(t) \wedge x_2(t)$, the *or* function
$z(t) \equiv x_1(t) \vee x_2(t)$, the *not* function $z(t) \equiv {\sim}x_1(t)$ and, finally, the *delay*.
$y(t + 1) \equiv x_1(t)$, x_1, x_2, z, etc. are here and in the figure used ambiguously
as labels for wires and as propositional function *variables*, just as in nerve
networks.

Delays are used to compensate for the *lack of lag* in the virtually instantaneous action of most *and, or, not* switches. In order to realize recursive
processes circuits for nerve networks or perhaps any conceivable logic organs

must be able to *remember* inputs. Thus suppose we desire to create a two-input switching system that emits a 1 at time t just in case it had 1 at input x_2, and *either* a 1 at input x_1 or an output of 1 at a previous time $t - 1$. Such a circuit would be designed as in the figure.

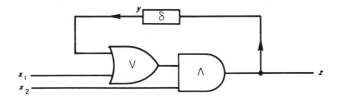

Now if $x_1 \equiv x_2 \equiv 1$ at time t, then z is 1 at time t. If $x_1 \equiv 0$ and $x_2 \equiv 1$ at time $t + 1$, then since y is 1 at time $t + 1$ in virtue of the delay, z is also 1 at time $t + 1$ as desired. Try it without a delay:

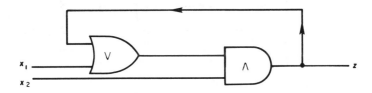

In this case every thing is alright at time 1, but at $t + 1$ $z \equiv 0$, as is x_1, and that's that. The thing doesn't remember anything and does not fulfill the wanted function. The built in latency of nerve cells, however, enables this sort of function without special organs. Using the diagrams of Figure 4, a *serial binary adder* has the logic of Figure 5.

If the reader cares to check how this works, imagine the two terms to be added arriving on x_1 and x_2, least significant bit (0 or 1) first. The terms are made the same length by filling in 0's at the high-order end of the short term, if there is one. The sum appears bit by bit at z_1, least significant bit first with the last (most significant) bit emitted at time $k + 1$ if the longest summand has length k and the action begins at time $t = 0$. y_1 is the *carry* line and at any time t is 0 or 1; these are the two states of the adder (in effect the circuit is in a *carry state* that remembers a carry when $y_1(t) \equiv 1$).

There are two formulas that represent this device, one for the sum at z_1 and one for the carry at y_1. These may be written in simplified form:

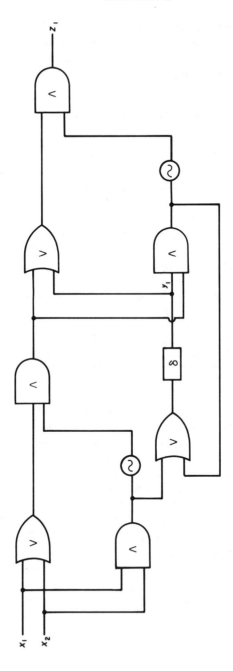

Fig. 5. Serial theory adder.

$$y_1(0) \equiv 0 \tag{3a}$$

$$y_1(t+1) \equiv [(x_1(t) \wedge x_2(t)) \vee ((x_1(t) \vee x_2(t))$$
$$\wedge \sim (x_1(t) \wedge x_2(t)) \wedge y_1(t))] \tag{3b}$$

$$z_1(t) \equiv [((x_1(t) \vee x_2(t)) \wedge \sim (x_1(t) \wedge x_2(t))) \vee y_1(t)]$$
$$\wedge \sim [y_1(t) \wedge (x_1(t) \vee x_2(t)) \wedge \sim (x_1(t) \wedge x_2(t))] . \tag{3c}$$

Inspection shows that (3a) and (3b) are instances of (2a) and (2b), p. 39. But here (3c) is function of both the y's and the x's unlike the general case of the nerve net (2c) on p. 39 where z depends on y only (although as we have asserted nerve nets and circuits are essentially equivalent concepts).

By an abstraction process reminiscent of the one used on nets, we see that the adder has four *inputs* (0, 0), (0, 1), (1, 0), (1, 1), — which are ordered pairs of values of the propositional functions x_1 and x_2, two *states* 0 and 1 which are likewise possible values of y_1, and two outputs 0 and 1 which are the values of z_1. In tabular form we may therefore express (3b) and (3c) as below.

TABLE V
Automaton adder.

y_1	x_1, x_2	M				N			
		(0, 0)	(0, 1)	(1, 0)	(1, 1)	(0, 0)	(0, 1)	(1, 0)	(1, 1)
0		0	0	0	1	0	1	1	0
1		0	1	1	1	1	0	0	1

Here M is the transition function mapping states and inputs to states, and N the output function from the same domain to outputs.

It would be very instructive for future application to see how one might work backwards from Table V to the Network of Figure 5 *via coding*. Let's do so in enough detail so that the reader who is familiar with truth functional logic techniques might fill in the holes. What we just did was ascend to the abstract automaton *via decoding* much as we did for the nerve net of Figure 3. The process of decoding from a net through formulas like (3a), (3b), and (3c) is unique for finite automata and produces just one abstract automaton up to an isomorphism. The reverse process, however, yields in principal an infinite number of nets although in designing artifacts one goes for the simplest according to some figure of merit. Before undertaking the derivation of the formulas (3b), and the rest let us take the final step to decode Table V, yielding the abstract adder of Table Va. The code (decode) mapping is

$$q_0 \leftrightarrow 0 \qquad q_1 \leftrightarrow 1$$
$$s_0 \leftrightarrow 00 \qquad s_1 \leftrightarrow 01$$
$$s_2 \leftrightarrow 10 \qquad s_3 \leftrightarrow 11$$
$$o_0 \leftrightarrow 0 \qquad o_1 \leftrightarrow 1.$$

The next table is

TABLE Va
Abstract automaton adder.

	M				N			
	s_0	s_1	s_2	s_3	s_0	s_1	s_2	s_3
q_0	q_0	q_0	q_0	q_1	o_0	o_1	o_1	o_0
q_1	q_0	q_1	q_1	q_1	o_1	o_0	o_0	o_1

Going backwards over the steps just covered, V is a coding of Va according to the given mapping. Here the encodment of the s symbol is not quite arbitrary because we wish to use symbols that square with the conventions of binary arithmetic. For this reason the design process in actual practice would start with Table V. In that table notice that what the N portion means is that when there is an input $(0, 0)$, for instance, and a carry of 0 (i.e., when the machine is in a state 0) there is a partial sum output of 0; in the M part the carry (next state) is 0. Another example: when the summands are $(0, 1)$ and there is a carry (when the machine is in state 1) the output is 0 and the next carry state is 1.

Back to the derivation. Recalling that 0 is a surrogate for F(alse) and 1 for T(rue), what we want to obtain are truth functional formulas that express M and N, which in coded form are just truth tables. So we obtain formulas in complete disjunctive normal form that express these functions in the arguments x and y. In the M part of V we get the condition for y_1:

$$((x_1 \wedge x_2 \wedge {\sim}y_1) \vee ({\sim}x_1 \wedge x_2 \wedge y_1) \vee (x_1 \wedge {\sim}x_2 \wedge y_1)$$
$$\vee (x_1 \wedge x_2 \wedge y_1))$$

noting that y_1 has the value 1 in the interior of the M table just under this disjoint condition. Likewise for z:

$$(({\sim}x_1 \wedge x_2 \wedge {\sim}y_1) \vee (x_1 \wedge {\sim}x_2 \wedge {\sim}y_1) \vee ({\sim}x_1 \wedge {\sim}x_2 \wedge y_1)$$
$$\vee (x_1 \wedge x_2 \wedge y_1))$$

which is derived from the N part of the table. Using truth functional equivalences these formulas simplify down to

$$[(x_1 \wedge x_2) \vee ((x_1 \vee x_2) \wedge {\sim}(x_1 \wedge x_2) \wedge y)] \tag{3d}$$

and

$$[((x_1 \vee x_2) \wedge {\sim}(x_1 \wedge x_2)) \vee y_1] \wedge {\sim}[y_1 \wedge (x_1 \vee x_2)$$
$$\wedge {\sim}(x_1 \wedge x_2)] \tag{3e}$$

(3d) expresses conditions for the next state of y_1 as a function of the inputs and y_1 itself. Therefore, in order to 'remember' these inputs and states it must be delayed one time unit as previously explained. Thus, explicitly introducing time and a delay of 1 for y_1 we obtain (3b) from (3d). '$y_1(0) \equiv 0$' expresses the fact the circuit always begins operating at $t = 0$ with a 0 carry. z, since it depends only on inputs and the present state and not on itself at a previous time, outputs at (roughly) the same time as the inputs are activated. Again explicitly introducing time we obtain (3c) from (3e).

The network diagram itself (Figure 5) derives more or less directly from the formulas (3b) and (3c). The internal state element y_1 is represented by the output of the delay. The input to the delay is the output of a network corresponding to (3b): that output is the output of the *or* component corresponding to the major connective of (3b). Similarly for the other subformulas. Then the network feeding the output z is constructed in a similar manner, using part networks, if possible, to represent identical tokens of subformulas. For instance '$x_1(t) \vee x_2(t)$' occurs three times in (3b) and (3c) while the corresponding net configuration occurs but once, at the upper left of Figure 5.

Philosophically it is of considerable importance, believe it or not, that the procedure just exemplified for FA and binary computing networks in effect *individuates* the net; or as one might say (still somewhat elliptically) the formulas individuate the net to within commutativity of $\vee$ and $\wedge$ and an intuitive step that allows, in a manner just indicated, one net part to stand for several tokens of subformulas. As we shall see in the next chapter this circumstance has implications for a kind of classical realism about the being of recursive rules.

A large scale digital computer, then, is nothing but an enormous table (set of rules) of this type as regards its logical function; but how the circuit scheme such as Figure 5 corresponding to Table V is actually realized in hardware is something else. The mode of operation of the adder (to stick to consideration of just this part of the computer) can be discerned by inspection of Figure 5, i.e., by 'chasing pulses' or by manipulation of a kind of algebra just discussed. For our purposes it is best to think of the adder as a system of recursive Post-type production rules. Switching circuits are not viewed this way by practicing engineers nor was the connection even seen until 1960. In that year, C. Y. Lee (Lee, 1960) of the Bell Telephone Laboratories observed that an idealized digital computer or equivalently an idealized nerve network is essentially a Turing machine which moves left (or right) only, with respect to external input, thinking of that input in time as a string on tape (not to be confused with internalized tapes, disks, or whatever in the Burks-Copi Model).

Hence a computer or nerve net is logically speaking nothing but an *embodiment* of a very large set of quadruples of the type (i) or (ii) on p. 19, or, alternatively of a set of productions as displayed on p. 32. In fact since motion is 'one way', we need only rules of the form

$$q_i s_j \rightarrow q_l s_k \qquad (4)$$

where q_i is the state at a certain present time, q_l is the next state, s_j is the input (which for a computer will be an enormous array of 0's and 1's) and s_k the output, likewise a large array. From Table V we construct the rules for the serial adder differentiating, as is necessary, states from outputs by use of parentheses. We write state 0, '(0)' and output 0, '0'. Here are the rules.

TABLE VI
Adder in form of production rules.

(i)	$(0) (0, 0) \rightarrow 0(0)$	(v)	$(1) (0, 0) \rightarrow 1(0)$
(ii)	$(0) (0, 1) \rightarrow 1(0)$	(vi)	$(1) (0, 1) \rightarrow 0(1)$
(iii)	$(0) (1, 0) \rightarrow 1(0)$	(vii)	$(1) (1, 0) \rightarrow 0(1)$
(iv)	$(1) (1, 1) \rightarrow 0(1)$	(viii)	$(1) (1, 1) \rightarrow 1(1)$

Suppose now that two integers in binary notation 1010 and 1100 are to be added. As the rules (see (4)) operate from left to right, we reverse the terms to 0101 and 0011. Then we write the terms (the 'addend' and 'augend') as symbol pairs (one component from one term to be added and the other from the other) yielding a string $(0, 0) (1, 0) (0, 1) (1, 1)$. This string should be thought of as precisely a string on a Turing machine tape. As in the case of Ernest's string reverser, we begin with the initial state – here (0) – written to the left of the string:

(1)   (0) (0, 0) (1, 0) (0, 1) (1, 1) (0, 0).

This is the initial instantaneous description in which we have added at the end the symbol (0, 0) for an ultimate carry, should there be one. So from (1) using rule (i) we obtain

(2)   0(0) (1, 0) (0, 1) (1, 1) (0, 0);

and from (2) using (iii)

(3)   01(0) (0, 1) (1, 1) (0, 0).

Then applying (ii), (iv), and (v) in that order we obtain

(6)   01101(0)

and the thing halts scanning a blank. Written in normal form the string of (6) is 10110, which is sure enough the correct sum (22 of 10 and 12 in decimal notation). Of course this is only of theoretical interest, exhibiting that indeed nerve-nets, switching and computer circuits, etc. are all at bottom systems of recursive rules — rules that specify which 'strings' follow which, and that apply by a purely effective or mechanical process.

The upshot of this historical discussion is that one can grasp a rather large number of phenomena ranging from logic, grammars and Turing machines to brains and circuits using one collection of extremely closely related ideas — indeed, of Post production systems. One is justified in suspecting that here we have found an idea which is not only pervasive but central to the understanding of a wide variety of intelligent or at least of information processing activities.[23]

6. GLIMPSES FROM PSYCHOLOGY

Before turning from our historical sketch completely, it would be of especial relevance to indicate three movements in psychology which rest on essentially the same ideas we have been describing. One of them arose in the work of Hebb (1949) in an attempt to develop a kind of neurophysiologically based psychology in which autonomous central activities are posited in order to account for certain facts observed in the behavior of animals. For example, psychologists had long known that men and animals respond to some events in the environment rather than to others which could be responded to just as well. With some reluctance, psychologists referred to 'set' or "attention" as some kind of factor beyond stimulus excitation that controls the response or psychologically significant properties of the response. Typically, psychologists attempted to account for behavior using a strictly stimulus-response (S–R) methodology, either to keep within the framework laid out by behaviorists or otherwise to avoid attribution of special mysterious faculties to the organism, while at the same time smuggling in the notion of a set or attention. Hebb explicitly introduced a theory of certain 'cell assemblies', complexes which emerge in the life of the organism and which when developed are relatively autonomous. According to Hebb, this means their activity is not to be the intervening effect of a stimulus in an S–R situation but rather to play a role in organizing the response to a stimulus. Abstractly, what we have is that animal behavior (responses, motor activity, etc.) is a function of both external stimuli and autonomous processes in preformed neural assemblies, which latter operate independently of the current stimuli. Viewed in this way a Hebbian organism embodies a function isomorphic to the output function N of some finite automaton. I hesitate to try for the next step, which would be to exhibit in his theory anything at all like the finite automaton transition function M, although if we count cell assembly states as internal states one might argue that any such state is a function of a previous state and input. Another contribution of Hebb's which strengthens our suggested interpretation is his theory of perception, which opposes the gestalt theory that organisms somehow grasp the whole independent of the parts, in favor of a theory of a serial, temporal process in which autonomous cell assemblies play an organizing part.

Of course one can squeeze almost any phenomenon, natural or cultural, into just about any preconceived mathematical mold, given enough latitude in one's mode of description of that phenomenon. My point here, however, is not to attempt any such feat but only to emphasize that the notion, roughly, of an autonomous internal state was in the wind at about the same time as the development in logic and machine theory, which I have been tracing, took place and was apparently under no particular influence from the latter.[24] If I am right, Hebb anticipated (without explicit recognition of the abstract underlying logical structure of his theory) Kolmogoroff by nearly a decade. Here is recognition of the crucial importance of inner structure in the behavior of the entire organism, a point of view which is essentially psychological. This position is near that of the present book, with the exception that we make no guesses as to the neural mechanisms realizing internal states and state transitions nor do we presuppose that all states or state components are brain states. In my theory the organism, not just the brain, has mentality.

Somewhat later another movement (Craik, 1943) arose in psychology that regarded thought as a symbolism of the same kind as figures in mechanical calculation (shades of Leibniz!). Thought in this sense was to be seen as a kind of conceptual planning using a symbolic model of reality in the head. This is very much the position of modern cognitivism in psychology and specifically appeals to machine notions although of course not to abstract automaton representations, as the latter theory was nearly a decade away (Kleene, 1951).[25]

Craik's ideas illustrate an approach to mind as a free system (as discussed in Section 3 above) analogous to a universal Turing machine or "instruction driven" hardware. By contrast, the nerve and computer networks just described *embody* algorithms. This is a good place to explore further the difference between free and embodied algorithms.

For Craik cognition is processing of internal representations — inner symbols of some sort — that are translations of external objects or processes. These symbols comprise an inferential system that translates out comes to bodily action; what we call "mind" is symbolism, and thought is construction of symbolic models of external reality and of the subject's own possible actions. Thus cognition is information processing.

One can not help but see the analogy between Craikian symbols, models in thought, and symbol influence on action and universal Turing machine inputs, quadruples of simulated machines and outputs (or input data, program, and output of a computer). If one were to count this conception of models as an anticipation it would have to be of systems of *free* rules or algorithms, as internal representations could presumably be fashioned into models of plans of action and abandoned at will. However the underlying processor as an effective system of some kind (it need not be!) would be a system of *embodied* rules. Contemporary cognitivism tends to construe mind and cognition in very much this way.

Another early idea is that of G.A. Miller and his collaborators (Miller, *et. al.,* 1960). Struck by the similarity between a cognitive plan guiding an organism's behavior and a computer program, and stimulated by the then very recent work in computer simulation of cognitive processes and by the work of Chomsky, they were moved to explore the relevance of cybernetical ideas to psychology. The key idea was that of a TOTE (acronymic for 'test-operate-test') unit, which is a model of a negative feedback controlled process.[26] Such a unit can be represented as in the diagram.

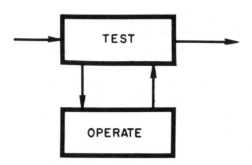

Fig. 6. A TOTE unit.

A stimulus signal entering the top left-most arrow causes the test (or control) part of the unit to check whether the operation is needed; if not, TEST sends an output signal (transfers control) to some other unit of the system (arrow going out to the right); if needed, the system operates and tests iteratively until the operation is complete. The hypothesis that Miller explored is that interconnected systems of these units can model intelligent skills and mental plans which seem to be beyond stimulus-response theories. Whether this early effort at application of cybernetical ideas can be counted as a success or a failure is really of no great importance. What is important here is that TOTE hierarchies are finite automata, and that the theory can in principle be formulated in such terms — putting one more early development within the circle of ideas we have been reviewing here.[27]

7. SUMMARY ON RULES

This completes my historical sketch to about 1960 of the development of several lines of theory in logic itself, neurophysiology, linguistics, circuit theory, psychology and computer science that rest on the concept of recursive rule. Although these rules are realized in the actual world in various guises, *they can all be regarded as kinds of rewriting rules or Post production.* Anything that realizes a collection of such rules is an automaton — which includes, of course, phrase structure grammars.[28]

Anything has a mind, we said, if it realizes rules of sufficient complexity to account for mental features (*not* occurrents!), especially intentional aspects of mind including language, and which is capable of consciousness. Of course we have seen no instance in the foregoing account, except for the brain, that is capable of managing natural language and that can think as we (or some of us, anyhow) do.

For the next chapter it will be helpful to review and in doing so to sharpen some of the central ideas of rules and automata introduced in my historical sketch. The key idea is that of an effective process, which I take to be a generalization of a computation. In ordinary English 'computations' arc operations on numbers or other mathematical objects; but we want this usage extended to Ernest's computations on symbols and still more generally to any enumerable entities and to polygenic or nondeterministic processes. Thus CT, which is central in Chapter IV, is to be used in the form:

All effective processes are recursive, and conversely. This involves three generalizations that remove us slightly from Church and Turing.

First, 'effectively calculable' function, which is Church's phrase, goes over to *effective processes* in order to avoid the limiting connotation of 'arithmetical function', as just said.

Second, 'recursive' now applies not only to functions but to relations over numbers, symbols, 'ideas', or whatever. This seems to me to be reasonable as all such things are either recursive functions, predicates, or sets, or become such under some kind of definite coding.

The third change requires more than a sentence. Strictly speaking a recursive function or relation is one from natural numbers to natural numbers that is formally definable by certain inductive means (there are variations), not by Turing machines, as I did in the previous section. It is a mathematical *discovery* that the functions defined by these means comprise exactly the same class as those computable via Turing machines (which is why it was all right for me to characterize one in terms of the other). The Turing idea is of course broader than recursiveness as Turing machines can operate on any discrete entities, not just numbers. But in addition to definition by induction or by Turing machines, there are ways of obtaining identically the same class of recursive functions: by systems of Post rules, certain formalized computer program schemes, the calculus of lambda conversion (due to Church), Markov algorithms, and others. To each one of these there corresponds a companion to Church's thesis: All effective functions are recursive (or Turing computable, or Post computable, or program computable, or definable by lambda conversion, Markov algorithms, or etc.). Now here's the third part of my generalization. I will use 'recursive' to cover the *whole family* of equivalent ways of explicating the intuitive idea of an effective process. When I say a rule or other relation or function is recursive I mean it to be an element of some member of this family, i.e., of the class of processes formulable by either automaton rules, Post-type rules, etc., or *perhaps in some language yet unknown*. The reason for this should be quite clear: as a mechanist I do not want to be saddled with a defense that mental features are literally, say, finite automaton rules (although I *will* argue that the individual *as a whole* is an NFA). All that is really at stake in my logic of mind is that these features be effective and hence by CT as just generalized expressible in some way equivalent to recursive relations, etc.; i.e., as recursive rules. Any such feature or composition of features is a *mechanism* and has a recursive logic.

It is absolutely essential to understand that recursive rules in this book are purely *syntactical.* A common error in cognitive science and philosophy of mind is to deny that computers (or abstract automata) really compute since, it is claimed, 'computation' is meaningful only for numbers, or what amounts to the same thing for interpreted numerals, other semantical encodements, or interpreted lexical items like in Table II.II. But the whole point of computability theory, which underlies this business, is to study functions *formally.* It is true that mathematicians and philosophers talk of addition of numbers and the like, which is no mere syntax. But this carries with it tacit semantical interpretations. The same can be done in reading about functions, symbols and rules in this book, but the semantics that is perhaps natural to our understanding of what is going on is *not* to be predicated of embodied automata. I am going to attempt to incorporate the intentional in the theory by other means, not by default!

Thus the pre-analytic idea is that of effective process; the explication is *recursive process* in some formalizable sense or other; and automata comprise the family of recursive processors. Mechanism is the doctrine that man is an effective processor which is the same as saying his mind is a system of recursive rules or an automata (plus the consciousness stipulation).

It is now time to discuss the sense in which a human being is or realizes a nondeterministic finite automaton. We will examine the meaning of this hypothesis in the next two sections which as we shall see require a careful consideration of the nature of representations and models. First, a more detailed examination is required of NFA. In particular, how can such a trivial-appearing structure handle natural language and such features as intentional attitudes? These automata, we saw, correspond to a trivial form of grammar, the finite state grammars of Chomsky, that are hopelessly *inadequate* for human languages. We are on the threshold of a paradox.

CHAPTER III

BEHAVIOR AND STRUCTURE

Philosophers and scientists frequently distinguish between the behavior and the structure of an organism. In automata theory the distinction can be made quite exactly, and provides for a concept of level of structure; at the low end is the material structure and at the high the abstract rule structure. Having developed the idea of various levels in relatively sharp form we go on to distinguish between rules that somehow guide and those that just describe a system, and also between models and theories. Finally I defend a realistic thesis: embodied automata rules are *really* in, or constitute, the mind.

1. SOME VARIETIES OF AUTOMATA

It is one thing to claim that we are automata and quite another to say what kind. The question is many-sided and has many answers depending on what concept of *kind* one has in mind. The key ideas are *behavior* (function) and *structure*. Behavior pertains to what a thing is able to do or is capable of. A universal Turing machine, for instance, can do anything any other automaton can do. That is its behavior, and in such terms is a certain kind. Some simple NFA can recognize sentences of a certain fragment of English; others can compose simple forms of music, take square roots, speak monosyllabic Anglo-Saxon, etc. and in respect of these capabilities are of many kinds. A human being has a great many capabilities and consequently is a combination of a great many different kinds of automata in some sort of composite whole.

Structure is a more difficult concept to elucidate as there are many levels of structure ranging from the stuff a thing is made of to the relational attributes it embodies. A computer, for instance, has a different material structure than a brain — one being composed of wires, chips, metal frames, etc., and the other of neural and glial tissues. Most probably the two also have different structures *qua* automata, the computer being a finite automaton which does one thing at a time very rapidly, and the brain being, so far as is known, a highly parallel relational structure of quite different complexity. Nevertheless the behavior of the two turn out to be similar in some ways. Conversely, two things might have the same structure in important respects while also having very different capabilities — an adder and a subtractor, for instance.

In this section one concern will be the question of capability: how can a person write poetry, compose music, or just manage ordinary language if she is only a finite automaton?[1] In this connection recall our earlier comment that the languages generated by finite state grammars or, equivalently, recognized by finite automata, are completely trivial and incomparably poorer than any spoken language in expressive power. Yet we are claiming that persons are NFA! The answer to this question is not particularly deep, but it will provide us with the opportunity to introduce other concepts that are useful in their own right.

For our present purposes I shall drop the general notion of NFA in favor of deterministic finite automata (FA) which are better models for describing function and structure. The ideas can be readily extended to general ones required for NFA (and even to Turing machines), a project which is not worth attempting here.[2] Recall that a finite automaton (with output) is a system consisting of inputs S, states Q, outputs O, and two maps, a next state or transition map M and an output map N, both maps on the domain $Q \times S$. These maps can, in simple enough cases, be presented by tables such as Table II.V above, p. 49 for a serial adder. We may think of the capabilities of such things in terms of their *input-output* behaviors. Roughly, what a thing can do is characterized by outward actions and reactions, specifically, sets of these. The linguistic behavior of a person is the set of sentences of a language she can speak or hear with understanding, and her musical behavior is the set of compositions she can compose or produce on some instrument or listen to with esthetic pleasure. For our purposes the behavior of an FA is the relation it computes, that is, the set of pairs of input-output strings on its alphabet S where the first member of each pair yields the second.

We can make this concept completely precise by extending the maps M and N to strings of symbols in the following manner. Let S^* be the set of all finite length strings of S including the *null* string Λ, and let x, y, z, etc vary over S^*. Λ acts like zero in arithmetic, e.g., $x\Lambda = \Lambda x = x$, which means that a string $x\Lambda$ with Λ at the end and one Λx with Λ at the beginning is just x. What we wish to do is extend the meaning of $M[N]$ so that $M(q, x)$ $[N(q, x)]$ with $x \in S^*$ is definite. Recall that when x is just a symbol s of S, $M(q, s)$ means the next state of an automaton starting in q and receiving s as input. What $M(q, x)$ is to designate, is the state the system settles in after it has received the whole input string x; and what $N(q, x)$ is to designate is the ultimate output after injecting x. The new definitions are:

$$M(q, \Lambda) = q$$
$$M(q, xs) = M(M(q, x)s) \tag{1a}$$

and

$$N(q, \Lambda) = \Lambda$$
$$N(q, xs) = (N(M(q, x)s). \tag{1b}$$

We are mostly interested in the second clause of (1b) which says that the output of the FA when xs is fed into it symbol-by-symbol is just that output mapped from the last symbol s and the state the FA is in after feeding in a string x. This state is of course computed by (1a).

(1b) expresses the *ultimate* output as a function of an input string. But in order to capture the preanalytic notion of behavior we want the entire output string resulting from an input; we want to define the function from *strings to strings*. One not especially elegant way to express this function is as follows. Let $x = s_1 \ldots s_k$; then the complete output function is

$$\mathcal{N}(q, x) = N(q, s_1)N(q, s_1 s_2) \ldots N(q, s_1 s_2 \ldots s_k) \tag{1c}$$

(1c), together with (1a) and (1b), is really just a compact way of representing a computation from $qs_1 s_2 \ldots s_k$ to $o_1 \ldots o_k$ on a one-way Turing machine, which we saw is the same thing as an FA (cf. pp. 52 above).

Finally, the behavior of the FA is the set of all ordered pairs of input-output strings, where the output is a function $\mathcal{N}$ of the input starting in some state q. If 'T' designates an arbitrary finite automaton, the *behavior* of T is

$$\beta_T = \{<xy>| (\exists q).\mathcal{N}(q, x) = y, \quad x \in S^*, \quad y \in O^*\} \tag{2}$$

where O^* is the set of strings on the output symbols O and S^* as before is the set of input strings.

Two FA T and T' have the same behavior if and only if $\beta_T = \beta_{T'}$.

I will illustrate these ideas with a *very* simple example. The reader should beware of taking the example as being typical of behaviors. β_T of (2) could be, in the case of an organism such as a human being, a composite of a great many subbehaviors including internal behaviors, if that is a coherent idea. But more of that later. Having posted the precaution let us consider the example of a certain human being, Peter, with respect to states being asleep (S) and being awake (W). Peter is susceptible to two stimulus *elements*, an alarm ring and a jab in the ribs, and is capable of emitting two response *elements*, a yawn and a striking out. There are thus *four stimuli* (shown in Table I(a)), and *four responses* (shown in Table I(b)).

TABLE I
Peter's stimuli and responses.

(a)	(b)
alarm, jab $- s_0$	strike, yawn $- o_0$
alarm, no jab $- s_1$	strike, no yawn $- o_1$
no alarm, jab $- s_2$	no strike, yawn $- o_2$
no alarm, no jab $- s_3$	no strike, no yawn $- o_3$

The four stimuli (pairs of stimulus *elements*) are labelled by s's as indicated and likewise the responses (pairs of *elements*) are labelled by o's. The automaton for Peter qua sleeper is shown in Table II.

TABLE II
Peter the sleeper.

	M_P				N_P			
	s_0	s_1	s_2	s_3	s_0	s_1	s_2	s_3
S(leep)	W	S	W	S	o_1	o_3	o_2	o_3
W(ake)	W	W	W	S	o_0	o_0	o_3	o_2

For example if Peter were asleep and someone jabbed him but the alarm didn't go off, he would awaken and yawn but not strike out $[M_P(S, s_2) = W$ and $N_P(S, s_2) = o_2]$. Incidentally Peter would fall alseep at any time unless someone were to poke him or were to ring bells $[M_P(W, s_3) = S]$; he is a sleepy-head.

Please note my deliberate phrasing of a piece of Peter's behavior in the subjunctive mode. Later on I will argue that to say he realizes the automaton of Table II is the same as to say his behavior is expressible as a set of subjunctive conditionals.

To complete the illustration, consider now a string $s_3 s_1 s_2 s_0$ applied to Peter in state S. One should think of this string of stimuli as occurring in successive instants (the string is a time sequence). According to (1c),

$$\mathcal{N}_P(S, s_3 s_1 s_2 s_0)$$
$$= N_P(S, s_3) N_P(S, s_3 s_1) N_P(S, s_3 s_1 s_2) N_P(S, s_3 s_1 s_2 s_0).$$

Using Table II and the relations (1a) and (1b) the output turns out to be $o_3o_3o_2o_0$.[3]

So part of Peter's behavior, which is one element of β_P, (2), is expressed by: If Peter were to be consecutively undisturbed (s_3), alarmed (s_1), jabbed (s_2) and both alarmed and jabbed (s_0) when he is asleep, then he would do nothing for two time intervals (o_3o_3), yawn (o_2), and finally strike out (o_0).[4] (1), (2), and Tables I and II together comprise a theory of Peter the sleeper. Its consequences comprise an infinite set of sentences of the sort just written above.

The devoted reader who has followed the details will perhaps now better appreciate the elegance of the original Turing-type computation using either quadruple or Post-production rules (see above, p. 21). The present notation, however, greatly facilitates our grappling with the complexities of structure, and besides affords quite a precise way of saying what we mean by 'behavior' or 'capability.' And it does illustrate what a very small part of a psychological theory might look like in the framework of an automaton logic of mind. The definitions (1) and (2) apply only to FA of course, but analogous definitions can be given for Turing machines, grammars, recognizers, etc., and we will supply them, in less rigorous fashion, when needed.

Now to structure. There are four senses of 'structure' that are nicely exemplified in FA terms, and that turn out to be conceptually of considerable service in cleaning up muddles which are quite regularly generated in discussions of function, structure, and innate structure or 'ideas', in mental philosophy. For the moment let's stick to the technicalities.

First, two FA have the same structure if their input-output computations match. In Turing machine style, let there be T and T' such that to every state a of T there corresponds an unique a' of T'. Then starting with *identical* input strings (tokens of the same type, symbol-by-symbol) on their respective tapes, with T, T' in corresponding states, the machines *match* provided that each successive instantaneous description (see above, p. 21) contains the same strings and corresponding states in corresponding positions. The same holds now for FA by simply imagining the tape limited to one-way movement (see above, p. 52). More mathematically expressed (for FA), two FA T and T' are *homomorphic* provided there is a map ϕ from the states S of T into S' of T' such that next states and outputs are "preserved," for any input s. Formally expressed, $\phi: S \rightarrow S'$ must satisfy

$$\phi M(q, s) = M'(\phi(q), s) \tag{3a}$$

and

$$N(q, s) = N'(\phi(q), s). \tag{3b}$$

M, N and M', N' are the transition and output functions of T and T' respectively. If (3a) and (3b) are true, then corresponding equations hold for any input sequence x, as can be shown by induction.

Suppose Paul, too, is a sleepy-head described by Table II, but with some inner structurally insignificant changes. (His nervous system might not be arranged exactly the same as Peter's.) Paul's awake state is W' and his sleep state is S'. Certainly $W' \neq W$ and $S' \neq S$ on anatomical grounds as just parenthetically noted, and yet the states correspond; that is, there is a one-one map such that $\phi(S) = S'$ and $\phi(W) = W'$. We represent Paul's sleep FA by an imaginary new table formed by replacing W by W' and S by S' in Table II in the M part, and retaining the N part. Let us consider $M(S, s_2) = W$ (Peter), and $M'(S', s_2) = W'$ (Paul). It is a simple matter to show that $\phi(M(S, s_2)) = M'(\phi(S), s_2))$, which satisfies (3a). The output tables are the same so (3b) is automatically satisfied. Checking that the comparable relations hold for all state and stimulus combinations, we see that Peter and Paul have the same sleepwise structure — the automata they realize are homorphic, in fact isomorphic, as the map is a one-one correspondence.[5]

Now Peter's and Paul's stimuli and responses certainly *do* differ. The actual events are slightly unlike.[6] For this more realistic case, we introduce new maps from Peter's stimuli and responses to Paul's. Let's call them g and h. And suppose again that they are one-one onto relations. Then the equations (3) appear in a more general form:

$$\phi(M(q, s)) = M'(\phi(q), g(s)) \tag{3c}$$

and

$$h(N(q, s)) = N'(\phi(q), g(s)). \tag{3d}$$

In as close to ordinary language as we can get it, (3c) means that the state in system T' (Paul) corresponding to the state we get to from q and input s in T (Peter) equals the state we get to in T' from the image state $\phi(q)$ and the symbol $g(s)$. (3d) says that the output in T' corresponding to the output we get from q, s in T is the same as the output we get to in T' from the image state $\phi(q)$ and the image input $g(s)$.

I shall not call on Peter and Paul further at the moment, but instead invite you to observe that the concept of *same* captured by the technical idea of the homomorphism is subject to various grades. For example, in (3c), (3d), the inputs s and $g(s)$, outputs o and $h(o)$ could be radically different, as could the states q and $\phi(q)$. Consider the butterfly afield. It flits about a bit, and then sits; again it flits. These alternating conditions are states in which the butterfly is variously affected by stimulus events, and emits certain responses, known only to butterflies. It is quite possible the butterfly thus taken as an automaton is isomorphic to Table II, and if so it has the same abstract structure as Peter and Paul.

You perhaps suspect, and rightly so, that two FA could be behaviorally equivalent by (2) and yet not be homomorphic. On the other hand two homomorphic FA with the same input-output sets (or organisms with the same stimuli as discussed in Note 6) that are homomorphic always have the same behavior. Here we see one quite precise way of characterizing the distinction between behavior or capability and structure.

A second kind of structure is discernable at a level in which inner detail is of scientific interest. Here there is a bewildering array of possibilities and I wish to consider just a few in order to convey the richness of the field and the great importance of clarity in discussion about structures – which level does one have in mind? Let us assume that all stimuli and response elements are propositional functions of time, such as Peter's stimuli. That is, 'yawn' means explicitly 'at time t the value of yawn is truth (or 1)' and 'not-yawn' means 'the value of yawn is falsehood (or 0)'. Then all inputs (outputs) will be tuples of 0's and 1's as will be explained in more detail in Section V.1. Now if FA states are also parametrizable by tuples of 0's and 1's, then the FA may be embodied in a logic net reminiscent of the adder of Figure II.5, which embodies the automaton of Table II.V. In Section II.5 we introduced the net first and then squeezed it into the abstract automaton version of the table. It turns out that this reduction is unique to an isomorphism, which is to say that any table like II.V produced from Figure II.5 will be isomorphic to any other, provided a certain minimality requirement is satisfied. But the reverse is not true. There are indefinitely many logic nets using the same kind of *and*, etc., elements as Figure II.5 does, which are significantly different, although each one embodies isomorphically one and the same FA adder. One of these dissimilar nets appears in Figure 1. This net is behaviorally the same as Figure II.5, and it embodies the same automaton (to within isomorphism), but is clearly a different net. So the abstract automata embodied have the same structure, while the logic net structures are unalike.

The butterfly could also be represented by a switching network using the same components as those of Figure 1, but it is more likely that its behavior is controlled by a neural network such as was described in the previous section, but perhaps of a more complex sort. The same can be said of Peter

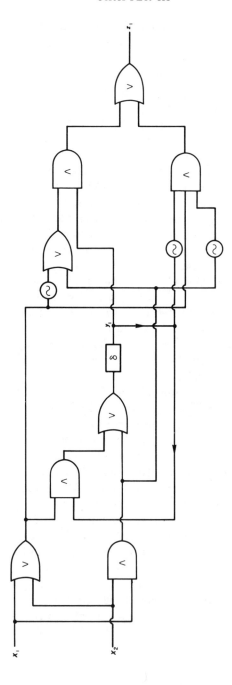

Fig. 1. Serial binary adder.

and Paul. If more were known about nerve networks of organisms, then they presumably could be represented by formulas in some kind of logic, and one would be able to associate formulas to neuronal systems in a manner analogous to formulas to switching circuits. One could then individuate neuronal systems via the syntax of logical formulas as we did for the adder in Figure II.5. Indeed, supposing that an appropriate formal language is known, we say *two neuronal systems* (or other relevant embodiments, whatever they turn out to be) are the *same* if and only if the expressing logical formulas have the same inductive derivation to within the order of terms in commutative operations.[7] It might turn out, however, that the right framework for an organism is a continuous underlying geometry rather than a discrete one, although the thing is indeed a finite automaton. This question will be taken up in Section 3 below, and again in Chapter IV when we turn to the evidence for mechanism.

In passing it is worth mentioning that abstract automata need not be embodied in binary logic nets, those using basic logic elements having the properties of propositional functions of time. Many-valued logics would serve as well and in some possible world perhaps do. Current neuroscience research, for example, has discovered that although the rest potentials of all axonal fibers of an animal, indeed a species, are the same (logical zero) action potentials can differ markedly as can the summations at synaptic junctions with other neurons (cf. Stevens, 1966). Thus if brains are to count as discrete state organs, something quite other than a two-valued system would have to be used for theory (cf. Schneider, 1974). On the other hand a brain would still realize an abstract automaton and perhaps one homomorphic to that of a two-valued system. This observation gives us yet another variety of structure, which for purposes of a philosophical logic of mind may be placed along side others on a level of net structure.

A third variety of structure is the material realization. Figure 1 could be realized in relays, microorganisms, vacuum tubes, transistors, or other kinds of solid state organs. Each one of these constitutes a different material structure. Moreover the very *same* material structure could occur in different net structures, and again in the same abstract automaton structures. All combinations are possible with the single restriction that same net structure implies same abstract automaton, as I previously emphasized.

In discussing function and structure I have consistently tried to write of material organisms (either natural or artifactual) as *realizing* structures such as nets and as also *realizing* abstract automata, while net-type structures *embody* automata. Thus an organism (or an organism part) realizes an automaton in some specific systemic embodiment. These ideas can be made completely precise, the first in terms of the technical notion of an interpretation, or model structure wherein the abstract automaton is strictly speaking a *formal system*, and the second in terms of *coding* (Section II.5 above). Rather than review the formalities here I will postpone them until the need arises in discussing specific questions such as the *reality* of rules, *innate* structure, and certain aspects of the *mind-body* problem.

A fourth level of structure above that of abstract FA and Turing machines concerns what I term the 'categorical'. All of the systems that we discussed in the earlier historical section were describable by Post-type production rules, and for this reason can be said to be of the same category. However there are many other ways of describing grammars of natural languages, ways that do not use production rules. Grammatical *transformations* act on trees or phrase markers, not on terminal and non-terminal symbols (see above, p. 30), and hence are of a different category of structure, but perhaps are still rules of a logic of mind. Another example is provided by grammars that do not directly employ the notion of nonterminal symbols in any way. Finally consider the rules for various types of programming languages, which can describe any algorithmic processes. Such categorical differences will be discussed in Section 3 below. The concept of a fourth level of categorical structure raises questions about the sense in which the logic of mind is *realistic*. For the time being I only want to encourage the reader to observe that *any* system of effective rules can, by CT, be equivalently rendered in the form of Post-productions; and the present point is just to indicate the existence of categories of systems of rules that are structurally different, but behaviorally equivalent. It is just the behavioral equivalence that permits recasting of systems of rules of one category into another.

Turning finally to a central topic of this section, how can an FA perform the operations of Turing automata with 'greater' capabilities. How can an FA, in particular, speak and understand English when the rules of its grammar as they are currently understood are of quite a different character and order of complexity than FA rules?[8] What about other complex cognitive functions?

The answer is that the rules of an ordinary language — or even of many languages for fluent speakers of them — can be a *parts* of an FA. Indeed, such rules will be parts in two ways corresponding to behavior and structure: (1) the rules of any language being finite in number and in length can be *stored* in an FA (when coded in some suitable way).[9] An FA can be described (see pp. 45–6) as a programmed automaton, not just as a table as in the previous examples. One may think of memory as consisting of a composition of FA (which is again an FA) in which programs can be stored in a way analogous to the inscribing of the quadruples of a simulated machine on a Turing machine tape (Nelson, 1987b).[10] In particular it can store free algorithms (p. 27) (which are distinguishable from the embodied algorithm that informs the fixed automaton structure), including recursive rules for any cognitive process, not just grammar. (2) Thus FA, except for the finiteness condition on its memory can compute approximately anything a universal machine can, provided input is *bounded*. An FA of sufficient complexity can generate all of the sentences, which are *shorter* than some given bound k, of any language. Some FA can generate all sentences of English of less than 100 words in length, say. This fact, which is really not very interesting in itself, shows that the NFA hypothesis is plausible — human performance is not up to all of English, but it can produce enough of it provided that we are sufficiently elaborate NFA. It seems to me this is as far as the logic of mind *qua* philosophy can presume to go. The distinction we are making here is between human linguistic *competence* and actual *performance*. Competence is reflected in the stored set of rules or some portion thereof, and performance in the memory-limited understanding and production of linguistic expressions. In psycholinguistics it is customary to say that the rules have been *internalized*, which means they have been stored in our finite memories. How they get there is the problem of language acquisition theory. This important distinction, which is due to Noam Chomsky in its contemporary form, will be explored more deeply in Chapter V.

In all of these cases it is quite tempting to use computer analogies, here the analogy of stored and executed rules of language or perception called by some stimulus, inner or outer, to computer subroutines. But we are almost completely ignorant of our own structures and we may not be organized in a way even remotely similar to computers. Our only assumption is that we are approximately NFA, and of course we already know that computers are NFA. Neither the basic thesis that the rules of mind are recursive nor that they are NFA imply that humans have random access memories or identifiable arithmetic circuitry. Nor do my subsequent plausibility arguments that use computer language or the programming idiom require that there be any similarity to the mind structurally.

Before leaving the topic of function and structure entirely, I want to say more about the *complexity* of structure. It should be clear that a serial adder or Peter the sleeper does not have the capacity to store anything. (The adder might be said to *store* a carry from one stage to the next, but that is all.) So the examples of FA we have so far used are misleadingly simple. A serial adder has two states as does Peter the sleeper. The human brain has $2^{10^{10}}$ states at least, counting axon potentials as state elements; and according to one recent analysis a neuron has *five* states, in which case the brain has at least $5^{10^{10}}$ (Schneider, 1974); and the brain *qua* neuronal system may not be all that underlies the mind! Counting the central processing unit only of a large computer of a half a million words of random access storage, there are about $2^{25\,000\,000}$ states, which is considerably smaller. Now automata of such complexity are quite beyond imagination though not beyond conception as the computer is a product of the human mind. What makes the the computer tractable and most probably what will cause the brain to be better understood than it is now, is its *decomposability into subsystems*.

A complex system, which the mind surely is, may be characterized as one having many qualitatively different components that are interdependent (cf. Simon, 1977; also Nelson, 1977). On this definition complexity increases not only with numbers of components but with variety and relation, so that division into subsystems depends on recognition of those relations which can be broken apart in theory without impairing our understanding. A neuron, as previously remarked, is an automaton, although this fact may or may not be of much theoretical interest. A randomly selected stretch of muscle could also be described without much effort as an automaton, but probably to no purpose, and might even distort our current understanding of muscle tension. This question of the relevance of taking a part of an organism as an automaton (or as realizing *any* kind of formalism) will be dealt with in Section 3. Here the sole point I wish to make is that automata might have parts that are again automata — depending on how we slice the thing up — and these parts or subsystems can be investigated without knowing much about the system itself. Of course the opposite is true as well: we know a lot about ourselves independent of exact science and without knowing anything of inner detail on the level of subsystems.

Any system with feedback represents one of the many different varieties of complexity. In real life Peter is a subsystem of a greater world including an alarm clock and a Roommate. Each of these is a subsystem and realizes an automaton. Moreover the three comprise a super automaton. This latter is hardly a mental system, but it does exhibit a kind of complexity in a concrete and relevant form for illustration and later use.

The alarm clock has twelve states labeled 1–12; two inputs, an alarm set (σ_0) and a nonset (σ_1); and two outputs, a ring (r_0) and nonring (r_1). Roommate has two states, in the room (I) and not in the room (0); input elements, 8 to 8:05 on the alarm dial (8_0), any other time indication (8_1), and getting hit (h_0) or not hit (h_1); and two outputs, a jab at Peter's ribs

(j_0) or not (j_1). Please note that r_0 is also the alarm element and j_0 the jab element in Peter's stimulus set, Table I.

The tables for these new automata appear in IIIa and b. Alarm clocks, besides being annoying, are not very interesting as they are input-free with respect to the transition map M_C (the next state is independent of input, as can be seen in the M_C table of IIIa) and exhibit no variety — they are clocks! Roommate *qua* awakener is a dull character, though effective.

TABLE IIIa
Alarm clock table.

	M_C		N_C	
	σ_0	σ_1	σ_0	σ_1
12	1	1	r_1	r_1
1	2	2	r_1	r_1
2	3	3	r_1	r_1
3	4	4	r_1	r_1
4	5	5	r_1	r_1
5	6	6	r_1	r_1
6	7	7	r_1	r_1
7	8	8	r_1	r_1
8	9	9	r_0	r_1
9	10	10	r_1	r_1
10	11	11	r_1	r_1
11	12	12	r_1	r_1

σ_0 = set; r_0 = ring;
σ_1 = nonset; r_1 = nonring.

TABLE IIIb
Roommate.

M_R				N_R			
$(8_0, h_0)$	$(8_0, h_1)$	$(8_1, h_0)$	$(8_1, h_1)$	$(8_0, h_0)$	$(8_0, h_1)$	$(8_1, h_0)$	$(8_1, h_1)$
I	O	I	O	I	j_1	j_0	j_1	j_1
O	–	I	–	O	–	j_1	–	j_1

$(8_0, h_0)$ = 8–8:05, gets hit; j_0 = jab (at Peter);
$(8_0, h_1)$ = 8–8:05, not hit; j_1 = not jab;
$(8_1, h_0)$ = other time, gets hit;   I = in room;
$(8_1, h_1)$ = other time, not hit;   O = not in room.

Some parts of IIIb are *undefined* (indicated by '—' in interior of table):
e.g., a situation in which Roommate is not in room and he is hit by Peter is
not possible in this world.

Now these automata are related in certain ways: Peter's stimuli (Table I)
are caused by the clock and the roommate. We still lack, however, the effects
of Peter's outputs $o_0 - o_3$. These are linked to the inputs of the clock and
the roommate via the following function ϕ, which is a kind of feedback link:

TABLE IV
Feedback to clock and roommate.

$$\phi(o_0) = (\sigma_1, h_1)$$
$$\phi(o_1) = (\sigma_1, h_0)$$
$$\phi(o_2) = (\sigma_0, h_1)$$
$$\phi(o_3) = (\sigma_0, h_1)$$

$\phi(o_0)$, for example, means that Peter's output o_0 (strike, yawn) is related
causally to nonsetting the alarm and the Roommate not getting hit.

Finally, we will make the extrasystemic assumption that when Peter is
awake and neither strikes nor yawns [$N_P(W, s_2))$] he actually gets out of
bed.

Consider the case where Peter is asleep (S), the alarm is set (σ_0) and
Roommate is present (I). At 8, the alarm rings [$N_C(8, \sigma_0) = r_0$] and presumably dwells in a ringing output mode at around 8. Roommate jabs at
Peter [$N_R(I, (8_0, h_1)) = j_0$] but remains in room [$M_R(I, (8_0, h_1)) = I$]. This
complex situation defines input s_0 to Peter (Table I); so Peter awakens
[$M_P(S, s_0) = W$] and strikes out without yawning [$N_P(S, s_0) = o_1$], by
Table II. By Table IV, $\phi(o_1) = (\sigma_1, h_0)$, viz., the clock is unset and Roommate is hit. The Roommate, still in state I, leaves room [$M_R(I, (8_0, h_0)) = 0$]
without jabbing [$N_R(I, (8_0, h_0)) = j_1$] thinking that Peter is awake. As
a consequence, there is an input (no alarm, no jab) and Peter, who is still
awake, falls asleep [$M_P(W, s_3) = S$] and yawns [$N_P(W, s_3) = o_2$].

This illustration prompts a few side comments: (1) The super automaton
differs from Rube Goldberg creations by being far more complex, incorporating state-to-state changes, whereas most Rube Goldberg's are 'if this then
that' schemes. The differences will be brought out sharply and analytically
in our examination of behaviorism in Chapter V. (2) It exhibits negative
feedback: Peter's response o_1 (striking but no yawning) gains him the desired
state of sleep; it reduces the irritating input to 'zero' in effect. Thus (1) and

(2) illustrate that purely discrete state systems can model the logical action of control devices, as one example of complexity.

The total system is one superautomaton having forty-eight states. It would be a useless *tour-de-force* to display this system as a single table (abstracting the timing relations in a suitable way is quite formidable), but it could be done. Basically, the sleeper system is again a rather complex collection of production rules of our fundamental sort as can be easily seen by way of the obvious interpretations of the several tables.[11]

There are functional or behavioral subsystems and structural ones as well; they need not correspond. Memory, for example, is an intellectual function which can be examined by psychologists from many points of view. It is thus isolable from other functions. Yet there is no known structure of the brain or mind that specifically houses it. It may be of some comfort to physiological psychologists to be told that this phenomenon is not limited to the mind. There are computer behaviors that correspond to no distinguishable subnetwork of a network, even though all such behaviors are automata behavior and hence realizable in some network or other. Any program for a calculation that is not wired in the computer is an example. For another, attachment of an exclusive or circuit as in Figure 2 to the x_2 input of Figure 1 converts that network to one that can perform either addition or subtraction.

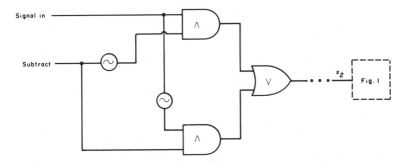

Fig. 2. Add-subtract network.

Thus if the input labelled 'subtract' in Figure 2 is sustained at value 1, then the signal input is inverted at the output of the exclusive or circuit, which is identical to input x_2 of the adder. The entire network consisting of the input modification and the adder performs subtraction.[12] If 'subtract' is sustained at level 0, the network adds. Now Figure 1 is a proper part of the whole network and corresponds to the function of addition, whereas no part of the network corresponds to subtraction.[13] *A fortiori* there is no automaton part of the abstract automaton informing Figures 1 and 2 that corresponds to subtraction. It does not follow, however, that there is absolutely *no* automaton for subtraction, and the reader is invited to find one. Likewise, although memory seems not to correspond to any particular neuronal structure in the animal brain it does not follow that there is no possible neuronal structure for memory. This example suggests rather strongly that even though memory is not embodied in a specific logic organ it might still be explainable in mechanical terms; the trick is to find the memory function in a super structure that has no decomposition including a specific memory structure.[14]

Behavior and structure in complex automata have no simple correlation, and nothing in the logic of mind presupposes that they do, nor does failure of a correspondence somehow default mechanism. This is all I want to say at this juncture about complexity. In later parts of the volume complexity of various kinds, such as direct product automata used to model perception, will be introduced.[15]

I have characterized behavior as sets of input-output pairs and distinguished behavior (or function) from structure. There are four interesting levels or strata of structure which may be summarized as follows:

(1)   the material constitution, which underlies;
(2)   the network (e.g., neural, logical, computer circuit) organization, which embodies;
(3)   the abstract automaton input-output-state structure, which is an instantiation of;
(4)   the underlying recursive rule structure (so far assumed to be Post production or Turing-type rules).

We use the terminology that the material organism (or artifact) *realizes* the network (2) and the automaton (3), and that the network *embodies* (3). (4) is the categorical level of effective structures. As I have indicated, but not yet discussed at any length, there are other categories of effective processors besides Turing machines or Post production rules which are nevertheless completely equivalent in the processes they govern.

Automata may be complex superstructures of other automata in a wide variety of forms, including those other than NFA. Of special interest to a logic of mind is the possibility that the production rules of automata having very rich behavior (for example grammatical rules of English) can be *stored* or otherwise *internalized* (we have not yet faced details) in an FA. This fact is one of the reasons for making a distinction between *competence* and *performance* in mental life. Finally I have shown that function and structure need not correspond in any obvious or direct way.

2. FITTING AND GUIDING

Future psychology might not establish that every mental feature is literally an NFA, but only that some aspects of mental life are equivalent to some automaton behavior and can be simulated, perhaps entirely, by computer programs. If this turns out to be true, you might say that a sufficiently complex NFA is a *model* of the mind or of the specific mental feature of interest in some inquiry. In Chapter I, I characterized the logic of mind as a system of recursive rules represented by NFA (p. 4), and in scattered passages wrote of humans as 'essentially NFA's'. I should not object, however, to saying simply that we *are* NFA, subject to a certain rather complex provisos.

What is at stake here is getting clear on the meaning and scientific status of a mechanist theory of mind and of *model* of mind, which latter concept we have already been using rather freely without labelling it as such. In order, I will take up (1) a discussion of what I mean by automaton type theories and models, and in particular of the distinction (which will disappear) between saying that a man is an NFA and that he is modeled by one; (2) a discussion of the metaphysics underlying the logic of mind, in particular the realism implicit in the theory; (3) a discussion of the use of models in philosophy of mind (as in this book) as contrasted with theoretical psychology and artificial intelligence.

The expression 'logic of mind' is ambiguous and may refer either to a certain theory — i.e., a system of logically inter-related statements — or to the 'rationale' of mental life itself (see above, p. 4). Traditional empiricism, especially in its positivist and instrumentalist forms, eschews the distinction I have in mind holding (as I understand it) that a difference between a model or a theory and what a thing really is in itself is either meaningless or a preferential distinction among theories. Theories are held to be true (or verifiable) if and only if they bear some kind of predictive relationship to observation or observation sentences, not because the conceptual manifold of the theory corresponds to outer reality. In its extreme Machian form, a theory is a conceptual short hand, a data-compressive bridge, from observation back to

observation. In early Carnap, the terms of a theory are accredited by definitional reductions to observations terms, and in later Carnap by the role they
play in a language of a theory that may be only partially interpreted in an
observational domain.[16] Theories, in these versions of empiricism, are pinned
to direct observation and from it derive all cognitively meaningful content.
In empiricist psychology this has been the dominant tradition from Hume
to logical behaviorism.

In mathematical theories, on the other hand, all concepts are on an equal
footing, more or less, and are interpreted in domains of abstract objects such
as numbers, sets, categories, or whatever is taken as primitive. Ideally mathematics has no observational terms except in its application. The point of
referring to mathematical theories here is that by contrast theoretical terms
in empirical science, according to conservative empiricist philosophy, do
not have direct interpretations in domains of 'theoretical objects' on pain of
being empirical nonsense, and are meaningful only when grounded in observational contexts. But since mathematics is analytic, interpretations of its terms
are factually innocuous − they commit us to no matters of fact. There are no
limits. Sets, for example, can be multiplied beyond mathematical necessity,
if you want.

A notable exception to this is physical geometry which (quite anomalously)
is a theory that gets interpreted in a physical domain, not a mathematical
one of abstract points and the like, exploiting all the privileges of formal
mathematical theories: *theoretical* terms such as 'point' and 'line' *refer* much
as 'number' or 'set' do in pure mathematics proper. Hence for empiricists
who accept this analysis of physical geometry, physics assumes real spaces
of points, lines and surfaces, which means that the domain of geometry is
not directly observational.

When the analytic-synthetic distinction is dropped, as it has been by
Quine and others, pure mathematics enjoys no special exemptions and is
seen to be up to its ears in ontology, as much as is physical geometry.[17]
Complementariwise, empirical science then need no longer be expected to
bend to *a priori* constraints on its employment of theoretical terms.

Logic of mind is empirical in the way geometry is in these open forms
of empiricism (although it has no pretensions of establishing more than
the initial plausibility of a conceptual scheme or framework hypothesis).
Various aspects of mind are interpretations of formal automata, just as
physical space is an interpretation of formal geometry. In both cases real
things realize formal theoretical structures.[18] In this spirit it does make
sense to distinguish between true descriptions of mental phenomena that

represent the rules of mind as they really are from true descriptions that do not. *Real* descriptions of mental states and their laws of development are not mere *façons de parler*. In psycholinguistics, alluding to an issue that has been at the center of lively debate during the past two decades, it has been argued that one can meaningfully distinguish between 'internalized' grammatical rules that actually govern speech and the rules basic to a description of a language which are true *qua* theory that explains or accounts for the empirically given linquistic corpus. There are rules that *guide* and *fit* behavior and rules that correctly *fit* only.[19] The grammar of a language is underdetermined by linguistic data just as a scientific hypothesis is underdetermined by the data appropriate to its domain. In general, a context free language, for instance, has an indefinite number of adequate grammars. One of them, G, might actually be the deep structure guiding some speaker of the language, and another, G', be a set of rules formulated by the linguist that fits the data but does not guide the mind. Generalizing, I claim there are rules that guide perception and cognition as well as language use and, in contrast, rules that merely fit the logic of mind. Here, however, I am limiting myself to making distinctions and not pushing doctrine until the next section.

In terms of the language-interpretation philosophy of science, we are saying that the following distinction is intelligible. Some theories are true of a given class of phenomena, while others are both true and in a certain sense *iconic* – they picture a structure or process in some quite literal way. I know of no general way of sustaining this distinction for philosophy of science against criticism, but I believe it can be done in a mechanistic philosophy of mind in a simple way. Table V(a) gives the automaton table of an abstract pulse divider (it functions to cut the number of occurrences of s_1's in an input sequence in half, and outputs the result). V(b) and V(c) stand for two actual automata embodied in electronic circuits. In each of the two physical cases inputs 0 and 1 denote zero and V+ volts respectively, and similarly for the outputs 0 and 1. The internal states are the electronic memory states of some kind of component (say, delay elements or flip-flops). Now a systems engineer looking at these circuits from the outside describes both (b) and (c) in terms of the automaton formulation (a) of which (b) is a realization (if the reader has not read footnote 18, it is strongly recommended he do so now). To the engineer the automaton description (a) is a hypothesis (verifiable in this case) accounting for the pulse dividing behavior of both circuits, which the reader himself can check out to be equivalent. However (b) is a realization of the engineer's abstract automaton, while (c) is not. So his description truly *fits* the behavior of both whereas it is *realized* only by (b).

TABLE V
Forms of pulse divider.

(a)

	s_0	s_1	s_0	s_1
q_0	q_0	q_1	s_0	s_1
q_1	q_1	q_0	s_0	s_0

(b)

	0	1	0	1
0	0	1	0	1
1	1	0	0	0

(c)

	0	1	0	1
0	2	1	0	1
1	1	0	0	0
2	0	1	0	1

In general, consider some mental feature P which an investigator describes by an automaton A: A is a hypothesis that is meant to explain P's behavior, and we suppose correctly does so.[20] Now another automaton B also explains P's behavior. But in addition P *realizes* B. A and B are equivalent abstract automata since they account for P's behavior equally, but only B is an interpretation for which P is true − not of just the behavior but of the whole state-to-state transition system. In such cases I will say that B, but not A, 'weakly guides P'. In particular an automaton T *weakly guides* a mental feature if and only if that feature realizes T.

It is possible to obtain a stronger concept of guidance by turning to the level of embodiment of an NFA network. Two objects P and P' both realizing A might be embodied in entirely different neural networks or other systems of organs of some kind. The logic nets of Figure II.5 and Figure III.1 above are, as explained there, associated to two different sets of formulas, the formulas being our ground for individuating nets (cf. footnote 7). Thus it seems reasonable to say that both formulas II (3b, c) and those of footnote 7 describe or fit both Figure II.5 and Figure III.1, while only II (3b, c) guide Figure II.5 and only the formulas of the footnote guide III.1.

Let us examine a simpler example, this time of a truth-functional net. Figure 4(a) corresponds to the formula $AB \vee A$, and Figure 4(b) to $A(B \vee A)$. Now these formulas are quivalent by truth tables and so express the same behavior and fit the same. Yet $AB \vee A$ differs from $A(B \vee A)$ computationally: The recursive definitions of 'formula' are applied differently in the two cases and the recursive definitions of the two nets are accordingly unlike. Informally, by chasing 0's and 1's (or T, F) through the net one can "see" that they guide differently; still, the behaviors are the same.

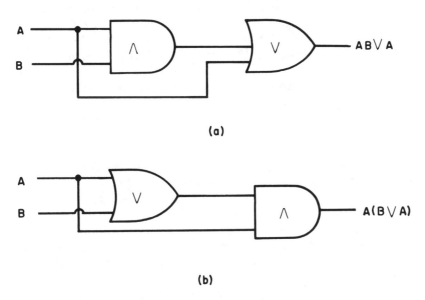

(a)

(b)

Fig. 3. Nonidentical, behaviorially equivalent networks.

A set of formulas corresponding to a network (such as II (3b, c) to Figure II.5) *strongly guides* an automaton if and only if the formulas individuate the net. Strong guidance implies weak. By a decoding procedure, sketched elsewhere, one can find the unique abstract automaton corresponding to the net. We then know that the derived automaton (production rules or table) weakly guides if the logic formulas strongly guide. Of course the converse does not hold as networks (or other comparable systems) are underdetermined by abstract automata.

Similarly a mental feature is *strongly guided* by a formula that corresponds to an embodiment such as a neural network if the formula individuates the embodiment. Whether there are in fact such formulas is not yet the issue, which we will turn to in Section 3 to follow.

Using the fit-guide notion it is quite natural to arrange possible true theories of mental logic in a hierarchy. We suppose that one goal of mental science is to account for human mental features in theories in which automata logic is central. Every such theory will satisfy three conditions at least, given a mental feature P of some system $\mathscr{S}$.

(i)   A specific collection of stimulus and response or input-output types (or equivalence classes of input-output) of $\mathscr{S}$ is designated with respect to which an automaton T is formulated.

(ii)   The feature P of $\mathscr{S}$ embodies an effective structure of some kind, not necessarily production rules, but possibly rules of another category (see above, p. 68) that involve the inputs and outputs of (i).

(iii)   The feature P of $\mathscr{S}$ is behaviorally equivalent to an *automaton* structure that realizes T.[21]

T is a *true* theory of P of $\mathscr{S}$ if (i)–(iii) are satisfied. For emphasis we also say that P is an automaton T *under description* (i) (cf. Putnam, 1967). Even though T be true of P, P need not realize T. In this case T captures the behavior of P while P is not guided by T.

T is *weakly real* if P of $\mathscr{S}$ is weakly guided by T, i.e., if P realizes T. It is conceivable that psychological theories might one day achieve this level of realism and that some experts in psycholinguistics, in particular, are nearly there.

T is *strongly real* if P of $\mathscr{S}$ realizes T and is strongly guided by T (i.e., given an encoding of T and a set of formulas in that encoding, the formula individuates the structural embodiment of T in $\mathscr{S}$). Perhaps there are no known strong theories of this kind except in computer engineering, given completely accurate logic diagrams.

The reader will recall that according to an observation of Section 2 above the mind might contain rules more complex than those of any NFA, while yet being only an NFA itself. It is for this reason that in characterizing theories I used automata (T) in general and not NFA. This already suggests a distinction between the sense in which the whole minded man is an NFA and that in which he perhaps has non-NFA parts. In (i)–(iii) you might think of system $\mathscr{S}$ as the whole individual. If so, the product, so to say, of all features P is just $\mathscr{S}$ and $\mathscr{S}$ itself becomes the object of the theory T in the definitions of 'strongly real', 'true', and so forth.

What I mean by a mechanist logic of mind can now be made more definite. It says that human beings *qua* minded are systems $\mathscr{S}$ of (i)–(iii) with T being an NFA. For short, *humans are* NFA. I will occasionally say that NFA (or other automata, if applicable) rules *represent* mental features such as 'knowledge' of language, and *vice versa.*[22] So a certain logic of mind (theory) represents an internalized logic of mind. What mechanism amounts to, then, is that the mind is a system of recursive rules of some kind represented as a whole by NFA.

This is an empirical though philosophical hypothesis (or 'framework' hypothesis) and as it stands is incomplete. As explained in the introduction and developed in the sequel, the NFA must be of enough complexity to account for intentionality in Brentano's sense (I must indicate how this is to be done) and must be sentient. The NFA must be capable of using and understanding language, music, and a lot else, and a part of the hypothesis is that these features *qua* rule-using are recursive structures that underly recursive processes. Other components (subsystems of rules) may be NFA or perhaps more complex than that, even full Turing machines, but still embodied somehow in a sufficiently large store or memory system which, as previously emphasized several times, is well within the resources of an NFA, in analogy to computers. The human NFA comprises stronger automaton parts.

By this time I am certain that the reader appreciates that the logic of mind need not be anything like a computer in organization or structure. Saying that the logic of mind is an NFA logic implies nothing whatever about the organization of human memory — whether serial (accessing one 'unit' of information at a time as in sequential computerers of the 1970s), parallel, or associative instead of indexical.[23] Moreover, brain state elements are not necessarily binary, but as seems likely in view of the most recent opinion, post synaptic potentials are n-ary for quite large n. Nor do we necessarily contain anything like a central computer or control; such functions might well be distributed throughout the nervous system, even at the cellular level, although the geography of certain abilities is known, such as the site of language skills in the dominant cerebral hemisphere, which controls speech in the normal individual.

To complete this section I must say something about *models* as promised. A model in this book is a weak theory, one that makes no claim to satisfying (iii); that is to say, the automaton T that figures in the theory might not be *equivalent* to one that truly describes the trait or feature one is trying to account for. For instance a model of visual perception might not behave in all possible ways an organism could, but still serve certain theoretical purposes, in general either to show that a mechanist explanation is in principle plausible (which will be the type of use in the sequel), or to elucidate a concept (such as isomorphism in the Peter-Paul story), or to provide a conceptual scheme or framework for a type of psychological inquiry.[24]

In general a model does not completely fit or describe actual inputs and outputs of organisms (i) or inner structures and processes (ii) and hence is not true but only suggestive of the truth; as I said, their main use is to support the plausibility of mechanism. Two questions arise in this connection: what is a 'plausibility argument', and why attempt what artificial intelligence (AI) already does better?

The two questions are related. My use of models, except as illustrations of technical concepts, is essentially *explication* in the sense of Carnap (1950, pp. 1–8). Briefly, I use models to explicate cognitive terms. However explication, in my less positivistic view of the method, is also theoretical; explication is not only a matter of cleaning-up and regularizing vocabulary but is an attempt to formulate hypotheses having content. As such my explications must, as Carnap required following Tarski, begin by writing down adequacy conditions, analyzing the concepts in question, and then showing that the analysis satisfies the conditions. I have argued elsewhere (Nelson, 1982) that AI often does not begin by framing adequacy conditions of any sort partly because its aim is directed more to getting computers to perform useful cognitive tasks than to model mind. This is not to deride AI in any way, which more than any other enterprise in the mental sciences has influenced thinkers to examine perception and cognition or in general mental features as kinds of information processes and has served to open wide a whole new conceptual world. I shall return to this theme again in Chapter XI and explain why AI at this time, despite its exciting achievements, does not replace the properly philosophical task of explication. My own use of models as tools of explication will appear step by step beginning in Chapter VI and further discussion of the method will be brought in there.

3. EMPIRICAL REALISM

Some readers might object that mechanism is so vague as to apply to anything, not only the mind. As several thinkers have urged in criticism of functionalism anything whatever can be construed as an automaton, depending on where one sets the boundaries and levels of description (Kalke, 1969). Peter, Roommate, and clock constitute an automaton in which the internal states are within the walls of a room. That is its boundary, and its description is on a gross, molar level. Joe's big toe is an automaton with respect to excess of or lack of, uric acid crystals in the gout joint; it is easy to find a description that identifies stimulus and response configurations. Here the boundary is the body surface, and the level of description is molar. Likewise congress sits or not, and thus can be construed as an automaton of two states, possibly input free!

This rather shocking observation, if right, would seem to reduce the main thesis of the logic of mind to an empty triviality. And so far as it goes the observation is correct. But it has no bite. No mechanist wants to claim that a person is any old automaton scheme you can squeeze her in to. Furthermore the argument seems to be quite innocuous as the same objection can be leveled against any abstract model. My pen at rest on my desk is a single state input-free automaton. My pen is also a semi-group or a group with respect to a stationary transformation; or even a finite topological space if described as a unit set. Indeed, under some description or other anything is a realization of almost any kind of an abstract model you please. Anyone who doesn't like semi-groups or whatever can always trivialize the subject in this way. So although the objection is in a way correct, the same can be said of a lot of abstract schemes which are useful inhabitants of the edifice of science and here to stay. The conclusion that mechanism is empty seems not to follow, although the theory might turn out to be quite useless on other grounds.

The trouble here is this. What mechanism claims is not that human beings are NFA under some description or other, but rather that given some description human beings are NFA or usefully modeled as such under precisely *that* description (condition (i) above). The order of the quantifiers makes all the difference in the world! If by 'description' is meant a true statement to the effect that an individual has a set of states that are automaton-related to sensory inputs and motor outputs in certain ways, then the NFA table which gives the transition and output relations is the specific automaton organization of the system under that description (cf. Putnam, 1967). Although it is quite doubtful that anyone will ever write down production relations for the whole woman, the possible stimulus inputs and responses thereto are identifiable in principle and do provide a level of description and a boundary (the body surface) of a definite automaton. A defense of this claim will be forthcoming in the next chapter using an argument due to Arthur Burks.

This brings me to special theories, ones that purport to represent some particular trait or component of mind. Here it is clear that a description at some level is established by the psychologist as a function of ongoing concern with the problems at hand. One begins where he is, with specified (or increasingly specifiable) stimulus and response patterns framed by the collective interests of the community of scientists. Again, the boundaries and levels of description within which a hypothesis is formulated are far from arbitrary. Our hypothesis is that *within* these frames mental features can be explained in automaton (or programming-like) terms. One of the ends of cognitive psychology, what Fodor calls a Phase I explanation, is to discover just what kind of and how complex, an automaton represents some specific trait is *under a given description.*[25] An NFA or more generally perhaps a transformational theory of language and language learning, for example, includes fairly well understood inputs (phonemes), and the space of states hypothesized is known to be a well-defined portion of the brain. This does not mean that a psychological theory of a mechanist form requires precise knowledge of neurophysiological events. On the contrary, with functionalism mechanism holds that the psychology of language in the early phases of development is quite independent of purely physical matters, and even that explanatory knowledge of brain mechanisms presupposes knowledge of the logic. The point is that boundaries and descriptions of data are given, not that the terrain has to be worked at all levels.

The foregoing account of the nonarbitrariness of NFA attributions insists that psychological explanations proceed from specified stimulus and response data patterns (condition (i)). But beyond this rather modest demand section (2) lays the groundwork for setting forth a thesis of *realism.* 'Logic of mind' is not a metaphor. Unlike some faint-hearted functionalists who fear that an outright automaton hypothesis makes clocks of minds or otherwise doesn't catch mental complexity, personality, the affective life, etc., I hold that the mind is strongly guided by recursive rules of some kind that are actually embodied in material systems. These embodiments are presently unknown. If they were known there would be no point in writing this book or indeed in doing large portions of theoretical psychology.

The claim of realism follows from mechanism itself combined with one additional premise saying that recursive rules are expressible in some formal language. Assuming the truth of these propositions for the moment, it readily follows that there are real theories, both strong and weak (as defined after (i)–(iii) in Section 2), implying that mind is guided by a certain recursive logic. These theories go beyond fitting descriptions. The weakly real theories are realized by definite structures equivalent to some automaton, and the strong by material embodiments of these structures individuated by formulas representing systems of organs of some kind, in analogy to computer nets or idealized nerve nets as discussed previously. I will briefly discuss these assumptions and then comment on the philosophical standing of this conception of real rules I am advancing.

The first premise is just a statement of mechanism itself: men are automata. The second requires some motivation; I take it that its justification is simply whatever arguement it is that philosophers might use to support the philosophical thesis that discursive knowledge is possible, plus a minor observation. I need to assume expressibility as I regard relevant mental phenomena as satisfying automata (or equivalent) formalisms, in analogy to physical geometry. The real is relative to theory − literally a *realization* − and I cannot claim the reality of a definite rule system without the expressing language. The idea of a guiding rule which is individuated by a formula makes this quite evident. Now the possibility of discursive knowledge is an article of faith that is supported by a considerable mass of inductive evidence. I am willing to admit this status for the proposition and ask the reader to do the same on pain of discrediting science itself if he does not. However for empiricists, all admitting this guarantees is that fitting not necessarily guiding theories are possible. What is needed beyond that is a small observation that we borrow from mathematical logic. Automata theory, including the transition and output functions of an arbitrary Turing machine, can be formalized in a consistent first order set theory with added nonlogical axioms specifying that machine. Moreover, the logic formulas that result from coding an automaton (as in the adder or nerve net examples) are all formulas of a certain recursive arithmetic.[26] In other words, the specific *embodiments* of such automata are all expressible in a formal language.

Now in analogy I maintain that any set of recursive rules in the generalized sense − even of a different category such as grammatical transformation rules or program rules − can be so expressed. And this is more than a bare analogy, as it is supported by our basic intuitions about recursive relations as ones that are computable by algorithms. All algorithms we know of are expressible linguistically (if, indeed, the proposition is not simply a tautology).

It seems to me that this establishes the expressibility of rules in a formal language at the level of nets or other organs and *a fortiori* in abstract form, analogous to finite or Turing automata, quite well.[27]

Realism of this type is not a theory of truth, although it might appear to have a certain similarity to Peirce, as what is real depends on scientific theory. Peirce said *the* truth is what is fated to be agreed on by the scientific community, and the real is its object (1934, 5.407, 564). But my theory does not say that any one will ever hit on the right effective language (we are not "fated"), and even if some one does, it does not follow that true (or highly confirmed) theories having properties (i)–(iii) will ever be discovered. What I claim to be true is that there are appropriate expressing languages, not that the true theories formulable in them will ever be discovered. We might *never* discover the rules that guide.

It seems to me that this is a truly empirical position although it does take sides on what has traditionally been a metaphysical issue. If there ever are confirmed recursive rule type theories, say of speech, where this appears to be increasingly likely, then it will follow by the realist principle that there are behaviorally equivalent guiding rules in the mind. Presumably these could eventually be isolated when more is known about brain systems and nerve networks; and this knowledge could falsify the theory. It might turn out for instance that there are infinite mental states not representable by automata in our exact sense of the word.

The existence of such guiding rules explains mental life without recourse to unwholesome powers or virtues or excessively fuzzy things such as dispositions to behavior or innate knowledge. At any rate so I hope to show. The theory of real rules is essentially an extension of Chomsky's views (if I do not completely misunderstand him) of descriptive adequacy stretched to include all mental features along with language (Chomsky, 1965). I depart from him however in denying that these rules are 'known' to the subject in any sense of the term having epistemic significance of any kind, instead using the relatively precise idea of *guidance* which in turn goes back to elementary mathematical concepts. Of course they are known to the psycholinguist who has a true theory. The guidance concept is still perhaps not sufficient to account for important differences between rules qua *followed* rules (tacitly or not) and mere habits or laws of mind (Quine, 1972, p. 443). Moreover, rules of mind are not, so far as the empirical evidence goes, common to all humans — e.g., the rules that guide perception need not be the same in all of us either at the level of abstract automata (or some equivalent structure of yet unknown category) or at the level of embodiment. These issues will be further attended to in Chapter V where I will conclude, *contra* Chomsky, that the doctrine of real effective rules has nothing to do with rationalism and in particular with Descartes.

As it stands this kind of realism bears a slight resemblance to Kantian philosophy, although some functionalists would give this more emphasis. But I myself see little point in pressing historical analogies very far unless one side of it genuinely illuminates the other or both. In theory of knowledge Kant's aim was to demonstrate the possibility of universal and necessary knowledge, which he claimed mathematics and the basic principles of physics already manifested. So far as I can see this has little in common with an empirical, naturalistic philosophy that accepts no aprioristic epistemology, transcendental or not, although if one tries hard enough he might trace the idea of rules *qua* informing mental processes (including belief and knowledge) back historically to the categories and transcendental schemata. But there's a lot that could go wrong here. Conceptually a form of judgment, for one, is a far cry from a recursive rule. And while knowledge does depend on antecedent mental conditions in both the principles involved are quite the opposite. For Kant, scientific theory (i.e., knowledge) depends on a priori constitutive transcendental categories or forms of judgment, while in the other case the rule of mind as a *real* entity is related to a theory that is true, if it is true, on empirical grounds. Of course if future psychology bears mechanism out, then the *latter* theory also depends on real guiding modes of thought. The scientist's thoughts are not exempt from the logic of mind she attributes to humans in general. There is no paradox here (any more than Gödel sentences that refer to themselves), but only an inevitable consequence of a naturalist epistemology that bootstraps itself out of psychology. Whatever be the rules that guide science they will be known only to science itself, not deduced (perhaps better *abduced*) *a priori*. There is no prior epistemology.[28]

There is a much more illuminating resemblance to moderate Aristotelian realism, perhaps closest to John Duns Scotus. I shall have more to say about this in Chapter XI and here just want to say enough to complete the sketch of what a rule of mind is like. A realized automaton is a form: It does not subsist apart from material embodiment, but is *formally distinct* from the body in the sense that it is individuated by formulas that really define it. And it is real in that it guides and not merely fits by some exterior description. The logic of mind is thus man's essence or in Chomskian terms his competence; it defines him as a natural kind, the kind adumbrated in Chapter I. On the other hand, as there is no reason to suppose that your logic is mine exactly, there are only material *individuals*, but individuals realizing sufficiently similar properties to ground a science of them as a unified species. If this be nominalism, then there is, nevertheless, a transcendental invariant core which is not merely 'conceptual' or 'subjective' although it is most certainly theory-relative. The theory is realistic, but still naturalistic and empirical. I find I am inevitably *led to* it from considerations of contemporary logic, computers, and cognitive science; and thereby *led back* to a stance in some important respects closer to classical thought than to modern.

CHAPTER IV

MECHANISM – ARGUMENTS PRO AND CON

There are two positive arguments for mechanism which will be presented in this chapter. The first is an argument from analogy which says that digital computers and human beings share an extremely large and ever-growing body of intelligent behaviors, and since a computer is an automaton so is a man. The second, which rests on a certain claim about psychological explanations to the effect that nothing counts as an explanation of intelligence that appeals to unanalyzable chunks of intelligence, says that automata descriptions afford exactly such noncircular explanations. A further claim, namely that a strictly behaviorist method cannot account for all mental features, will be laid in the next chapter.

Other arguments in support of mechanism are made later in the book by way of establishing the *plausibility* of mechanism. The reflections of Chapter VI, meant to establish the coherence and plausibility of an automaton analysis of perception and, indeed, of gestalt perception, makes up one such argument. The sketch of theories of belief, desire, and meaning is another.

Before persuading the reader both of the force of the computer analogy and of the sufficiency of automaton theories of mental features, it will be necessary to disencumber his mind of the pervasive and pathogenic idea that a mechanist philosophy of mind entails that computers can think.

1. THINKING MACHINES

Turing published a paper in 1950 which has had more impact on philosophers and on practitioners of artificial intelligence than any other single source (Turing, 1950). Many philosophers were introduced to computers, Turing machines, and the fascinating question of the capabilities of machines for intelligent tasks through this paper. Perhaps you wonder why reference was not made to it in the section of Chapter II above on the historical development of contemporary mechanism. The reason is that Turing was considering the question whether digital computers can think. This is quite a different issue than the one posed by mechanism, namely whether men are indeed

89

machines, i.e., automata. In particular Turing did not claim, at least in that paper, that men are machines although certainly if machines can think that fact lends a kind of inductive support to mechanism. All of Turing's arguments in defense of the proposition that computers can think (or play his 'imitation game'), if they hold, help here. However, if they do not hold, they do not necessarily count against mechanism. There has been so much confusion of the idea of mechanism with that of thinking machines and robots in the philosophical literature that it is time to untangle the issues, if for no other reason than to obtain reasonable clarity. My main reason, however, is to remove one more possible misunderstanding of what mechanism actually says.[1]

Consider the following argument:

(1)   Computers cannot think,
(2)   Men can think,
(3)   Therefore, men are not computers.

Now contrary to Turing, (1) could be true — either one could defeat some of his arguments, such as the one against the popular view that Gödel's incompleteness results refute mechanism, or one could use an ordinary language argument against the expression 'thinking computers.' If so, granting that (2) is true, (3) is also true and therefore mechanism is false.

Now whether you accept *this* argument or not it serves to illustrate one way in which the issue about thinking machines is presumably related to the truth or falsity of mechanism. Whether persons are machines stands or falls with the proposition that computers think. What is wrong with this sort of argument and its interpretation is its use of a tacit assumption that all machines are computers or artifacts of some kind used to perform tasks sometimes performed by people. There is, of course, a perfectly common usage of 'machine' which connotes electronic computers or rods and levers arranged in complex configurations. Not even classical, La Mettrian mechanism held that everything was a machine in the first sense mentioned. At any rate in the logic of mind as we have seen at some length 'machine' means 'automaton' in the sense of a system of rules. Digital computers are machines embodying such rules, as Burks and Copi have shown, and so are animals and men, according to the hypothesis we are defending. The hypothesis, then, which the argument (1)–(3) is meant to discredit if it is to be philosophically relevant is that

(3')   Men are machines.

And (1) should be replaced by

(1′)   Some machines (*viz.* computers) cannot think.

From this and the ingenuous (2) nothing whatever follows about (3′).
There is a more sophisticated argument which replaces (1) by

(1″)   No machines can think

in which 'machines' has the present technical meaning; that is to say, (1″)
means something like "nothing whose central activities can be explained
entirely in terms of effective processes can think". From (1″) and (2) the
falsity of (3′) does follow. But this last argument no longer hinges on misunderstanding of the thesis of mechanism and may well be sound. I hope
the reader will forgive me for laboring what is really a very clear issue. But
it is extremely important that one not be taken in by antimechanist arguments that conflate 'machine' in the philosophically important sense with
'computer'. For concreteness I will briefly list and comment on some of the
largely irrelevant attacks on mechanism that stem from this confusion. At
one time most of them were taken seriously by philosophers, and some of
the may still be. They include a few which Turing answered, but usually by
a different kind of argument from mine. I will use 'machine$_1$' for the abstract
sense of a system of recursive rules and 'machine$_2$' for artifacts including
digital computers and other kinds of information handling hardware. Of
course some machines$_2$ are machines$_1$, but not all machines$_1$ are machines$_2$.

Persons like strawberries, fall in love, and think consciously. So mechanism
must be false since machines do not like strawberries, etc. If 'machines'
means machines$_2$, then there is a point here; if it means machines$_1$ then
the argument shows nothing.[2] Satisfying certain rules, if mechanism is true,
is a necessary condition for being human, not a sufficient one; and there is
no incompatibility between being rule guided and being conscious, in love,
or liking strawberries.

A closely related objection is that man cannot be a machine because
the latter are unable to immitate human perception. Some who raise this
objection may concede that computers can do a fair job of playing checkers
or theorem proving or other 'higher' cognitive tasks, but strongly question
their ability to imitate 'lower' mental functions (Dreyfus, 1972, pp. 151–
55). But again, if the reference here is to machines$_1$, the objection comes
to nothing. When Dreyfus argues that pattern recognition schemes have
in fact failed he pretty clearly has in mind actual computers and attempts
to program recognition schemes. As of this date this alleged empirical fact is

quite disputable. In a later chapter I will argue that this objection, even for machines$_2$, is wrong *in principle*.

There is also an argument against recognition by machines$_1$ (just as there was one against machines$_1$ thinking noted earlier). However let us limit our attention at present to objections that turn on the ambiguity of 'machine'.

Two other arguments, which are hard for me to attribute to any serious philosopher, can be disposed of quickly. The first, which Turing calls the 'theological objection' is that thinking is a function of man's immortal soul. Machines do not have souls: ergo, etc. This argument refers to machines$_2$, for certain. If it is meant to apply to the other, I might reply as follows. Although I do not believe in souls immortal or otherwise, and indeed take one of the virtues of mechanism to be its power to account for mental life naturalistically, there is no incompatibility whatever in the concept of being recursive rule abiding and immortal. Mechanism seems to be compatible with idealism or even Cartesian dualism so far as I can see. No part of the concept that the logic of mind is a realization of abstract automaton formalism requires that the mind be materialistic or even naturalistic. In fact I can readily imagine that a Thomistic philosopher might find a recognizing automata quite attractive for explicating the medieval notion of the active intellect (see Chapter VI).

The second is the objection that the consequences of machine thinking would be too dreadful. This objection is a kind of inverse will to believe à la William James. If the consequences of a belief are dreadful and insofar forth do not 'work', then they are false. Although this kind of argument might not be entirely without merit for emotional or religious purposes it has no standing as philosophy; besides it appears to do solely with machines$_2$, and hence is entirely irrelevant. It seems to be related to a strong anti-technological animus dominant in some quarters. Technology, computers, science, government data systems, etc. dehumanize and mechanize us. Man's real nature is being twisted and corrupted, it is said, by the machine. I find myself partly in sympathy with this attitude, although the simple-mindedness it manifests probably does more harm than good in the long run. Unfortunately many persons opposed to science, technology, and machines for apparently humanistic reasons often glorify certain irrational elements of life that defeat the highest human aspirations.

2. THE ARGUMENT FROM ANALOGY

According to Smart (1963, p. 107), with whom I otherwise find myself in broad agreement, the scientific plausibility of physicalism gives good grounds for accepting the hypothesis that men are physical mechanisms.[3] Strong support, he says, also comes from cybernetics, presumably including automata theory, which suggests ways of explaining the purposefulness, adaptiveness, and appropriateness of human behavior. The importance of control and automata theory is clear, but physicalism does not provide any better grounds for a mechanical theory of mind than idealism does. I think that what Smart has in mind is something like this. Since physics is the only science having a body of universal laws, any science that rides on physics, such as psychology, need not assume entities beyond those of physics, and hence it is reasonable to take the hypothesis that men are purely *physical* machines − one does not need souls or ghosts to account for mental phenomena. In fact Smart identifies conscious events with brain processes. But, as already indicated, the version of mechanism I am advocating is not committed to elimination of mental entities (occurrents) such as sense data, but only to the recognition of and the (tentative) separation of, two kinds of problem of mind. It may tun out, for example, that mental occurrents should be identified with physical brain states, but that logical states, in turn, are not identical with physical brain states.[4] Or, considering that Leibniz is the progenitor of mechanistic$_1$ type philosophy, we might well follow him all the way and adopt pluralistic idealism. Presumably, then, logical states would be awareness states of the monads. Realizations of abstract automaton systems are in no way limited to the physical.

I am compelled, therefore, to reject physicalism as a support for mechanism because a machine$_1$ is not *necessarily* either a physical, material, or epiphenomenal entity. (However, see Section XI.1.)

It should be mentioned here in anticipation of later discussion that I also reject Smart's version of physicalism in its explicit claim that psychology, or for that matter biology, consists of empirical generalizations but has no irreducible universal laws of its own. If a logic of mind is right, then in principle psychology will be founded on a theory comprised of law-like statements, indeed, an essentially *logico-mathematical* theory. So the arguments for mechanism here will depend largely on what boils down to questions of logic.

Let us now consider the argument from analogy. Digital computers are automata, and, further, individual computer programs are automata in the sense that they are free algorithms. Now there is an extremely large number of behaviors mean and other animals have in common with computers or computer programs. These behaviors range from primitive stimulus-response and other lower biologic phenomena to higher cognitive activity and include the conditional reflex, reproduction, growth and self-repair, simple learning, learning to play games, sentence parsing, looking up references, proving theorems (either heuristically or by algorithm), doing arithmetic, composing music, doing office work, drawing pictures, planning itineraries, carrying on conversations in fragments of English, writing stories and poems, etc. Hence since computers are finite automata there is a reasonable likelihood that men are, too.

It is not hard to find weaknesses in this analogy to pounce upon. There are those, myself included, who are troubled by the use of such locutions as 'computer composition of music', or of 'thinking machines'. The analogy does seem to attribute questionable powers to computers (machines$_2$), such as the capability of doing things intentionally and being conscious in what they are doing to boot. However, I have only *indicated* an analogy, which pivots on common *behaviors*. We could express the argument less deceptively, perhaps, by replacing the objectionable expressions by topic neutral terms that indicate recursive functions only. For instance 'doing arithmetic' or 'adding' or even 'calculating sums' could be replaced by 'mapping pairs of input strings to outputs such that the output is the sum of the input' for those who want to go so far as to deny calculating skills of machines$_2$ (cf. Matson, 1976, p. 90). There is no readily convenient and understandable substitute vocabulary for the kind of terms I used in the sketch of the argument. However each offending expression could be appropriately replaced, in principle, by introducing notations for the input-output functions involved in each case. In effect we could construct a mathematical language of recursive functions which would do the job, which is in effect what we did in previous chapters (see Section II.7).

From the opposite side, the companion complaint might arise that when human beings add, persisting in the same simple example, they are doing something quite different than taking input, performing a mathematical transformation on it and ejecting output. Although this is a plain case of begging the question, I'll let it pass, asking only that the reader accept that addition by people, for example, *necessarily* entails such a transformation. To see this one might use Turing's device of communicating with people though a slot in a wall using punched cards: introduce a card having two coded integers together with the instruction 'add'; then recover the same card with the sum punched thereon. An infinite stack of such cards represents the addition function, which is precisely the *behavior* in question stripped of accidental conditions. Similarly for poetry writing etc. Some humanists, probably not poets, might boggle at the idea of a punched card carrying a poem but in this argument the *poem's* the thing.

Having made adjustments on each side we are left with an analogy depending on similarity of behavior. That computers are machines₁ we mentioned in our historical sketch, and even indicated what the Burks-Copi demonstration looks like. Assuming that the foregoing discussion has cleared the air about the appropriateness of using expressions like 'composing,' etc., we are left with just two objections, which I can think of, that could still be raised. One has to do with the strength of the analogy itself, and the other with the comparability of the set of musical compositions on the computer side with that on the human side, of the set of theorems proved (or theorem provings) on one side with that on the other, and so forth. These collections are certainly not the same. I will take up the first objection first, assuming that the second has been met. (See Section 4 below.)

That automaton behavior is the behavior of an organism does not imply that the organism is an automaton. This is a point which I raised before (in Section III.3) in my stressing that mechanism makes a metaphysical claim about what a person is. Here, however, the issue is not the meaning of the doctrine but its ground. A man could, for example, be a kind of infinite list and compute a response (behavioral output in our stripped-down representation of behavior) from a stimulus or stimulus sequence by a kind of look-up or associative process without use of any feedback mechanism or internal state structure; or there might be a set of environmental conditions playing the same logical role as internal states, so that although the animal is not an automaton, it is part of an organism-environment system that behaves exactly like one. What I am alluding to here is the possibility of a system of such a kind that the internal state role is cast in external objects. For example, consider an experimental psychologist who has discovered that a rat sometimes respond to an electric shock in a leg by flight behavior and sometimes not, even after a long series of experiments that uniformly produced flight. Chances are that the experimenter would either get a new rat, assuming the rat is healthy, or look for an emergent environmental side condition. A strict S–R theorist would not make the obvious step of attributing internal states to the rat such that the flight response is a function of both the stimulus and the state. Although I will give what I believe to be a definitive argument against the environment state line in a later discussion of behaviorism, it nevertheless does constitute an objection to the analogy.

Both of the foregoing alternatives to the automaton hypothesis tacitly accept the discrete state character of input and output entities as posited by mechanism and perhaps of state entities if any as well, but reject the internal structural organization. In particular what is being rejected are the transition and output functions of finite automata. For, the first objection argues for direct input-output correlations of discrete entities, the second for external-ization of the transition function mapping discrete things to discrete things. A third objection explicitly rejects the whole business: it either maintains that mental processes are not discrete state processes at all; or, if they are, are of a far more complex order than is pre-supposed by the oversimply conceived automaton models.

I must confess that I see no way of satisfactorily responding to the first version of this third objection, except in part. An answer would require a book about some of the most difficult problems of epistemology and philos-ophy of science – one I do not know how to write, especially at the beginning of an enterprise which I hold to be prior to a refined epistemology. So the following will have to suffice.

Within the broad naturalistic tradition which provides the background for our remarks the scientist or philosopher is free to slice up the actual world in any way that pays off in inquiry. This includes a choice of *con-tinuous* versus discrete geometry as framework for the objects of study. In theoretical physics, as we all know, certain phenomena are explained in two or more apparently contrary theories, the one explanation sufficing for one class of application and the other a different class. Thus if the physicist is concerned with the bending of light rays he uses a wave theory while if he is concerned with a photo-electric effect he explains in terms of quantum theory. In the language of wave theory color is a question of wave length and in the other of the energy of light quanta. These theories are incompatible inasmuch as 'wave' and 'quantum' are contraries. Similarly an input stimulus to an organism may for some theoretical purposes be regarded as a con-tinuously varying signal and for others as a discrete pulse – fit to be taken as a realization of an automaton symbol, s. Consider the degree of dilation of the pupil of the eye as a function of the luminous intensity of a light source and its distance from the eye. Here the stimulus, light intensity, is a continuous variable, and the pupil response is also a continuous variable. But consider also a worm which wriggles when it is irritated, provided that some time in the recent past it was exposed to light of a certain intensity or above but not to heat of a certain level or above. Now the 'variables' here are wriggling or not wriggling, light at a certain level or not, etc. These variables are in fact propositional functions of time with values 1 or 0 (or T or F) and are hence discrete. It is easy to see that this worm is a finite automaton;[5] i.e., when light, heat and mechanical irritation are taken as propositional functions, they are automaton inputs while wriggling, similarly taken is the output. Moreover, the worm must have at least two internal states, possibly two states of a neuronal axon, which are its logical states. One of these states serves as memory that the right levels of heat and light exposure occurred recently.

Unlike the light quanta-wave example the light stimulus is interpreted in two ways which are not contrary although the mathematical schemes are radically different: in the one we use continuous functions of real variables and in the other the logic of automata. There are those who would no doubt argue that the light is *really* continuous in its intensity levels and that the automaton-type description is somehow provisional or heuristic or at any rate 'reducible' to the physical. In my opinion this is a serious mistake and I will argue the point later. For the present, however, I will appeal to an argument of Arthur Burks to the effect that all of the worm inputs, in fact all the entities in the study of natural human (*a fortiori*, animal) functions are *discrete*. Each natural function is defined in terms of the set of responses to the set of all possible input stimuli.[6] Now there is a smallest difference "between stimuli intensity to which the organism can respond". Likewise there is a time interval so short that an organism cannot respond to physical changes within it, and there are spatial volumes so small that the organism cannot detect quality variations within them. "Consequently there is a quantum of space-time such that the organism can react to only a finite number of quality differences within it" (Burks, 1972–73, p. 51). Since the human body is finite it follows there can be only a finite number of stimuli [classes] among which it can distinguish. So inputs are discrete.

To prevent later misunderstanding, note that nothing in Burks' argument to the finiteness of possible stimuli assumes that stimuli (or receptors or internal states) need be 'on' or 'off' (or T or F) in character. There could be many stimulus levels – a question for the neurophysiologist, not the philosopher or even the theoretical psychologist to decide. Nothing in the concept of finite machine implies binarity, even though many natural phenomena relevant to the study of mental processes are binary, such as the firing or nonfiring of neurons. Of course the automata we know most about, namely digital computers, are binary. We have already allowed for this flexibility in the theory in the manner in which we generalized from Pitts-McCulloch nerve networks to finite automata (in Section II.4).

Similarly, Burks argues, there is only a finite number of responses possible. Finally, the transformations of man's input histories to output is mediated by discrete states. There is a minimum size of physiological part that has any significance in internal processing; for example each genetic nucleotide stores a finite amount of information. And since, again, the human body occupies only a finite volume, only a finite number of internal states are possible.[7]

This argument, which draws on essentially physical-physiological facts, shows that the concept of stimulus and others has significance only relative to the organism. 'Stimulus' is really short for 'stimulus-to-the-organism'. Even light luminosity, reverting to our example of the reaction of the pupil, must *qua* stimulus come in discrete levels, if Burks is right. However assuming that we want to keep to the view, convenient in most physical applications, that luminous intensity is continuous, then we stimpulate that the function mapping intensity to degree of dilation be a composition of three functions as follows: the first is a step function, which assigns discrete levels to intensities as determined by the eye's discriminative characteristics; the second is a finite function over these levels to a set of a finite number of degrees of pupil dilation, likewise determined by physiological constraints; and the third interpolates and smooths the range of the second. On Burks' view that intermediate function is a finite automaton input-output transformation.

I believe that this argument shows that mental processes (as well as other natural functions in Burks' terminology), provided we accept a physical interpretation of mental features, are indeed discrete.[8] And the simplest way to take the organism as a whole is as an NFA. At the same time it shows one way of reconciling the presumed conflict between those advocating continuous mathematics and those the discrete in the pursuit of biological and psychological phenomena. In the light-pupil example, one interested in intensity studies the composite function; one interested in the etiology of a response studies the mediating function.

An extremely influential viewpoint in contemporary cognitive science and artificial intelligence that on some points seems to be opposed to computationalism in any form is *connectionism*. According to its proponents (e.g. Rumelhart, McCelland, *et. al.*, 1986; Smolensky, 1988), the most fruitful models for perception, some types of learning, and problem solving are not digital computers or Turing machines but networks of interactive computational devices, connected by weighted excitatory and inhibitory pathways, some of which are analogue, hence entailing an underlying continuous geometry. These models incorporate content addressable memories, and data is represented in a "subsymbolic" systems, which means the counterparts of algorithms are *embodied,* not free.

If connectionism is right, the familiar one-step-at-a-time digital computers or "von Neumann Machines" or universal Turing machines are not adequate for explaining perception, etc. These machines are not capable of parallel operation, it is said; they are instruction-driven and manipulate separable symbols under free algorithms. The technical reasons why these traits seem to make the models unsuitable are pretty far from our concerns. All I am moved to discuss here is that the critics are both right and wrong. As will be seen in due course (Chapter VI et. seq.) perception, perceptual belief, intentionality and semantics seem within the grasp of something like a connectionist model; so that extent they are right. However they are wrong in thinking (if they do) that embodied algorithm FA do not have all the properties they need in connectionist modeling.

There are two points, one concerning parallelism and the other geometry. I will take up the parallelism question in the next chapter and *exhibit* parallel systems still later in this book. As to continuity, models that use the concepts of analysis – real functions, differential equations, probability theory and analogue devices – probably can *not* be *realized* by networks using analogue computers. If the number of parallel inputs is large enough, there is no analogue device adequate to store the information need for computation (See Minsky and Papert, 1969). Moreover any required computations can be sufficiently approximated digitally by networks of logic devices or idealized neurons (not necessarily as simple as McCulloch-Pitts nets, of course; see Nelson, 1988b).

This is no recommendation that connectionists drop the analytic and statistical models, but only that the question of the actual nature of the *embodied* system can be answered by FA, for much the same reasons that partial differential equations (for example) don't (can't, as a practical matter) be integrated on analogue computers. So none of the hypotheses, including connectionism, if construed in a realistic way, have the plausibility of mechanism so long as we recognize a distinction between free and embodied algorithms and give up the idea that everything can be done with programming models. There remains the objection that the hypothesis may be *too* simple. It could be argued that the discrete input-output model is on the right track but (against Burks) that the human processing system is something more complex than a finite automaton or indeed than any conceivable system within our family of abstract processing systems, including full Turing machines. This kind of objection returns us to a discussion of Church's Thesis.

3. PSYCHOLOGICAL EXPLANATION AND CHURCH'S THESIS

C. D. Dennett has sketched an argument to support the claim that mechanistic explanations are adequate for psychological theory, which I should like to adapt to my purposes here (Dennett, 1976).[9]

Any non-question-begging psychological theory, the argument goes, will not attempt to explain cognitive phenomena by ultimate appeals to unexplained intelligence — in other words whatever parts a theory decomposes its subjects into, the smallest or fundamental parts must not presuppose little homunculi that order and execute mental processes. (Dennett, 1976, p. 181). If so the fundamental procedures fall within the class of those procedures which we intuitively regard as effective or recipe-like. Dennett defends this assertion by drawing an analogy with the methods of artificial intelligence (AI) researchers. AI programmers in effect make a complete analysis of a process (say, solving a puzzle) when they find a program that works, even in a high order language such as LISP or MACLISP.[10] Such programs effectively translate down to machine language programs, thence to hardware processes all of which are realizations of Turing-type rules, as we have already indicated. These correspond to fundamental procedures (whatever they may turn out to be in the human physiology) that do not require any intelligence. Then by CT these processes and procedures are Turing computable processes. Our conclusion from this line of argument is, then, that that the simplest way to account for these latter phenomena is to hypothesize that the psychological subject is an abstract automaton.[11]

One possible objection to this argument, anticipated by Turing (1936, pp. 136–138) is that the fundamental or atomic procedures a human computist follows might not be anything like Turing machine or finite automaton operations. There is no reason to believe, the objection continues, that Dennett's fundamental processes, even though analogous to atomic computer operations are that simple. A human computist seems to be much less restricted in behavior than a machine. However in response Kleene (1952, p. 377) following Turing's line has enumerated the possible ways in which additional complexity may arise:

(a)   [A human computist] can observe more than one symbol occurrence [input] at a time.

(b)   He can perform more complicated atomic acts than a machine.

(c)   His symbol space [medium in which input is presented] need not be a one-dimensional tape.

But, he goes on to argue, all of these more complex forms of behavior – observation in parallel in a multidimensional space, and processing by less simple atomic acts – are reducible to Turing machine computations by strictly *effective* procedures. Hence by our definition of the family of recursive processing systems (which includes all mutually effectively intertranslatable systems which compute the recursive functions) the human computist is included. To cover other cognitive processes in this type of argument we simply note that inputs, states, etc of the organism need not be symbols on paper, but any discrete entities that could satisfy automaton formalisms. In other words the complexity we find in Kleene's 'less restricted behavior' does not entail the existence of entities other than those fit to satisfy formal systems. Again the best evidence for this is Burks' argument combined with Dennett's analogy of fundamental parts of psychological processes with atomic computer acts.

The Turing-Kleene argument is really an argument for CT based on a kind of rough and ready analysis of the way in which human computists manipulate symbols in doing a computational problem. Numerous attacks of a more formal, logical kind have been leveled at the thesis, which would take us too far afield to consider (cf. Nelson, 1987a). Those who are not impressed with the earlier arguments to the effect that mental processes and features are discrete in nature (a necessary condition for effectiveness as usually construed) or with the Turing-Kleene arguments perhaps will agree to take CT as an underlying assumption for our remaining discussion.

4. ON THE DISSIMILARITY OF BEHAVIORS

The era of 'can computers think?' questions in recent philosophy generated a number of arguments which seem to be directed more against the view that human and computer behaviors are *shared* than against the view that a human being is an abstract automaton. Our analogy premissed that a large number of cognitive behaviors are held in common. But, this next objection might go, the theorems proved by computers (e.g., large portions of *Principia Mathematica*) is a trivial sub-collection of the corpus of real mathematics. Assuming that this kind of objection is not guilty of confusing what has been proved with what is machine provable, which is what is at issue, the point is that computers considered as machines are severely limited. Indeed, man might even be a kind of discrete machine (remember Post's comment) but not one limited to the realm of the recursive or the constructive. However, the foregoing argument for CT casts doubt on the possibility of such more advanced machines, and greatly weakens the Nagel-Newman argument to be presented now.

The most famous argument of this type is the argument from Gödel's theorem. Let us examine a popular version of this due to Nagel and Newman (1956).

... in the light of Gödel's incompleteness theorem, there is an endless set of problems in elementary number theory for which such machines are inherently incapable of supplying answers, however complex their built-in mechanisms may be and however rapid their operations. It may very well be the case that the human brain is itself a 'machine' with built-in limitations of its own, and that there are mathematical problems which it is incapable of solving. Even so, the human brain appears to embody a structure of rules of operation which is far more powerful than the structure of currently conceived artificial machines. There is no immediate prospect of replacing the human mind by robots.

To put the argument in the most favorable light we will assume that the authors' reference to computing machines is to machines$_1$. Now since all a Turing machine can do is enumerate theorems of a formal system such as number theory, it doesn't have any way of seizing the truth of a certain formula of number theory that we can. Briefly, the rejoinder is that there is no evidence whatever that the human mind is capable of perceiving the truth of any sentence a machine cannot prove. Nagel and Newman beg the question.

In somewhat more detail, this argument seems to go as follows. Gödel proved that every consistent formal system which is rich enough to express recursive functions is incomplete. This means that there is a well-formed formula of the system without free variables which is not provable, nor is its negation. This formula in effect expresses that it itself is unprovable.

Now, it is claimed, *we can see* that this self-referring unprovable formula is indeed unprovable: namely, we can see that it is *true*. On the other hand a machine, which is capable only of enumerating all of the theorems of the system, given enough time, cannot 'see' that this formula is true — all it can do is grind out sentences; and it will never get this one.[12]

The latter part of this argument is essentially correct, although it is known that a formal system can be extended to another formal system in such a way that the true formula in question of the first is a theorem of the second. But then a new undecidable formula can be produced (which Lucas claims we can see the truth of) and so forth. Smart (1963, pp. 116 f.) has made an argument out of this fact in support of mechanism. A machine, he contends, given a formal system presented in a language L_0 having an undecidable Gödel-type formula F_0 could formalize the semantical metalanguage L_1 of L_0, and within L_1 deliver a proof of F_0 (assuming L_0 to be consistent). But then L_1 would have an undecidable formula F_1; however this would next lead to construction of the metalanguage of L_1, and so on. The trouble with this line of argument lies in the notion of construction. Smart believes it is not *a priori* implausible that a machine could be built which could discover the rules governing the language it uses, say L_0. It would have to have this capability in order to go on and formulate L_1, which of course embodies these rules. This kind of 'inductive' construction is in fact known to be possible for a very restricted sub-family of the context-free languages. But the predicate calculus, to begin with, is not context-free, and so far as I know the problem of the limits of inductive machines in this sense, which is strictly mathematical in character, has scarcely been attacked. I strongly suspect that this process is *not* in general algorithmic in which case the relevant question for mechanism becomes the question of the capabilities of *human beings* for this construction and for the requisite consistency proof.

Returning from this slight digression to the Nagel-Newman argument we see that they conclude that the superior human brain knows, from Gödel's discovery, that there are formally indemonstrable arithmetic truths (Nagel, *et al.*, 1956, p. 1695). But as Hilary Putnam (1960, p. 153) has pointed out this is simply a mistake. All a human being can prove is that if the formal system is consistent, then the Gödel formula is true. He can 'see' the truth of the self-referring formula only in this sense. In the instance of formal number theory, a person can produce an intuitively true interpretation from which it follows that the systems is consistent, and hence from the above proposition that the Gödel formula is true. But this supposedly true interpretation can be established as such only by somewhat precarious, nonrigorous methods, and for any arbitrarily chosen system to which Gödel's result applies, probably not at all. Indeed a consistency proof for number theory which is generally acknowledged to be one that would satisfy strictly formalist requirements has not yet been obtained. So given the facts about consistency proofs and known methods of obtaining them, the claim that human beings can 'see' the consistency of an arbitrarily chosen logical system having a Gödel incompleteness theorem is entirely gratuitous. The argument is like saying that an existentialist couldn't possibly be a mathematician because mathematicians can't write down a complete decimal expansion of Pi; or that a horse can't possibly be an elephant because an elephant can't knit.[13]

A related argument is that machines$_1$ cannot do anything creative. This is a variant of the objection that machines can only do what they are told to do by a programmer and is known, following Turing, as 'Lady Lovelace's objection'.[14] Before coming to the main reply we should notice that there is a certain confusion about mechanism which is bound to arise when we consider that effective processes of the type we are attributing to the mind are characteristically *deductive*. Post systems, or alternatively Turing machines, which we have seen underlie certain linguistic, nerve network, and computer network theories, are generalizations of ordinary formal deductive logics. How, then, can a hypothesis which claims that all mental activity reduces to effective procedures account for nondeductive skills such as writing poetry, heuristic problem solving, or day dreaming? Focusing for now on heuristic procedures the situation is this.[15] Many problems people are faced with and sometimes solve require ingenuity, experience, extraordinary preseverance, luck, inspiration, the ability to grasp complicated inter-relationships and patterns. On the face of it none of these mental attributes are algorithmic. Indeed, it is just those cases in which no list of deductive-type instructions would guide one to a solution for which these mental traits and skills are required.

Now to say a problem is nonalgorithmic does not mean it cannot be solved by a computer program or universal Turing machine. The relatively high success of computer programs for learning and playing games (especially checkers as presently to be described) where no practical algorithm is known belies that. Yet even a heuristic program is a *program*; and a program is essentially a composition of *deductive* rules. So we are faced with paradox.

But the paradox is only apparent and is resolved by observing that a heuristic program, say, a learning program is algorithmic sure enough but is not an algorithm for the complete solution of the task at hand. For instance chess is nonalgorithmic (at least in a practical sense) in that there is no sure routine for producing a win.[16] Yet heuristic programs for chess are plentiful. What the latter do is to (algorithmically) determine moves which the programmer (and eventually the learning program) believes to be good by some reasonable programmed or learned standard and which *may* lead to a win. But this program does not give a winning computer move as response to every move of the opposition – that is to say, it is not an algorithm for winning every chess game.

Similarly, in principle, there is no reason whatever for believing that discovery of scientific hypotheses or writing poetry or music is not programmable even though there is probably no algorithm for the formation of serious hypotheses and almost certainly not for composing music that could pass for

Bach or Mozart, even in Albert Hall.[17] In short, heuristic programs may exist for all of these and inasmuch as they are programs they are algorithms *for*, in the sense of unerringly producing, hypotheses or poetry of merit.[18] In this book when there is occasion to make the distinction we will use 'closed algorithm' and 'semi-algorithm' for the strictly decisive routines and the heuristic procedures respectively.

The relative success of heuristics and the possibility of programs for simulating the highest intellectual skills including artistic creativity suggests another approach to the problem broached in the last chapter: how can a finite automaton, either a human being if he is such or a computer, perform tasks requiring powers of, say, a full Turing machine? In particular how can a system limited in principle to using finite state languages handle a natural language such as English, which is believed to follow rules of far greater complexity that account for self-embeddedness, transformations, and the like (cf. Section II.1)? The answer that suggests itself is of course that these tasks may be accomplished, not by closed algorithms for there are none for the finite automata, but by heuristic semi-algorithms. The limits of such procedures are unknown, but they are, if nothing else, still systems of effective rules. By trading decisive certainty for heuristic (even hit or miss) groping the capabilities of a theoretically underendowed organism can reach the heights. Incidentally, the reader is encouraged to reconsider the Gödelian argument in the light of these remarks. Perhaps using heuristic methods (which is what Lucas may have in mind) we come to 'see' truths; but if so, the same is available to anything with the powers of machines$_1$, including computers (see Nelson, 1980, pp. 441ff.)

We are now in a better position to assess Lady Lovelace's objection that computers can only do what they are told to do and can do nothing new. Well, a computer can learn, and moreover can learn to perform a task better than its programmer can. The outstanding example of this phenomenon is Arthur Samuel's checker program originally written for an IBM 704 (Samuel, 1959). It would take us much too far afield to attempt to describe how this program works or even to give the history of its career. Suffice it to say that the program has developed strategies through experience so that it plays at a level far superior to its programmer. It has defeated top-ranking players, the first of which (in 1962) declared " . . . I have not had such competition from a human being since 1954, when I lost my last game".[19]

Learning is programmed into a computer according to various possible schemes which are usually variations on the following theme for learning to play finite board games. Every legal arrangement of pieces is called a configuration. When a player, either machine or human, makes a move, the result is a new configuration. In other words one can think of a move as change from one configuration to the next. If the computer is to move, it makes a large number of virtual or trial moves and examines the resulting configurations for goodness. In simple games like tic-tac-toe, it tries all possible moves and checks out all the resulting configurations. In complex games like chess it tries only those that are not completely absurd (here of course the programmer is utilizing his own knowledge of the game); it next tries nonabsurd responses of the opponent, its own response to that, and so on up to several levels or 'plies' of play. The program next evaluates the resulting configurations against weighted criteria established by presumably good theory, and makes a choice, going to a random number table to break ties or to effect choices when the available criteria are inapplicable. The opponent moves, and the computer repeats, and so on to the end of the game. The moves and corresponding configurations (or, simply, configuration pairs) are stored for the entire game. At the end, if the machine wins it alters the criteria or the weights associated thereto (in tic-tac-toe the criteria are the weights themselves associated to each game configuration) so that the likelihood of using winning configurations in future plays is enhanced. If it loses, it alters these criteria oppositely, in some way.

Even from this very imperfect sketch it should be clear that if the machine begins its learning career with reasonable built-in criteria, it will very likely eventually improve its skill during plays of the game. Improvement will depend on the level of play of its opponents and on program modifications as the programmer himself comes to a better understanding of the game and the learning capabilities of the ever-changing program. There is a not-too-far-fetched analogy here with learning situations involving human teachers and learners; and just as in the human case the computer can and in some cases does, surpass the teacher in playing skill. The key point with regard to the philosophical issue we are considering is that the computer does not do just what it is told to do; its program governs its operations, and the program in game learning is altered and even improved by the vicissitudes of the play, not by the programmer. In principle there is no reason whatever why a computer could not learn to perform extremely elaborate cognitive skills beyond those attainable by people. For us, however, this just attests to the scope and power of a machine$_1$ as a conceptual tool for understanding mind. The remarkable performances of actual machines$_2$ are a side matter.

It would be unfair not to mention that there is another side to the question of the capabilities of machines for playing difficult games using semi-algorithms — although the issue involved is not that computers only do what they are programmed to do, but that they cannot play on the same level as humans. Chess, for instance, so far has not submitted to programming analysis to the same extent as checkers, although there is no shortage of programs that can play at about the expert or master level.[20] It is just possible that no one will ever produce a chess learning routine that performs at a level comparable to Samuel's checker program. If not, the question then arises whether the relative failure is attributable to poor programming, to lack of sufficient analytic understanding of chess, or to the limitations of machines$_1$ — chess might be beyond any algorithm, heuristic or not. But if the last alternative turns out to be right, then mechanism would be shattered, and, unlike the argument from Gödel, we would have a clear case where superior man can do something that the machine can't touch.

One argument against the *possibility* of chess programs contends that strong chess play depends on a player's ability to perceive complex patterns having a significance that cannot be captured by the kind of recognition open to computers. In short, winning chess depends on a player's having the ability to grasp *gestalten*, pattern wholes not reducible to constituent parts (cf. Dreyfus, 1972, p. 17). The trouble with this argument is the same as the argument from Gödel. It attributes to man an unanalyzable skill he may not in fact possess and then argues that since machines do not have it either they or their programmers are doomed to failure at the relevant tasks. This seems to be an extremely weak argument, and boils down to the simple assertion that A cannot do B because it lacks an inexplicable property which B is presumed but not known to require. We will reopen the question of gestalt perception and machines in Section VI.1.

There are a couple of other objections, going back to Turing's paper, to the position that machine behaviors of the relevant kind are co-extensive with those of humans. They can be given short shrift here, because they appear to be based on lack of information about machines$_1$ which is easily available to anyone who is serious about the question. The first is that machines cannot be their own subject. This is false. It has been known since 1960 that there are self-describing Turing machines — machines which, given an input, can compute and then print output including a complete coded description of their own quadruple rules.[21] Moreover, actual computers constantly alter their own programs, e.g., in learning something; moreover they can *trace* their own operations and can print out during computation or in a batch at the end of computation a record of all transactions made in doing a problem.[22] If there is a disparity here between computer and human self-knowledge the computer would seem to have the edge. Human beings seem to lack this kind of direct access to their own cognitive performances.[23] Turing, in his answer to this objection concerning self-knowledge, did not note that there is a sense in which it is perfectly sound. If this criticism means that machines$_2$ are not aware of themselves, then it is correct as machines$_2$ are not *aware* of anything. An event of awareness, on my view, is a mental occurrent – in the same cateogry as a pain – and machines$_2$ do not suffer such events. However *some* machines$_1$, namely animals, or at least men, do have awareness of themselves. Turing did not make the distinction we are observing between features and occurrents and hence did not recognize that machines$_2$ could share features, e.g., behaviors, with men without feeling anything. Of course the distinction is only a working one and has yet to be somewhat more thoroughly defended, as does my rather dogmatically expressed position that computers are without feeling (Chapter XI).

The second of this last pair of objections says that machines cannot make mistakes. The force of this objection is, I think, similar to that of the objection from alleged lack of ingenuity. Machines, after all, are *machines*; they inexorably grind out whatever is put in. Whatever mistakes a computer makes can be traced to the programmer.

Unfortunately this is not true. As Turing pointed out computers make mistakes all the time to the great distress of programmers and operators, and in many cases it is practically impossible to tell who or which made it. There are hardware failures and random errors in electronic circuit performance, which facts are sufficient to answer the objection. Moreover *learning machines* can make mistakes where in principle the mistake is traceable to a bad program, and where the program is the computer's own creation in a sense just explained above. The essence of learning is mistake making, and computers learn. So aside from the trivial hardware case, computers do make mistakes of their 'own making'. In effect our answer to the objection reduces to the one about machine ingenuity and learning.

A much deeper objection here comes to mind that concerns computers, determinism, and free will.

5. COMPUTERS, DETERMINISM AND ACTION

Many philosophers will boggle at the idea that computer and human behaviors are comparable, as required by the fundamental analogy, because computers cannot act: they are not free agents, not capable of action, playing social roles, etc. "Your device of stripping activities people engage in down to behaviors completely reproducible in holes of punched cards [as I did in the last section], is a travesty on human activities even such dull ones as adding numbers or proving theorems. Adding two and two is an action revealing intentions taking on full significance only in the context of personal and human affairs and is qualitatively unlike anything a computer does. For this reason alone the notion that man is a machine even one of your abstract automata is an absurdity and a corruption." Shorn of the rhetoric, this objection still undeniably shakes the basic man-machine analogy at its weakest joint. The allegedly common set of behaviors of computers and men on which this analogy turns is admittedly an abstraction: to make the argument stick we were compelled to replace (or indicate the possible replacement of) terms such as 'compose' or 'planning' or 'drawing' with neutral expressions in a purified language of recursive functions and we supposed that the human creation of a poem could be represented in punched cards without loss, thence also transformed to the function language. All the discussions, pro and con, of the above sections and of the associated literature on the topic use the tacit assumption that behaviors whose commonality we are now troubled about are adequately expressed in a 'purified' language. Even those who are unswervingly devoted to the idea that the cognitive and perceptual processes are really continuous do not question the premise of common behaviors except possibly for Gödel-type issues and the like.

This type of complaint against comparisons of behaviors has been frequently lodged by philosophers and psychologists usually but not solely of a behaviorist stripe. For a person's knowledge, intentions, expectations, hopes, skills, actions, deliberations, and free choices are kinds of behavior. These mental features are not mysterious ghost-like entities that get expressed in behavior but are dispositions to act in certain ways or are complexes or clusters of acts themselves in their social, cultural and moral contexts. Thus Ryle (1949, pp. 226–227) argues that a person *knows* a tune if he can whistle it or, failing that he can *recognize* it when he hears it; and he recognizes it if he has appropriate *expectations* about it:

He expects those bars to follow which do follow; . . . he does not erroneously expect the previous bars to be repeated; . . . he detects omissions or errors in the performance; when several people are whistling different tunes, he can pick out the one who is whistling this tune. . . . And when we speak of him expecting the notes which are due to follow . . . we do not require that he be actually thinking ahead. Given that he is surprised, scornful or amused, if the due notes and bars do not come at their due times, then it is true to say that he was expecting them. . . .

These episodes of whistling, recognizing, detecting omissions, etc. ultimately reduce to *behaviors* which are *actions* not mechanical bodily movements. These actions are manifestly different than the programmed movements of computers and robots. According to Ryle denial that there is a ghost in the machine does not degrade man to a machine. "He might, after all, be a sort of animal, namely, a higher mammal" (Ryle, 1949, p. 328).

E. C. Tolman has put forth a similar view in his version of behaviorism. According to him, psychological behavior "is an 'emergent' phenomenon that has descriptive and defining properties of its own" over and above stimulus-response behavior at the physical and physiological levels (Tolman, 1932, p. 9). "Behavior as such cannot be deduced from a mere enumeration of the muscle twitches, the mere motions *qua* motions, which make it up" (Tolman, 1932, p. 8).

Now there is nothing in this concept of 'molar' behavior that precludes it from being an abstract automaton behavior; molar behaviors, in other words, could perfectly well be interpretations or realizations of automaton input-output vocabularies. As we emphasized only a few pages back in the discussion of discreteness questions, molar entities are as discrete as Burks' *molecular* entities and are just as easy to accommodate within a mechanist framework.[24] So the main point evidently cannot be that the concern of the psychologist is molar rather than molecular behavior but rather must be that the former has properties we cannot attribute to *computer* inputs and outputs. Some of these identifying properties of 'behavior-acts' are goal-directedness, engagement with objects as means to ends, and "selectively greater readiness for *short* means activiites as against *long* ones" (Tolman, 1932, p. 11). These behaviors are intentional and have little in common with computer input-output behaviors which are mechanical movements wholly analyzable in strictly physical terms.

Our reply will have two parts, one a rejoinder and the other an objection to the behaviorist views on intention and purpose found in both Ryle and Tolman.

We deliberatley chose as a background for discussion typically cognitive behaviors — theorem proving, checker playing — because of their fitness as examples for many of the issues raised by the users of Gödel, those who find something peculiarly human in mistakes, and Lady Lovelace. These issues had to do, roughly, with the 'cognitive' and 'intellectual' limitations of machines as they stand on the floor. But in principle we could build a robot (incorporating an abstract automaton) capable of walking, talking, etc. and not just of taking in and putting out tape, punched cards or print.

As has been argued many times there is no end (except for money) to the detail and refinement that could be built into a humanoid so perfectly constructed that it would be taken to be fully human and to exhibit typically human purposive behaviors in almost all situations. It seems to me that this is undeniable, and that in time such robots will be built (a good deal fancier than C3PO). A music-loving robot could be built to show knowledge of tunes by whistling or other performances sufficient to attribute recognition, expectation, and the rest to it. I am arguing that in most situations the *same* observations which would establish a human's behavior as intentional would also establish the robot's. On the other hand, we would very likely decide that Burks' (1972/73) automatic sweetheart, to take a sufficiently fancy case, does not have a mind, but not because of any lack of intentionality in the behavior but because she would not be alive and hence would not feel anything.

I am aware that this rejoinder may not convince everyone, the main trouble with it (and with the objection itself) being that none of us are sufficiently clear about our meanings: when is a movement or action intentional or purposive or goal seeking and when not? I see nothing clear in Ryle's view that men are intelligent while machines are not (except possibly not machines$_2$) and that expectations, for example, are somehow observable in behavior. Nor are Tolman's 'emergent' features particularly enlightening theoretically. The same emergents could occur, I would argue, in the humanoid sweetheart. Neither thinker gives us the slightest idea how to decide when there is intentional activity and when not. Moreover I strongly suspect that if psychologists are like other people they tend to *attribute* purposes to human behavior in tacit analogy to themselves, and given a realistic enough humanoid they would do the same. But this is no *analysis*.

These remarks concerning the lack of individuating principles for the attribution of intentional terms to overt behaviors brings me to the main objection I have in mind against behaviorist accounts of mental features. By now the weaknesses in the account are an old story, often told, but I do want to dwell on only two closely related points. The first has to do with the *externalization* of mental features and the second with the *analysis* of them.

Using the input, inner space (box), output model we can see that what the behaviorists have done, from various motives, some methodological and some metaphysical, is to remove mental entities from inside the box to the external input-output realm, roughly the realm of the publicly observable. It was the presence of the mental in the outer world of observable behavior that led our critics to object to comparisons of human and machine input. The removal of pains and other mental occurrents to this realm is an out and out mistake, as I think is generally agreed by all except possibly the most extreme behaviorists (cf. Fodor, 1968, p. 71); and perhaps occurrents need no underlying mental substance to exist in, Descartes notwithstanding, whence we can push them back in the box identifying them with neural events or whatever. At any rate I'll leave them wherever they are for the time being.

Now let us consider features. In some cases the externalization of features is plausible but, I argue, only at the expense of rendering them *unanalyzable*, unanalyzable bits of intelligence, to lean again on Dennett's phrase. For the behaviorists they turn out to be dispositions or emergents of some kind mainly — in any case fuzzy and mysterious — and not much better off than when they were simply in and of the mind. Indeed I suspect that almost any good analysis that could be given would apply just as satisfactorily to a real enough robot. This seems to me to be certainly true of analyses of disposition in terms of subjunctive conditionals (which have the notorious disadvantage of being as obscure as dispositions), or of analysis of emergents in terms of Hempelian style explanations (Hempel *et al.*, 1948). If I am right, bringing features out into the light costs the behaviorists something — either these mental predicates are held to be unanalyzable or otherwise they must be just as applicable to sufficiently complex computers and robots as to men (except for the restriction on the use of locutions like 'feel' normally reserved for living things).[25,26]

This leaves the choice of embarking on a suitable analysis since we want more than ascriptions, and poses the most crucial argument against mechanism. Is analysis of deatures, in particular intentional attitudes in terms of recursive rules even *possible*? John Searle in a widely discussed paper (1980) maintains it is *not,* and that intentionality is a property of brains, not of "digital computer programs." I think, if he made the distinctions, he would include machines$_1$ and embodied algorithms. For Searle, as for me, programs are strictly "syntactical" and blindly direct movement of meaningless symbols around. The denial of his claim, that is to say, that features can be really explained by syntactical rule systems is precisely the thesis of this book, and we should be grateful to have at hand a counter-thesis, finally, that really challenges mechanism.

Unfortunately the details of Searle's argument are weak. He argues that a person (Searle) or a machine using an imaginary but writeable program in English for answering, in Chinese, questions written in Chinese using a purely formal Chinese character dictionary doesn't understand Chinese. This is meant to be a familiar Turing-type test. He's right. But he's wrong if he supposes as some do (Simon and Newell, 1963) that every computationalist believes symbol-pushing under such a simple table-look-up program para-adigm explains human cognition. I for one don't, and I will give Searle further answer after developing some theory.

We have yet to face one last related objection, which is that man is a free agent and a computer not. This, too, is a sort of objection to the premise that there is a significant group of common behaviors between man and machine. Some philosophers would wish to argue that robots, even fancy ones, could not possibly manifest intelligent behavior, have expectations, perform actions, or carry moral responsibility, because they are not *free*. Actions, unlike mere bodily movements, imply freedom, exemption from causal law.

Without taking sides on the latter issue and without attempting to untangle the bewildering assortment of issues involved in the concept of freedom, let us just consider the question of determinism. Let us suppose that freedom implies indeterminism (denied by Hume among others); then since machines₁ are not necessarily deterministic, it is at least possible that they be free. In other words being an abstract automaton does not imply any lack of freedom (under the present assumption).

The first thing to get over is the crippling notion that 'nondeterministic machines' is a *contradictio in adjecto*. As we have already seen in some technical detail in our historical sketch of the development of the mechanist hypothesis, both recognizers and language generators might well be *polygenic*, that is to say, they might, like the propositional calculus, be governed by rules which are applicable in more than one way. Such systems are non-deterministic in the precise sense that the relation of input symbols and present state to the next state is not a map. My version of mechanism says that men are such nondeterministic systems. Whether this turns out to be true or not is a strictly empirical question which is to be decided by whatever criteria emerge as psychology develops, and not *a priori*. If acceptance of a nondeterministic model fits the facts that need to be explained better than a deterministic one (whatever that exactly turns out to mean) then we adopt the theory that man is a nondeterministic automaton. These criteria may include philosophical components. For instance Harman thinks that psycho-logical states do not follow one another in rigid deterministic fashion and hence that explaining why someone believes something is "like explaining why a nondeterministic automaton is in a certain state" (Harman, 1973, p. 51). So the appropriate model here is nondeterministic.

The fact of nondeterminism, if it is one, does not conflict with a thorough going determinism in physics, although it necessarily does with metaphysical determinism. As I understand the latter, every event, physical or mental, is caused by some antecedent chain of events, and occurrences of that chain (if more than one is possible) do not produce one effect at one time and another at another. Hence there could be no nondeterministic explanation of any event. But physical events could be rigidly determined while the mental are not, *even though our ontology include only physical things*. Our *theories* of the mental need not reduce to the physical, and indeed mechanism in its modern formulation does not. A simple example will illustrate, although perhaps not yet clinch, this point. We do not even have to ascend to complex human examples to make it.

Consider the worm. Part of its behavior is wriggling when it is mechanically irritated on its surface provided that in its past it was exposed to light of a certain intensity or above but not to heat of a certain level or above. This thing is a deterministic automaton, which we show as follows. It has three *input elements*: Light above a certain intensity which we denote by x_1; heat above a certain level which we denoted by x_2; and mechanical irritation by x_3. For convenience we code each of the eight possible inputs determined by states of the input elements as in the following table:

TABLE I
Worm stimuli.

x_1	x_2	x_3	
0	0	0	$-\ s_0$
0	0	1	$-\ s_1$
0	1	0	$-\ s_2$
0	1	1	$-\ s_3$
1	0	0	$-\ s_4$
1	0	1	$-\ s_5$
1	1	0	$-\ s_6$
1	1	1	$-\ s_7$

In this table s_0 is the input of no light, no heat, no mechanical irritation; s_1 no light, no heat, but presence of mechanical irritation, and so forth. The s's constitute the input alphabet to an automaton. Similarly the wriggling response will be denoted by z and has value 1 (response) or 0 (no response).

Now from the description of the worm we know that the worm reacts to an irritating touch by wriggling only if it recently — at the past moment, say – has been exposed to light but not heat. In other words the worm's response behavior to the irritation stimulation depends on its *internal memory states*. We do not know what these states are physiologically, but we posit them as theoretical entities to explain the *differences* in response to the *same* stimulus conditions.

Having thus introduced states, call them q_0 and q_1, the latter indicating memory or recording of a previous stimulus event of sufficient light but no heat (either s_4 or s_5 of Table I), we again appeal to our behavioral description and set up an automaton table which shows a transition and output function for the worm. Suppose the worm is in state q_0 i.e., has not been earlier exposed to a stimulus of enough light but no heat. Also suppose there is an input event s_0. What happens? Well, she will not wriggle, because she's in the wrong state. So the output is 0. Moreover she will *stay* in state q_0, because she goes to q_1 only from an input condition in which light is high and heat low. So we write 'q_0' in the interior of the transition part of the table, first row first column. Similarly for the output 0 which is written in the output part. Proceeding in this manner we fill in the entire table, and obtain

TABLE II
Worm automaton.

q \ s	M								N							
	s_0	s_1	s_2	s_3	s_4	s_5	s_6	s_7	s_0	s_1	s_2	s_3	s_4	s_5	s_6	s_7
q_0	q_0	q_0	q_0	q_0	q_1	q_1	q_1	q_1	0	0	0	0	0	0	0	0
q_1	q_1	q_1	q_0	q_0	q_1	q_1	q_1	q_1	0	1	0	1	0	1	0	1

What we have done is formulate, via the table, a theory of the worm's deterministic behavior.[27]

We are next going to transform the worm to a nondeterministic one. When the new worm is in state q_0 and receives stimulus input $s_4(1, 0, 0)$ the next state to which she transits is to be *either* q_0 or q_1. Sometimes she remembers the light stimulus in the presence of no heat and no irritation (q_1) and sometimes not (q_0). The transition part of her table, which is derived from the other by entering the pair (q_0, q_1) for q_1 in the first row, fifth column of the table of her ancestor is no longer functional, but only relational. The thing is polygenic. So suppose that the new worm in state q_0 is exposed to a short sequence of stimuli s_4, s_1 (light, no heat, no irritation followed by no light, no heat, irritation). Inasmuch as we created the worm we are not particularly astonished if she does not wriggle although her ancestor would have.[28] However if we were actually to find this worm in nature we might be somewhat upset by the uncertainty especially if it persists. Perhaps many of us would hunt for an additional environmental condition present in the wriggling case but absent in the other in order to achieve a satisfactorally deterministic explanation. Or, lacking discovery of that, we might hunt for some internal physiological condition present in one case but not the other.

So now suppose that a naturalist turned on by *annelida* comes upon this worm, conducts experiments, constructs a theory much as we did, and discovers that it fits all the worms of the variety investigated. He finds that they are all nondeterministic. Moreover although each worm has some varying internal *physiological* condition which deterministically accounts for the differences in the behavior from one time to another on selecting the stimulus pair s_4, s_1, these conditions are *different* for each pair of worms. Here we are of course leaning on the fiction that the investigator would be able to discover the exact neurophysiological locus of the state element in each worm. This probably wouldn't be too difficult for the case of worms but is of course out of the question for anything much more complex.[29] Clearly the worms, in the relevant respects here, have *exactly the same behavior*, which is nondeterministic in all cases. They all realize the same abstract automaton. Yet from the point of a physiological or even molecular level of description they are deterministic or, perhaps, depending on one's interpretation or understanding of modern physics, indeterministic. In any case, as Harman puts it, either an indeterministic or deterministic worm can instantiate a nondeterministic automaton.

I claim this argument shows that organisms including men *qua* abstract automata, i.e., as subjects of psychology or philosophy of mind, might be *free*, that mental states might be part of a system, which is nondeterministic. And again, whether it is nondeterministic in this sense is an empirical question, although in the hypothetical framework of the logic of mind we are of course holding that men *are* NFA. The above argument shows the plausibility of the position which is for the moment enough, I think, to answer the objection that prompted the discussion in the first place. We would no doubt withhold use of 'free', 'mental', and 'mind' for the worm, but that is only because the worm-automaton is not complex enough to have language, intentions, etc., not because his internal states, whatever their instantiations, are less mental in some ontological sense.

There is much more that can be said in defense of the position that psychological processes could well turn out to be nondeterministic. But even if it be true that attribution of nondeterministic automaton structures to men is not scientifically justifiable, there are still grounds for saying he is 'free' in any sense liable to have important implications for the study of human conduct and certainly in a meaning in accord with the best usage. These further issues will be considered at some length in Chapter XI.

6. SUMMARY OF THE MAIN ARGUMENT FROM ANALOGY

Some of the arguments against mechanism have what little force they have by playing on an ambiguity of 'machine'. We resolved the ambiguity and in doing so defused the attack by marking off machines₁ (abstract automata) from machines₂ (hardware devices including digital computers). Thus machines₁, e.g., human beings, like strawberries, make love, perceive gestalt patterns, and perhaps have souls, although machines₂ certainly do not like (or dislike) strawberries or indeed anything at all.

The main objections to the argument from analogy can be listed and, I think, adequately met in the following way: The analogy attributes mentality to computers as it uses intentional terms like 'compose' music or 'prove' theorems. This is question begging.

Answer. In principle the analogy can be restated in a topic neutral vocabulary, perhaps in a language of functions, domains and ranges. Analysis of intentional vocabulary in automata terms then becomes a project for later pursuit (especially in Chapter VIII).

Automaton behavior of an organism does not imply that the organism is an automaton. (1) Behavior could be understood in strict S–R terms as a kind of infinite list; (2) there might be state-to-state transitions, but all of them being external environmental states so that the organism again would be strictly an S–R system; (3) the processes underlying behavior could be continuous, not discrete.

Answer. (1) and (2) are disposed of in detail in the next Chapter. As to (3), the underlying geometry chosen for a theory of a domain is a function of the purposes of the scientist and of the ongoing character of the scientific discipline. For some purposes classical analysis, which assumes a continuous domain, is best. For others, discrete spaces are suggested by the subject matter, here such entities as phonemes, intentions, sentences, thoughts, hopes, etc. All bodily S–R functions take off from just noticeably different signals. Bodily states come in a finite set of quanta; and responses likewise are discrete.

Another argument for mechanism stems from the idea of a mechanical explanation as follows: Any noncircular psychological theory must ultimately explain cognitive (and perceptual) phenomena in primitive terms that do not assume intelligence or intentionality. Such explanations account for intelligence in terms of effective, step-by-step procedures. By CT these procedures are Turing computable; and the simplest hypothesis, given our realistic stance, is that these processes are guided by automaton rules.

Gödel's incompleteness theorem has been used to argue that the class of cognitive behaviors of automata and human beings are not coextensive. Omitting details, we showed that the argument from Gödel assumes that persons have powers (like proving the consistency of any formal system in which recursive relations can be expressed) which they are not in fact known to possess. Again, heuristic (semi)-algorithms may be sufficient to establish whatever we can 'see' but that a computer can only calculate.

This latter objection is closely related to Lady Lovelace's objection that says that computers (interpreted as machines$_1$) can not do anything creative and especially can not go beyond strictly deductive operations. This can be answered by pointing to learning programs that transcend the skills of the programmer for the programmed task, and to computer heuristics.

Machines can discover their own blueprints, i.e., their guiding rules, which refutes the complaint that machines, unlike persons, can not be their own subject. Machines$_2$, however, are not consciously aware of anything (a topic to be considered in the final chapter of this book).

Our recommendation of a topic neutral way of talking about computers in the basic analogy gives rise to another objection to mechanism: Computers are not capable of actions, while humans are, and the distinction between actions and bodily movements appears in behavior itself. One cannot 'strip' behavior down to holes in punched cards or abstract talk of function and still have *human* actions.

The reply is that a fancy enough robot might cause one to attribute expectations and the like to it. The computer of the main analogy doesn't have to be bolted to the floor nor be all that ugly either. Either the psychologist must analyze such behaviors in terms that do not assume intentional aspects of mind as primitive or he must grant that the same behaviors are attributable to sufficiently complex humanoids.

If free will implies nondeterminism, then machines can quite possibly be free. Whether certain organisms are nondeterministic is an *empirical*, not an aprioristic metaphysical question. Nondeterminism in psychology is compatible with determinism in the physical and biological domains.

CHAPTER V

FUNCTIONALISM, BEHAVIORISM, AND RATIONALISM

Many of the notions of rule of mind, behavior and structure, and arguments for mechanism apply broadly to other theories of mind that are usually referred to collectively as 'computationalism'. On the whole these do not have anything much to say about sentience — mental occurrents — while all of them claim that mental features, dispositions, etc. are subjects independent of biology and physics. They differ in nontrivial philosophical detail while still sharing a common distrust of ghosts and other mental substances, and a fondness for autonomous, essentially irreducible, cognitive psychology. My aim here is to bring to the fore key philosophical issues about individuation of mental entities and how they fit into overall cognitive anatomy.

At one time I thought that the ideas that set my mechanism apart from various forms of cognitivism (following very much in the tradition of Craik) were inessential to either view. But this appears to be not so. Mental representation theories wed to Chomsky's rationalism, although computational in spirit, construe Turing rules and models in a way very much at odds with my own. As we shall see soon, the issues come down to a choice of free versus embodied rule paradigms, especially in theories of intentional attitudes and semantics.

In the following I will:

(1) disengage the logic of mind from those forms of functionalism that invite various puzzles about the relationship of psychological to automaton states and that tend to assimilate awareness and intentionality directly to role-playing machine states;

(2) fulfill the promise made in IV.6 to lay behaviorism to rest, showing that it is essentially false as a doctrine about psychological method, and in particular that stimulus-response, operant conditioning, etc. methods are not sufficient to account for cognitively directed behavior;

(3) describe cognitivism with respect to the issue of cognitive organization and internal representations, and indicate its relationships to Chomsky's neorationalism;

(4) outline the main features of mechanism, as it will unfold in ensuing chapters, in contrast to the other computationalist views.

The reader might want to read (2) before (1), unless he thinks behaviorism in a radical Watson-Skinner form is done for, in which case he might skip (2) altogether.

1. PSYCHOLOGICAL AND AUTOMATON STATES

A mark of mechanism is that the same formal automaton can be instantiated in many different ways. If to have a mind is to be a sufficiently complex conscious automaton, then psychology is in part at least the study of mental phenomena *qua* rules of mind, and the material realization is of little moment. Mind is mind, no matter the funny ears or the printer for a mouth. This much mechanism shares with functionalism, which I hesitate to define beyond the ascriptions made in the following critical remarks.

Functionalism is also marked by its conception of internal mental states as role-playing or purposive, and definable implicitly in terms of inputs, outputs, and other states — by machine tables, in the mechanist version.[1]

A third mark of machine functionalism (from now on, simply 'functionalism') is that all mental states including occurrents, paradigmatically pains, are functional or automaton states and as such are neither physical nor special phenomenal nor epiphenomenal entities.

Following the provisional distinction of Chapter I between mental features and mental occurrents such as pain events, I will consider only features here and defer consideration of pain and other kinds of awareness to Chapter XI which contains a kind of addendum on the classical mind-body problem. In the present section, however, we shall need to consider occurrents stripped, so to speak, of sentience: we shall treat the phenomenal qualities or *qualia* indifferently. In earlier passages I suggested that we call events which have no phenomenal quality (say, a state in the production of a sentence) or which are taken in abstraction from qualia, simply 'occurrents' (p. 12).

The first characteristic, which makes psychology relatively independent of physical questions such as the nature of the actual embodiment of mental processes in the brain, is quite intimately related to my realistic views and to questions of reducibility, and will be considered in the chapter on the nature of psychological theory. For the time being let us simply admit that the same mental features (a disposition to solve puzzles, for instance) can be realized in a great number of ways.

The second mark deserves some comment beyond that of the Introduction where I already registered a complaint against sneaking in intentionality with the concept of state. Some thinkers *assume* that states play roles: states, they say, intermediate between inputs and outputs, and hence intentional attitudes can be accounted for by associating mental states with automaton states (interpretations of q-symbols). Since automaton states are individuated according to their 'roles' in linking inputs to outputs and themselves to other states, and since psychological states such as belief and desire are (or are correlated with) automaton states, it follows, so it is claimed, that psychological states must be characterized implicitly, if at all. Thus assuming that belief is a disposition to act, to say that X *believes* that *p* seems to mean something like, whenever X *wants* E he is disposed to act in a way that will produce E given that *p* is true. Likewise X *wants* E just in case X is disposed to act in ways he *believes* will realize E, etc. (cf. Grice, 1974–75, p. 24).[2] Here, for the functionalist I am concerned about, *belief* and *want* are states that play causal roles with one another, and any definition that would entail these assertions about belief and want must be implicit.

Jerry Fodor and Hilary Putnam at one time thought of machine states as 'role-playing' or 'open to rational criticism' or as 'functionally [relative to ends] equivalent' (or inequivalent) to one another. (I take it that the terms in screech quotes are the material counterparts of the formal notion of implicit definition).

. . . relays will play the role of neurons: e.g., . . . the closing of a machine relay [a state event] should correspond to the firing of an organic neuron [a state event], and so on . . . the machine's relay should be functionally equivalent to the organism's neuron (Fodor, 1968, p. xviii).

Quite similarly, for Putnam

. . . states seem intimately connected with verbalization . . . in the case of rational thought (or computing), the 'program' which determines which states follow which, etc., is open to rational criticism (Putnam, 1960, p. 162).

Putnam's point here is that the behavior of a computer governed by a program is subject to rational criticism — i.e., whether or not it achieves its proper ends, is efficient, etc. — and not merely that the *design* of the program is open to criticism. The criticism is directable to the program, not the programmer. A similar view is Dennett's (1978, p. 4) regarding what he calls the 'design stance' or strategy one might adopt in accounting for the moves of a stored program computer. One's explanations or predictions would rely, he says, "on the notion of *function*, which is purpose-relative or teleological". As computer programs fall into the family of systems of recursive rules this again is tantamount to asserting that states play roles.

In principle I agree with the spirit of these suggestions, but not the letter: surely if there is anything to Fodor's and Putnam's view it is not to be found in the bare idea of a state or sequencing of states but in the concept of *very complex* programs or automata. If states play roles, then state S(leep) of Peter in Table III.II has a role. But I am fairly certain that the reader will balk at the suggestion that when Peter is asleep, suffers no alarm ring or jab in the ribs, stays asleep, and produces no overt behavior, his sleep is playing some role *vis à vis* the alarm set-up unless she is one infected with the kind of functionalism I am criticizing and *reads* a purposive role into it.

Returning to programs: Any program is equivalent to a Turing machine, which is nothing more than a pair of finite mathematical transformations. Hence a program can be completely explained in terms of its equivalent automaton table without invoking reasons in any way; and if the program does not work, it is because it realizes the 'wrong' table or because the underlying hardware system it guides fails or is subject to noise. In other words, the purposive connotation of 'functional' has no special place in characterizing automaton behavior, which can be done strictly in terms of logico-mathematical structures (rules) together with terms referring to the underlying hardward stratum. An automaton state is 'functional' or 'role-playing' only in the sense that it is an element of a state space, the latter being but a set A for which there exists another set B such that there is a map from the product of A and B back to A (for us, a transition function). If one insists that such states play roles, then in all consistency he must admit that position-momentum pairs in mechanics play roles![3]

My own view is that automaton states no more play roles than physical states do and that intentional features of the mind should be treated explicitly: part of my programme is to deny Brentano's thesis that intentional phenomena are primitive. Perceptual belief, for instance, I associate with an automaton, not an automaton state, and in such terms is explicable (in Chapter VIII). The intentionality of belief resides according to my theory in being a very complex automaton, namely one that encodes its own structure. The next part of my discussion of functionalism opens the way to some of the underlying issues.[4]

One could, of course, deny the role-playing virtue of automaton states and still insist on correlating psychological states with such. Then intentionality would have to be accounted for in some other way, if I am right in my criticism above. But there would still be plenty of room for confusion. Not all psychological states are (or are correlated to) automaton states. But then, what are they?

The answer to this question must scrupulously distinguish among four parts: (a) the ontological question; (b) that of the type-identity of automaton states; (c) that of the relation of automaton to psychological states; (d) that of the type identity of psychological states.

(a) An automaton state of an organism is a physical entity (or mental, depending on one's ontology). But an automaton state *qua* state is not identical to any cluster of physical properties. It is a state in virtue of a certain type of description. It is a state considered in abstraction from physical qualities in virtue of its being an element in the interpretation of a formal automaton (Cf. Section III.2 and 3; also Section XI.4 esp. p. 329).

(b) There are several ways of taking the type-identity of automaton states, and how this is done depends on the use we contemplate.[5] Here are three ways. (i) Using the fact that an automaton state is such relative to a description, we say two states are type-identical if they are co-referents of a q-symbol of a formal automaton in a true interpretation.[6] (ii) Two states are type-identical if they correspond 1—1 in an isomorphism, or in the case of a single automaton, an automorphism.[7] (iii) Two states are type-identical if they are behaviorally equivalent, that is, if any string x beginning with automata in either state produces the same output string.

(i) will not do as it precludes two states of the same automaton being type-identical. A q-symbol has but *one* referent because the interpretation is a map, not an arbitrary relation.

(iii) does not appear to be adequate since according to the behavioral equivalence criterion two states could be identical and yet be instantiated in different state-to-state sequences, that is to say, be part of two quite different computational streams. This violates the spirit of functionalism. And in effect it would be the same as saying that every state in a formal automaton system of rules that guides an organism is type-identical to a state in a system that merely fits! This option is incoherent. *Structure*, not behavior, seems to be the right concept for explicating type-identity. This leaves (ii): states are the same if they are 1—1 in an isomorphism.

(c) Functional state identity theory (FSIT) as Block and Fodor call it maintains that psychological states are in 1—1 correspondence with automaton states, which means either they are contingently identical or related by biconditionals (Block and Fodor, 1972, p. 174). This view is wrong, but its consequences are interesting for a lot of reasons.

If every psychological state is contingently identical to a machine state, then the answer to part question (d) is (ii): two psychological states are type-identical if they are 1—1 in an isomorphism. If the relation between psychological and automaton states is a biconditional, then two psychological states are type-identical if their corresponding automaton states are isomorphic.

Let's back up to (iii), the behavioral equivalence theory of type-identity, and combine it with FSIT. This leads to instructive trouble that is not avoided by (ii) either. The trouble is that if psychological states are type-identical because they are behaviorally the same, then that identity condition is too fine-grained. If your anger when you stub your toe causes you to say 'damn' on one occasion and 'darn' on another, then by the behavioral criterion the two anger states are not type-identical (Block and Fodor, 1972, p. 174). If, on the other hand, we adopt (ii), as we already have, then identity is allowed when behavior is drastically different materially. Remember Peter and the butterfly (Section III.1). If we allow the liberal version of isomorphism of III.(3a) and III.(3d), it seems that we let in too much, and some butterfly state (even when it is flying) is psychologically identical to Peter's sleep! The situation is seemingly mitigated by going to III.(3a) and III.(3a) which *does* require identity of input-output for two systems to be isomorphic. But if so we're back with the 'damn' − 'darn' problem on our hands. Are the two the *same* response?

These questions suggest that the 1−1 theory of psychological states is wrong. What we are saying is that if stimuli and responses are individuated by their interrelationships with psychological states, then those states can not be 1−1 with automaton states. In a moment I'll argue that features such as belief are not *states* at all! But a more basic philosophical point here is that stimuli and responses are not individuated by their relationships to each other and to automaton states (*a fortiori* to psychological states in the 1−1 theory) alone. The condition may be necessary, but some reference to nonrelational attributes is also required. There is a fundamental asymmetry in all functionalist theories. Mental features including states are determined by relationships to each other and to stimuli and responses; but stimuli and responses are not determined only by relationships to each other and to mental features. The solution to the 'damn'−'darn' problem requires other determiners.

I see no way of getting around this by some automata-theoretic or other formal ploy, which does *not* mean we are in hot water. What enables us to keep out of it is the theory of method in psychology which I used to answer the mistaken complaint that anything whatever is an automaton (in Chapter III). This, of course, is of a piece with the view that something is an automaton under a description of inputs, outputs, etc. logically antecedent to new theory. Sameness of response, like *same phone* or *same phoneme*, depends on a prior determination of what counts as input and output, and this depends on some given properties or other. Inputs and outputs are *types* (or equivalence classes modulo some determiners or other).[8] If 'damn' is in the same class as 'darn', then the two anger states (if anger is a state) are identical. If not, not. If we don't know what to make of it, we don't know what to make of the state identity question, and that's that. Type-identity of inputs and outputs requires quite a different analysis than that of states.

Block seeks a characterization of inputs and outputs that does not start with the stimuli and responses of received science. For one type of functionalism, neural impulses would be such givens. He terms this 'chauvinist' as it rules out strange beings from having 'functionalist descriptions' and hence from having psychological states ascribed to them (Block, 1978, pp. 314 ff.).

I share Block's attitude, although I think there are other paths to relief from chauvinism besides individuating responses solely in terms of generating inputs and inner states. One is that if we are inclined on *other* grounds to attribute sentience to a thing, then it also makes sense, by the analogies leading to that attribution, to identify what counts as input and what output. This way out of chauvinism again makes use of the doctrine of prior determination of nonrelational stimulus and response properties and also meets the philosophical requirement, which I take to be fundamental, that only sentient things are minded. Economic systems (his example) or the Congress of the United States are excluded from the family of minded things (as are other features not here at issue). This path, however, is not open to functionalists who identify feelings, pains, and other mental occurrents with automaton states. For them, if an economic system is discrete-state and automaton isomorphic to a pain-enduring animal, it has pain.

Returning to the main question, if psychological states are not 1−1 to automaton states, then they are related to some other properties of an automaton, but perhaps nothing so simple as a state. The question, it seems to me, is not even answerable prior to doing some psychology or, failing that, some deeper speculative philosophy. So the pay-off thus far is almost all negative, although perhaps we have succeeded in weeding out some confusions. Automaton states as such are not purposive, and psychological states (and features) though perhaps in some sense 'functional' are not only automaton states. Those that are are type-identical if they are isomorphic or correspond in some way to isomorphic automaton states. Stimuli and responses can not be individuated solely in terms of the states they express but in addition are determined by their nonrelational attributes. None of this implies that mechanism fails; it does tell us, however, where not to look for certain psychological entities.

If psychological states are 1−1 to automaton states after all then we are in trouble, it is said, because a machine can be in only one state at a time while a human being can be in several psychological states – say believing and desiring – at the same time (Block and Fodor, 1972, p. 171).[9] But this is a misunderstanding of 'state'. In network embodiments, states as well as inputs and outputs are made up of state *elements*. (See page 39ff. where we constructed an abstract automaton from a Pitts-McCulloch net, and p. 49ff. where we constructed an adding network from an abstract automaton via a coding procedure.) In the network of Figure II.3 there are *three* state elements represented by three neuronal axons, and a *state* is determined by the firing or nonfiring of each of the three, giving a total of eight states. Here each q-symbol is a decoding of a triple (y_1, y_2, y_3) where each y_i is 0 or 1 according to whether it fires or not.

Let's consider a more interesting example, namely Jones and m of her state elements. These elements are toes that curl or not, a breast that heaves or not, palms that are damp or not, neurons $c_1, \ldots, c_n$ that fire or not, etc. Now a state might consist of curled toes, heaving breast, damp palms, $c_1, \ldots, c_{100}$ firing, $c_{101}, \ldots, c_n$ not firing, etc. According to our naturalistic ontology the indicated values of these state elements are physical states, while the state comprised of the components is an automaton state in virtue of some appropriate tabular description that relates it (the m-tuple) to inputs, outputs and other states. Now let us suppose pain correlates to curled toes, being happy to heaving breast, and feeling flushed to damp palms (I don't believe in any such correlation, but some such is what the $1-1$ assumption amounts to that I am using to explore the consequences of the one-state-at-a-time theory). Then although it is true that Jones can be only in one automaton state at a time if she is an NFA, she can at once be in pain, quite happy, and feeling flushed, conditions which are components of one state depending on the values of the several components.

Complex automata like Peter, Roommate and alarm clock are often composed of parts that are themselves automata so that what is a single state of the complex is a multiple state if you think of each automaton as a unit. Thus in that example (again avoiding the nontrivial exercise of actually synthesizing the three into one system) a single state of the complex might be (I, 8, S) which is a triple of states of the ingredient machines – roommate in room at 8 o'clock AM, Peter asleep. Obviously, if organisms are at least as complex as this they might be in many states at once in one respect or in a single state in another depending on what you take to be the whole. So the argument that if all psychological states $1-1$ correlate to automaton states and FA can be in but one state at a time then the organism can be in only one state at a time, contrary to empirical fact, fails. The underlying construal of FA is too simplistic as it neglects the distinction between states and state elements and the possibility of complexity of automata.[10]

Another question closely related to that of one-at-a-time states concerns simultaneous interaction of states and parallelism of mental processes. FA and Turing machines are essentially sequential devices. However behavior can result not only from a series of states but from parallel interaction as well. The best examples are drawn from gestalt perception. Organisms, some anyway, can perceive a thing to be of a kind under extremely nonstandard conditions and yet act appropriately on the spot. There is no scanning or trait analysis apparent to introspection or to any experimental test, so that the effect must be got by some kind of synthesis of parallel operations. Another example: " . . . what an organism does at t may be a function of what it is feeling at t and of what it is thinking at t. But FSIT [or even straight FA mechanism without the 1−1 condition, as a matter of fact] provides no conceptual machinery for representing this state of affairs" (Block et al., 1972, p. 170).

Let's see whether this is really the case. We've already had an example, namely Jones, wherein feeling and thinking can occur in parallel as components of a single automaton state. Let us denote Jones' states by the m-tuple of variables $(y_1, \ldots, y_m)$ so that one of her coded states is given by $y_1 = 0, y_2 = 1, y_2 = 0$, etc., that is, by $(0, 1, 0, \ldots)$. Let us also denote her possible stimuli by $(x_1, \ldots, x_n)$. Then using the basic formula scheme for automata in coded form, we have that each state element y_i is a truth function (or perhaps some multivalued function of time functions) of $(x_1, \ldots, x_n)$ and $(y_1, \ldots, y_m)$. Thus, with time made explicit:

$$y_1(0) = (\text{or } 1)$$
$$y_1(t + 1) = f_1(x_1(t), \ldots, x_n(t), y_1(t), \ldots, y_m(t))$$
$$y_2(0) = 0 \ (\text{or } 1)$$
$$y_2(t + 1) = f_2(x_1(t), \ldots, x_n(t), y_1(t), \ldots, y_m(t))$$

$$\vdots$$

$$y_m(0) = 0 \ (\text{or } 1)$$
$$y_m(t + 1) = f_m(x_1(t), \ldots, x_n(t), y_1(t), \ldots, y_m(t)).$$

Each y_i is a function, not quite instantaneously, but at the next time, of all other state elements including itself. Therefore on this model (FSIT) feeling at $t + 1$ depends on thinking and feeling (and other elements) at t and so does thinking itself at $t + 1$, and all the rest. This is simultaneous interaction save for one unit of delay and shows that parallel interactions can be conceptualized in FSIT unless its 'state' is taken very narrowly in the decoded version.

Unfortunately the model does not fare so well for the gestalt zap. Computer 'perception' does necessarily rely on sequencing for our current models and for programmed information processing as well. There does not seem to be any way at present to grasp such processes conceptually. Perceiving a Necker cube in one of its two aspects may be a single zap through the optic nerve, analogous to grasping that 010101 . . . is a string of alternating 0's and 1's in one swoop rather than by checking off 0, going to a state, checking 1, going to another state, etc. in time as would be required of an automaton 'recognizer' (these machines are defined in the next chapter).

But the lack of a decent FSIT theory is no sign of an impossibility. No one is irretrievably stuck with FSIT, and although humans are NFA by hypothesis we know next to nothing at this time of the structures of the parts beyond their embodying effective processes. Within this framework we may appeal to several pieces of evidence in favor of the proposition that the parallel zap is captured by automata in our more liberal sense (see p. 176).

The first is Kleene's argument already appealed to in Chapter IV to the effect that observation of symbols in parallel in multidimensional space is Turing reducible. The second is the design of completely parallel Pitts-McCulloch type networks that simulate the retina (Culbertson, 1963; Minsky and Papert, 1969). The third is the existence of truly parallel computer networks.[11] And the fourth is the beginnings of a theory of parallel computation.[12] These, and possibly more, suggest strongly that mechanism does, after all, provide a right conceptual apparatus for understanding highly interactive, parallel psychological processes.

Functionalists and their opponents sometimes think of dispositions to act as psychological states. Thus Rorty on occasion writes of logical (automaton) states as being like some dispositions, not others, while Block and Fodor refer to 'dispositional states' and even to states being identical (for behaviorism) when certain dispositions are. Although the confusion here is understandable in the light of a behaviorist tradition that attempted to reduce psychological phenomena to dispositions to behave in certain ways we ought to do our best to avoid it.[13]

For, one can be in a state and have a disposition, the former being an event and the latter not. Jones' disposition to be angry under certain circumstances is sustainable through any stretch of time during which she is in an angry state, or through any stretch during which she is not in an angry state.

She need not be angry to have the disposition. If states were dispositions, Jones could have a disposition to anger at the same time she does not, which is absurd! A state, as the reader knows, is an element of a set X that maps from the product of that set and another back to X via a transition function. Stated in the linguistic mode, a state is whatever corresponds to a q-symbol under an automaton description, independent of its material qualities. A disposition, on the other hand is more like an automaton itself. An organism is disposed to behave in certain ways if and only if it contains a certain automaton structure – a set of recursive rules. Of course, I mean *psychological* behavior. Peter has a disposition to strike out when awakened (he has an automaton in him), and he actually strikes only when in a certain state coupled with the right input. But this does not make the disposition the state nor the state the disposition. Again, an organism is capable of or has a disposition to, perceptual belief in x only if it contains or 'internalizes' a system of rules of an acceptor automaton (cf. above, p. 214). This is precisely the 'place-holder' view of dispositions.[14] But the unknown seat of the disposition according to mechanism will be a rule-structure not a specific physical-chemical structure of the organism, although it will be instantiated in a material stuff. This much of the nature of dispositions the logic of mind carries over from functionalism.[15]

Another question about psychological states and their circumstances that is closely related to the one about states and dispositions concerns what I will call the *mathematical* versus the *historical* way of doing psychology.[16] Under the totally unreal assumption that you know Jones' machine table, you could deductively explore her possible reactions to various stimuli in essentially the same abstract way that you could do other mathematical deductions, in principle. This may not be flattering to Jones, but yet is essentially what we do when we talk about her in a crude, ordinary every day subjunctive language. To say in this mathematical sense that q_0 = (curled toes, . . . , $c_1 - c_{1000}$ firing, . . .) is in Jones' state space Q is not to say anything about the *historical* Jones, namely about what state she is in now or was in ten minutes ago. And to say she would sigh if she were in a certain state of Q with certain designated input is not to say anything about the historical Jones who might never sighed in that way in her life. Such talk is meant to show her dispositions and capabilities, not her history, and incidentally displays a connection between psychological subjunctive conditionals and systems of recursive rules that we will exploit later.[17]

It is important to emphasize that *events* can be thought of subjunctively, i.e., mathematically. A mental event (which is an occurrence stripped of sentient qualia, according to our conventions) − such as a state event is a mapping from an instant of time to True or False (to 1 or 0). However, one can speak of events without committing one to historical fact. For instance the adder network of Figure II.5 is describable mathematically using II(3b) and II(3c) in some such wise: "If input x_1 to x_2, ... were activated at time t then the state of the network − the output of the delay, δ, − would be 1 at time $t + 1$ ... " This mentions times but is not historical (as it is universally quantifiable).

Now having cleared this possible confusion out we can face *part* of the difficulty Block and Fodor raise concerning occurrent and 'dispositional' beliefs (wants, desires, etc.) i.e., features. They distinguish between dispositional belief and occurrent belief in terms of states the organism *has* mathematically and states it is *in* historically. This device (which we already have reason to doubt because it still assumes that psychological are 1−1 to automaton states) works pretty well for dispositions like *speaks French*, and for the occurrent *is speaking French*; but they claim it does not work in a parallel way for *believes that P*, in as much as there is no occurrent *is believing that P*. It seems to me that this is a false issue rising in part from the 1−1 assumption, which Block and Fodor also call into question, in part from supposing beliefs are anything like states at all, from taking locutional peculiarities of ordinary English too seriously, and from collapsing various kinds of belief into one. I think we can go along with the application of the mathematical-historical distinction which is implicit in their analysis. But in addition, we should, I think, identify the disposition with the rule structure, and also discriminate between standing beliefs (and other attitudes), to borrow another Quinian expression, and perceptual beliefs. First, note how this works for 'speaks French' and 'is speaking French'. 'Speaks French' connotes an automaton subject to mathematical talk − a system of recursive rules of French grammar − , while 'is speaking French' connotes an historical state-to-state process. Similarly for perceptual beliefs such as is expressed by "Jones believes that she sees a cat". I am sure almost anyone would say such a belief is an occurrent, despite the oddness of 'is believing'. There is no oddness that "Jones believes at t that she sees a cat", which certainly connotes an historical event; and the same seems to me to be true of all perceptual beliefs. *Perceptual belief* on the other hand is not a good parallel to *speaks French*, for I doubt that a perceptual *belief* is a disposition at all! To be capable of perceiving a cat or especially of anticipating the emergence of a cat on a roof or in an alley is a disposition and therefore entails the presence of a certain automaton in the observer. This capability might well be captured by the phrase "Jones believes that cats have certain properties", and might apply to dogs or other dumb animals. Perceptual belief itself is a very complex relation among a time, an organism, a state, a disposition and objects (see Chapter VII).

Not all those beliefs, which we might characterize as expressible by standing sentences such as "Jones lives on 10th St." or "π is greater than 2," appear to be the sorts of thing that are grasped by the automaton concept, which implies they are not dispositions and certainly not automaton states. Some beliefs appear to be intimately connected with verbalizations; and how their theoretical status is to be secured is certainly a mystery. Nevertheless I'll have something to say about them in Chapter VIII. Roughly the idea there is that certain 'core' beliefs are 'mental representations' (a most popular locution nowadays!) of a schematic sort that are stored in automaton structures; further beliefs are generated deductively from them in a way reminiscent of the generation of sentences in grammars. For the present we can say with some certainty that such beliefs are *not* 1–1 states and do not seem to be even remotely like dispositions to act in many cases.

The upshot of this overly long discussion is that mechanism in my version suffers none of the shortcomings of certain forms of machine functionalism, especially FSIT, except for the problem of mental qualia of we keep putting off. While both accept FA models, FSIT is wrong in identifying features with logical states, which are *not* role players either except in a formal, mathematical sense; dispositions (in Ryle's sense or any other, as a matter of fact) are not states; automata can be in more than one state at a time, and this fact is related to the one that you can get as much parallelism as you please out of automata — contrary to FSIT (and, incidentally, to connectionism, cf. p. 99 above). Both mechanism and machine functionalism have nothing to say about cognitive meanings, beliefs, and other intentions as things now stand. I have issued a promissory note in behalf of mechanism; and FSIT mistakenly identifies purpose (and hence intentionality) with the formal role playing of states.

2. BEHAVIORISM

Most philosophers of science long ago gave up the idea that science can be boiled down to observables like *yellow, long, hot, right, left*, and *sour*.

Extended to psychology, most doubt the sufficiency of observables such as *stimuli* and *responses* for building a science of the mind. The main present day tendency, I think, is toward a view holding that purely 'theoretical' terms and concepts like *atom, belief*, or *mental state* are not reducible to observables and either do refer to real entities or are a part of a scientific corpus that has real significance on the whole. Science begins in observation, but goodness only knows where it might end and still count as science, especially in psychology.

In this environment behaviorism, which accepts most of the empirical *dicta* of another day, hardly seems worth arguing about. It is an anachronism.[18] Yet the writings of Skinner, Quine, Ryle, and Wittgenstein to name a fairly hefty quartet, are extremely influential. And now also a younger but not tenderer ensemble has sprouted that stands for the same old cause. These thinkers claim that behaviorists are right (in a sense) after all: functionalism, including mechanism, is subject to essentially the same difficulties as behaviorism because they reduce to the same position (see Chapter XI)! So there is good reason to renew the attack.

Behaviorism comes in several varieties, none of them entirely palatable. One says mind is nothing but a collection of dispositions to behavior. With this I have no quarrel if dispositions are rule structures. On the other hand if dispositions are conditional ways of behavior and that's all there is to it, I demur: Rules involving internal states are real and mind is *not* wholly external. If mindedness, by which I mean intentionality, is manifest in behavior, then the same goes for fancy robots or else it is in principle unanalyzable, and no better off dangling on the outside than dwelling in some ghostly domain. However, I do not wish to repeat the argument (of Chapter IV) here, but to supplement it. In this section the indispensibility of internal logical states is the issue.

Another version is not so much a metaphysical (or anti-metaphysical!) doctrine like Ryle's as an advocacy of method. Led by Skinner, it says that intelligent behavior including use of language and all manner of mental skills can be accounted for in observational S–R terms. If this doctrine, called methodological behaviorism, is false, then so is the metaphysical version; so it is sufficient to work on the former.

A third variety, logical behaviorism, is quite technical and says that 'functional' terms or those referring to automaton or more generally mental states are explicitly definable in input-output vocabulary. This position adds up to a kind of revival of an older empiricism that sees theories as instruments and eschews the theoretical in any other role; it represents a radical step beyond (or back from) mere questions of metaphysics and methodology. I will touch on it here and consider it more thoroughly in Chapter XI on the nature of psychological theory.

Minimal behaviorism, which is the core of the methodological version, claims (A) External behavior can be explained in terms of external variables alone: stimuli, responses, response strength, reinforcing event, operants, glandular secretions, verbal utterances, and the like. In particular, if this is right, input-output behavior in our sense (Formula III(2)) can be described in a language using as nonlogical terms just the s's and o's for inputs and outputs without recourse to internal state terms q. Put in the terminology of the discussion of psychological states and their identity, such states or features or other mental attributes are individuated by input-output relations alone. Reference to the internal is eliminable.

(B) Second, minimal behaviorism is sufficient for all intelligent behavior, where the relevant observables are simply what psychologists say they are. It may countenance in addition to discrete molar phenomena descriptions of intensities of response, drive reduction, and so forth, that use nonfinite mathematics, in particular probability, statistics, and other portions of analysis. But this does not affect the picture as all we are concerned with are the parts that mechanistic theory purports to comprehend *viz.* the *intentional* or mental features (see (B$'$) below).

(C) Third, minimal behaviorism in advocating a certain kind of explanation of mental behavior is not concerned with logical reconstruction, the idea we are putting off until Chapter XI. It does not argue that terms for internal states, for example, can be defined away in some reductionist language. Rather, behaviorism argues that psychology does not require the *use* of states in any way. All it insists on is a preferred method. Direct observables and 'intervening variables' are clearer, more subject to empirical tests, more relevant to the explanation of behavior, and less liable to conceptual confusion than theoretical entities. The psychologist's aim is to establish theory, not to analyze terms.

Let's see how far (A), (B), (C), go. For some very simple organisms, those which have initial states, this methodological surmise about the sufficiency of external variables is correct. An *initial state* FA is one that is always in a certain distinguished state at the start of input. The convention in initial state machines is that q_0 is this state. For coded machines (cf. Formula II(3a)) the initial state is specified by fixing the value of the state elements y_i at $t = 0$; so in general the *definition* of y for an initial state machine is by the schema

$$y(0) \equiv a$$
$$y(t + 1) \equiv f(y(t), x(t))$$

where a is a constant 0 or 1 in the binary case and f is as usual a truth function.

A *general* FA is one in which $y(0)$ is *not* constant; it is a *noninitial state*. If an automaton is general (as assumed in Formula II(2b)), then the state-to-state sequences will depend on the arbitrarily chosen start state at the beginning of the stimulus sequence.

To illustrate, let us consider the worm who appeared in raw form in Table IV.II. This organism, we suppose, has an initial state q_0. Whenever we observe his behavior by imposing a sequence of stimuli to which he is susceptible he 'resets' to q_0 at the start of the experiment. Now it turns out that his behavior is accurately described in a certain first order language containing '$<$' (less than) and quantifiers ranging over time. To see what this description is like let us use the coded form wherein inputs have elements x_1, x_2, x_3, as in Table IV.I, and the output is z. Then it turns out the output at t is given by

$$z(t) \equiv (\exists u)\,(0 \leqslant u < t \wedge x_1(u) \wedge x_3(t)) \wedge$$
$$\sim(\exists v)\,(u < v < t \wedge x_2(v)). \qquad (1)$$

This formula says "the animal wriggles when it is irritated, provided that in its past it was exposed to enough light but not too much heat". From this the behavior in the sense of Formula III (2) can be deduced, in principle. If the worm were not initial state one would require another expression similar to that above for the behavior of the worm when it starts in state q_1. For comparison, in the automaton formalism again using Table IV.I, Table IV.II can be expressed in the formulas

$$y(0) \equiv 0$$
$$y(t+1) \equiv x_1(t) \vee (y(t) \wedge \sim x_3(t))$$
$$z(t) \equiv y(t) \wedge x_3(t).$$

(One substitutes for the s's according to IV.I, uses the normal form expansion, and simplifies; for help see discussion pp. 49ff.). In more or less ordinary English this set of formulas says that the inner state (say, a nerve fiber stimulation) is quiescent at time 0. The nerve fiber fires at time $t + 1$ iff the animal is exposed to sufficient light at time t; or the fiber fired at t and the animal was not exposed to too much heat at t. It wriggles at t iff it is mechanically irritated and the fiber fires at t. Close reflection should convince you that the two ways of expressing z are equivalent. Also observe that y can not be eliminated in the latter pair of formulas by substitution.

Unfortunately it turns out that one can not always dispense with state expressions in this (1) or any other relatively simple way short of using a rather formidable array of logical techniques, and for noninitial state automata not at all, unless the automaton table is already known. Now animals are not initial state FA (or NFA) although they probably have initial state parts. For if they were so limited they couldn't learn anything. At any rate a supposition that they have initial states (beyond biological states involved in embryonic development) is extremely risky and has no empirical support whatever that I know of. This already suggests severe limitations for behaviorism. If we broaden 'description' from a statement about inputs and outputs (above p. 133, and (i) p. 80) to 'collection of statements which entails the behavior of an FA' (III(2)), then there are automaton behaviors that are not entailed by languages satisfying behaviorist methodological requirements. Behaviorism is therefore not true as a methodological proposition. This conclusion follows from two key premises:

(A′)   Automaton behaviors are animal behaviors,

and

(B′)   Languages satisfying behaviorist requirements are inadequate for describing automaton behavior.

(A′) is easily established by the observation that any automaton behavior is codeable as a recursive function. Since all recursive functions are computable by some human being in the sense that if he is given an argument value of the function and enough time he can compute the function value, it follows that for any behavior of an automaton there is an animal that can perform it.

We get at (B′) by way of the concept of *intervening variable*. No behaviorist, with the exception of B. F. Skinner and his group wishes to exclude reference to inner entities entirely. Neural, glandular, muscular or even purely theoretical 'hypothetical constructs' are permissible provided they are no more than 'intervening variables'; these, by the tenets just reviewed before the worm exercise, are theoretically dispensable, but useful.

Originally 'intervening variable' referred to elements of a domain somehow between external stimuli and responses. In a now classical paper, Kenneth Spence (1948) enumerated the possible inter-relations among intervening variables and stimuli and responses thus: response-to-response: stimulus-to-response: organic-to-response: stimulus-to-organic: stimulus-to-state: state-to-state: and state-to-response.[19] Adapting our automaton notation in order to facilitate comparisons, let us use R for response, O for output, S for stimulus, and Q for intervening variables, either organic or hypothetical. Then one can represent these relations by the following functional schemata:

$$
\begin{aligned}
N' &: S' \to R' & M' &: S' \to Q' \\
\alpha &: Q' \to R' & \beta &: Q' \to Q'.
\end{aligned}
\tag{2}
$$

N' corresponds to the output function N of automata, M' to M, while α and β represent functions from internal entities of some kind to responses or just from internal entities back to themselves. Now assuming that the domain of α includes the range of M' and of β, $\alpha(M'(S')) = R'$ certainly exists as does $\alpha(\beta(M'(S'))) = R'$. Both of these reduce to

$$
N'(S') = R'.
\tag{2a}
$$

For automata, on the other hand, the relevant relations are

$$
M: (Q \times S) \to Q, \quad \text{and} \quad N: (Q \times S) \to R.
\tag{3}
$$

Outputs are given by

$$
N(M(Q, S), S) = R.
\tag{4}
$$

Schematically, (2) and (3) are radically different as is shown by comparing (2a) and (4). In (2a) there is no dependencey on internal states.

As pointed out many times, the variables Q' in the behaviorist schema are logically dispensable; Skinner himself (1963) has argued that they simply clutter up inquiry. If he is right and if behaviorism as characterized here is right what goes on in the body has no relevance to behavioral science whatever. Whatever you can get by positing intervening variables you can get without. Their only conceivable use would be for the heuristic fixing of ideas in some way. If intervening variables were the only concepts of a theoretical sort allowed, then we would already tend to show (B') owing to the discrepancy between (2a) and (4). This satisfies our intuition that automata states are quite different *items* than intervening variables, but I'm afraid its short of a demonstration. The proposition that intervening entities are simply the domain of a composite function $\alpha M'$ or $\alpha\beta M'$ (as above) entails that they are 'dispositions' in a sense made famous by Carnap long ago (Carnap, 1936, pp. 44 ff.). Given any systems $\mathscr{S}$ and appropriate domains and co-domains of functions schematically like M' and α, if $M'(x) =$ q when $x = s$ and $\alpha(y) = r$ when $y = q$, then the following conditional holds:

> If $\mathscr{S}$ receives input s, then $\mathscr{S}$ is in intervening condition q if and only if its output is r.   (5)

Scheme (5) is that of Carnap's *bilateral reduction* sentences. What we see is that if intervening variables refer to the elements of the mediating domain of a composite function they are definable by reduction sentences of this classical positivist kind. Moreover, since q in (5) enjoys this logical status and the same treatment applies to so-called disposition terms elsewhere in science (like 'soluble', 'fragile', 'ductile', 'flammable', etc.) intervening variables are frequently termed 'dispositions.' In order to avoid confusion with dispositions as place-holders, let us refer to terms introduced by a schema (5) as 'pure dispositions'. This is strictly a terminological device and we will drop it all together in due course.[20] The question now arises whether automaton states are pure dispositions. If we violate behaviorism principle (C) by using some method that admits concepts of the internal to discover an automaton structure, then given the complete automaton table beforehand it is possible to eliminate q terms. But this is reconstruction in a new language. Even then, however, the situation is complex, and if the inputs s of (5) are restricted to single automaton symbols, the thing can't be done. Moreover, if whatever information the psychologist might have about a realized automaton is short of the entire table, he's stuck with internal states in any case, contrary to (A).

The worm story leads to the surmise that some states are dispositions in Carnap's precise sense, because we get its behavior in an input-output language. This is correct. Going back to Table IV.II consider input s_1 and state q_0. By the table we write the conditional

> If the worm has input s_1 in state q_0, it outputs 0.

Likewise for state q_1,

> If the worm has input s_1 in q_1 it outputs 1.

Now since the worm either wriggles or not but not both and is in either state q_0 or q_1 we conclude

> If the worm has input s_1, then it is in state q_0 if and only if it outputs 0,

and

> If the worm has input s_1, then it is in state q_1 if and only if it outputs 1.

These are bilateral reduction sentences, and by the positivist convention, the state q_0 and q_1 are therefore pure dispositions. These sentences serve as eliminative definitions of q_0 and q_1 in the partial sense that if s_1 actually occurs the outputs are necessary and sufficient for identifying states. However even with a full table to work from it is easy to produce counterexamples showing that states are not dispositions to respond to *single* inputs (sequences x of length 1) and *à fortiori* are not intervening variables.

Consider Table I

TABLE I
States not pure dispositions.

	M		N	
	0	1	0	1
q_0	q_1	q_2	0	0
q_1	q_1	q_0	1	0
q_2	q_0	q_1	0	0

Here I use $s_0 = 0$, $o_0 = 0$, etc. to keep the symbolic clutter down. q_0 and q_2, according to the foregoing definition, are the same pure dispositions as they both output 0 for an input 0 and the same output for input 1. (Formally, $N(q_0, 0) = 0$, $N(q_0, 1) = 0$ and $N(q_2, 0) = 0$, $N(q_2, 1) = 0$). But q_0 and q_1 are not *state equivalent*: it is false that for every sequence x of inputs, $N(q_0, x) = N(q_2, x)$. For instance $N(q_0, 00) = 1$, and $N(q_2, 00) = 0$, as you may check for yourself using the recursion formulas III (1a, 1b). So the FA does not behave the same for all inputs, hence we infer that dispositions to respond to single inputs do not individuate states in general.

What happens if we generalize to finite input *sequences*? The answer depends almost wholly on what the investigator knows. If a psychologist already knows a table an organism realizes, then he certainly knows the *number* of states. If the number of states is n, then sequences of length $n - 1$ are sufficient to differentiate states (Nelson, 1968, p. 155). Another way of expressing this fact is: no two inequivalent states q and q' will yield the same output for every sequence of length $n - 1$ or greater. That is to say, for some x if the length of x is greater than $n - 2$ then

$$N(q, x) \neq N(q', x). \tag{6}$$

On the other hand, if the states are equivalent then no sequence of any length will distinguish them.

An FA is *reduced* if the equivalence of two states implies they are *identical* (not type identical, but the same *symbol* type (cf. Nelson, 1968, p. 155)). For reduced FA it is true that sequences that are long enough to individuate states determine true bilateral reduction sentences. Table I is in fact reduced, and so this result must hold for it; specifically $x = 0$ is sufficient to distinguish q_0 and q_2 both from q_1 and we already know that q_0 is inequivalent to q_0 using $x = 00$ immediately above. Consequently

If the FA has input 0, it is in state q_1 if and only if it outputs 1

and similarly for q_0 and q_2 using input 00 in the antecedent.

The upshot of this exercise is that if one knows Table I, then state terms are eliminable by reduction sentences in the same way as pure disposition elsewhere in science provided that we use sufficiently long input sequences. I still prefer not to use 'disposition' for 'state' for the reasons registered in Section 1, and will have no reason to use the locution 'pure disposition' in this book again.

This circumstance, however, does not help the methodological behaviorist's cause very much. The true issue is, can he *find* true description of the automaton behavior of an organism without employing an internal state concept? If he can, then he does not violate (C) (or (A) or (B)) and our demonstration (B') fails.

The situation he (Burry) is faced with centers around noninitial state organisms. One avenue he could take would lead to testing an organism's reactions to stimuli and attempting to obtain laws like (1). And if the organism suffers n states, from any one of which a sequence of tests might start, then Burry will have to find n such laws in order to *describe* the organism in the required sense of entailing its behavior (on pain of violating (A) otherwise). Each such law he assigns to a unique state symbol q which represents the beginning state for which the law holds.

Now let us suppose that Burry has actually succeeded in grasping the behavior, β, of the organism. From his description he can immediately calculate the N part of a table for the FA because he knows the output resulting

from each input sequence for a given state. Such a partial table appears in
Table II. In order to derive the M part, Burry knows that it is

TABLE II
Partial automaton.

	M	N
q_0		
q_1	Unknown states	Known outputs
q_{n-1}		

sufficient to test the organism with sequences of length $n - 1$. In fact there
is an algorithm: construct all possible $n^{m \cdot n}$ M tables, test each table against
the function $N(q_1, x) = o_j$ using formulas III (1a, 1b), with sequences x of
length $n - 1$ or less. We know that this finite set of sequences is all that is
needed to reveal inequivalence of states and hence to individuate them (up
to an isomorphism). Hence, if Burry can describe the behavior β, he can
derive the complete automaton table, and conversely.

However, given an unknown automaton, it is *impossible* to identify
states by any bounded finite number of tests. In fact, after injecting an
input x it is impossible for Burry to tell what state the organism was in
initially, unless it has a distinguished initial state, which is not what concerns
us here (Moore, 1956; Nelson, 1975).

TABLE III
Backwards indeterministic automaton

	M		N	
	0	1	0	1
q_0	q_3	q_2	1	0
q_1	q_0	q_2	0	0
q_2	q_3	q_3	1	1
q_3	q_1	q_1	0	0

Table III has a certain peculiar 'backward indeterministic' property which is
reminiscent of indeterminism in quantum mechanics. Consider *any* input
string of 0's and 1's that *begins* with a 0. It is easy to see that the FA of Table

III yields exactly the same output string starting in state q_0 as it does starting in state q_2 — in effect, q_0 and q_2 are 'equivalent' with respect to all strings headed by 0. Similarly, every string beginning with 1 yields exactly the same output from q_0 as it does from q_1. Despite these partial equivalences it is possible to show that the four states of the automaton of Table III are *pairwise inequivalent*.

From these results we may conclude states are not reducible via bilateral reduction sentences with respect to inputs that are *arbitrary length finite sequences*.

The mechanist is in a different position to the extent that for him the desired description, from which he can get a table, is *possible*. He has open to him formulating hypotheses about the *M*-structure, computer models and simulation, results of neuroscience as they come in, his own intuition, introspection, and the like. But the behaviorist position is not good. For him complete descriptions are out in principle.

In earlier writings I considered the possibility of eliminating automaton state terms in organic, most probably neural terms. I will do so again in Chapter XI, but drop the topic here as the kind of behaviorist I am worried about does not seem to be much concerned with the possibility of reduction of psychology to neuroscience. There is, however, one other behaviorist ploy that should be considered. It says that all the conditions that constrain inputs to different outputs are *environmental*, and that behaviorism is not restricted to a narrow functional (in the sense of many-one relation) view of stimulus and response. For example, a certain rat sometimes responds to a lower level electrical stimulus in the cortex by a beta pattern of much lower amplitude than normal. It is quite tempting to attribute the abnormal response to the presence of some internal condition — or otherwise get a new rat. But an alternative is to look for *external* side conditions (or one could look for both, of course). It is just barely conceivable that for FA-like organisms, all behavior to which the mechanist might attribute internal state structures can be equally well explained by ascription of external states. More precisely, suppose one entertains an hypothesis to the effect that an organism is *fitted* in part by an automaton with the usual M, N functions and stimulus, state and response sets S, Q, and O. Then instead of attributing to it the states Q, one might recommend that a set E of environmental conditions be looked for so that the automaton with E replacing Q can be iso-morphic (behaviorally equivalent is good enough) to the first. An immediate objection is that organisms appear to maintain their behavioral integrity (pretty much) in a wide variety of environments if not varied too radically.

Whether or not this last conjecture stands with future progress in psychology, we can argue *à priori* that this kind of move to eliminate completely the internal and to save behaviorism thereby *is doomed*. Years ago Claude Shannon (1956) showed that Turing machine internal states can be stored on tape so that almost any machine can be replaced with another having fewer states and more input symbols. He also demonstrated, however, that a Turing machine requires *at least two* irreplaceable internal states. If it does not have these it can no longer find the appropriate marks (surrogates for states) in its tape environment. It follows that there is an automaton that is equivalent to no replacing automaton and hence that there is a behavior not describable in terms of an environmental replacing scheme, contrary to (A).

Our conclusion must be that as states are not dispensible (unless by logical reconstruction of a known given automaton) by reduction via reduction sentences – *à fortiori* via explicit definition – nor by externalization, the conclusion (B') holds. Behaviorism as prescriptive of method can not describe all animal behaviors and therefore can not explain them.

3. NEORATIONALISM

Any theory meant to settle the problem of the nature of mental features must pave the way to a theory of intentional attitudes. This can not be done by the simple expedient of identifying features with machine states (FSIT). Mechanism proposes to solve the problem by identifying features, including belief and other intentional attitudes, with automata systems, not with states. Cognitivism in its several forms tends to identify them with inner mental representations of some sort.

More than one critic of computational theories of mind (e.g. Searle) has pointed out that computers don't believe (or disbelieve) anything, although there might be sense in saying they execute or emulate certain mental skills. We might (and we often do) *ascribe* grasp of meanings and the having of attitudes to machines, but ascription is not *predication* with truth. You can ascribe evil intentions to a motor that won't start or to a computer that won't print on command; but your will to ascribe doesn't license a proclamation of intentions in fact.

A peculiarity of intentional attitudes is that they might be about no actual object and depend only how things are thought of, not on how they are. Jane believes Bach wrote Bach's 203rd church *Cantata,* although there probably is no such piece. Thus beliefs can address the "inexistent", to use a widely loved but untamed notion of Brentano's. If a belief about a Bach cantata is a relation between Jane and an inexistent, it is not easy to see how it could be identified with any part of a rule system in a mind, anyone of which, from a functionalist viewpoint, is realized in a physical embodiment of some kind. There are *no* physical inexistents.

The first of two sorts of cognitivism I want to discuss is Noam Chomsky's, which boldly accepts intentions, propositions and other intensional objects along with a commitment to eventual explanations of key ideas in species-specific biological terms. Since psycholinguistics in the Chomskian tradition is the most highly developed of the cognitive sciences, and since that pursuit exploits the concept of recursive rule, it will pay dividends to see *both* how a machine approach fares as a supporting philosophy, *and* what a theory that largely eschews ontological modesty looks like.

The philosophy of Noam Chomsky and his followers is one cornerstone of functionalism, historically and conceptually. Chomsky, being a linguist, has naturally concerned himself with those aspects of philosophy closest to philosophy of language and psycholinguistics. Still, his views on mind and the nature of man are general enough and are of notable philosophical substance. Indeed "language is a mirror of the mind", and this is what most intrigues Chomsky about the study of language (Chomsky, 1975b, p. 4). I am not aware of his having written or said that mind as such — not just mind *qua* mastering language — is a system of recursive rules. And although I am placing on him a doctrine about mind, rules, and the like, he has more specifically allied himself and his teachings through the years with Cartesian rationalism. This affiliation, which is not identification and is the reason for my using the rubric 'neorationalism', has generated a lot of heat when brought into contact with contemporary empiricism. Much of it, I think, is based on misunderstanding which, in turn, is in part attributable to Chomsky's attempt to fit his thoughts into a vocabulary of 'ideas', 'innateness', 'knowledge', 'freedom', 'creativity', and 'mental', that is burdened with centuries of accumulated philosophical baggage. For instance one scarcely avoids bicker if he writes of *mental* rules, and also of exorcising ghosts *à la* Ryle without explanation; or of Cartesian 'automata' one time and Turing machines on the other without saying something about the radical gap that separates the conceptions. Still, throughout the twentyfive years of disputation a persistent and unambiguous claim of rationalism runs unbroken through the writings of Chomsky, Katz, and others.

According to neorationalism (NR) animal communication operates on a principle of 'strict finiteness' (among other principles not relevant here). This means that the communication consists of a finite number of signals, "each produced under a fixed range of stimulus conditions" (Chomsky, 1975a, p. 303). Human language, on the other hand is entirely different. Human speech production is free of external stimulus and is creative: a normal child who has mastered his mother's tongue can easily produce sentences she never heard before and she can do this without external prompting of any kind. Her linguistic output during her lifetime is a potentially infinite body of utterances. If she lived forever there would be no bound that could be placed on her linguistic originality. As a listener she effortlessly (for the most part) understands an indefinitely large number of sentences, most of them new, in all kinds of situations and without conscious awareness or control of how the process works. (We are of course not talking about learning a second language during which understanding often follows deliberate and painful translation.)

The key idea in explaining this remarkable human phenomenon is that the speaker-listener has *tacit knowledge* of a grammar of the language she speaks. This grammar consists of several systems of rules: *syntactical* rules, which include phrase structure rules of the kind exemplified by the example of Table II.II together with certain 'transformation' rules; rules of meaning or *semantical* rules; and *phonological* rules (Chomsky, 1965, p. 15). Most of what is rather securely known in the psycholinguistic theories that have emerged from Chomsky's basic work has to do with the syntactical part. Very little is known about semantical rules, and in fact the field is marked by considerable disagreement among the linguists who work more or less within an NR framework. My own sketchy suggestions concerning meaning will be set out in later chapters. So what I have to say now should be understood as taking grammatical rules to be strictly syntactical.[21] For the time being the reader would probably be safe to keep Table II.II in mind as a simple example of a grammatical system, although it includes no transformational rules (which, approximately, operate on entire trees, not just on a vocabulary of primitives). It generates an infinite collection of sentences, and illustrates well enough the principle that production of a sentence is not a mere association of data in concatenate fashion. Even that trivial fragment of English provides for self-embedment (a sentence within a sentence), nesting (clauses within clauses), multiple branching, and ambiguous readings, which are among distinguishing traits of human language (Chomsky, 1965, p. 12).

Knowledge of the rules of a grammar is the same thing as 'competence' in the language, a term Chomsky at times prefers as it does not ring out all the epistemic overtones of 'knowledge' which has induced, as I already remarked, much misunderstanding.[22] A person's linguistic competence represents what she can do with the language in principle. Of course her actual *performance* does not always measure up to her competence; she makes false starts, hesitates, makes grammatical slips occasionally, can generate sentences of bounded length only (unless she's James Joyce), and can neither generate nor understand nested constructions beyond a depth of three or four without use of a scattering of grammatically superfluous anaphoric devices, and so forth.[23] The study of performance is an entirely different matter, although psycholinguistic models of performance as they are developed will somehow contain representations of competence (Chomsky, 1965, p. 9). One's competence or tacit knowledge is the proper subject of the grammarian; a grammar (system of rules) is a theory of the language. This theory is an adequate one if it correctly describes and accounts for the generation and understanding of the language by the human speaker.

Learning a language is perhaps the most extraordinary feat a human being can ever perform, although "feat" here is something of an abuse of normal English; the thing is done effortlessly by the child. I am exaggerating slightly – the child does intently watch her mother's lips, utter sounds, is gently corrected – but still the learning is more by example than instruction. On Chomsky's view the growth of a language in the mind of the child is analogous to the development of a bodily organ (Chomsky, 1975b, p. 11; 1980). This development requires the acquisition of a system of extremely complex rules, beyond the complexity of those for good chess strategy, say, or for performing at the piano on a world class level. But unlike acquired special skills acquired linguistic competence is essentially the same for all children, for a particular language. This human capacity is universal.

. . . One of the faculties of the mind, common to the species, is the faculty of language that serves the two basic functions of rationalist theory: it provides a sensory system for the preliminary analysis of linguistic data, and a schematism that determines, quite narrowly, a certain class of grammars. Each grammar is a theory of a particular language, specifying formal and semantic properties of an infinite array of sentences. These sentences, each with its particular structure, constitute the language generated by the grammar. The languages as so generated are those that can be 'learned' in the normal way. The language faculty, given appropriate stimulation, will construct a grammar; the person knows the language generated by the constructed grammar. This knowledge can then be used to understand what is heard and to produce discourse as an expression of thought within the constraints of the internalized principles, in a manner appropriate to situations as these are conceived by other mental faculties, free of stimulus control (Chomsky, 1975b, pp. 12–13).

The key to the rationalist character of NR is the theory of the nature of the innate structures that inable acquisition of a grammar during the learning process. There are two preliminary main points concerning the nature of any kind of animal learning that counts as being cognitive to some degree. Animal learning is *not* a matter of associating a stimulus to the appropriate response or, in other words, of internalizing a functional relation from a stimulus set to a response set. On the contrary, learning is a two-part affair that involves the development of a cognitive structure from experience together with a functional relation that maps stimulus conditions given that cognitive structure to actions. This, Chomsky holds, is what is required at *least* if any progress is to be made in analyzing behavior (Chomsky, 1975b, pp. 16 ff.; Chomsky, 1965, pp. 30–34). Now when the organism is a human being and the domain of learning is language, the learned cognitive structure is the grammar (in part) and the relevant experience is a sample of the language. The crucial question is, how much does it take to internalize such a complex thing as a grammar from a relatively small finite sample? Chomsky has fruitfully compared this achievement to that of the formulation of explanatory hypotheses in science where, obviously, an enormous amount of information and cognitive prowess is demanded (Chomsky, 1972, p. 90). Here the counterpart to whatever latent instincts we have that allow us to guess the laws of nature (a kind of Peircean view) is knowledge of a *universal grammar*. It is this tacit knowledge that enables the individual to select the right grammar that explains, so to speak, the language sample experience has thrust upon him. Every person has knowledge of the universal grammar as a system of rules, conditions, and principles that constitute the elements of all human language. The learned natural language must, by a kind of biological necessity, conform to the universal grammar (Chomsky, 1975b, p. 30 *passim*).

The precise character of linguistic universals is of course still highly speculative, and what Chomsky has to say about this is tentative and changes, as it should, over the years. Examples which are probably safe to use are that a grammar must be generative (like Table II.II) have a transformational component (e.g., to transform a sentence in active voice, which has already been generated by a phrase structure component into passive voice); use basic noun-verb-categories; and use structure-dependent (such as recursive) rather than structure-independent (such as sequential stringing) rules.

According to Chomsky, all organisms possess innate cognitive structures of various degrees of complexity for learning. But possession of a universal grammar is a distinctive mark of man. It is species specific: this innate cognitive structure differs *qualitatively* from anything present in lower animals.

Both the individual's acquired linguistic competence and the underlying universal knowledge that he must have to get the right rules are beyond anything that can be grasped by behaviorist, S–R theories, strictly classificatory linguistic methods, mathematical communication theory or simple (FA) automata theory (Chomsky, 1972, p. 4). Speech behavior of lower animals, by contrast, is induced by simple conditioning and reinforcement, guided by external cueing, is stimulus bound, and is constituted by a small finite corpus of acts. This sustained view of Chomsky's is being vindicated today in the discovery of the wrong-headedness of exaggerated claims about 'speech' in apes, claims that have received widespread attention in recent years.[24]

Now these paragraphs, I take it, pretty well outline the main features of NR thought regarding language and mind. Not all of the group agree with Chomsky on all the details, but I think the sketch is broadly enough drawn and close enough to the right spirit to catch those who would style themselves 'rationalists'. Before going ahead with the suggestion that mechanism provides a comprehensive framework for it, something should be said about aspects of this picture that are clearly metaphysically relevant and that agree with the point of view of this book. Chomsky's thought does not include a mind-body dualism, or any other explicit metaphysics so long as we stick to issues about rule complexity. Over and over again he declares that the theory of universal grammar which is an innate property of the human mind is in principle accountable in terms of biology (Chomsky, 1972, Chapter 5). So the basic philosophy is strictly naturalistic. Moreover Chomsky never, so far as I am aware, concerns himself with the question of mental occurrents, sentient events, and their ontological status. Therefore the basic presuppositions and concerns are the same as those of mechanism, although he might not be as worried as I am about the mind-body problem. I am stalling off, while he does not seem to be concerned with the issue.

NR, despite my opening remarks about its antecedency, sometimes reveals itself as a one-way functionalism. All neorationalists believe that linguistics is a branch of psychology as it is intrinsically a theory of mind, and believe that it has methodological autonomy from biology. Whether linguistic theories are irreducible is not clear in view of Chomsky's insistence that innate capacities can be accounted for biologically. One way to construe this emphasis on biology is as follows: Only a specific kind of brain, namely the human, embodies the necessary knowledge of universals to learn a language; computers don't, and no conceivable robot could. If so, the functionalist idea which is really present in one respect is partial in that it does not, like

Putnam's version, see the possibility of mind-like realizations in almost any variety of material from brains to silicon chips. If species specificity is taken that seriously, *viz.* not only specific with respect to biological taxonomy but in a broader context of *physical* categories, then Chomsky could not consistently be a mechanist — a system of recursive rules regardless of any special embodiment would be insufficient for the presence of mind.

It is quite possible to be a full functionalist with respect to competence but not performance, although I do not recall that any neorationalist has raised the point. Mental performance as manifested in the use and understanding of language by a person as a living organism in a socio-environmental context could well be reducibly biological except for the internalized rules *qua* rules that could find, perhaps, equivalent counter-parts in nonbiological systems, Chomsky himself does refer to his position as 'realist' (Chomsky, 1977, p. 37).[25] Exactly the same sentiment is evinced in earlier writings in the distinction between the descriptive adequacy and the explanatory adequacy of a grammatical theory. A theory of language is *descriptively adequate* if it generates the sentences of that language with corresponding trees — "assigns structural descriptions to the sentences" — , and distinguishes grammatical from grammatical in a way that accords with the linguistic intuitions of the native speaker. Such a theory has *explanatory adequacy* if it accounts for the innate linguistic structures that make learning language possible (Chomsky, 1965, pp. 24–26). Although not enough is known for anyone to give a detailed description of these latter structures or of what a universal grammar is like, the very distinction between a descriptive theory and an explanatory theory in Chomsky's sense, shows a commitment to the reality of underlying mental processes. 'Internalized rules' and 'innate structures' are not metaphors. But the underlying reality may not be a domain of formally distinct rule structures that are irreducible to biological categories. In any event the whole question of reducibility in NR functionalism poses questions that are not much different than those we already must face in a more general way when the time comes to examine the nature of psychological theory. There is basic agreement therefore with functionalism in philosophical outline.

Psycholinguistics at least in the early stages is an autonomous discipline even though the ultimate locus of inner structure is of course biological. NR is realistic, and I should go so far as to say that everything Chomsky says is *compatible* with my own version of realism as reflected in the fit-guide distinction. Fitting corresponds roughly to descriptive adequacy and guiding to explanatory adequacy.

Even if the NFA hypothesis is correct and it finite automaton structures are far from adequate for anything like human language an NFA can store or otherwise contain in its organization any finite system of recursive rules (see Section III.1). Hence the competence-performance distinction is naturally made, and competence or "what is known" is represented by the learned grammar that is somehow stored. Performance is represented by the finite 'limitations' of an NFA immersed in an earthbound biological organism. Nothing that I am familiar with in studies of the psychology of language along NR lines conflicts with this construal of performance; and contrariwise, appeal to purely formal constructions, computer models and analogies and the like are consistently made by NR. Likewise the fact that a language is potentially infinite and that the user has the capacity both to generate and to grasp cognitively the elements of such an extended domain is captured by automata. All but the most trivial automata process infinite collections in the mathematical (not historical!) sense. Indeed any automaton is the instantiation of an algorithm for processing recursive functions. Finally, for the straight-forward questions, a necessary condition for creativity, mainly nondeterminism, is built into the model.

Of course, all of these observations are too sketchy to give the slightest idea of the detailed work that has already gone into an understanding of linguistic performance and creativity, but these remarks are meant only to indicate a compatibility of principle.[26] Two *hard* questions remain: (a) Does the qualifier 'recursive' that modifies 'rule' impose too many restrictions on NR linguistic theory? (b) Are certain key rationalist commitments intimated by *knowledge* of rules, *innate* ideas, and à priori *universal grammar* completely incompatible with an avowedly empirical logic of mind?

(a) The universal grammar as well as learned rules selected by application of that grammar to linguistic data are part of a *discrete* communication system (Chomsky, 1975a, p. 301). This eliminates any worry over a possible interpretation of NR that says the underlying processes are continuous. So the only relevant issue for comparison with mechanism is whether the linguistic domain − sentences, acquired rules, etc. − are the results of computations of some kind. If so, all the rules of concern are recursive and fall into the class of automata. If not, one or more of the following, presumably, would be noneffective: (i) phrase structure rules; (ii) transformation and phonological rules; (iii) learning; (iv) universal grammar.[27]

(i) All phrase structure rules of concern are, like those of Table II.II, by definition equivalent to Turing machine rules and hence recursive. In recent developments (Chomsky, 1981) less significance seems to be given to the role of phrase structure rules, and there is an added concern with referential dependence of anaphora. But still, all the rules might be thought of as machine programs (Chomsky 1986, p. 48).

(ii) It is certainly not known whether transformation rules, which transform generated trees into trees, are recursive. The linguistic facts are not in. *À priori* it seems hardly possible that any psychological process would not be step-by-step effective, but this may be nothing but a dogmatic extension of our conscious cognitive powers such as they are, especially of reasoning as reconstructed in logical theory. Some philosophers have argued that grammatical theory has no need for transformational rules (Harman, 1963). A stronger case has been made by some mathematicians who have claimed that the theory of *tree* automata, which is in the domain of the recursive, can provide everything transformational grammars can for linguistic theory (Rounds, 1970).

Besides this slight support the best that can be said, I think, is that no hypothesis as fruitful as a mechanist or computationalist one is really in sight. At least there is no positive evidence I know of that tends to demonstrate an incompatibility between NR and mechanism on the issue of the recursiveness of transformational rules. The bet is that the whole theory, when there is one, will be programmable.

(iii) *Learning* presents a really serious problem for our austere form of mechanism. Learning games, indeed perfect chess, is theoretically trivial for a full Turing machine, although it would take more time or memory than would be practically available; but chess is a far cry from language. Finite state languages, which are at the bottom of Chomsky's hierarchy of languages, which will be characterized a few paragraphs on, can be learned at asymptote by an organism having the properties of a rather simple stimulus-response learning model (Suppes, 1969). This is learning clearly within the limits of animal learning that associates stimulus conditions to response with reinforcement. One ought to be able to conclude by an *à fortiori* argument that these things are learnable by an automaton. This is true, but it takes some work to do (Pao, 1969).

Whether a recursive device of some kind, given a generous language sample, can construct full linguistic competence (represented by a finite set of rules) is completely unknown. There are some purely mathematical facts that appear to be relevant and thus provide a basis for a presumption that a device equivalent to a very powerful Turing machine could do the job. The first is a theoretical result showing that there is an algorithmic construction — and therefore a machine — that can construct a grammar for an arbitrary context-free language of a certain rather restricted class, given only a small finite sample of the language whose grammar in unknown, and a reinforcement regimen (Pao, 1969). If natural languages such as English do turn out to be context-free after all then such rather preliminary results suggest the plausibility of a mechanistic account of learning.

Another theoretical development is that of self-reproducing and self-describing automata.[28] A self-describing automaton is one that carries a code of its own table within the table itself, much as a living organism contains a code of its own genetic structure within each of its cells. So far as I know there is no work being done relating language acquisition to automaton self-description; but this could be a fruitful field. In the next chapter I will argue that *expectation* contains an ingredient of self-description. Furthermore, it is almost certain that learning of complex tasks involves expectation. This, I take it, is something like saying that learning is not *inductive* so much as it is *abductive* and resembles hypothesis formation, which is just Chomsky's insight. In science one advances a theory on the basis of expectations of what *would* happen under such and such circumstances, and then trims and adjusts that theory if the expectations are not fulfilled. Since expectation entails self-description, as I shall try to show, the von Neumann-Lee theory could be extremely relevant.

A closely related point is that learning is possibly heuristic in the same sense as game playing or other cognitive computer programs discussed in Chapter IV. Recall my final shot at those who use Gödel against mechanism. Heuristic methods, I said, might allow a mechanism to 'see' the truth of an unprovable formula much as Professor Lucas claims we can. If so, similarly unconstrained procedures might account for language learning. The facts of artificial intelligence research show that semi-algorithms hit on solutions to cognitive problems *much* faster, in many cases, then full algorithms, although there is high risk: they miss sometimes.

I hasten to add that puzzles about the existence of learning *algorithms* certainly make the innateness hypothesis of NR very plausible. A parallel with self-description theory is brought to mind once again. It is relatively easy to give a theory of animal expectation if one takes self-coding in the nervous system as *there*, as built in. If a system must learn its own description one can still account for expectation but the overall mechanism must be much more elaborate. There is a trade-off in complexity between a thing with a built-in self-code and one that must discover that code in order to get on with its business. Roughly and approximately, the more complete the native structure, the less elaborate need be the mechanism for cognitive tasks like learning.

Looking up a solution to a puzzle in a book is a lot easier than solving it. In particular, then, if sufficient innate structure is there already, then the sufficiency of algorithmic language learning — by a system of automaton rules — is quite plausible. This is not what Chomsky says, but it is in the right spirit and goes some distance, I think, to exorcise the ghost in the machine (Chomsky, 1975b, p. 23).

(iv) The question whether man's linguistic gifts are *qualitatively* different from anything existing elsewhere in the animal world is purely verbal. Mathematical linguists, following Chomsky, have been interested for years in a certain hierarchy of languages that falls into the range of what is called a 'subrecursive hierarchy' in mathematical logic. At the top are full Turing machines: there is a universal machine that can imitate *any* effective process, by Church's thesis; and at the bottom are the FA, which are behaviorally equivalent to one-way-tape Turing machines, as discussed in Chapter II. In the middle of the hierarchy are certain families of languages including the main subdivisions of context sensitive and context-free languages (Chomsky, 1959b). The latter, which is exemplified in Table II.II, characterizes what linguists have recently referred to as a 'deep-structure' basis for natural languages. Its rules are of the form,

$$q \rightarrow r_1 r_2 \ldots r_n$$

where q is a *nonterminal* symbol (such as NP or V) and $r_1, r_2, \ldots, r_n$ are either *terminal* symbols (such as 'words' in English) or nonterminal. The propositional calculus is context-free as is a certain normal form of FORTRAN, lots of English, parts of the first order predicate calculus, and so forth. Is all of English context-free?[29] Where in this hierarchy is English (Chomsky, 1975a, p. 302)? Are there other subrecursive (below Turing languages) hierarchies that might shed more light on English? Questions such as these are of serious concern to Chomsky-type linguists for the light they might shed on the question of transformations as well as for an interpretation of 'qualitative difference'. Is separation in a set-theoretic hierarchy 'qualitative'?

Now the behavior of our favorite worm falls at the low end of the hierarchy and is, indeed, a finite state language, viewed purely formally and abstractly. The behavior of this thing can be learned at asymptote as you would probably expect, by the S–R model of Suppes we discussed earlier. The learning involved is a very simple form of conditioning. Does this make the language *qualitatively* different than English? In a way, I suppose, it does.

On the other hand this language, though on the low side, is still in the super class of those generated by recursive rules. Does this make it *qualitatively* different?

(b) We still have not squarely faced the question of 'tacit knowledge' and of 'common knowledge' of rules, universal grammars, ideas, and so on. The issues here are somewhat muddy as different neorationalists make different claims about what they mean by these terms and say different things at different times. In another place I inventoried over fifteen theories of competence that have been put forward, some of them quite off-handedly, by linguists and linguistic philosophers (Nelson, 1978a). I don't think there is any point in going over this ground again here. Perhaps it will suffice to say that competence is represented by tacit knowledge of the rules of the language, is ideal, and never wholly manifested in performance. So what is meant by 'tacit knowledge'? is it the same for all? And what does the NR answer to these questions have in it for rationalism rather than empiricism?

First of all a rule of the type we are concerned with is a recursive relation much like a rule of logic, as sketched out in Chapter II. As such it does not *refer* to anything; it doesn't *state* anything, although it could be part of a statement. For instance

$$S \rightarrow NP + VP$$

is a rule, does not state anything, but does allow a kind of inference: "from S one may derive NP + VP by rewriting the second for the first". Such rules are not true or false, hence are not propositional. If one is known, what is known is not "S → NP + VP" but rather something like ' "S → NP + VP" is a correct rule of the base of English [of French or maybe any language universally]'. Keeping this elementary logical observation in mind, it seems that a good analysis of 'Jones knows English' is that she has acquired the rules which are now stored in her head. To say her knowledge is tacit means that she can not write out the rules if asked and might not even identify a rule as a rule of English if shown one, although this is rather unlikely if she is fluent and the rules are not presented in some opaque guise. Chomsky, at least quite recently, means exactly the same, assuming that the question of the recursiveness of rules of grammar has been settled: " . . . to know language is to have internalized [i.e., learned, acquired] a generative grammar [a system of recursive rules] . . . ". (Chomsky, 1975a, p. 314).

Let us call this knowledge, 'knowledge of'. Harman (1967, p. 82) claims Chomsky means by 'knowledge', 'knowledge that' or propositional knowledge, but that the proper interpretation of knowledge of language is 'knowledge how' to do something. Over and over again Chomsky has denied this and affirmed the view above quoted, which is also that of mechanism (Chomsky, 1969, p. 153). Consider the following two sentences:

A knows the rules of L (7)

A knows that such and such are the rules of L (8)

(7) does not imply (8); the two sentence are inequivalent. (7) is equivalent to 'A knows L' or to 'A is fluent in L' and the latter does not imply (8). If it did linguistics would be completely trivial. If, however, the knowledge expressed in (8) is *tacit*, then presumably a case could be made out for equivalence; if A knows the rules of L then he tacitly knows that such and such are the rules of L; (8) implies (7) in any case.

This appears to be precisely the position Jerrold Katz embraces (See Graves *et al.*, 1973). It is very doubtful, according to Katz and his group, that propositional knowledge can be analyzed in computer terms (Graves *et al.*, 1973, p. 326). An organism that has knowledge and understanding of language is not a mere robot clicking away under the governance of recursive rules. If competence is propositional knowledge, then it is very likely that mechanism is false, and functionalism along with it (Graves *et al.*, 1973, p. 32). Moreover, if linguistic knowledge, including innate knowledge of universals is propositional, then most certainly there is a commitment to something mighty like Cartesian rationalism. However, I do not think the view that knowledge of language is tacit knowledge *that* can stand up under close scrutiny.

'Tacit knowledge' of rules internalized or stored in the brain seems to me to express a clear enough idea even though it is hardly a part of ordinary ways of talking. But tacit *propositional* knowledge is not. If you have tacit knowledge that such and such are the rules of English, why is it so devilishly hard to elicit them? The true rationalist argues that if you know L you would not always be able correctly to identify a rule of it if it were presented to you. But I think that to say you can have tacit knowledge that R is a rule of L and then to go on and claim you can make a mistake about what you know when it is laid out in front of you is simply incredible. A necessary condition for *knowledge that*, it seems to me, is expressibility, although none of it might ever have been expressed.

Secondly, if competence is knowledge *that* some truth about rules is the case, the rules we learn must be *communal*. As Katz puts it, linguistic communication proposes a *common* system of internalized rules (Katz, 1965, p. 592). I am not certain that this is true as stated but if knowledge is propositional then knowledge of rules must be communal, that is to say, be held in common by everyone fluent in the language. They must have the *same* competence (Chomsky *et al.*, 1974, p. 349). For if not, then members of the speech community must have internalized different systems, whence there is more than one body of knowledge *that* about the same domain. A phenomcnon like this does occur in quantum theory, leading in some quarters to acceptance of a wave-particle duality; but in psycholinguistics the existence of two diverse theories would hardly lend support to rationalism! The problem of course boils down to the meaning of 'same competence'. I don't have anything pat to say about 'same' in this regard, but I have made detailed suggestions elsewhere all of which lead away from the doctrine that grammatical tacit knowledge is propositional. I think a complete review of this line of argument here would lead us too far astray. *Very* briefly if we require that two grammars be point-by-point equivalent in order to count as the same, and if we consider the embodiment of rules to be on the level of organic structures (we employed the term 'networks' earlier with an idealized neuronal network as an example) then there is no *à priori* argument from the nature and success of human communication that requires sameness of competence (Nelson, 1978). Two grammars could be strongly equivalent (but not isomorphic or point-by-point the same), could have incomplete overlap of domain, be embodied in radically different organic structures, and be acquired in radically different environments (so that demands on innate capacity and 'knowledge' of universals would be very different) and still enable the interpersonal linguistic performance that in fact obtains. The conclusion that is suggested by these several observations is that there is individual competence, a proposition entailed by the doctrine of real guiding rules, while there is no call to posit the 'same competence' for all in a sense strong enough to support the idea of propositional knowledge of rules and at the same time account for the empirical data, the facts of language communication. As I emphasized in the referenced article, linguists would go out of their minds if they were to seek a grammar *cum* theory for every person (or for a sufficiently large family of competence-groups of persons). Perhaps all mental science has to be content with the theories that are more or less true for everyone. But to reify any theory as the *one* realized by all, which seems to be required by the knowledge *that* position, is completely unwarranted.

A much stronger argument derives from the idea that linguistic competence underlies skill or ability to perform linguistically. The rules in our collective heads *guide* performance. A realistic logic of mind can explain this common sense intuition about our linguistic acts while a propositional knowledge theory of competence does not. Propositional knowledge does not guide anything. Scientific and mathematical knowledge do not guide behavior except quite indirectly, and conversely, many intelligent behaviors are guided by rules or mechanisms that contain no propositional element whatever. They are more like imperatives or regimens with built in options, as we initially remarked.

The concerns about knowledge of and knowledge that, (7) and (8), arising in this review might be allayed by calling on the notion of an *inner* language, although it is not clear this would apply to other rationalists such as Katz. An acquired language L has instantiations in an inner I-language that corresponds to an outer, community-wide external E-language. An individual learning L acquires the inner I-language which she *has.* "... for P to know L is for P to *have* a certain I-language" (Chomsky, 1968, p. 8, ital. mine). On the other hand knowledge of a universal grammar is knowledge *that* certain rules and principles hold for any possible spoken language. Knowledge *of* is the theoretical concept relevant to languages acquired, and knowledge *that* to universal grammar.

I wish this were as clear as we'd like. Concerning the I-language, Chomsky repeatedly says it *represents* the external E-language of L. The weasel word 'represents' could mean 'stand for', which I take it has no semantical force, but only indicates the system of guiding, generative rules (certainly not the whole generated, infinite corpus); this is the language *had.* Or it could mean the I-language has propositional content; that is to say, 'represents' could mean 'refers'. In my opinion the choice should be settled in favor of 'stand for' since I don't see how an I-language that refers to an E-language could have anything whatever to do with governing speech unless it somehow guides as well.

On the other hand a universal grammar — knowledge that so and so are constraints on possible I-languages — is plausibly propositional and realized in some sort of tacit language.[30] Its range of objects is a set of candidate grammars some of which will never be actualized; they are "inexistent". If this is right the neorationalist is really a rationalist, as he is too happy to insist he is. His theory is in part one of innate rules having a built-in semantics of propositions and in part of a speaker having native intentions, inasmuch as propositional knowledge is a species of (tacit) belief. If propositions are objects of sentences, in agreement with the conventional semantics discussed earlier, there must be a native grammar language (not the I-language) which expresses the propositional content of universal grammar. The language can not be anything like an E-language as the knowledge it represents is tacit.

Thus for Chomsky an adequate theory predicates knowledge of a universal grammar to members of the human species, which is knowledge of *propositions,* linguistic input data, parameters fixed by the data, an acquired spoken E-language used in communication, and a representing I-language which might again be one having tacit propositional content or, on another interpretation, might be a guiding system of rules for the acquired E-language. It would seem there must also be an innate internal language of universal grammar, for reasons just given.

Insistence that this composite linguistic "state" (embodied in a species specific organ-module) will eventually be accountable in strictly biological terms comes down to a demand to accept a somewhat compromising promissory note. The neorationalist can probably get along with recursive rules to deliver an adequate account of syntactical characteristics of spoken languages (to this extent the theory is computational), while the semantical dimension of the theory is speculative indeed.

4. COGNITIVISM

A feature of neorationalism interpreted this way is that it holds the question of what it is that *does* the rule executing open, except for the claim that the working mind/brain, the underlying causal agency, is biological. It also attributes native propositional knowledge to potential speakers as an explanatory hypothesis of language acquisition. One type of cognitivism, perhaps the most influential, can be characterized as an expansion of this theory to all of cognitive science, not limited to psycholonguistics, making explicit the functional view that the underlying agent is a computer and striving for a purely naturalistic, causal explanation of intentions, reference, and meaning. Chomsky himself does allude now and then to the possibility of computer programs emulating performance or even acquisition — suggesting, in a theory of universal grammar, separation of a system of cognized program rules together with input data from a speech community, from an embodied hard-wired mind/brain executive of some sort.

If the latter is an automaton system, what we have is essentially the idea of a free algorithm — the universal grammar — as an embodied algorithm which guides the biological computing agent in acquiring language, using input cues. Of course this is just to draw the picture of a universal turing machine or programmed computer, and I have no business literally to attribute it to Chomsky.

The overall scheme is, however, very much that of Jerry Fodor's cognitivism (1981). According to him, the representational theory of mind (RTM) is concerned with information processing systems realized, as in functional theories, in the brain. He leaves questions of specificis of structure open, although Turing machines provided *canonical languages* for expressing the causal *cum* computational properties of cognitive process. So the cognitive architecture is analogous to that of a programmed computer or universal machine that operates on turing input symbols under the control of an executive driven program. From our point of view this is of course just an FA described so as to have a discriminable tape (see p. 68 above).

In Craikian style, mind is thus to be thought of as processing mental representations (MR's) which are turing symbols having *semantical content* and which comprise a language of thought, *Mentalese,* common to all language speaking communities. Mentalese should be understood as including the internal language of a Chomskyian universal grammar, but certainly not as an I-language, which for Chomsky represents a specific E-language like English. Moreover the RTM language is not merely an internal image of external type languages, but is the vehicle of all thought: problem solving, planning, appraising the attitudes of others, making decisions, formulating sentences, making decisions, evaluating art, contemplating the self, and so forth.

As Fodor often remarks in his writings, MR's are essentially Lockean ideas construed so as to refer to objects of attitudes: they express meanings — propositions and intensions — in Mentalese, and some have reference to natural objects much as names in English or Russian do. The notion of MR comprehends individual concepts like BACH and GOD and universal concepts like HOUSE, DOG, PHILOSOPHY, and propositions like BACH WRITING BACH'S 203rd CHURCH CANTATA and that SENTENCES MUST HAVE NOUN PHRASE AND VERB PHRASE CONSTITUENTS. Note that MR's include representations of inexistents, which supposedly resolves one of the problems posed by Brentano.

This version of cognitivism quite naturally combines with computationalism. Mental features, in particular beliefs, are now identified with computable relations from subjects to MR's, not with states as in primitive functionalism's finite state identity theory (FSIT). The causal network of attitudes — belief, desire, actions, and so on — which FSIT hoped to explain as role-players (p. 121f above) is now to be explained as interwoven relations; and the contents of belief are to be expressed, for the cognitive theorist, as Turing machine symbols *bearing meaning*. These are precisely the MR's. For added emphasis observe that for Fodor and company the notion of information in 'information processor' is *displayed* information in a contentful sense, not just causally *transmitted* information (Fodor, 1986);[31] that cognitions are indeed causally interrelated, but also bearing of meaning; that thoughts have content and are about objects, actual and possible. Cognitivism in this semantical form should, in principle perhaps, meet Searle's (1980) objections to digital computer program theories of the mind that we noted in Chapter IV.[32]

Eventually the semantics of natural language is to be founded on the semantics of Mentalese. Lexical items of English such as 'dog' or 'house' refer according as they are associated to mentalese MR's DOG and HOUSE; and truth conditions of sentences in English derive from those of sentences in Mentalese. The mystery of nonactual propositional contents of dependent clauses like 'that Bach wrote the 203rd cantata' is solved by identification of the content with that of a mental sentence.

So far so good. But what about the semantics of Mentalese itself? What are MR's and where do they come from? They are functional entities under a canonical description and are identical to some brain entities or other. But where does the semantical content come from? Fodor's most recent position is that semantical significance is to be found in a causal theory of mind-world relations (Fodor, 1987).[33]

Very briefly, interpretation of Mentalese symbols, is determined by causal relations to the world. The Mentalese symbol corresponding to the spoken 'water', 'eau', 'wasser', or 'voda' expresses the property H_2O. Precisely how this causal relation is to be analyzed is speculative and controversial. But Fodor is quite definite about its relationship to other issues in RTM, that is, about intentionality and semantics." ... the intentionality of the attitudes reduces to the contents of mental representations. Given a truth definition (for mental sentences – essentially laws of combination of veridical primitive lexical items such as correspond to 'red' and 'ball' to form veridical phrasal items like the MR corresponding to 'red ball'), the content of mental representations is determined by the interpretation of the primitive, non-logical (lexical) vocabulary of Mentalese that's at the bottom of the pile." (1987, Chapt. 4). These interpretations are causal.

In some such wise meaning-bearing MR's arise in cognition; and presumably the theory applies across the board, among other things to Chomsky's mind/brain linguistic state. Mental features including skills and abilities of various kinds are computational relations, and in particular beliefs, desires, etc., are relations to MR's. Mentalese explains meaningful thought and planning, and encodes universal principles of grammar. In short Fodor presents a partially fleshed-out Craikian conception of cognition which in comprehensiveness establishes a very interesting philosophy of mind for all mental features, and a foundation for cognitive science. If his causal psychosemantics program works out, RTM should be able to help pay off the promissory notes issued by neorationalism.

However as it stands cognitivism places an almost unbearable load on a direct causal theory of meaning. If as Fodor says intentionality reduces to contents of representations and if perception is intentional, then perception reduces to content; put in another way, depends on meanings. But this puts the cart before the horse. Take reference. A necessary condition of ostensive Mentalese reference to a cat is to perceive a cat. So to claim a contentful MR must be present as an object of the attitude of perception one has to show that reference is something other than the causal order of object to MR. But this either contradicts RTM or skirts terribly close to one.

Of course Fodor often seems to espouse something akin to an inferential product theory of percepts elsewhere. But either his causal theory is now the official one or he is open to charges of circularity in his theory of MR's. The having of semantical objects for MR's just assumes what one is looking for in semantics of natural language, or assumes little knowers or referers (Dennett, 1978) unless the theory can be invaded using an idea like causal reference.

Setting this opinion aside, the trouble with the direct causal theory is the idea of a free algorithm operating on turing *input* symbols.[34] A program style model is the wrong one, I think; yet cognitivists on the whole assume computation *cum* cognition presupposes interpreted data. Mechanism holds just the opposite. Some interpreted data − a percept, e.g. − is the *result* of a process guided by an embodied algorithm.

The mechanist claim must be then, that computation, at least perception is *syntactical*; intentionality of perception must be found not in a semantically antecedent MR but in the processes of mind; in perception, anyway, MR's must be *products* of computations − outputs, not inputs; and semantics of natural language must be grounded in a theory of intentionality not the other way around.[35] Finally, intentions must be individuated in terms of computations (rule systems), not in terms of mental objects. The following chapters develop this idea in great detail.

CHAPTER VI

THE LOGIC OF ACCEPTANCE

According to the naturalist philosophy I pursue, perception is a relation between objects and a perceiving organism. This relation falls within the domain of ordinary science; and epistemology, having no prior claim on the subject, occupies no especially privileged vantage-point. I reject the old empiricist view that one can not use ordinary observation and theorizing in order to understand perception and that correct philosophy demands a grounding in pre-scientific principle.[1] For any one bred into the tradition of the 'problem of empiricism' — how do you get from phenomenal objects to the real thing? — this view may be hard to take, and my use of 'perception' misleading; but then the tradition has no corner on the commodity. We do not have to burden ourselves with a model in which "there is immured in a windowless cell a prisoner, who has lived in solitary confinement since birth. All that comes to him from the outside world is flickers of light thrown upon his cell walls and tappings heard through the stones; yet from these observed flashes and tappings he becomes, or seems to become, appraised of unobserved football matches, flower gardens and eclipses of the sun" (Ryle, 1949, p. 223). Instead, using the objective approach, I will try to show how some of the puzzles, such as the separation of private subject and outer thing that give rise to the problem of empiricism, originate.

I do not claim that the following reflections add up to a complete theory. The aim is narrower and perhaps can best be steadied by back-reference to my views on models. In this chapter and the next two a model is used to show how a mechanist approach can deal with problems of perception and belief. A model provides an argument for philosophy as much as it offers a tentative venture into scientific theory. The idea is to set out certain key problems, here of perception, in the form of conditions. For example a model should offer a 'solution' to the problem of perceiving a universal in a particular — a token in a type, in contemporary jargon. If the model entails that universals can be grasped in instances by minds having a certain recursive logic, it is adequate and in so far forth shows mechanism's plausibility as a framework hypothesis. A bonus of the exercise might be that the model is in some respects close to a true theory. But the main point is to construct an automaton model that satisfies an array of conditions that have been isolated as important by both epistemologists and psychologists. These conditions are set forth in Section 1.

In outline the theory can be briefly sketched out as follows. There is a physical object, the *perceptual object*, that the organism (the 'perceiver') processes. This object acts on the perceiver and produces a surface irritation which her *reception* system works on to yield a *stimulus pattern*. This pattern, which is composed of *stimuli*, is either *accepted* by the perceiver as a *type* τ in virtue of the perceiver assuming a *perceptual state*, or is *rejected*. If the perceptual object is indeed a τ and the perceiver accepts, then I will say that the organism *perceives* it.[2] It is possible that the perceiver accept the object as a τ while it is in fact not a τ or reject it as a τ when in reality it is a τ. A pattern type, τ, is an observable or *sensible* physical property which the perceptual object instantiates. The object is the 'cause' of the stimulus. The concepts *perceptual object, type*, and *cause* should be take at the moment in a vague, ordinary way without any special philosophical credentials. We will not use these ideas officially until they are given passports: and in the meanwhile 'token' and type' are used ambiguously for objects and stimuli or stimulus patterns. Again, I will frequently write of 'perception' and 'perceptually' in a pre-analytic sense − the official expression in this section is 'acceptance', which is a kind of map from stimulus pattern to perceptual state as detailed below in Section 2.

The logic of perception includes an analysis of *expectation*, a most basic intentional feature of mental life. It is in terms of this trait that I try to account for the perceiver's ability correctly (and sometime incorrectly) to recognize indistinct, shaded, lost, and even inexistential objects. Then I identify (Chapter VIII) fulfilled expectation with tacit *perceptual belief*, and ordinary expressible perceptual belief ('I see a cat') with a pair consisting of that belief and the expressing sentence. Perceptual belief is related to desire, which is separately characterized, again in terms of expectation. Knowledge is *evidenced* belief à la Plato's *Theatetus*, and I face up here to Gettier examples. Finally, the objects of belief, the perceptual object and the propositional object land us squarely in the midst of problems of meaning (Chapter X). Roughly the idea will be that intentionality and meaning are already present in the activities of an organism capable of 'tacit' belief and desire, and that the meanings of linguistic entities are derivative − they are the meanings of the underlying cognitive processes language 'expresses'. In twentieth century idiom, it makes semantics depend on pragmatics − the theory of the sign user. In classical thought it makes language meaningful in virtue of its dependency on antecedent perceptions, beliefs, and cognitions of the speaker-listener.

1. UNIVERSALS, GESTALTEN, AND TAKING

All the knowledge we shall ever get enters through the senses and exits in actions that enable us to cope with our surroundings. This basic pragmatist premise stands behind all theories of a naturalist stripe and motivates slogans such as "belief is a disposition to act" or "perception is a disposition to act". Combined with the idea that dispositions are rule systems, naturalism projects the following picture: perception, belief, and other mental features somehow involve underlying automata that process input stimulations and generate responses. The fact that automata are *active* in the sense that they respond to the same thing differently at different times, depending on past histories (unlike the passive intervening variable model of behaviorism) makes it likely *à priori* that what counts as a stimulus to an organism with a specific make-up depends in an essential way on how it is able to act. Dependence of stimuli on the organism and its repertoire of response movements appears to be of two kinds, one related to reception, or the definition of stimuli, and the other to perception, or operations on stimuli (cf. Quine, 1973, pp. 16 ff.). In terms of automaton formalities for model construction, reception is *constitutive* of stimuli or input symbols $s_0, s_1, \ldots, s_m$, whereas perception presupposes stimulus patterns (sequences of stimuli, denoted as usual by 'x') in an *inferential process* (a computation of a sort) that places the organism in certain mental states.

Let us dispose of reception rather quickly here giving it enough attention to furnish a background for model construction of perception and at the same time acknowledging some important problems that once seen can be relegated to the neuroscientist. In automaton modeling we want to take the inputs as *given* (with some notable exceptions we will make) and not as problematic.[3]

The constitutive character of reception is borne out by modern neuro-physiological research. Eye movement in a frog is very restricted and occurs only as compensatory response to gross body-movements; frogs can not visually track their prey as many other organisms can. Detectors in the visual apparatus of the frog thus respond to stimulus patterns of a limited variety — e.g., sharp, convex, moving boundaries between contrasting grey fields — and ignore or 'throw away' the rest (Lettvin et al., 1959). This is a clear indication that visual sensing in organisms is a function of behavioral capability; and the observation is general; it holds for other sense modalities *and* for other things than frogs and cats.[4]

Thus some of the problems that trouble computer scientists who attempt to simulate human perception or 'pattern recognition', as they term it, do not trouble the organism, who imposes innate delimiters on receptive fields to make the elements fit for perception. There is a built-in pre-processing. A computer's input must be carefully prepared while in contrast a woman continuously exposed to a welter of data can abstract relevant patterns from it.[5] She can spot a melody in the clamorous ambience of a party — a modulated sine wave in noise — or a sharp line in a blurry field of dots. The receiver's ability to isolate interesting stuff is at one with her "prior tendency to weight qualitative differences unequally" (Quine, 1960, p. 83). A child, Quine remarks, is amenable to linguistic training, to respond verbally in the right way to stimuli and reinforcements only if she already has a built-in "pre-linguistic quality space". She must be able to classify things in similarity classes in order to be trainable by reinforcement. And to accomplish that she must have a built-in filter that cuts out the trash that is irrelevant to what she is equipped to respond to. Just as the frog's neural anatomy determines four basic similarity or equivalence classes of stimulations it can respond to, so the child has perhaps untold thousands of similarity classes of stimulations; it heeds those of one class uniformly (given a fixed state). These equivalence classes of stimulations are *stimuli*, and correspond to our automaton s-symbols or symbols elements.[6] I hope the reader will keep in mind that the s's themselves are (classes of) vectors of stimulus elements. The stimulus can have many components. Further, a stimulus pattern (a sequence of stimuli in most of our models) is a composite of vectorial composites — which is quite a complex article. For our purpose we need rarely descend from abstract automata to the network structural level, however.[7]

Anything not in a receptual class is meaningless to perception unless the organism *takes* the thing to be in a class at the perceptual level. But this phenomenon, which I'll treat of in detail in due course, is not receptual. Fuzzy stuff that the innate filters fail to cut out probably does not stimulate the frog at all; it goes by. But perception in higher organisms can *take* fuzzy items to be of a type due to context, interests, intentions, and purposes. If Jones *knows* a melody and hears it sung out of tune, she still recognizes it as that melody or close to it. If she doesn't know any tune that resembles what is sung then of course her filters relegate it to the nonstatus of disposable noise.

Before dropping reception it is important to recall the place of attention. In computer circles a particularly recalcitrant problem for simulation of perception arises in *scene analysis*. This is not the same problem as stimulus constitution, but rather one of focus on the *significant* perceptual pattern among many that are all defined. Read the county names scattered throughout the welter of road markings, route numbers, town designations, etc. on the map of a state. This operation is almost impossible to program, but is fairly easy for *you* once you get the hang of what to look for and how to look. The knack of performing this task is a receptual or pre-processing skill and appears to depend on the ability to focus attention selectively on different items according to one's ends. Perception also presupposes attention, and although it is not a problem for mechanism (it is similar to pulling out a subroutine for use in a main computer program, or for circuitry gating in a subprocessor), I mention it here only to complete my sketch of what reception is responsible for, not to set up an issue for settlement.

The outcome of receptual pre-processing corresponds roughly to the epistemic primitives of modern philosophy, but more distally situated, closer to the surface of the body and strictly a physical complex. It is an *automaton* input in virtue of a description that relates it to state and outputs. Just where the stimulus figures in the logic of perception will be naturally determined as the model is developed. We shall see that it must be distinguished from both perceptual objects, the 'real thing' that 'causes' perception, and perceptual states. Anatomically the stimulus must be inward from raw irritation as it is, as we have just observed, the result of construction during reception. It is hard to see how to fit Lockean ideas into the scheme, but we will try when we rummage through that miscellaney of raw feels, sentience, datable thoughts, and the like in Chapter XI.

Now to perception proper. An adequate theory or model must show how perception is related to belief, desire, and action. But for the present we may safely abstract from all such considerations in favor of an analysis of the path from stimulus to a perceptual *state*. Then later on that analysis can be fitted in to a more complete one including perceptual objects, propositions, beliefs, wants and overt behaviors. So using the NFA model our object of study is the M relation of an automaton T, a relation of the pairs (q, s) to q' where q is interpreted to be an initial state (of a *subautomaton*) and s is a prepared stimulus. q' is interpreted to mean an internal mental state, a *perceptual state*.[8] The transition function M is a perceptual relation or, more properly, the *accepting* component of the relation.

What conditions must an automaton T with M relation satisfy to count as *perception*? First, perception reduces the 'manifold of experience' to unity. How, Aristotle asked, "is it possible to obtain knowledge of an infinite collection of individuals if there is nothing apart from individual things?" All things we know we must come to know by some unity and identity and "insofar as some attribute belongs to them universally" (*Metaphysics*, 4.99a 25–31). This condition means T, which models the perceptual link, must be able to assign *types* to *tokens*, universals to particulars, and must be able to accomplish this feat over a potentially infinite domain.

There are two parts to this condition. If T can perceive an apple as an apple, it must be able to do so for *any* apple, even fringy ones, red ones, sour ones, green ones, and so forth; and it must be able to discriminate among apples, pears, peaches, wax apples, pictures of pears, and so forth. It must assign types from among many types over a very large domain. Let us call this condition the *condition of universality and discrimination*.

Second, a person on some occasions perceives any member of a collection of individuals as coming under a type τ and on others under a different type τ'. Typal variation is one aspect of *gestalt* perception. Consider the set of Necker cubes, an instance of which we see in the familiar figure below. One way of looking at it puts the cube under type τ: face *abcd* to the front in a two dimensional projection. Another way puts it under type τ': $a'b'c'd'$ to the front. All two dimensional cubic projections fall under *two* types depending on the perceiver's way of looking at them (which for the most part is not under conscious control).

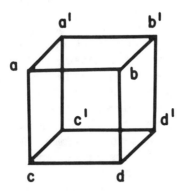

Fig. 1. Necker Cube.

A similar phenomenon can be found in the auditory world, but usually in somewhat untidy though more delightful form. Let the reader consider

Pousse y gâte, pousse y gâte
Et Arabe, yeux bine?
A ben, tout l'on donne
Toluca de couenne.
Pousse y gâte, pousse y gâte,
Oh, a dit Dieu d'hère?
Y fraternelle Lydie Moïse,
Honneur de chair. [9]

Let us call this condition the *one-token-many-type* condition. Any model of perception must provide for *T*'s that can perceive a token under many types.

If the reader has not already thought of it himself, it is worth noting that this variety of gestalt phenomenon completely rules out any theory that construes perception as a *function* or a *map* from stimulus object to state; objects do not map to one state. For example, a standard approach to pattern recognition (i.e., perception) in artificial intelligence circles is to consider the perceptual field to be represented by a *d*-dimensional Euclidean space. Every pattern (for us, type) is an open region in this space, and individual instances thereof are *d*-dimensional vectors in the region. The regions corresponding to patterns are non-overlapping and the boundaries count as external to all regions. In this model perception is essentially a map from the regionalized space into a set of 'category numbers' that represent the type of each specific region. [10] A little reflection shows that this scheme can not in itself model the two-dimensional Necker Cube phenomenon, nor can any other mapping scheme. Condition II can be read simply to say that the perception model must be *relational*.

Third, human beings are able to perceive one and the same type in totally different sets of tokens. This property of perception is a kind of opposite to the *one-token-many-type* property just embodied in our second condition. This is also a Gestalt type phenomenon. The nicest examples come from music. A musical (but perhaps not too musical!) ear can recognize the C Major Fugue of the second volume of the *Well-Tempered Clavier* when it is played in E major by a brass choir. The phenomenon is harder to detect in pictures as visual characteristics seem to be preserved intact under geometrical, but not qualitative, transformations. Pictures retain many of their intrinsic esthetic properties when they are blown-up, rotated, displaced over their backgrounds, or are homeomorphically transformed (pretty much), but not when their colors are permuted. Do you get the *same* Arles scene when you interchange the blues and yellows in a Van Gogh? Similar visual type-assignments, it seems, are frequently made on rather abstract structural features more than on material quality. At any rate, there must be some automata able to perceive the elements of a single type from any one of several disjoint sets of tokens.

Let us call the condition to be satisfied arising from this phenomenon the *one-type-many-token* condition. *Caution*: this condition, though perhaps superficially similar to, is not to be confounded with, *universality* and *discrimination*. In the Bach example, universality and discrimination simply means a good model should be able to tell the difference between the C Major Fugue in Volume II of the *Well-Tempered Clavier* and that of Volume I and should, in other words and more generally, identify all and only renditions of the first when it 'hears' them, whether deriving from an Altnikol, Kirnberger or other manuscript. However, using the same example, *one-type-many-token* means that the same perception rules apply to different *acoustical primitives* – here different keys and instrumental timbres. The universality condition says any token of a set goes to a type. The third condition says there is a *family of disjoint sets*, and one and the same type is the type for each set of the family. Of course the partitioning into disjoint sets is made modulo some characteristic such as key. Renditions of the Bach in C, D, E^b, etc. induce separate receptual clauses of the same type. In a sense the universality and type-token conditions are quite the same, but the considerations leading to adequate models for the two conditions are conceptually very different. The issues intimated here will come in for more thought in the sequel.

Fourth, there are perceptual episodes in which a true perceiver can correctly assign a token to a type even though the individuating properties are *degraded*. The phenomenon corresponds to that of grasping verbal meanings pretty well even in vague utterance. For our purposes better examples would be perceiving faces in cubist concoctions, hearing melodies in cocktail lounges or supermarket Muzak. Consider Goodman's mark which vaguely belongs both to type *d* and to *a* of a notation (Goodman, 1968, p. 133 f.). Let us suppose an organism's quality

Figure 2

space consists of similarity classes of *d*'s and *a*'s along with the rest of the English alphabet. Strictly speaking Figure 2 falls into no class, i.e., it is partly degraded, although it is vaguely a *d* or an *a*. Now we guessed earlier that any thing as simple as a frog would simply throw Figure 2 out as trash. But more elaborate animals can transcend the tight categories of their receptually defined stimuli. Anyone of us, for example, would immediately *take* the second mark from the left in Figure 3 to be '*a*' and the third mark in Figure 4 to '*d*'. These takings, I claim, would be correct if the intentions

bɑ́d   baɑ́

Figure 3    Figure 4

of the writer of the two strings of inscription are what I think they are, namely to write 'bad' in each case.

The condition this leads to will be called a *taking condition*. Any model *T*, to meet it, must be able to filter the perceivable stuff out of the very bad or degraded or, as I shall say introducing a technical term, must be able to *take* degraded input to be other than it is and to be in some sense *correct* in doing so.

These four conditions arise from consideration of psychological facts. People do assign types to tokens − perceive universals in things − , do see more than one picture in a scene, hear the same melody in different keys, and take fuzzy things to be good, sometimes mistakenly. Any theory must account for these facts, and a model must at least meet the adequacy conditions while yet it might not be literally true of the mind. To show that Gestalt perception is possible for a recursive system is not the same as giving a true theory, although one might hope for glimpses of one.

For later reference I list the four conditions here:

I.   *Universality* and *Discrimination*. A model must assign types to tokens over an indefinitely large domain.

II.   *One-Token-Many-Type*. A model should provide for assigning a set of tokens to more than one type. The model must be relational, not functional.

III. *One-Type-Many-Tokens*. The model should provide for many distinct sets of tokens sharing a single type.

IV.   *Taking*. The model must be able to take input outside the given receptual categorization and assign a type under certain circumstances of context.

There are fundamental problems about development of perceptual capacities and about their working synthesis in the economy of the mind. But the emphasis here will remain on the in principle plausibility of accounts of I–IV separately with scattered comments here and there about these properly psycho-neurobiological integrative and global problems.

2. ACCEPTANCE

We begin by constructing automata that meet condition I and work upward to ever greater complexity. We suppose that the s-symbols refer to (are interpreted as) received stimuli and variables x, y, etc., which are strings of s's standing for stimulus patterns or pattern *tokens*.

A *finite state acceptor* (FSA) is a finite system of rules of the form

$$qs \rightarrow q' \tag{1}$$

where as usual the q's are states and the s's inputs. A subset of the q-symbols is called the set of *final* or *perceptual* states, and a certain symbol q_0 is the *initial* state. If a restriction is added that no two rules may have the same pair of symbols q, s on the left, the acceptor is *deterministic*, or otherwise *nondeterministic* (NFSA). A simple example of a nondeterministic acceptor appears in II (3). For the time being we will develop the model using FSA.

For all kinds of reasons it is easier to treat systems of FSA rules set-theoretically. In this form an FSA is a system $T = \langle S, Q, q_0, M, Q_F \rangle$ where S is the set of s-symbols; Q of the q-symbols; q_0 the initial state; M the transition function which is defined from the rules (1) and presented in the now familiar tables; and Q_F is the set of final states, where $Q_F \subseteq Q$.

An FSA is just an FA deprived of its output and extended by designating certain states to be final. We suppose as in formulas III (1a) that M is extended from arguments like (q, s) to (q, x) where x is a string of S^*, the set of all finite length strings made up of symbols of S.

T *accepts* x, if and only if $M(q_o, x)$ is an element of the set of final states Q_F, i.e., $M(q_0, x) \in Q_F$. $\tag{2}$

An acceptor T corresponds to a stimulus pattern type: indeed it is easy to see that every T determines a set $\mathcal{U}_T$ of strings that it accepts; and conversely every set $S^+ \subseteq S^*$ of a certain family, of regular sets (see Section II.4), is the set accepted by some T: there is a T, in other words, such that $S^+ = \mathcal{U}_T$. Essentially an acceptor divides all the strings of S^* into two subsets, those *accepted* and those *rejected*. The rejected set of T is $\overline{\mathcal{U}}_T$, the complement of $\mathcal{U}_T$, and, quite obviously, for every rejected set $\overline{\mathcal{U}}_T$, of T there is an automaton $\overline{T} = \langle S, Q, q_0, M, \overline{Q}_F \rangle$ that accepts the set $\mathcal{U}_{\overline{T}}$. $\overline{T}$ differs from T in just the respect that its final state set is the logical complement of Q_F of T.

An acceptor thus in effect serves as a characteristic function on the domain S^*. Technically the subsets in the dichotomy $\mathcal{U}_T$, $\mathcal{U}_{\overline{T}}$ are *recursive* sets, and the acceptor is the embodiment of a decision procedure for membership in $\mathcal{U}_T$ (or $\mathcal{U}_{\overline{T}}$ in the opposite case). It was, of course, the concept of a decision procedure that led to this model.

For full Turing machines the situation is much more complex. Some sets $S^+ \subseteq S^*$ are such that there exists a Turing machine that *accepts* S^+, whereas there is *no* machine that accepts $\overline{S}^+$. The machine will scan back and forth across a string, but never go into a final state; it can't make out what the thing is (Nelson, 1968, pp. 121–122). Further on we will also use this more general concept of acceptor. These ideas are quite close to basics already discussed in Chapter II; but if they are not crystal clear to him the reader is encouraged to sharpen them in terms of the following example.

Let us suppose Jones likes a very simple melody which her auricular reception system converts from continuous sound wave patterns to digital sequences in time. Let the melody pattern type be '*Air in X*', which is a property of certain acoustical complexes and not of any others. Further, suppose a play of the melody generates, via conversion, digital sequences consisting of stimuli $s_0 = 0$ and $s_1 = 1$ such that 1's occur in *contiguous pairs* only. *Air in X* is *very* plain and not particularly listenable; but Jones is musically naive and her needs are easily satisfied. The example is just right for illustrating principles.

Each such sequence of the kind described corresponds 1–1 to a play of the *Air*, and the set of plays is infinite. 11, 011, 0110, 0011011, etc. are all patterns in the set, while 00, 01, 0111, 01, etc. constitute non-Air-in-X strings.

An FSA T that accepts this set appears in the next figure.

TABLE I

A finite acceptor for 'Air in X'.

| | M | |
	0	1
q_0	q_0	q_1
q_1	q_4	q_2
q_2	q_3	q_4
q_3	q_3	q_1
q_4	q_4	q_4

q_0 = *initial state*
q_2, q_3 = *final states*

It is easy to prove about T that all the strings x such that $M(q_0, x) \in \{q_2, q_3\}$ are precisely the ones that correspond to plays of the Air in X. For suppose a string x begins with a head of y 0's; then $M(q_0, 000 \ldots) = q_0$ is easily verified; if this block of y 0's is followed by exactly two 1's, then $M(q_0, y11)$ = q_2 by the table; if this is followed by another block of 0's, z, of arbitrary but finite length, then $M(q_0, y11z) = q_3$; then tack on another pair 11 and see that $M(q_0, y11z11) = q_2$; and so on. As q_2, q_3 are both final, *any* such string (got by varying the x and y) is accepted. Hence the set of such strings $\mathcal{U}_T$ is the stimulus version of the Air, and q_2, q_3 of T are *perceptual* states. T goes to such a state if and only if the Air is played. T is an '*Air in X*' automaton corresponding to that type of acoustical pattern. Perhaps the reader recalls our discussion of a version of functionalism, FSIT, that seeks to correlate mental states with automaton states 1–1. One of the reasons this is wrong is exemplified by Jones' *Air in X* acceptor. Either of *two* automaton states corresponds to (is) a perceptual state.

As I said, there is a T for any family of sets of a certain rather restricted kind. Now let us consider any set of observations (tokens) of a visual scene, playings of a tune, etc. that instance observable physical properties. If these properties, whether visual, auditory, olfactory, etc., are *effective*, that is to say are graspable or perceivable by step-by-step operations then there always exists a Turing machine that will accept digital encodings of the instance. (The definition of a full Turing accepter is not difficult, but it is preferable to deal with simpler automata). Each such accepting machine in effect reduces an infinite aggregate of instances of a physically observable kind to a final, perceptual state, *viz.* to a kind of unity. A realized automaton of this kind plays the same epistemic role as the *intellectus agens* of medieval philosophy and its product is the *intelligible species*. Thus Turing automata, assuming the mechanist hypothesis that perception is effective, satisfy the *universality* condition.

An FSA such as T also discriminates, but not much. Jones doesn't have much going for her if all she can discriminate is the *Air in X* from everything else. In order to approach her true capabilities we therefore consider for each sense modality a product of many automata. Switching the example to just the visual properties of fruit, Jones can tell apples from pears, pears from oranges, and so on for n kinds of fruit. On the other hand she can only tell the *Air in X* from *Three Blind Mice* owing to her extremely low musical tastes and sensitivities, and all other tunes fall into her musical *omnium gatherum*.

The model for n discriminable types consists of n FSA organized in a single *product* or *parallel* automaton which can be deplicted as in the next figure. A stimulus pattern processed by the reception system enters the accepter, which is a product of n FSA T_i, $i = 1, \ldots, n$. Each one computes its M_i function in a manner exactly as in the case of a single T, and each of the T_i assume final states $q^i{}_F$ indicating acceptance of the stimulus token as a type. This situation can be handled set-theoretically, but with not much benefit here except

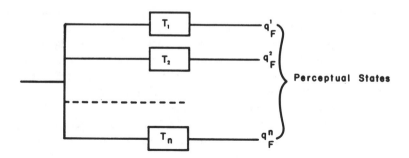

Fig. 5. Parallel automaton

to see better what is being constructed into the model operationally and to see its limitations. $T_1, \ldots, T_n$ are the *components* of the product T. Each T_i is a structure $\langle S, Q^i, q^i{}_0, M^i, Q^i{}_F \rangle$. T itself is $\langle S, Q, q_0, M, Q_F \rangle = T_1 \times \ldots \times T_n$ where S is fixed (one sense modality, say), $Q = Q^1 \times Q^2 \ldots \times Q^n$, $q_0 = (q^1_0, q^2_0, \ldots, q^n_0)$, and similarly for Q_F; $M(q, s) = (M^1(q^1, s), M^2(q^2, s), \ldots M^n(q^n, s))$ (Nelson, 1968, p. 187 f.). When s is extended to sequences (stimulus patterns) we assume the components of $M(q, x)$ compute in the same time. For FSA this assumption presents no problem, although it will when we come to condition IV.

To illustrate for $n = 2$ consider Table II which I'll call T'.

TABLE II
Alternating acceptor.

	$M_{T'}$	
	0	1
q_0'	q_1'	q_2'
q_1'	q_2'	q_3'
q_2'	q_2'	q_2'
q_3'	q_1'	q_2'

$q_0' = $ initial state
$q_1', q_3' = $ final states

This automaton accepts just those strings on $\{0, 1\}$ instantiating the pattern: begin with 0 and then alternate 0's and 1's; e.g., 0, 01, 010, 0101, etc. Now let us turn our attention to the product of T (Table I) and T'. It would be arduous and senseless actually to write down the direct product machine table (20 states), as we may easily see how things come out by running computations together. Note that M_T is the transition function of T and $M_{T'}$ of T'.

Consider $x = 010$. A parallel computation (you do one, and a friend the other, simultaneously) yields, using III (1a), $M_T(q_0, 010) = q_4$, not final; and $M_{T'}(q_0', 010) = q_1'$, final; hence as q_1' is final for T' while q_4 is not for T, 010 is correctly 'perceived' to be an instance of the pattern-type alternating 0's and 1's.

This kind of construction entails by a straight forward argument that automaton models are available that *discriminate*, completing the demonstration of the full condition I. Of course there is nothing in the construction that prevents one string from being of many types.

Models that satisfy Condition I have rather gross limitations. They presuppose no ambiguities amongst the stimuli S; but this is a consequence of the assumption that all receivers, like frogs, divide their quality spaces (per each modality) into disjoint classes of stimuli. This limitation will be lifted in considering Condition IV. Likewise it assumes simultaneity of the parallel computational steps, as just exemplified. This limitation, too, will be lifted — and quite easily, simply by permitting delays, when we come to IV.

The product construction represents truly *parallel* operation in one of the senses we pulled out of the ambiguous concept 'parallel operation' in our criticism of functionalism in Chapter V. However, each automaton component of a product operates serially by symbol, i.e., sequentially. Such a model fits music pretty well, hence the banal Air; but it doesn't seem to fit cases wherein one perceives something *qua* type at one swoop or zap. My own introspection tells me that I perceive the cup on my desk as a cup *instanter*, although to verbalize my ensuing belief takes some time; it is again a sequential act. But assuming my intuitions, which most others seem to share, are right we may incorporate parallel acceptance into the model by assuming our anatomy is such in the cube or picture case as to compute the recursive nestings implicit in an expression like $M(q, x)$, x a string, *virtually at once*. This is hardly a theory of zap perception. But the device (ruse?) of construing 'parallel' operation of this type as extremely fast in comparison to 'sequential' operations will do for us, and reduces one problem to another — here by timing. Incidentally this can not be entirely wrong as most certainly the excitation of ganglion cells from the reception of retinal images followed by pulses down the optic nerve (to take a stock example of parallelism) and onto the occiptal lobes takes *time*.

Gestalt psychologists will object to that property of our model which makes acceptance of an object as a type a process of 'running down a list' and checking off those parts essential to a whole. Perception, they say, is not attained by marking typical part-wise features of wholes but by a kind of total grasp of the intrinsic nature of the thing.

There are wholes, the behavior of which, is not determined by that of their individual elements, but where the processes are themselves determined by the nature of the whole (Wertheimer, 1944, p. 78–79).

So far the objection is on target. If one counts, properly I think, *s*-symbols as parts and strings as wholes, then perception of a whole as a type *does* come down to checking off characterizing traits and the model fails to accommodate one aspect of gestalt perception.

Another objection worth mentioning is that the positing of an automaton for each kind of fruit is 'unrealistic'. I fail to see how any one could know this much in view of the rather limited scope of existing psychology and neuroscience. It can hardly be an objection to mechanism as such. But the concept *is* somewhat inelegant, and as a sop to the critic, let me remark that many automaton functions can be embodied in complex networks that enjoy no 1—1 correspondence of net parts to discernible automaton behavior (remember the adder-subtractor of Figure III.2). A multiplicity of component automata of a system entails almost nothing whatever about net structures. For instance, some strings are *parts* of others and consequently *one* automaton can comprise several acceptors depending only on how final states are assigned. Table I, for instance, altered simply by designating q_4 a final state along with q_0, q_2, and q_3 is an acceptor for recognizing all strings containing at least one occurrence of a 1 in it. You can distinguish between the two acceptances by mapping q_0, q_2, and q_3 via an *or* switch to a symbol α meaning type: contiguous occurrences of 1's; and q_0, q_2, q_3, and q_4 via an *or* switch to a symbol β meaning type: at least one occurrence of a 1. Of course β will occur whenever α does but not vice versa as β indicates the accepted string is a part of a kind indicated by α. Again, you obtain different acceptors, in general, by redesgnating *initial* states. In Table II, if you designate q_1' initial, you get an FSA that accepts just those strings alternating in 1's that begin with 1, not 0 (as in the case wherein q_0' is chosen as initial). Also an FSA beginning always in q_2' accepts any string on 0 and 1 whatever. At the present time, so far as I know, there is no very developed theory of part-whole automata; but clearly the possibilities for many behaviors being contained in one relatively simple structure are almost endless. An ability to discriminate perceptually among a billion types (if that is at all reasonable) does not imply the existence of billions of little separate organs in the nervous system, although on my model it does imply a billion discriminable abstract automata.[11]

I want to give very brief attention to two other matters that bear on the receptual and perceptual definition of a type.

In automata theory it is shown that if T_1, T_2, etc. are FSA corresponding to pattern types, $\mathcal{U}_{T_1}$ and $\mathcal{U}_{T_2}$, then there is an automaton $T_1 \cup T_2$, which is the union of T_1 and T_2 and which accepts just the strings of the collection $\mathcal{U}_{T_1} \cup \mathcal{U}_{T_2}$. Since there is an automaton that accepts the set-theoretic complement of $\mathcal{U}_T$ for any T, it follows that the set J of all the subsets of S^* accepted by FSA comprise a boolean algebra (Nelson, 1968, p. 293 f.). In less abstract terms what this means is that if a subject can tell an apple when she sees one and a pear when she sees one, she *might* also perceive the type nonapples and nonpears, the *type* pear-or-apple, the null type pear-and-apple and so forth. Then again she might *not*, depending, if Piaget is right, on how old she is (12—14), and whether, given the right age, she has acquired the appropriate network embodiments of the respective automata (Piaget and May, 1957, Chapter III). If all this is correct (I do not know that it is) then some elementary logic operations already obtain logically prior to language acquisition in perception. I suppose perceptual capability can and possibly has been inculcated in subjects by simple reinforcement. Of course *after* learning language and logic these operations become central to thought and conception.

The converse might also hold true. A rather extreme form of Whorfian theory might establish that both conceptual and *perceptual* structures are influenced by language. If so, linguistic practices influence what is seen and heard. It is a commonplace observation that laboratory scientists must be trained to perceive patterns in X-rays, and that only trained musicians (or listeners) can hear complex harmonies or contrapuntal patterns. And training in these skills entails prior acquisition of a linguistic sophistication and a technology or, in the second example, the ability to express musical theories and principles. I do not know whether these are strictly perceptual, conceptual, linguistic, or mixed phenomena. At any rate the *genesis* of perceptual capability is no area for much philosophical speculation. I am claiming that what skills we have can be adequately modeled by automata, and can only express a rather vague hypothesis that perceptual facility, if it is not entirely native, is acquired by strictly mechanistic means.

Finally the model, so far, is neutral on the question of mixed sense modalities. Does one 'directly' perceive a sour green apple or are sourness and green appleness associated at some 'higher level'? In our terms are there automata whose primitive symbols include elements (stimulus components) of modally different alphabets? Quite obviously this presents no theoretical difficulties; we take the union S of S' (visual, say) and S'' (gustatory) and generate mixed sequences $(S' \cup S'')^*$. Then for every recursive set in this ensemble there exists an accepting Turing machine. Whether organisms instantiate such things is the question. No one has the slightest idea whether such structures are realized on the perceptual level we are talking about. The 'higher level' operation would presumably entail some kind of 'conceptual' synthesis; or, oppositely, the division of sour from green might be the result of conceptual analysis, grounded in linguistic usage, of an essentially unified perception. It might be of interest to construct the several indicated models in some detail, thereby suggesting useful lines of investigation. But this is clearly more appropriate to psychology or artificial intelligence than it is to philosophy.

Condition II. The condition should be read as meaning 'one *set* of tokens' in as much as it is completely trivial that one stimulus pattern say of a globe-shaped apple, is an instance of a globe and of an apple. Similarly the string

11 is a token of type: all 1's occur in continguous pairs; and of type: at least one occurrence of a 1. The problem to be faced, rather, is automaton acceptance of *one set* in two ways. More precisely, is it possible that there be one set instantiating two distinct pattern types, such as the set of Necker cubes, each type being accepted by distinct automata, one that accepts one type and the other the other? If the accepted set $\mathcal{U}_T$ is of type τ and $\mathcal{U}_{T'}$ of type τ' and $\mathcal{U}_T = \mathcal{U}_{T'}$, then can it be that $T \neq T'$? The question, although it helps locate condition II in our philosophical scheme of things, is unclear as it stands. What is meant by 'distinct type' or 'distinct observable physical property' and 'distinct automaton'? In Chapter III we did get a line on *same automata*, one explication being *same behavior* and the other *same structure*, but neither one provides exactly the right idea for approaching the condition II problem. We will end-up a few paragraphs on using the idea of *same recursive function* in a somewhat unobvious way.

We're worse off with 'same property type'. How are sensible (here stimulus) properties individuated? If there were an answer to this available we could then also settle the question of automaton types: two acceptors would be the same type if they accepted the same pattern. Let us see briefly that this approach goes nowhere and that a far more fruitful idea is to characterize *same property type* in terms of *same acceptors*.

Try: two types τ, τ' are the same if they determine the same tokens. But this simply ignores the problem posed by condition II. An equally unsatisfactory dodge is to engage in 'semantic ascent' and try: τ and τ' are the same if the predicates P, P', of some language L, that designate τ and τ' have the same extension. Then there is a Carnapian way: τ and τ' are the same if their designating predicates are L-equivalent (Carnap, 1956a, p. 18). Besides the well-known difficulties surrounding any known theory of meaning of a Carnapian type, a semantical approach relativizes a question of perceivable properties to a specific language. It is at least conceivable that two individuals perceive disparate patterns in one set of tokens while making no corresponding intensional distinctions in ordinary language whatever.

The opposite approach, which is the one I will take, is to count stimulus types as distinct if they are not recognized in the same way; then we can show that condition II is satisfied by demonstrating the existence of automata that accept the same sets in different ways. This reduces the puzzle to obtaining a suitable analysis of 'same way'. We can eliminate immediately any analysis that makes 'same way' depend on hunting for 'same features' of a pattern, as that route leads straight back to the puzzles about 'same property' we have eschewed. Also if 'same way' means 'same structure' we seem to

get nowhere. The proposal implied by taking 'same way' to mean 'same structure' is to reduce the question to that of a homomorphism. If two acceptors
are homomorphic, one to the other, then they accept the same patterns. However, it is easy to construct two Turing acceptors that are not homomorphic
but that differ very minutely in their computations – one taking an extra
vacuous step to the left at a certain point, while the other not. Anyone's
intuition would boggle at the proposal that two such automata significantly
discriminate dissimilar types from within a collection of individuals (see
Nelson, 1976, p. 34 f.).

A good solution, it seems to me, must depend on divergent responses to one
and the same stimulus. Jones is asked to respond to a stimulus favorably if it is
a two dimensional diagrammatic projection of a cube and unfavorably if not.
Further, let A be one Necker cube aspect and B the other. Jones is asked to
respond by 'Yes-A' or 'Yes-B' according as she perceives A or B, if the presentation is a cube, and 'No' if not. This illustrates what I mean by saying Jones
responds in different ways to A and B. I think it is reasonable to say that there
are two systems of rules involved, one C_A and the other C_B, and that rules for
being a cube (in either aspect in two dimensions) is the union $C = C_A \cup C_B$.
Now let's pin this insight down and submit it to a more careful analysis.

We will use some elementary facts about recursive functions (Nelson,
1968, p. 121 f.). In Chapter II we characterized recursive function of nonnegative integers as those computable by Turing machines. Now some functions of the nonnegative integers are *partial*; they do not yield values (they
are not 'defined') for all possible argument values. For instance subtraction,
which is an arithmetic function of two variables, is not defined for the pair
$(1, 2)$ – there is no nonnegative integer equal to 1 minus 2.

When it comes to computing a partial recursive function, one of *three*
things can happen: the Turing machine will print out the function value for
defined arguments; it will print-out some indicator equivalent to NO VALUE
for the undefined arguments; or it will, alternatively, run on in a nonterminal
loop forever – it will never halt. The defined arguments constitute a *partial*
domain.

Every numerical set accepted by a Turing machine, *a fortiori* by an FSA, is
the domain of a partial recursive function. Moreover each such set is the
domain of an *infinite* number of *different* functions, i.e., functions having
different ranges. To illustrate, suppose f is defined as follows:

$$f(x, y) = \begin{cases} x - y & \text{if} \quad x \geqslant y, \\ \text{undefined otherwise.} \end{cases}$$

Let α be a nonnegative parameter, and ϕ_α a function variable. Then

$$\phi_\alpha(x, y) = \begin{cases} (x - y)\alpha & \text{if} \quad x \geqslant y, \\ \text{undefined otherwise} \end{cases}$$

represents an infinite family of functions depending on α. By our generalization from numbers to strings on arbitrary alphabets (Section II.3), this fact implies that every set of strings, given an alphabet, that is accepted by an FSA is the domain of a computable string-function — a map from strings into strings. For example, there is a partial string function whose domain is the set of tokens of the type: all 1's occur in contiguous pairs. Again, by extension, there is an *infinite number* of such functions from any such set, and any such function is computed by its own unique Turing machine. In the psychological interpretation, from any collection of stimulus patterns, i.e., of tokens, there is an infinite collection of distinct recursive rules that produce distinct sets of responses.

What all this conceptual apparatus provides us with is a new way of marking off *same* and *different* automata and hence of understanding "perceive in the same (different) way". Two automata *compute in the same way* provided that they compute the same function. Two automata compute *differently* provided that they compute different functions. In particular, under the psychological interpretation, two automata compute differently from the same domain of string patterns if and only if they produce different responses, that is, different ranges. Of course in the organism these responses might be internal, not external and overt; no one has much of an idea what the neural upshot of distinct computational processes from a retinal image is like (there must be distinct processes, or there would be no Necker cube phenomenon!) But no matter. We can truncate (ignore) the responses in the following way and still retain the idea of deriving "perceive in the same way" from "compute in same way". Every Turing machine that computes a partial recursive function f with domain D can be used to construct an acceptor T without output (such as an FSA) such that x is accepted by T just in case the Turing machine computes a function value. The acceptor is just the full Turing machine equipped with a routine to obliterate the function value and to assume a final state. The acceptor retains all of the structure (the precise set of recursive rules) required to compute the function wherever it is defined. Let us suppose that all Turing acceptors in our theory are obtained in this way. Then let us call the Turing machines from which acceptors are derived *base* machines.

Now for the explication of 'accept in the same way'. Let D be a common domain accepted by T and T'. Then T and T' *accept D in the same way* if and only if their base Turing machines compute the same functions. Hence such T and T' virturally respond in the same way to the tokens of the same type. If the basic machines compute different functions, then the acceptor's virtual responses are different and they 'perceive' in different ways and thus the *types* differ.

Our result of course relativizes *types* of stimulation properties to automata, if mechanism be true.

> τ and τ' are the *same type* if and only if the accepting automata T_τ and $T_{\tau'}$ accept in the same way, i.e. their basic machines compute the same functions on D.

D is the union of the tokens of both types τ and τ'. In particular, different gestalt patterns are accepted by automata that accept a common domain of different functions. But this relativization is of a piece with the naturalist idea that perception is a "disposition to respond". Where there are two *Gestalten*, there are two dispositions; and dispositions in the logic of mind are automata.[12] These conclusions about types apply to *sensible* properties only and any extension to all physical properties is *forbidden*.

Condition III can be met with our type of model by some additional fussing with the concept of a base Turing machine. Most people can recognize faces in entirely different instances than the 'standard' ones, under certain circumstances, and can perceive melodies to be such and such under various key changes, moderate changes in tempo, inversions, and the like. For purposes of discussion of many sets of tokens of the same type music appears to offer better illustration than almost any other aesthetic structures.

We just argued that patterns are of the same type if they are accepted in the same way; and of course you can accept one and the same set of tokens in different ways. What is wanted to meet condition III is a model that postulates two qualitatively different sets of tokens and yet can intelligibly ascribe a single type to both.[13] To this end it seems that a likely move is just to extend *same computation* (on a base machine) to processing of the two sets of tokens. And that 'likely move', up to some slightly distressing complications, can properly be made in terms of the mathematics of *diagrams*. The idea we will use is close to that of homomorphism. The discussion is mathematically technical although it still uses only concepts of sets, functions, and automata, and the reader won't miss much if he skips it, except the heart of the argument.

Suppose that S and S' are two Turing machine alphabets not necessarily disjoint. For an example think of S as produced by all the musical elements — tones at various pitches and of various durations and timbre, rests, etc. — that go into your favorite composition $\mathcal{K}$. S are the stimuli that our receptors constitute from playings of $\mathcal{K}$. Let S' be a set in another key, or at a different decibel level or whatever you fancy to be qualitatively different. Let $S*$ and $(S')*$ be strings over S and S' respectively. Now your favorite piece $\mathcal{K}$ can be regarded extensionally as a subset of $S* -$ it is a set of sequences of the musical elements of $S -$ and when we say $\mathcal{K}$ is a set we refer to all of the *plays* of $\mathcal{K}$. This is 'straight' $\mathcal{K}$.

$\mathcal{K}'$, which is similarly a subset of $(S')*$, is the same piece as $\mathcal{K}$ but in another key or on instruments other than the ones intended by the composer. What we are after is 'same tune', even though it is not played straight. As in the construction of the model for II we first want a concept of *accepting in the same way*, again from which we will then derive *same type*, the same tune.

A listening to or hearing of $\mathcal{K}$ is a map k from $\mathcal{K}$ to internal responses $\mathcal{R}$ of some kind and similarly one of $\mathcal{K}'$ is a map k' from $\mathcal{K}'$ inward to $\mathcal{R}'$. Suppose that T_k and $T_{k'}$ compute k and k', that T and T' are Turing acceptors (constructed as described in the previous section) that derive from the base machines T_k and $T_{k'}$; suppose that $\mathcal{K} = \mathcal{U}_T$ while $\mathcal{K}' = \mathcal{U}_{T'}$ that is to say, that $\mathcal{K}$ and $\mathcal{K}'$ are the sets accepted by T and T' respectively.

Now for emphasis, note that k is a map from $\mathcal{U}_T$ to $\mathcal{R}$ which we depict:

$$\mathcal{U}_T \xrightarrow{\ k\ } \mathcal{R}, \tag{3a}$$

and likewise k' is one from $\mathcal{U}_{T'}$ to $\mathcal{R}'$:

$$\mathcal{U}_{T'} \xrightarrow{\ k'\ } \mathcal{R}'. \tag{3b}$$

Finally let ϕ and ϕ' be one-one correspondences from $\mathcal{U}_T$ to $\mathcal{U}_{T'}$ and from $\mathcal{R}$ to $\mathcal{R}'$:

$$\mathcal{U}_T \xrightarrow{\ \phi\ } \mathcal{U}_{T'}$$

$$\mathcal{R} \xrightarrow{\ \phi'\ } \mathcal{R}'. \tag{4}$$

Now pick a play x of $\mathcal{K}$ out of $\mathcal{U}_T$ and compute a response y via T_k in $\mathcal{R}$; determine $\phi(x) = x'$ in $\mathcal{U}_{T'}$ and compute y' via $T_{k'}$ in $\mathcal{R}'$. If $y' = \phi'(y)$, then we say that T and T' *accept in the same way in the extended sense*. T and T' use the same *listening recipe* for the tunes $\mathcal{K}$ and $\mathcal{K}'$. In mathematical jargon, T and T' accept in the same way in the extended sense if and only if $\phi'k = k'\phi$, that is, if the diagram

$$\begin{array}{ccc}
\mathcal{U}_T & \xrightarrow{\ \ k\ \ } & \mathcal{R} \\
\phi \downarrow & & \downarrow \phi' \\
\mathcal{U}_{T'} & \xrightarrow{\ \ k'\ \ } & \mathcal{R}'
\end{array}$$

(5)

commutes. (5) is obtained by pasting (3a), (3b), and (4) together. If our main mechanist assumption is that T and T' do in fact 'perceive' $\mathcal{K}$ and $\mathcal{K}'$ respectively, then they *perceive* in the same way — 'hear' the same tune — in the *extended sense*, i.e., in different keys or whatever provided the foregoing construction is satisfied. As to types, $\mathcal{K}$ and $\mathcal{K}'$ are the *same type in the extended sense* if and only if T and T' accept the same in the extended sense. Here also same type for the case of stimuli is relativized to same way of accepting.

Is this adequate? Well, there are both pleasant and unpleasant things that can be said in behalf of the model. *In its favor*: if it is reasonable to say that two acceptors accept the same — their base machines compute the same function — then it seems to me it is equally so to claim that they accept the same type in the extended sense if in reacting to qualitatively different tokens they compute the same function. This can be made even more precise for the Pythagorean under the assumption that the functions in the case are sets of pairs of numbers (not numerals or notations or strings) and that accepting music is processing numerical relationships.[14]

The foregoing treatment works nicely for sequential processes such as music perception, except for the simple-minded notion that perceiving a play of music is just perceiving it to be or not be a given piece. I get more out of a play of a Bach number than just recognizing it! Exactly the same truncated treatment would be given to perception of sentences which, again following Chomsky in the main, would be Turing business, but producing final states that say, in effect, "Yes, this is English". Knowing a sentence in English is a far cry from knowing what it says, just like knowing $\mathcal{K}$ is a Bach Fugue is by no means understanding it. But presumably the state-to-state sequence induced in the accepter T_{Bach} by the listening and the responses, whatever they are, suppressed in the hypothesized base machines do give an abstract representation of what goes on provided that T_{Bach} *guides*. If it doesn't, the mechanist hypothesis still suggests there is some other type of unknown recursive structure that does. All we seek here is a conclusion that mechanist concepts work, in principle.[15]

Against: the model prescribes a possibly separate set S of pattern token elements for each qualitatively different version of a type. In effect in our constructions what we are doing is starting with a set of accepter rules then making uniform substitutions for the s-symbols yielding rules with the same structure and same behavior, except for the material quality of stimuli and responses. This compels us to posit a unique accepter for each type variant. There was a similar complaint against our way of meeting the *universality and discrimination* condition by stipulating an automaton for each type (not type variant). But there I could retort, with some credibility I believe, that the one automaton for each of n types (yielding an n component product) does not commit us to n little organisms or subnetworks in the brain. However I'm afraid the multiplicity of alphabets might so commit one, and this is very inelegant besides being *prima facie* wrong. There's no end to the qualitatively diverse ways in which I can listen to Bach, and I certainly didn't have to learn each one (cf. Fodor, 1968b, pp. 24–29). It is possible, of course, that a structural scheme, such as an embodiment of a Turing machine for a tune, could be biased under some kind of tacit control to work with different symbols S, just as axiom schemes can be instanced in an infinitude of axioms all differing in the constituent well-formed parts. But unfortunately this is foreign to any way I know of handling recursive rules.

In jotting down these remarks I am assuming that the S's, the stimuli pattern constituted by reception, are distinct for each sense modality and for each 'significant' qualitative shift such as key changes in music. The nervous system, on the other hand, possibly could be so arranged that stimuli constituted for perceptual processing are already qualitatively neutral. If so there need by only one recipe for $\mathcal{H}$, not one for each qualitative mode. If programs rather than Turing machines are our paradigm models, then the difficulties are relieved somewhat in another way. The *same program*, which presumably could in principle be made a precise concept in a manner similar to our way with same acceptor, can operate on all kinds of data, some representing tokens of quality Q others of Q' and so forth. A fourth possibility, in my estimation the most promising, is that learning a melody is like learning a grammar (I already just noted another analog between music and grammar in point of the distinction between *identifying* a piece of music or a sentence of English and *understanding* either one). The basis of the analogy is that musical elements – tones of various pitches and qualities, rests, accents, etc. – correspond to phonemic elements of language; and just as one somehow learns certain phrase structures independently of specific terminal ingredients (e.g., rules, $R_1 - R_6$ of the grammar of Table II.II together with those that derive therefrom by rewriting such as S → (NP + VP) + C + (NP + VP)) one might learn melodies independently of the musical elements to some extent. Of course this is not an original observation about music-language parallelism. Perhaps similar remarks could be made about learning to identify visual and other pattern types in the extended sense, *mutatis mutandis*.

Further objections: The model is far too liberal. (5) says that the maps k and k' ((2) and (3)) from stimulus tokens to responses are the same if corresponding elements of $\mathscr{U}_T$ and $\mathscr{U}_{T'}$ map via k and k' into corresponding elements of $\mathscr{R}$ and $\mathscr{R}'$ respectively. $\mathscr{U}_{T'}$ could be any old jumble of acoustic stimuli and $\mathscr{U}_T$ good Bach, and so long as there is some sort of correlation T' would be hearing Bach in a new variant! (I am assuming *at least* that both sets are stimuli of the same sense modality). A strengthening requirement would be to require *isomorphism* of base machines T and T' so that the computation from the $\mathscr{U}$'s to $\mathscr{R}$'s would be point-by-point the same. What this would mean is that state-to-state transitions correspond, the 'same recipes' are followed; such a condition would be much less liberal than mere correspondence of arguments and function values of k and k,. But an isomorphism requirement of this kind might rule out the sameness of inverted melodies or sameness of those played backwards to straight tunes, or of upside down photographs to right side up ones. You might lose serial music, in particular, if you happen to think that would be a loss.

But there is a wide range of mathematical tools that can be used to shape up a mechanical model so that it accounts for the fact of same type in distinct sets of tokens. What model is right surely depends on empirical considerations, not *a priori* philosophical speculation that probes any further than (5). Some kind of a morphism concept is just the ticket, I claim, and a mechanist approach can deliver it in principle as just shown.

3. EXPECTATION

Gestalt theory places wholes over parts: perceivers grasp the whole of things, not parts — indeed, parts are frequnetly *determined* by wholes. I know the bulbous purplish blob is a nose because I know the indistinct, pink, oval is a face; and I know the flatted singing is a play of *Noel* because I know *Noel*.

The basic accepting automata constructed for conditions I–III do, in a way, hunt for defining features of strings although they do not check off items of a list or match parts against labels, even tacitly. Moreover there is certainly an independence of simple part accounting in both II and III: II models can find two or more types in a token, which does hint at a transcending of token and token parts by *ways* of accepting; likewise III models can find

Wertheimer's intrinsic wholes (p. 176 above) such as tunes independently of key. Still, all these models are grounded in an *analytic* concept of perception in as much as they presuppose good, undegraded component parts of tokens. Can automata satisfy Condition IV? Can these models cope with degraded characters like Goodman's wayward *d*? I hope to convince you that they can and that the way they do it involves a major ingredient of intentionality.

Philosophers and psychologists from behaviorists to phenomenologists seem to agree that human perceivers have expectations about objects and frequently *take* things to be other than the way they are on the basis of 'global meaning' or an intuitive grasp of the 'intrinsic whole'. When you read 'b *d* d' you expect the middle character to be an 'a' and take it to be an 'a', correctly. When you expect an event to occur you are in a psychological state that has a history, however short, that leads to that event.

Suppose T is scanning a string $u = wx$ such that $M(q_0, w) = q$ at time t and $M(q, x) = q_F$, a final state at some time $t' > t$. This models Jones who is listening to a tune (let us suppose she has graduated from *Air in X* to *Noel*), has heard a part of that tune, w, followed by another part x that completes it. We want to make precise the idea that Jones has been led to expect the tune by the fragment w and that her expectations are fulfilled or disrupted by x. The fundamental notion is that of a winner, which does wonders for the theory.

> A *winner* is a state q of T such that there is an x for which $M(q, x)$ is a final state. (6)

In Table I all the states save q_4 are winners. The initial state q_0 of any automaton is of course always a winner except for uninteresting cases wherein that state connects to no final states via inputs, and final states are winners except for automata having inputs of bounded length. In the table q_1 is also a winner, although it is neither initial nor final.[16]

There are two reasonable explications of 'expectation' each capturing senses of ordinary usage. On some occasions you expect an *individual* as when you expect a friend to turn up at a certain place; on others you expect a *type* to be instantiated. If you expect a *type* you don't expect any particular instance to occur, while if you expect an individual of a type you also expect the type.

Let τ be a type. The first explication says,

> T_τ *expects* x at t if and only if T_τ is in some winning state q at t and $M_\tau(q, x)$ is also a winner. (6a)

The second says,

> T_τ *expects* τ at t if and only if T_τ is in some winning state q at
> t.   (7)

(7) seems to me to be more natural: even when we expect a person we do not expect this or that phenomenal appearance of her, that is, a particular event. At any rate (7) better fits our later theory of reference of names.

If Table I is in state q_1, which is a winner, then any string that takes it back to that state itself or to q_2 or q_3 fulfills the automaton's expectations. Some of these strings are 1, 10, 1011, 10110, etc. These are not the same as the *accepted* strings, all of which contain 1's in contiguous paris only; but to be in q_1 *means* that T must just have received a single 1; and so all of the strings resulting from concatenation of these string examples to the right of that 1 are fulfilling strings. This suggests the following:

> x *fulfills* T_τ at t if and only if T_τ is in some winning state q at
> t and $M_\tau(q, x)$ is a winner.   (8)

Similarly,

> x *disrupts* T_τ at t if and only if T_τ is in some winning state q
> at t and $M_\tau(q, x)$ is not a winner.   (9)

If Table I is in winning state q_1 and either 0, 01, 0011, etc. occur, then it is disrupted in state q_1; $M(q_1, 0) = q_4$, which is not a winner, and similarly for the others. It is clear that if T_τ expects τ at t and x is input at t, then either x fulfills or x disrupts at t.

For the time being our interest is mainly in fulfillment of expectations in situations where expectations are not literally fulfilled but are taken to be. Thus the next order of business is to modify (8) for vague input. Consider Jones who has just heard the first three notes, she thinks, of *Noel*. She is now in an expecting state, hears a few more notes that fulfill her expectations and is quite sure that what she is listening to is indeed *Noel*. However her expectations could be disrupted by a continuation that renders *Three Blind Mice* instead of *Noel*. This turns her off, whereupon she turns off the source or shifts her attention to the round. But a third possibility is that the fourth note in the musical sequence is *flat* and still later parts of the piece are missing or distorted in some way. Yet this play is *virtually* or 'nearly' *Noel* and she still 'hears' *Noel*; she expects it, and she *takes* the bad stuff to be true.

In setting up a model meant to capture this phenomenon the key idea will be that when one takes something x to be other than it is she reacts to x as if it were a y that fulfills expectation, i.e., a y that x resembles. Thus we shall say that x is *taken* to be in a set A of a certain type or is a *virtual* element of A if there is a y such that x resembles y and $y \in A$. What we have to do, in automaton terms, is obtain an adequate notion of resemblance and of reacting. Now from recursive function theory set A is equal to an accepted set $\mathcal{U}_T$ for some Turing machine T, and if R is a computable relation (which means that if $R(x, y)$, there is an effective way of getting y from x), then the set of virtual elements x of A is also the set accepted by some Turing machine. Thus theory tells us that if R is constructed to be computable then there are T's that virtually accept or perceive. R is constrained to be a resemblance in terms of expectations, and T'reacts' by going into a winning state.

We can obtain such a resemblance relation by use of Dr C. Y. Lee's idea of self-encodement of automata (Lee, 1963).[17] This remarkable theory, which stems from John von Neumann's work on self-reproducing machines in the late 1940s, shows how a Turing machine can be built that can discover its own table, including of course the part that does the discovering, and print it in coded form on its tape. We use this idea to establish that there are machines that have access to their own structures and can realize expectations in vague contexts by looking up what they *would do* (looking up 'mathematically' in the terminology of the last chapter) if they were in a winning state and had defined input, i.e., input from the symbol set S rather than the degraded input that we are puzzling about. The scheme is technically somewhat formidable and is worked out in considerable detail elsewhere (Nelson, 1976b). In this book I will present enough of it to show how you can plausibly satisfy condition IV.

Begin with an acceptor $T = \langle S, Q, q_0, M, Q_F \rangle$ whose accepted set is $\mathcal{U}_T$. As always the elements of set S are symbols all of which T can 'sense' clearly and which correspond to equally well-defined stimulus classes as previously discussed. Let B be a finite set of degraded symbols (like flatted notes or $\mathcal{d}$) none of which are accessible to T; that is, the intersection of B and S is empty, $B \cap S = \phi$. Recall that to say a symbol b of B is not in S means there is no rule of T that applies to b if b occurs in a string x. T gets hung up.

$T' = \langle S \cup B, Q', q_0, M', Q_F' \rangle$ is a super Turing machine that includes T as a submachine and that has the production rules that constitute T coded in its memory for reference; that is to say, T' has self-coding capabilities as per Lee's theory. An organism realizing T' might have been born with this self-script, which would be part of its genetic code structure. To say that T is a submachine of T' means that Q is included in Q', M in M', and Q_F in

Q'_F and of course $S \subseteq (S \cup B)$ while the initial states are the same, q_0. T' has another part that computes the resemblance relation (say a d from Goodman's $\mathcal{A}$), R, a part that determines what state it itself is in; and still another part that determines whether the present state is a winner. These latter two properties call for some side commentary. Any Turing machine can identify what state it is in at time t using a coded table of itself. A crude procedure would be to print present state q (using a new rule $(q, s) \to$ print q) and match against the table (cf. Putnam, 1960, p. 155).

To decide whether a state is a winner presents a serious problem for this type of approach to virtual acceptance. For arbitrary Turing machines T the winner problem is reducible to the halting problem; and the latter, which asks whether there is a way of telling whether the Turing machine will compute and stop (the 'halting problem'), is recursively unsolvable (Davis, 1958, p. 70). What this means is that there is no algorithm or no other Turing machine that can tell whether T can compute a function value for a given argument. Hence by reducibility the winner problem is unsolvable — there is no winner detector of the type we want in our construction, in general. However, there is a winner detecting procedure, fortunately, for FSA and even for more elaborate perception models called 'pushdown automata'. If these latter models, however, turn out *not* to be adequate for human perception and full Turing machines or ·the equivalent are required, then either mechanism is false or expectations are satisfied in some entirely different way than the one proposed in this model.

Returning from this digression. Note that (T')'s alphabet is $S \cup B$ and that elements of B are meaningful to T': one of its main roles in life is to say of any b of B that b is not in S. In a version truer to the capabilities of perceiving organisms T' would contain a product of FSA's like T, not just T alone (see Figure 5). But we shall have plenty to do just describing the performance of one such T'.

We are now in a position to see how expectations can be fulfilled by taking fuzzy input to be, to resemble, well-defined stimuli. Suppose x is a string on $(S \cup B)^*$, which is a set of strings x having b's mixed in with s's. Recall that T is the part of T' that does the accepting. If the scanned symbol of x is a valid symbol s of S, then T computes according to its table. If the symbol scanned is a degraded item b of B, T of course is hung up as its transition function is undefined. T', however, is constructed so as to initiate the following chain of events: the appropriate part of T' determines the present state, q, and the winner detector decides whether q is a winner. If it is not, T' has no expectations and it does not accept x. If q is a winner, call it q_w; then

T expects any string y that would drive it to another winner, that is to say, such that $M(q_w, y)$ is a winner. In particular, it expects *any* symbol s in place of the bad stuff, b, that would take it from q_w to another winner. Accordingly T' goes to the self-coded table and collects all those rules of T in which q_w occur on the left and such that q on the right is a winner. This collected set of rules defines a subset A of symbols of S, any one of which will take T to a winner, i.e., will fulfill its expectations. T' next lists all of the pairs (s, q) such that s is in A and $q = M(q_w, s)$, the next state from q_w and s. T' next selects one of the s's of A at random, overprints b with s and places T in the state q that was paired with s in (s, q).[18] T then scans the next symbol of x and repeats the algorithm.

To illustrate this rather complex process, suppose the automaton of Table I is fed the string $00b11b$, b being degraded, which is an element of $(S \cup B)^*$. According to our routine, T in state q_0 first scans 0; since $0 \in S$, it computes $M(q_0, 0) = q_0$, by Table I; likewise it scans the second 0 and computes q_0. The situation is now that T is in q_0 scanning b. As there is no rule (as $M(q_0, b)$ is not defined by the table), T', the super automaton, takes over and determines that q_0 is the present state and is a winner. So T' checks the table, which is encoded in memory, and determines that both symbols 0 and 1 take q_0 to winners, namely q_0 and q_1. This determination defines two pairs $(0, q_0)$ and $(1, q_1)$. Now let us suppose that T' picks $(1, q_1)$ by some random means; then by the recipe being followed it overprints the b, which it is scanning, by 1 yielding the string $00111b$ and assumes state q_1. The situation is now that T is to compute $M(q_1, 11b)$. By the table, T will be in state q_4 scanning b in a few steps. Since q_4 is not a winner and not a final state, T ends in q_4 without accepting $00b11b$ and with expectations disrupted.

Going back to the crucial point where a random selection was made, T' could have picked 0 instead of 1, overprinted b with 0 and would have assumed state q_0, yielding $00011b$. Next $M(q_0, 11b)$ computes out in a few steps to $M(q_2, b)$. But now as T is hung up again, it is determined that q_2 is a winner and that 0 will drive T to another winning state. Accordingly 0 is overprinted for b, T goes into a winning and final state q_3, expectations are fulfilled, and T accepts $00b11b$. Depending on the random choice made, the input $00b11b$ is transformed by this type of computation either to $00111b$ (effectively 00111, which is already rejected) or to 000110. Therefore what results depends on the actual historical computation and can not be read off from T's table.

The computation of y from x at time t when T is in state q will hereafter be denoted by 'K_q':

> T in state q *takes y for x at t* — $K_q(x, y, t)$ — if and only if superautomaton T' in state q computes y from x at t using the table of T.   (10)

From any input x defined for T several different y's might be computed at different *historical* times t. That is to say, we could have both $K_q(x, y, t)$ and $K_q(x, y', t')$ with $y \neq y'$ if $t \neq t'$ as exemplified in which case taking reduces to acceptance immediately above. If $x \in S$ we stipulate $K_q(x, x, t)$ for any t

> The *resemblance relation* $R_q(x, y)$ is the relation on $(S \cup B)^*$ $\times S^*$ such that y is derivable from x by T' in state q by the foregoing program.   (10a)

Using the same example, $00b11b$ *resembles* 00110 because 000110 can be computed from $00b11b$, although it *could* be taken otherwise. This is the relation sought at the outset of our discussion of perception of vague, degraded items. Note that it is a mathematical not an historical relation and that (T')'s table (if construed as a theory) entails R. In the discussion of taking, if the time parameter t were not understood historically but as ranging over numerical indices of possible computations, then R_q could be defined as the projection of K_q on its first two components.

In order to wind up the technical part of this discussion we summarize our new concepts of fulfillment and disruption as follows:

> x *fulfills* T_τ at t if and only if T_τ is in some winning state q at t and there is a t' and a y such that t' is greater than t and $K_q(x, y, t')$ and $M_\tau(q, y)$ is a winner.   (11)

> x *disrupts* T_τ at t if and   only if T_τ is in some winning state q at t and there is no t' and y such that t' is greater than t and $K_q(x, y, t')$ and $M_\tau(q, y)$ is a winner.   (12)

Using these revised and improved notions of fulfillment and disruption we are able to deduce from (7),

> T_τ expects τ and x is input at t implies either that x fulfills T_τ at t or x disrupts T_τ at t.   (13)

(13) will play an important part in my later argument that this analysis is adequate for expectation as an *intentional* term.

In (11)–(13) and all later formulations where T involves taking we suppose that T is part of a sypersystem T' that checks winning, takes in behalf of T, and so forth as described in the construction of T' on p. 189 ff.

Note once more that in the case of disruption, although the y computed from x at t does not take T from q to a final state ($M(q, y)$ not a winner) there might very well be a computation of a y at a *different* time that would yield a winner $M(q, y)$. Hence, it is quite possible that x disrupt T while still $R_q(x, z)$ for some z, and $M(q, z)$ be a winner. In this case there is *mathematically* a computation of y from x but it did not occur *historically*.

To nail down acceptance in the general sense of virtual acceptance involving taking we need a specialized notion of fulfillment involving the initial state and passage to a final state:

> T *virtually accepts* x at t if and only if T is in state q_0 at t and there is a y and a t' greater than t such that $K_{q_0}(x, y, t')$ and $M(q_0, y)$ is a final state.   (14)

The reason for this cut back in generality is, of course, that one can expect fulfilling fragments of pattern tokens that are not the full pattern. Fulfillment from state q_0 guarantees that $y \in \mathcal{U}_T$ while it is definitely possible that $M(q, y)$ is a final state while $y \notin \mathcal{U}_T$, if $q \neq q_0$.

We also obtain an analysis of 'acceptability', using (14):

> x is *acceptable* to T_τ if and only if there is a y such that $R(x, y)$ and $M_\tau(q_0, y)$ is final, i.e., if $y \in \mathcal{U}_{T_\tau}$. Alternatively we say x is a *virtual element* of $\mathcal{U}_{T_\tau}$.   (15)

According to our concept R, there need never have been a computation K of y from x, and acceptability is just a disposition to take on a final state (or in a full FA, to respond). Similarly the subjunctive conditional 'T would assume a final state, if x were input' is, I claim, fully analyzed by the analysans of (15); but that is another story we must postpone the relating of. We will have central use for (15) in the context of reference and truth in Chapter IX.

The model T' demonstrates, I think beyond much doubt, that perception of indeterminate, degraded stimuli is explainable in terms of recursive rules owing to incorporation of intentional traits, expectations, in the structure. T' will not always take bad stuff to be as it really is, for instance a shadowy, indistinct apple as an apple, but on other occasions it will take it aright. But this uncertainty of taking is also true of human beings. When we come to it a more complete analysis will show how *desires* affect expectations and how the perceptual object in its relation to stimuli also intrudes in the taking scheme. Human beings often take things to be what they desire; and a real object, I submit, that satisfies expectations will not normally be taken to be other than it is. These propositions must of course be defended in the context of our discussion of belief.

As it stands the model for meeting condition IV has the consequence that a perceiver who realizes the parallel automaton, Figure 5, might take one and the same input ambiguously: α, for example, is a virtual element of both type a, for T_a and of type d for T_d. We note parenthetically that a product of acceptors might, therefore, have several simultaneous expectations. It seems to me that this is correct. If I begin listening to an unannounced tune that I know middlingly well I do seem to have different expectations at once, some even fulfilled in mid-play; usually all but one is disrupted somewhere on after the beginning. If not, there is some question concerning what it was I just heard. Resolution of ambiguities of this kind might come in part from the context of desire as just noted or perhaps through taking another look or another listen. But within the formalities of the model as we have now got it, without issuing any promissory notes, these ambiguities can be managed by consideration of syntactical contexts in the following manner.

Suppose a bank of automata as in Figure 5 accepts the lower case letters a, b, c, etc. of the English alphabet while another product automaton recognizes words in the English dictionary. Call these T_L and T_W. T_L is a product $T_a \times T_b \times T_c \ldots$, while T_W is a product automaton $T_a \times T_{an} \times T_{aid} \times T_{be} \times \ldots$. T_L's automaton alphabet is $\{0, 1\}$, and the letters a, b, c, $\ldots$ are strings in $\{0, 1\}^*$. Similarly T_W's automaton alphabet is $\{a, b, c, \ldots, z\}$ and the words of English are strings of $\{a, b, c, \ldots, z\}^*$. Hence the 'atomic' symbols of the automata of T_W are just the accepted strings of T_L. T_L and T_W are both contained in a super-automaton T' as in our earlier taking construction; besides, T' includes, as before, automaton means for identifying current states, winners, and encoded tables of T_L and T_W. Now let us reconsider Figures 3 and 4, which appeared as below.

$$b \, \alpha \, d \qquad\qquad\qquad b a \alpha$$
$$(3) \qquad\qquad\qquad\qquad (4)$$

T' operates as follows: T_L scanning $b \, \alpha \, d$ accepts b (that is to say, its component T_b goes to a final state). T_W computes $M_{bad}(q_0, b)$ via its component T_{bad}. Next T_L takes Goodman's character to be an a (T_a goes into a final state) and simultaneously takes it to be a d (T_d also assumes a final state). T_W computes $M_{bad}(M_{bad}(q_0, b), a)$, which is a winner; however, $M_{bad}(M_{bad}(q_0, b), d)$ goes into a nonwinner and will eventually go to a nonperceptual state at the end of the string $b \, \alpha \, d$; moreover there is no automaton T_{bdd} in T_W. So the overall yield is that $b \, \alpha \, d$ is taken to be 'bad'. By a similar process the system takes $b a \alpha$ to be 'bad' as well.

4. FAMILY RESEMBLANCES

The adequacy of the model for meeting condition IV is underscored by the manner of managing one more type of gestalt phenomenon and of facing the rather extreme nominalist Wittgensteinian claim that much of perception is recognition of *family resemblances*. As to the gestalt phenomena, Hubert Dreyfus maintains that digital machines (I assume machine$_1$ – p. 91 or the claim is not interesting) can not determine *values* of parts of whole patterns, while people can;

> ... in recognizing a melody, the notes get the values they have by being recognized as a part of a melody, rather than the melody's being built up of independently recognized notes. Likewise in the perception of objects there are no neutral traits. The same hazy layer which I would see as dust, if I thought I was confronting a wax apple might appear as moisture if I thought I was seeing a fresh apple. The significance of the details and indeed their very looks is determined by perception of the whole (Dreyfus, 1967, p. 17).

I interpret this rather reckless denial of the role of parts to mean not that wholes determine parts, as we have already been discussing at uncomfortable length, but that wholes determine *kinds* of parts. Dreyfus thinks machines$_1$ cannot do this. To the contrary, assuming that wax apples are *apples* (assuming that one is confronting apples *via* the sight faculty only), then both the wax and the fresh apple are of the same type in the *extended sense* of condition III; They are accepted in the same way by systems of recursive rules that differ over their alphabets only. Now as we have observed there is an acceptor for the *union* of wax and fresh types, which we incorporate in our now familiar superautomaton T'. Put the apples in Dreyfus's haze. An indeterminate token with a hazy layer could then be taken either as a dusty wax apple or a moist fresh one depending on context, using the device just described, with possibly other determiners.

According to Wittgenstein and his followers, one can know this is a leaf and that is a leaf even though the things have no common defining or essential properties.[19] People perceive family resemblances when no two individuals of the family have exactly similar traits in common. According to Dreyfus, you can "recognize such similarities by picking out a typical case and introducing intermediate cases", while a system of recursive rules can 'recognize' only by use of a specific list of traits.

This is not so, as can be shown by reducing the resemblance problem to taking.[20] The problem can be reduced by using the set of paradigms of the family to construct, in effect, an incomplete property. Of course, no leaf contains all the properties of leaves, not even the essential or defining ones because, the claim is, there are none. Nevertheless, we may take the union of the properties of paradigms, defining traits or not, upon which resemblance depends and take *these* as patterns. This is not to suppose we have found a 'common' property, which would be to 'play with words' (Wittgenstein, 1953, par. 67). Now the fact that Wittgenstein rules out the union as a true essential property implies that the doctrine of family resemblances attributes a certain indeterminacy or vagueness to objects. At least some of the parts of wholes must be vague (stimuli not in receptual classes); otherwise, it seems to me, the union of properties clearly *would* comprise a defining property (individuated, on my theory, by a *way* of accepting it) albeit not one literally *in* all instances. But our models can *take* a thing to have a property; all that is needed is to put the union of automata (which we know exists) for accepting the canned property into a superautomaton of our kind T'. In this way we show that family resemblances can be accepted by models that satisfy condition IV.

There appear to be many uses of the word 'resemblance' in English, most of them analyzable in acceptor terms. For instance, if T_τ accepts things of type τ then any two elements of τ resemble each other as they are the same type. Again any two things x, y accepted in the same way in the extended sense resemble each other (two plays of Bach in different keys). A stronger version of the second meaning of resemblance, which exploits the fact that there are models satisfying condition III, would require that x and y be correlated under ϕ of (4) (In this connection, however, see the 'Further objections', pp. 186 above).

Family 'resemblances' are different. The Wittgensteinian point is that two things resemble without common 'defining' properties, unlike 'resemblance' in the two foregoing classical senses. In order to understand how this cluster idea is to be analyzed, first consider our official R relation of (10a). This relation is non-reflexive, since for degraded x it is false that $R(x, x)$ in general. However, as a step toward resemblance we may simply stipulate that R be extended to a reflexive relation R' by defining R' as the union of R and the identity relation $I = \{<x \ x> | x \in (S \cup B)^*\}$. R is not symmetrical either; but I do not think it should be.[21] In the kind of resemblance underlying taking we do not, it seems to me, say y resembles x where x is taken to be y, although x does resemble y. A photograph resembles the face photographed, but the face does not resemble the photograph; and the hulk in the hazy fog perhaps resembles your uncle, but your uncle not the hulk. Clearly R is transitive. For if x is taken to be y, then y can only be taken as itself. Thus R satisfies reasonable formal requirements of this concept of resemblance.

If my surmise that Wittgenstein's demurring over terming the union of paradigmatic properties a 'property' is correct and that membership in a family depends on taking, then 'resemblance' in 'family resemblance' is characterizable in terms of R. Suppose we let $\mathcal{V}$ be a family virtually accepted by our Wittgensteinian automaton T', which was a taking automaton containing a union T of paradigm-accepting machines. Then x *resembles* y in the family sense just in case both x and y are in $\mathcal{V}$, i.e., both x and y are acceptable to the union. By (15) this says that there is some z such that $R(x, z)$ and $M_T(q_0, z)$ is a perceptual state and likewise there is a w such that $R(y, w)$ and $M_T(q_0, w)$ is a perceptual state. Thus x and y resemble each other in the family way because they are taken to resemble (in sense R) paradigms.

It seems to me that in ordinary discourse when you say one thing vaguely resembles another what you do mean is that one can be taken for the other (or, tacitly, both taken to resemble a paradigm) and thus to fulfill expectations. A construal of resemblance along this line is more natural than one determining resemblances by some kind of *matching* against paradigms, which seems to me sneaks in a *same property* or *same type* presupposition that is totally foreign to Wittgenstein. To say x resembles y because a person's way of perceiving things operates to let x fulfill y-ish expectations is nicely in accord with the psychological facts as we know them as well as with Wittgensteinian intuitions, and strengthens the plausibility of my mechanistic way of managing vague acceptance.

The several models used in showing how the conditions I–IV are mechanically satisfiable can be built into a composite machine and then paralleled in some fashion as depicted in Figure 5, including all sense modalities. Presumably stimulus patterns as we have considered them would be the products of the reception system operating on different transductions and digitalizations. Such processes are quite outside the range of anything I am going to attempt to consider here, but evidently are natural functions of perceiving organisms, given the known facts of neuroscience.

A composite model of this kind would incorporate, in particular, the taking function for each property type in its perceptual repertoire and provisions for taking advantage of context levels as described in connection with the example of 'bad' above.

A weakness of the take concept, which the reader might have noticed, is that no restrictions of any kind have been placed on what can be taken to be a type τ. If you will glance back to the design of the superautomaton T' which includes an acceptor or product of acceptors T you will see that the part B of the alphabet $S \cup B$ of T' is *any* set of 'symbols' disjoint from S. Jane takes flatted *notes* to be true; but T' might take a bass drum boom at the right moment to be a true Beverly Sills A^b two octaves above middle C if that is what it expects. Normal listeners would be thoroughly shattered. The model would not take a clod of clay to be an A^b because we have imposed a minimal demand that a product acceptor work over a single sensory domain. But this still will not do.

Second, it may seem reasonable to include stimulus patterns that are not fuzzy or degraded — *viz.* those that are certified inhabitants of receptual categories — in the taking scheme. For instance 010101010100 is in some sense so 'close' to being a string of alternating 1's and 0's that a perceiver would not be far wrong in taking it to be one. In this instance, unlike the degraded A^b there is nothing wrong with the stimulus parts, but the organized whole does not really instantiate the pattern. Shouldn't a theory of taking, especially one that purports to include contexts, provide for acceptance in such cases? My suggestion will be 'no'. The reason is that an acceptor which contains a component for alternating strings that terminate in double 0's and which expects such a string would not take it to be something else without radically changing the logic of the model. But the changes it would require seem to demand a giving up of too many features that appear to satisfy our adequacy demands for a theory of perception. At one time I thought probabilistic automata (see Note XI.6) might be used to model closeness in this new sense. But given an intuitively suitable notion of closeness it turns out that there are cases in which the closer the string to an exemplar, the lower the probability of acceptance (Nelson, 1984). These problems lingering around the take are best dealt with in the context of perception (as are our residual questions about property types, the causal character of perception, and perceptual objects) to which we now turn.

CHAPTER VII

PERCEPTION

Acceptance of stimulus patterns taken in some way by a perceiver is not yet perception, for according to main stream epistemology perception is veridical while acceptance could be illusory. When they can be said to perceive at all, organisms perceive objects in the world, not stimuli or sensory transductions. So our theory must be extended to real objects of which acceptance is in some sense true.

Provisionally, let us try: T perceives x to be a τ at time t just in case x is τ and T accepts x at t — in the sense of virtual acceptance, VI (14) — and x is understood to be a perceptual object, not a stimulus pattern. This formulation commits us to a propositional version of perception as it makes perception *veridical* acceptance. So what we seek is a completed analysis of 'T perceives that x is τ'. Nonpropositional perception, in case one is interested, is just presentation of x to an organism; it is the result of stimulus reception without the taking computation.[1] The reader will recall that 'virtual acceptance' unpacks in terms of 'fulfilled expectations,' which goes back to 'winning' and 'taking'. In the psychologist's jargon what we have is therefore a 'transactional' theory of perception, so far as it goes.

The first section of this chapter fills out this sketch with the main focus on objects. What little I shall have to say about veridicality, which is of course an epistemological concern, will come out in the context of perceptual belief, and is to be considered in the later chapters. Perceptual belief comes down to fulfilled expectation that is linguistically expressible.

1. PERCEPTUAL OBJECTS

The business of extending the concept of acceptance to full perception is fairly intricate. I wish I knew how to make it simpler; but my deeper concern is that the model is already too idealized and has abstracted away from relevant aspects of organism-environment systems. A central problem is the taking relation, which is liable to radical misconstruals of stimuli, as just briefed at the end of Chapter VI. Our approach to it will be to place the organism in the context of an environment.

A possible solution might be to cut down on the set B of vague symbols that could be taken as S's for some T so that the unwanted acceptance of a drumbeat as a vocal high would be precluded. But this would require retreat to a notion of resemblance or type-similarity that I do not know how to manage. The restriction to symbols of one modality already assumes more than empirical science warrants (organisms have been wired-up to hear what they see, for example). So we are forced to take a closer look at expectation itself. As we shall see, an analysis of the adequacy of the account pushes us inevitably toward perceptual *objects* and so to a realist or representationalist view of perception in which the object is causally related to the stimulus pattern. Indeed, the argument at this stage coupled with naturalism suggests an *evolutionary* theory; the naturally selected relation of object to stimulus pattern excludes wild takings.

Another quandry about taking that survived the discussion of the last chapter is this: why not take a string such as 01010100 that is close to 01010101 to be the latter? Given the naturalist background, our answer will be that such a generalization of the taking function leads to an incoherent theory.

Thus we shall have arrived at objects and at a theory of their relation to the organism's stimulations. The remaining problem of this section then is property individuation. We have already argued that stimulus patterns are the same type provided they compute to perceptual states in the same way. Using the evolutionist thesis, the final step then will be to stipulate that sensible properties of objects are the same provided that the causally related stimuli are of the same type.

According to Chisholm, who has cogently discussed many of the relevant issues about intentionality and who has summarized for us a number of conditions that any theory must satisfy, a reasonable definition of 'expectation' would be, schematically

> 'T expects E to occur' means that T is in a bodily state q such that either (i) q would be fulfilled if and only if E were to occur, or (ii) q would be disrupted if and only if E were not to occur (Chisholm, 1957, p. 182).   (1)

(1) is not the same as our definition VI (7), but we want to use it as the starting point for eventually formulating conditions our definition should satisfy to be an adequate account (beyond what we have already done in Chapter VI) of expectation and perception. In our terms (1) is formulated equivalently (close enought): given any input x

> 'T_τ expects τ at t' means that T_τ is in some winning state q
> such that either (i) x fulfills T_τ in q at t if and only if x occurs
> at t or (ii) x disrupts T_τ in q at t if and only if x does not occur
> at t. (1a)

Of course Chisholm's (1) is a scheme in barest outline as 'fulfilled' and
'disrupted' are essentially without content. He considers the possibility of
defining 'fulfill' in terms of reinforcement and 'disrupts' in terms of surprise
or shock, which would be a behavioristic tack. But, he points out at once,
"it is easy to think of situations which, antecedently, we should want to
describe as instances of expectations but in which fulfillments or disruptions
do not occur in the manner required" (Chisholm, 1957, p. 182). As we
ourselves might say, Jones could meet someone other than her uncle and yet
take that someone to be her uncle. But also, Chisholm asks, what if Jones
were to expect her uncle, meet him, and yet take him to be someone else?
These are real eventualities, and to provide for them we might modify (1a)
to read as follows: given any input x,

> 'T_τ expects τ at t' means that T_τ is in some winning state q
> such that either (i) x fulfills T_τ in q at t if and only if x occurs
> at t or x does not occur at t but T_τ takes x to occur; or (ii)
> x disrupts T_τ in state q if and only if x does not occur at t or
> x occurs at t but T_τ does not take x to occur at t. (2)

This appears to be a satisfactory statement of an adequacy condition for
an explication of 'expects' to meet provided that 'fulfill' and 'disrupt' in
turn can be explicated in nonintentional terms. But this has already been
accomplished in VI(11) and VI(12) in automata-theoretic terms.

It is fairly easy to show that our theory satisfies (i) of (2) under the
assumption that 'x' in (2) denotes a stimulus pattern, not a perceptual object.
For if 'x occurs' means in my theory that x is computed at t by the K function and is accepted, i.e., that '$K_q(x, x, t)$ and $M(q, x)$ is a winner' is true,
and 'x does not occur but is taken to occur' means '$K_q(x, y, t)$ and $M(q, y)$
is a winner' is true for some $y \neq x$, then VI(11) entails (i). However, things
do not run so smoothly for (ii). (ii) says that a possible case of disruption
would be for x to occur while T would not take x to occur. My model entails
a condition which is close: a string *could* have been taken to occur while it
did *not* occur, viz., there is a z such that $R(x, z)$ while in fact at t, during
an actual computation, neither $K_q(x, y, t)$ holds nor is $M(q, y)$ a winner, for
any y. But 'could have been taken to occur' does not mean 'x occurred'.

In fact in the model for a string to occur but not be taken to occur even if expected is a flat-out contradiction. For, if T expects x then by Definition III.(6) $M(q, x)$ is a winner, and if x occurs, then by the construction of K, x is taken to occur, that is, $K_q(x, x, t)$. Furthermore it seems that on anybody's theory the proposition that expectations of events are not satisfied by those very events is a nonlogical contradiction if there ever was one.

What is wrong of course is that the x's of our theory are *stimulus patterns*, not perceptual objects, and indeed must be other than perceptual objects for Chisholm as well. If he is right in putting forth the condition that favorable occurrences can be disrupting (experience shows that he is) then we are driven to posit perceptual objects out beyond the inner patterns. I suppose any one would agree on naturalistic grounds that the stimulus object is not the outer, physical thing, the perceptual object. We perceive objects, not our own stimulations (I am aware that on traditional epistemological grounds this is disputable; but it is not under the assumption of naturalism, given the circumstance that perception involves expectations, as we are in the process of discovering). In line with the naturalist view what our theory requires is a distinction between the external object and the stimulus pattern and a relation between the two that is subject to singularities or *lapses*. Jones accepts a circle as an ellipse thereby frustrating her expectation to see a circle. There is a 'mistake' here but not in our sense of 'take'. There is, rather, a lapse in the correspondence of circles to the stimulus pattern.

Let us first consider the relata and then the relation. I have consistently written of the interpreted strings x as stimulus patterns. But when a degraded y is taken to be x, it perhaps seems more natural to consider x to be some kind of inner event not a surface phenomenon; but this is a matter for neuroanatomy, not philosophy.[2] At any rate for convenience and without sacrificing anything of importance, so far as I can see, I will count all x's and y's degraded or not as stimulus patterns. The good ones are in receptual equivalence classes as discussed in Section VI.1 and the bad are not. Thus all of these stimulus entities are in a set $(S \cup B)^*$ and K is a relation in $(S \cup B)^* \times S^* \times$ time.

Second, for each modality we need a relation between real objects and $(S \cup B)^*$, a relation which I will write '*Rep*' and which may be read 'is represented by at t'. *Rep* is a *relation*, not a function, as an object x that is τ could well be Rep by some stimulus pattern y that is not degraded, *viz.*, is a member of $\mathcal{U}_\tau$.[3] Or, there could be a lapse owing to environmental interference or positioning of the object *vis à vis* the perceiver so that x would be *Rep* by some not degraded y (a circle appears as an ellipse) that is not in $\mathcal{U}_\tau$; or there could be a contingent lapse as in the second case such that x is *Rep* by a degraded y. The representing entity y is *not* a Fodorian MR as it is a purely causal entity and does not carry information, except to an external observer who delves into cognitive science. It represents only as a surrogate for the object in taking-to-be, only as an entity demanded by (2).

The notion of a lapse from object to a good though untrue stimulus seems to be forced upon us by the common sense observation that one might expect an event that does occur and still accept it wrongly, i.e., in such a way that it disrupts expectations. This extension to objects now squares the theory perfectly with (ii) of (2) provided only that x be an object, not a stimulus pattern, and 'expects' and the other technical terms be modified. This is fairly easy. Using our new *Rep* relation and letting x range over real perceptual objects, y over stimulus patterns of $(S \cup B)^*$ and z over patterns in S^*, the definition of 'expects' in S^* in VI(7) is the same as before. This is worthy of comment. VI (7) means that T expects τ if and only if some stimulus y would lead to acceptance. It says nothing about the existence or inexistence of a real object.

The new definition of 'fulfills' is

> x *fulfills* T_τ at t if and only if T_τ is in some winning state q at t, there is some y such that $Rep(x, y, t)$ and for some $t' > t$ and some z, $K_q(y, z, t')$ and $M_\tau(q, z)$ is a winner. (3)

And the definition of 'disrupts' is

> x *disrupts* T_τ at t if and only if T_τ is in some winning state q at t, there is some y such that $Rep(x, y, t)$ and for every $t' > t$ and every z, if $K_q(y, z, t')$, then $M_\tau(q, z)$ is not a winner. (4)

Using these new meanings of 'fulfills' and 'disrupts' we obtain a new version of VI (13)

> T_τ expects τ and x is input at t if and only if either x fulfills T_τ at t or x disrupts T_τ at t.

which follows directly from VI (7) and the definitions (3), (4).

In our unsuccessful cut at (ii) of (2) we assumed 'x occurs' means 'x is computed, etc.'; but this stipulation is to be shelved now along with the considering of stimuli to be real objects. In order to show that our analysis of 'expectation' satisfies (2) we now interpret 'x occurs at t' to mean 'x is τ and T_τ in winning state q goes to a winning state $M_\tau(q, z)$ for some z, y and $t' > t$ such that $Rep(x, y, t)$ and $K_q(y, z, t')$'. Also, 'x does not occur at t

but T_τ takes x to occur' means 'x is not τ and T_τ in winning state q goes to a winning state $M_\tau(q, z)$ for some z, y, and $t' > t$ such that $Rep(x, y, t)$ and $K_q(y, z, t')$'.

We interpret 'x does not occur at t' to mean 'x is not τ and T_τ in a winning state q does not go into a winning state $M_\tau(q, z')$ for some z, etc.'; and 'x occurs but is not taken occur' to mean 'x is τ and T_τ in a winning q does not go into a winning state $M_\tau(q, z)$ for some z, y, $t' > t$ such $Rep(x, y, t)$ and $K_q(y, z, t')$'.

With those meanings in mind, (2) now follows from our new (3), (4) wherein x is a perceptual object.[4]

The ground we have gained can be summarized in this way. Our explication of 'expectation' in the sense of 'expectation of events' — x being τ at a t — appears to be adequate as it satisfies (2); the concept covers perceptual objects, not stimuli, as required. We also have obtained a better idea of the taking function and can set about removing our concern about taking drumbeats for soprano highs and good stuff for something other than what it is.

Let us dispose of the second issue first. Suppose that we are dealing with a composite automaton (Figure VI.5) that contains automata T_τ and $T_{\tau'}$ such that instances α and β of τ and τ' respectively are Rep by strings x and y of S^*; these strings have no parts from the vague class B, the degraded things. Assume that α fulfills T_τ and β, $T_{\tau'}$. To make the problem interesting let us also suppose that the sets of instances of τ and τ' are disjoint. Assume that x, contrary to what we want to show, is taken to be y at some time t'. Then since $M_{\tau'}(q, y)$ is final for some q, $T_{\tau'}$ is fulfilled by α, by (4). But T_τ is also fulfilled by α. Hence although τ and τ' are incompatible properties, both T_τ and $T_{\tau'}$ are fulfilled by the same stimulus pattern x. If x were degraded this would be a tolerable conclusion. But it is *not* degraded; and hence taking can not be extended to objects whose representations are nondegraded — i.e., to members of well-defined reception classes.[5]

The decision not to take good things for good gets independent support from naturalism as the following considerations show. We are near the end of a formulation of a causal theory of perception the *formal* nature of which has emerged in the analysis of expectation. Whether 'causal' is the right expression for a nonfunctional relation of a thing to a stimulus pattern is perhaps moot, especially when one considers that that pattern is in part constituted by the organism and can be taken in a variety of possible ways by a self-describing mechanism. *The organism fashions its own representations.* If we had stuck rigidly to formal talk of symbol strings x and states q instead of irritated organisms and stimulus patterns and perceptual (bodily) states we would have been free to choose an essentially idealistic or dualistic interpretation. In that case 'cause' would have been inappropriate if used in its ordinary sense. But our inclinations are naturalistic; and it is for this reason that 'cause' seems correct for the relation of object to organism even though the latter be active. Nautralism therefore imparts a material content to 'cause'. The object causes stimulus patterns that represent the thing to the subject, and those patterns must be good (not necessarily veridical in each case) or the organism would not survive. This kind of picture presents a view of perception that is both representational (causal) and evolutionistic.

According to evolutionism, human perceptual abilities are a result of natural selection, with "selection generally favoring improved recognition of objective featues of the environment in which our prehuman ancestors lived" (Shimony, 1971, p. 571; Edelman, 1987). This theme can be developed along lines that are clearly directed toward epistemological concerns as well as to the psychology of perception. Indeed, Shimony claims knowledge of the world is explained in terms of the knowledge — "principles of the natural sciences" including evolutionary principles — itself (Shimony, 1971, p. 582). Although I am essentially in agreement with Shimony my aim here is only to strengthen the claim about the taking of stimulus patterns, not to push for a general epistemological theory. It is implausible, I say, that 'clear' stimulus patterns (I am not insisting that I know what this might turn out to denote) fulfill expectations of incompatible property types if the representation of objects by stimuli is a product of evolutionary selection.[6] A thing can be taken for itself, or, if vague, for another; but not for another contrary thing if it is distinct. A mouse that takes a clear case of a cat stimulus to be a rabbit stimulus won't last.

If one thinks this play upon vague and precise has a cartesian ring to it she misunderstands the argument. I suspect that almost all human stimulation is vague, in which case there is no issue; but if there are clear, precise cases it is still perfectly possible on my view that one accept the clear and distinct ellipses stimulations as ellipses and be wrong — they might be circles. But this has nothing to do with taking. Lapses are one thing and are among the epistemic facts of life; taking good for good is not possible on evolutionary grounds, although the logic of expectation itself denies the possibility.

Evolutionism is, however, the *only* remedy for the other taking quandry. I consider it a fact that people do not take elephants for fleas except possibly when under the influence of some potently contractive drug. Formally, the set B of degraded sound stimuli could not map via the taking relation to S in such a way that a dull boom be taken for an expected bright, high A-flat by an evolved listener, that is, one that survives. I am not saying that a woman could not listen to music that pumps out booms and highs at once — witness punk rock — , and discriminate both until addled. But she would not *take* one for the other and *last*.

The remaining point to be settled about perceptual objects and stimulus patterns is the criterion for *same observable physical property*. We remind ourselves of the problem by finally setting down the definition of 'perception'. Except for VI(14), all of our formulations of 'expect' and the other terms have been general as they stipulate only that an expecting T be in in some winning state or other. But in order to go through an accepting computation for an entire object (even in a parallel fashion) automata begin in reset or initial states, q_0, which are always winners. Therefore (3) and (4) above can be simplified to

> x *fulfills* T at t if and only if there is a y such that $Rep(x, y, t)$ and for some t' greater than t and some z, $K(y, z, t'$ and $z \in \mathcal{U}$.
>
> (5)

> x *disrupts* T at t if and only if there is a y such that $Rep(x, y, t)$ and for every t' greater than t and every z, if $K(y, z, t')$ then $z \notin \mathcal{U}$.
>
> (6)

where K is short for K_{q_0} here and hereafter and of course $z \in \mathcal{U}_\tau$ means $M(q_0, z) \in Q_F$. Using the amended 'fulfills' VI(14) becomes

> T_τ *virtually accepts* x at t if and only if x fulfills T_τ at t.   (7)

Likewise (15) of Chapter VI becomes for the amended dispositional case of acceptance:

> x is *acceptable* to T_τ if and only if there is a y such that $Rep(x, y)$ and a z such that $R(y, z)$ and $z \in \mathcal{U}_\tau$.
>
> (8)

Then at last

> T_τ *perceives* that x is τ at t if and only if x is τ and T_τ virtually accepts x at t.
>
> (9)

So (propositional) perception is virtual acceptance of x when 'x is τ' is true and acceptance boils down to fulfilled expectation.

In these definitions the subject is always an automaton T_τ. However we normally speak of an organism or person as perceiving, etc. So to conform more closely to our ordinary ways let us amend VI(7), (7) and (9).

> $\mathcal{S}$ *expects* τ at t if and only if $\mathcal{S}$ realizes an automaton T_τ such that T_τ expects τ at t.

For (8),

> $\mathscr{S}$ *virtually accepts* x to be τ at t if and only if $\mathscr{S}$ realizes an automaton T_τ such that x fulfills T_τ at t. (11)

So for perception:

> $\mathscr{S}$ *perceives* that x is τ at t if and only if x is τ and $\mathscr{S}$ virtually accepts x to be τ at t. (12)

Also,

> That x is τ is *perceivable to* $\mathscr{S}$ if and only if x is τ and $\mathscr{S}$ realizes an automaton T_τ such that x is acceptable to T_τ. (13)

In these definitions T_τ might be thought of as a schema that can be filled out by names of all the kinds $\mathscr{S}$ is capable of perceiving. These automata are either parts of a product or themselves are embedded in networks in some manner or other as previously discussed (see pp. 76–81).

Now our question about sensible properties is, "what right do you have to take all occurrences of 'τ' in (12) to denote the same"? Earlier (p. 182) we individuated τ in terms of partial recursive operations on stimulus patterns x. But since x is an object now and not a stimulus and since it is highly unlikely that inner patterns (neuronal conditions of some sort) are brown, or lovely, or salty, the individuation principle does not directly apply. However it seems reasonable that two sensible properties be considered the same if their stimulus representations are of the same type, i.e., are computed the same in either the strict or the extended senses of Chapter VI. Thus two Necker cube aspects are different in that their sets of stimulus instantiations are domains of different partial recursive functions. This way of understanding 'same property' applies only to *sensible* physical properties and is entirely consistent with and even abetted by an evolutionist form of naturalism. It assumes just that objects *are* of the same type if responded to in the same way (from initial states). An organism that grappled with exigencies of the same kind via different perceptual responses (i.e., by going to final states outside of Q_F) would not seem to have much change of surviving. If there are no types but only resemblances, then the organism would respond pretty much in the same way to all members of the family, as can be seen from our manner of handling acceptance of resemblances.[7]

Finally, the notion of family resemblance itself naturally extends to ordinary things. If $Rep(x, y)$ and $Rep(x', y')$ and y' *can be taken for y,* then x *resembles* x'. And aside from the formal force of the theory the definition gets partial warrant on evolutionist grounds.

2. PERCEPTION PERSPECTIVES

Conditions I–IV of the previous chapter and Chisholm's conditions on expectation are all satisfied by my automata models and in so far forth mechanism is supported as a hypothesis about perception. A logic of recursive rules does appear to afford a plausible account of this aspect of the mind. I have not yet said much of anything about the intentional character of perception, although the ingredients are all there, and a more complete theory must continue on to other mental features and their ties to perception.

Before tracing these ties I want to discuss the above views on perception, in particular the logic of acceptance, in relation to certain current issues in computer science, psychology and philosophy of mind. There are two of direct relevance: (1) whether machines can be said to perceive or recognize anything; (2) whether human perception is some species of classification or template-matching.

(1) It is almost impossible to tell whether philosophers who complain about machines and their inadequacies for stimulating human intellectual skills are opposed to machines$_1$ or machines$_2$.[8] To give these persons the benefit of the doubt I will assume that their views are directed against machines$_2$ that embody machines$_1$, in short, against digital computers.

According to Matson computers do not compute, much less perceive anything (Matson, 1976, p. 89 f.). This follows from an ordinary language argument to the effect that 'perception' does not apply to insentient beings. I agree. Nevertheless the expression applies to *some* machines$_1$, namely to organisms of sufficient elaborateness. And I see nothing objectionable in employing the word 'perception' in automata modeling of organisms. A related issue is whether insentient beings can have intentions; and the same answer may be given: No, (so far as I know), if the thing is a *hardware* machine$_1$, and Yes if it is a living organism (which is exactly what I am trying to achieve in this and the next chapter). But this is old ground not worth dwelling on.

Of course there is a difference between being sentient and having intentions on the one hand, and being sentient with sentience somehow being an ingredient of intentionality on the other. The latter does call up a substantial issue (which I suspect is at the heart of questions of epiphenomenalism *vs* the identity theory) which I am avoiding, admittedly, in dividing off the theoretical treatment of mental occurrents from features. We shall have to face it as well as we can when the time comes to discuss the classical mind-body problem.

Questions about the possibility of perception for machines₁ have been raised by Hubert Dreyfus and others in a spirit that seems to be independent of the sentience question as such. Thus Dreyfus thinks that those who wish to model perception via computers are stuck with an assumption, related to logical atomism, "that everything essential to intelligent behavior can in principle be understood in terms of a determinate set of independent elements" (Dreyfus, 1967, p. 14). Similarly, Kenneth Sayre claims that (programmed) mechanical recognition depends upon "distinct features of a pattern to provide identifying criteria for inscriptions of that pattern" (Sayre, 1963, p. 170).[9]

In view of the results about Conditions I–IV of the foregoing chapter these claims are seen to be groundless. Turing machines can cope with indeterminate elements, can take advantage of informational contexts and even *determine* 'elements' on the basis of 'knowledge' of the properties of a gestalt whole. Since digital computers are equivalent to Turing machines with bounded tape the same is true, in principle, of them.[10] However my main concern is the defense of mechanism, not thinking machines, against unwarranted and frequently misguided attack.

(2) In view of the facts of perception some of which, at least, are captured in Conditions I–IV and the adequacy conditions for expectation which I am inclined to believe that anyone who has thought seriously about the subject would accept, it seems almost incredible that anyone might understand perception as a kind of matching against templates stored in the head, or as a kind of measurement — "as if recognition always consisted in comparing two impressions with one another" (Wittgenstein, 1953, par. 604). If this surmise were correct the human memory would be an overstuffed closet; in fact it would need to contain an infinite number of data bins. Each perceptual act would require an infinite number of matches, which of course is completely absurd. For this reason some cognitive psychologists think of perception as a kind of pattern-analysis that forms hypotheses on the basis of sparse evidence (Kolers and Perkins, 1975, p. 229; Kolers, 1974, pp. 51–52). Other psychologists, however, still find it fruitful to model perception by measurement: place a test pattern in a well-defined category if its distance from a paradigm or a prototype is less than its distance from a prototype of another pattern category (Reed and Friedman, 1973). Unfortunately, as we already pointed out in the previous chapter, this sort of

procedure would violate Condition II, which prescribes that a satisfactory model must be *relational*. However there is nothing to prevent the possibility that actual perceptual processes combine both inferential and matching-type of operations.

A benefit of my theory is that it shows how an 'inferential' or 'operational' process might be structured. Fodor draws an analogy between theories of conceptualization and theories of perception, and I agree with him on the appropriateness of it. "Perception is essentially a matter of problem solving. . . . Conceived this way, models of perception have the same general structure as models of concept learning; one needs a canonical form for representation of the data, . . . , a source of hypothesis for the extrapolation of data, . . . and a confirmation metric to select among the hypotheses" (Fodor, 1975, p. 42). In my logic of acceptance the stimulus patterns x are representations; the taking relation is an operation of hypothesis formation; and a formed hypothesis is (is represented) by a perceptual state that fulfills expectations. The 'confirmation metric' is a component of the total process that is still left open; I shall try to narrow the gap in the next chapter on belief and desire.

I should like to emphasize once again that stimulus representations of objects are not MR's (mental representations) in Fodor's sense, as they are syntactical entities from the point of view of the subject and probably totally out of consciousness. My final states – in the next chapter *outputs* – are, however, analogous to MR's and do have an intentional significance arising in perception (cf. the very end of Chap. V). This idea is developed in Chap. IX. But whether they are part of a language, assuming there is an internal language of mind at all other than unvoiced spoken language, is moot.

The doctrine that perception is inferential does not apply at all, it seems to me, to animals down on the scale that do not take – whose receptual machinery puts incoming presentations into a small number of sharply defined equivalence classes (frogs, e.g.; cf. Section VI.1) 'Perception' at that level is 'mechanical' in the popular, naive sense of the word; and it is simply an abuse of language to talk of frogs 'expectations' (although as a preliminary step I did introduce the term for any automaton having winning states, even before introducing the taking function). If this is correct, any information-process that looks like a truly intelligent process – I should say one that uses abduction or hypothesis formation – involves vagueness, taking, and a certain randomness. Without these, no intentionality and no mind. Of course human perception involves both direct, sharp, 'unproblematic' acceptance, and vagueness *cum* taking; the former is shared by the nonintelligent and the latter not (cf. Anscombe, 1974, p. 214).

Finally, I can not refrain from making the remark that this theory, if it is anywhere near being right, refutes the popular dogma that hardware machines$_1$ must, by their very mechanical nature, recognize by template matching and not the way we do (although I am far from certain exactly how we do do it) (Matson, 1976, p. 133). It is a perennial source of wonderment to me how phenomenologists and ordinary language specialists are able to issue pronouncements about the in-principle capabilities of machines$_1$ without doing any work, that is to say, without presenting any arguments at all. The fact (if it is any longer a fact) that computers have not been successfully programmed for hard recognition tasks tells you no more about what can be done computationally than the fact that man's failure to fly before the twentieth century tells anything about aviation.[11]

In summary of the theory of acceptance and perceptual belief of this and the previous chapter, a finite state automaton (FSA) *accepts* a stimulus pattern if it computes *via* a transition function to a final state (VI(2)). A group of FSA's in parallel (p. 174) can assign types to individuals (universals to particulars) and discriminate among types as well as do gestalt perception (conditions I–IV in Chap. VI). To show adequacy for these conditions the idea of a winning state — one for which there exists a stimulus input sending the automaton to a final state (VI(6) — was introduced. In terms of winning state, the idea of expectation of a type and fulfillment or disruption was introduced for a primitive, oversimplified case (VI(7–9)). Using the idea of a self-describing automaton (included in a superautomaton) the notion of taking one thing for another (VI(10)) was used to obtain a concept of resemblance (in the sense of taking one thing for another, not in the sense of matching) (VI(10a)) and revised notions of expecting, fulfillment and acceptability. The notion of resemblance built up in this way was shown to accomodate Wittgenstein family resemblance.

By introducing real objects that have causal relations to stimulus patterns one can satisfy rather strong conditions (VII(2)) on any suitable notion of expectation of perceived events. All the basic notions of expecting types, fulfillment, and taking can be redefined for the realistic case (VII(3–11)). A subject (a person) perceives an object to be of a type if and only if it realizes an automaton that virtually accepts (accepts *via* taking a stimulus representation as being of that type (VII(12)). In a nutshell: perception is a tacit computation by a subject that *takes* objects to be such and such.

CHAPTER VIII

BELIEF AND DESIRE

It is a short step from perception to perceptual belief, which is just acceptance of a sensible thing as a type. However, a *general* theory of belief is a long step from an abstract model of the perceptual, and I have no very constructive theory to present. A study of the relationship of perceptual belief to other intentional attitudes, in particular to immediate desires, is alone enough to keep us quite busy except for assorted programmatic remarks that I will offer in the last section of this chapter.

There is a psychology of belief and a semantics of belief, and the two should probably be kept apart until more is known. I do not mean there are two subdisciplines dividing a subject called 'belief' housed in a university department in some possible world, but rather that there is a psychological way of philosophizing about belief and a semantical way. Both ways, it seems to me, are in a rather sorry condition, especially when mixed. Your typical philosopher says belief is *of* sentences or propositions and is either a relation between a subject and a sentence or proposition, or otherwise is a functional state. The first of these considers belief in the context of the semantics of belief sentences and the second, which can be traced back to pragmatism and behaviorism, considers belief in the context of adaptive action. The semanticists have lately dipped into something called 'pragmatics', which in the heyday of logical empiricism was supposed to study the relationship of signs to users. In the newer subject the user is a pretty dull, opaque fellow who usually turns up as just another degree of freedom in a metalanguage or a somewhat to be poked at, a thing to worm assent or dissent out of. The cognitivists, who are fighting their way out of a bog of states and dispositions, seem to be concentrating on more or less programmatic efforts in role-playing and mental representations, the latter smacking of propositions. They appear to be giving up on the believer and concerning themselves more with the locus of propositions in the head.

I agree with Hartry Field that it might be a good thing to keep these tendencies separate even though, as just indicated, they are falling together (Field, 1978, p. 44). One of the tasks of psychology is to state laws "by which an organism's beliefs and desires evolve as he is subjected to sensory stimulation", and also to state the laws of how these features affect bodily movement. In formulating these laws there is no need to intrude questions of the meaning and objects of belief. Thus in the model of acceptance and perception $Rep(x, y)$ is indeed a representational relation. But one can go a long way, if we are right, toward understanding the psychology of perception without concerning ourselves about the meaning of y to the organism or about other semantical issues. This seems to be the case with perception as is attested to by the foregoing analysis. We did separate stimulus patterns from perceptual objects (which certainly do have an epistemic hence semantic significance!); but the object stimulus dichotomy is really a kind of formal trick to make a theory of expectation come out right. Rep, so far, is just a formal relation, but *causal* if one adopts a naturalistic ground. This does *not* mean Rep does not contain a seed of reference; it does. But the whole point is to continue to deal with the problems of perception and belief and other features in *stages*. Even expectation, which is a prime case of intentional phenomena, has been dealt with formally up to this point and the only hint of reference or meaning lies perhaps in the notion of *winner* and of *taking*. Although there is no meaning without intention there does seem to be something like intention without meaning, that is to say, intention in a nonlinguistic environment.

These preliminary reflections suggest that we keep on the incremental approach and deal with belief more or less independently of meaning questions and go from one stage to the next as the model naturally directs. So we begin with formal definitions. Then we shall consider *true* perceptual belief but only to the extent of getting a line, on the level of perceptual belief, on so-called Gettier counter-examples to Plato's views on knowledge. We shall see that there is indeed a natural way of illustrating the concepts, but this is hardly a foundation for full blown epistemology. Then we turn again to the functionalist claim that belief is not explicitly definable in a nonpsychological vocabulary, thus rounding out the 'formal' and relatively nonsemantic foundations of a psychology of belief.

1. PERCEPTUAL BELIEF

The relation of language to belief presents an open question as to whether language is essential to belief or not. Most of us often attribute beliefs and desires to dumb animals; mechanists can do so without fear of anthropomorphism as there is nothing in the theory of acceptance, including expectation and taking, that precludes application to higher animals. My own intuitions incline me to rule out everything up to about birds. But whether animals experience perceptual beliefs is strictly an empirical question not to be settled by presence or absence of substantial minds or speech, or on the basis of intuitions (including mine) or ordinary language considerations. If some animals do believe then it is patently wrong that belief is an attitude toward sentences. But we do normally think of human belief as *expressible*; for to say that Jones believes τ of some passing event x is just to say that she has fulfilled expectations — she virtually accepts x as τ — and knows at least one sentence of English that could be used express that x is τ.[1] Accordingly for human perceptual belief we add to acceptance a requirement of expressibility; thus we have similarly to VII(12),

> $\mathcal{S}$ *perceptually believes* that x is τ at t if and only if $\mathcal{S}$ realizes some T_τ that virtually accepts x is τ at t, and $\mathcal{S}$ knows a sentence in some language that expresses that x is τ.[2]   (1)

T_τ is part of an organism that is capable of many other perceptual beliefs, each corresponding to some T; these T's are not necessarily isolable organs or neuronal networks of some kind, but each one is an automaton, not a state, and represents a disposition that might or might not get exercised on a given occasion. For the time being I suggest that we maintain an attitude of indifference toward the qualifying clause on sentential expressibility. If you wish, think of 'knowledge' of such sentences as a correspondence between sentences and perceptual (final) states of the T's and of the sentences themselves as deliverable to overt expression by gating means of some sort. The semantics of belief sentences will be deferred until Chap. IX.

Beliefs are not states, and hence to individuate beliefs in terms of states is a mistake. A suitable notion of 'same belief' borrows the idea of *base machine* from the discussion of Condition II in Chapter VI. Let $\mathcal{S}$ perceptually believe that x is τ at t, and $\mathcal{S}'$ perceptually believe that x is τ' at t. Then

> $\mathcal{S}$ and $\mathcal{S}'$ *have the same perceptual belief* at t if and only if $\mathcal{S}$ realizes T_τ and $\mathcal{S}$ realizes $T_{\tau'}$ and the base Turing machines of acceptors T_τ and T_τ compute the same partial recursive function on the common domain $\mathcal{S}$.   (2)

If $\mathcal{S} = \mathcal{S}'$ the definition covers the case of one person having beliefs that are the same; while if $\mathcal{S} \neq \mathcal{S}'$ it covers the case of two persons holding one belief. T_τ and $T_{\tau'}$ need not be structurally the same either in the sense of isomorphism or of same network embodiment, nor need they compute by the way of the same algorithm (see Note VI.12). If you like propositions, then $\mathcal{S}$ and $\mathcal{S}'$ believe the *same proposition*, which is expressed in English by either 'x is τ' or 'x is τ'', and the two sentences are *synonomous* although they certainly need not be inscriptionally the same or even have the same surface structure. Although somewhat premature, this remark about propositions does suggest a natural way to pass on to the subject of meaning.

Still keeping to a more or less formal approach, certain features of the model illuminate some aspects of the foundations of knowledge. Perceptual belief stands to perceptual knowledge as acceptance of an object does to perception; knowledge is true belief, and perception is veridical acceptance.[3] Now by taking 'true' as an unanalyzed predicate of sentences or propositions, one can get some insight into the epistemology of belief by heeding the role of *Rep* and the K relation in the definition of 'belief'. In the logic of perception, 'knows' in the case of perceptual knowledge is analyzable as follows using (1).

> $\mathcal{S}$ *knows* at t *that* x is τ if and only if x is τ and $\mathcal{S}$ realizes some automaton T_τ, such that there is a y, $t' > t$, and a z such that $Rep(x, y, t)$, $K(y, z, t')$, and $z \in \mathcal{U}_\tau$; and T_τ knows a sentence in some language L that expresses that x is τ. (3)

(The occurrence of 'knows' a sentence in the analysans means 'correlates to a final state' as heretofore explained.)

Now philosophers generally make the condition that belief must be justified (or reasoned belief, supported by evidence, etc.), more explicit. The reason for this is that they do not want to count a belief as knowledge when there is nothing but an adventitious relation between the believer and the true facts. Jones believes there is life in another galaxy, and there is, let us suppose; but she doesn't know it for she does not have evidential support. Or, she conjectures that the number of twin primes is infinite, but she doesn't have a proof, so she doesn't know it even if the conjecture be true. Let us suppose that on the level of perceptual belief the evidence for the belief is just that of sense experience, which is a basic thesis of traditional empiricism. The presence of this type of support is built into our model: x causes y, and the evolutionist thesis makes y *representational* in our surrogate sense; also, z is *taken* to be y on *evidence* which is shown by the fact that T_τ is in a winning state with expectations being fulfilled, or the taking does not occur.

Now the further epistemological problem is that this type of formula for knowledge is not sufficient. Our analysis of perceptual belief displays enough of the etiology of knowledge to expose the trouble. Edmund Gettier has shown that one can satisfy all of the conditions for knowledge – P is true, T believes P, there is justifying evidence in support of P – and yet not have a warranted claim to knowledge (Gettier, 1963). For suppose that Smith and Jones have applied for a certain job. Smith has been told by her boss that Jones is the most likely candidate for the position, and Smith knows Jones has ten dollars in her purse as she, Smith, just saw Jones count it out. Thus Smith has evidence for

(a)   Jones is the person who will get the job and she has ten dollars in her purse.

(a) entails

(b)   The person who will get the job has ten dollars in her purse.

Meanwhile, unbeknownst to herself, Smith has actually been appointed to the job and happens to have ten dollars in her purse although she doesn't know it as she has not counted recently. From this data it follows that Smith believes (b); (b) is true; and (c) Smith is justified in believing (b) is true because she has been told by the person who decides, that Jones will most likely get the job; and she just saw Jones count ten dollars. But Gettier contends she doesn't know (b) because she bases her belief on a count of dollars in Jones' purse and she falsely believes Jones to be the person appointed.[4]

Perceptual belief presents a simpler and perhaps less interesting example because the false evidence does not entail the true proposition but only gives inductive evidence. But the peculiar gap between evidence and the belief is still manifest. Jones who is driving her car past a farm yard on a misty morning sees an animal she takes to be a sheep but which is really a goat. Unbeknownst to her, there is a sheep nibbling grass behind a shed in that yard. So her belief that there is a sheep in the yard is true and is based on strong visual evidence, while the evidence does not support the truth that there is a sheep in the yard because the thing furnishing the evidence is a goat.[5]

In terms of the automaton model, let τ be a sensible property, x a perceptual object, y a pattern in $U = (S \cup B)^*$, and z a pattern in S^*. T_τ is the accepting automaton and $\mathcal{U}_\tau$ is the set of accepted z's where as usual $\mathcal{U}_\tau \subseteq S^*$. Finally suppose that $Rep(x, y, t)$ and $K(y, z, t')$ for the appropriate t'. (These are just the notations of (3) and earlier and are included here for quick reference.) There are eight initially plausible cases of T_τ believing or not believing x is τ. They are listed in Table I.[6]

TABLE I

(1) x is τ	$y \in \mathcal{U}_\tau$	$z \in \mathcal{U}_\tau$	$y = z$; no take; T_τ believes x is τ; and x is τ.
(2) x is τ	$y \in \mathcal{U}_\tau$	$z \notin \mathcal{U}_\tau$	Impossible.
(3) x is τ	$y \in U - \mathcal{U}_\tau$	$z \in \mathcal{U}_\tau$	$y \neq z$; take; T_τ believes x is τ; and x is τ.
(4) x is τ	$y \in U - \mathcal{U}_\tau$	$z \notin \mathcal{U}_\tau$	$y \neq z$; take; T_τ does not believe x is τ; but x is τ.
(5) x is not τ	$y \in \mathcal{U}_\tau$	$z \in \mathcal{U}_\tau$	$y = z$; no take; T_τ believes x is τ; but x is not τ.
(6) x is not τ	$y \in \mathcal{U}_\tau$	$z \notin \mathcal{U}_\tau$	Impossible.
(7) x is not τ	$y \in U - \mathcal{U}_\tau$	$z \in \mathcal{U}_\tau$	$y \neq z$; take; T_τ believes x is τ; but x is not τ.
(8) x is not τ	$y \in U - \mathcal{U}_\tau$	$z \notin \mathcal{U}_\tau$	$y \neq z$; take; T_τ believes x is not τ; and x is not τ.

Line (1) appears to be a case of knowledge, for 'x is τ' is true, T_τ believes x is τ and did not take the representing string to be another string z. For the belief to be evidential, however, we might have to count *Rep* not only as causal but as otherwise epistemically coupling x to y.[7] For the moment let us agree that (1) is knowledge for comparison with cases (2)–(8) even though we are not able to characterize *Rep* fully.

(2) can not obtain for reasons already used in arguing against the extension of the taking function to 'pure' patterns y.

(3) is a Gettier case. The string y is not in $\mathcal{U}_\tau$, and yet is taken to be; it could not possibly 'represent' or be complete evidence for x, as it could be exactly the same y (of the *string*-type) as the occurrence of 'y' in (7), and in *that* case x is *not* τ! What makes (3) Gettier is that y fulfills expectations, which is a kind of psychological evidence but of little epistemic force.

(4) is a nonproblematic case of x being τ but not taken to be τ as y is 'degraded' and taken otherwise than a τ.

(5) is a case of a lapse in *Rep* wherein something not τ, τ', say, is represented as a τ. This is a clear case of τ' occurring but taken to be other than τ', a situation that led us to posit perceptual objects as distinct from stimulus patterns.

(6) is immpossible for the same reasons as (2).

(7) is the case wherein the expected event does not occur but is taken to occur.

(8), finally, is a Gettier example parallel to (3); what makes it such is that y could be exactly the same y as in (4); again, y is psychologically evidential but of slight epistemic force for the attribution or disattribution of τ to x.

It seems to me that this case-by-case analysis of perceptual belief might be of some use in epistemology, although I want to claim only that it clarifies issues, not that it solves any. If a mechanist logic of mind is on the right track, perceptual belief is abductive, and in C. I. Lewis' terms is of the nature of 'nonterminating' judgment. Ultimately what qualifies (1) as knowledge and what defeats Gettier counterexamples (so that knowledge is justified true belief after all) is community assent and induction − taking another look and still another. Further, as belief plays some role in natural man's adaptive pursuits a less truncated view of it might tend to facilitate an empiricist epistemology.

2. DESIRE

Most philosophers in the naturalist camp think that belief is a disposition to act or respond in some way. If this is true, then the foregoing analysis misses belief *qua* belief because it treats the individual organism too abstractly. The model not only considers him in isolation (except for the *Rep* relation to objects) but doesn't even give him a response repertoire, only hypothetical internal entities called 'perceptual states'! Furthermore beliefs as dispositions to act in certain ways involve wants or desires, since action entails desired ends to be achieved. Again, it is often claimed, 'belief' can not be explicitly defined in any way, including automata-theoretic terms because of its unbreakable semantic ties to 'desire'. 'Belief' can only be defined in other terms expressing intentionality and specifically in terms of 'desire', and *vice versa*.

True or not, these claims introduce a flood of difficulties that plague contemporary mental philosophy. I number among them (i) the problem of subcategorizing beliefs: it seems to me there is a *radical* difference between perceptual belief and beliefs that have an *essential* tie to verbalization, for example belief that grass in the yard is green versus belief in the Hahn-Banach theorem of analysis. (ii) There is little agreement as to the *sort* of thing a belief is: a state? disposition? relation? avowed idea? a sentential operator? (iii) Is 'belief' explicitly definable? (iv) If so, are there any conditions that any two philosophers would agree must be satisfied by a definition? Although there is plenty to do in attempting to construct one line of theory even on a very elementary level, there seems to be no choice but to engage in some preliminary distinction-making regarding (i)–(iv).

(i) Current philosophy makes few distinctions among the welter of *kinds* of beliefs. For just consider perceptual belief, mathematical belief, linguistical belief, physical belief and philosophical belief. I am not only saying the *objects* of these several kinds are different; rather I suspect that the psychology may be different from one family to the other. While perceptual belief is or entails a disposition to act, the same can not be said of beliefs that seem to have some essential dependence on language, such as mathematical belief. 'The continuum hypothesis is true' expresses a belief of mine that has no relation to any particular action I know of except, vaguely, writing something down in a discussion of set theory. But there certainly is no *unique* act associated to it. Must there always be an action that has fixed relation to belief like this?[8] Does an associative or illative relation to another belief count as an act? Do mental acts count? They do not for behaviorists; but perhaps they ought to in all consistency for cognitivists. Likewise, 'there are no unbounded sentences' is something I believe, but it has no force to it except to restrain me from looking around for infinite strings or trying to utter one. One might insist that there *must* be some action implicit in belief, in order to preserve the theory that belief is a disposition to act; but such a move would simply convert the disposition to act dogma into a pointless redundancy. I am inclined to think that the beliefs-are-dispositions-to-act stance is of a piece with the dogma that every bodily movement, including intentional acts, has an identifiable antecedent stimulus – a dogma shattered by Chomsky in regard to language behavior many years ago.

(ii) Perceptual belief, however, *is* a disposition and as such is built into automata. Moreover I suspect that in this case there is a law-like connection to action, which as Hume argued long ago would imply that action is not part of the meaning of belief. And concerning the nature of belief queried above, the answer is 'none of the above'. As we have seen, perceptual belief, which is probably the simplest variety of belief, is a very complex relation among a person, an automaton, a final state, a perceptual object, a stimulus pattern, a taken stimulus pattern, and possibly a 'proposition'. It is not a 2-ary relation or a state or a disposition in any of the numerous vague behaviorist or functionalist construals of the terms. If my view is wrong, it errs on the simplistic side.

(iii) The problem of explicit vs implicit definition is closely related to the *synthetic* character of the belief-action relation just alluded to with reference to Hume; specifically it brings to mind Brentano's thesis. According to the nineteenth century German thinker Franz Brentano intentional attitudes like belief characterize the mind *essentially*; as the mind can direct itself on an 'object that is inexistent' such as mermaids or round squares, mental phenomena are irreducible to the physical (Brentano, 1924). For this reason psychology must be autonomous; it studies mental relations having inexistent correlates, which is not possible in a strictly physicalist or materialist ontology. A consequence of this thesis (or another way of putting it) is that intentional concepts such as *belief*, which might relate to the 'inexistent', can not be defined except in other terms of psychology, that is to say, in other intentional terms (Chisholm, 1957, Chapter 11; Quine, 1960, pp. 219–222). In principle the circles of definition, if anyone ever manage to construct them, could be quite large or even broken if psychologists were able to settle on ground terms, such as 'mass' in classical physics. Belief and desire, however, are at the ends of a diameter of vanishingly small length – at least so it is maintained by many functionalists.

Now a way to defeat Brentano is to externalize intentions in the style of British behaviorism. Belief then is a disposition to behavioral acts of certain kinds that are strictly observable; there is no inner phenomenological world of mind *à la* Brentano or Descartes irreducibly set-off from ordinary science. But it is generally held for various other reasons, some of them already discussed earlier in Chapters IV and V, that behaviorism is a failure. So a next move is inward to some variety of central state theory or functionalism. Whatever be the specific logistics of the move, the typical result is a doctrine of belief and other attitudes that either clings to Brentano's insight but 'naturalizes' belief-talk in some way so that it is about physical organisms and their behaviors or that introduces belief objects in an ontologically innocent way.[9] The first typically makes beliefs functional states (as we have already seen), such states being nothing but material items, ontologically, but owing their character *qua* states to relationships to other states (beliefs to desires, e.g.) and inputs. This is precisely the role-playing view rejected in Chapter V in favor of the present programme. For the functionalist, then, belief is still a disposition to act, in the spirit of behaviorism; but dispositions are now states (leading to the inevitable confusions marked in Chapter V) and beliefs *cum* states or events of some kind are only implicitly definable. The second construes belief as a relation, but unlike Brentano's mental relations, which have no material correlates, relate the organism to a sentence token or mental representation of some kind or to possible worlds. Thus one avoids Brentano by appeal to functional states, which are ontologically material, while retaining the role-playing property; or by construing the mental relations as spanning persons and purely material or mathematical things after all.[10]

In both of these approaches the ontological bite is taken out of Brentano's thesis, but the doctrine of an autonomous science of the mental still threatens. For some thinkers, Grice and Dennett among others, explicit definitions of features in terms not presupposing the intentional does not seem possible. So belief must be defined in terms of intentions or acts in some way that presupposes want or desire, if they are right; and likewise desire must analyze in terms of belief. This is a contemporary form of holism.

Despite its popularity and deep entrenchment in contemporary thought this position is quite mistaken, it seems to me. The mistake stems from a failure to distinguish evidential conditions of belief and desire (which might require reference to other beliefs, hopes, and so on, indefinitely), and explicative definition. The confusion can in part be traced to Grice (1974) but perhaps more influentially to Quine. Individuation of intentional attitudes *qua attitudinal* is one thing, while the holistic intercausal connections of attitudes is another (cf. Loar, 1981, p. 4). If you merge the two you get Grice's Brentano. If you deny the possibility of individuation owing to holistic interplay of meanings (a.k.a. indeterminacy of translation) you get Quine. Perceptual belief is a disposition to act given certain desires. This requires explications of the relata *and* a theory of their functional (causal) interactions in machine terms.

(iv) I wish to perform the kind of exercise suggested by this example by introducing certain conditions, which I take would be the sort philosophers would accept, then going on to explicit definitions of 'desire' and 'acts' that together with the definition of 'perceptual belief' entail those conditions. Here a difficulty of obtaining adequacy conditions arises. It is a distressing fact that anything like firm conditions for analysis of belief and desire to satisfy can not be garnered from the uses of 'perceptual belief' or 'desire' in ordinary speech or from the writings of philosophers. So the enterprise of stating conditions I have in mind is filled with exegetical risk. To compensate, there is perhaps less risk in writing definitions themselves as there is so little in the way of received conditions to satisfy. At any rate let's begin with an example from (Dennett, 1978, p. 18) which I take it he would support as a condition (or, for him, as expressing a schema for implicit definition):

A man's standing under a tree [an act] is a behavioral indicator of

his *belief* that it is raining, but only under the assumption that
he *desires* to stay dry, and if we look for evidence that he *wants*
to stay dry, his standing under the tree will do, but only under
the assumption that he *believes* the tree will shelter him [italics
mine].   (4)

According to Grice (4) would be incomplete if meant as an implicit definition. The man can be counted on to stand under a tree only if there is no
condition he *wants more* than staying dry. "But the incorporation of any
version of this proviso into the definiens for wanting will reintroduce the
concept of wanting itself" (Grice, 1974–75, pp. 24–25). And then of course
the new concept of wanting would require a further proviso, *ad infinitum*.
It seems to me, however, that this confuses a putatively psychological phenomenon about conflict and competition of desires with the question of the
meaning of 'desire'. We simply do not need to add this proviso to any definition, explicit or implicit, as the following considerations show.

Think of (4) as telling a *closed* story. The subject intends to keep dry even
though he might be thinking about dinner, picking his ear, vaguely worrying
about the meaning of the Indeterminacy Principle, and running through
the second movement of Beethoven's Opus 3, No. 2 in the back of his head.
Nevertheless the story is closed; his attention is focused on keeping dry —
none of the other mental stirrings are at a level sufficient to disturb the
small belief-act-desire loop. If this were not so he would never successfully
act to get anything done. This kind of closure property of the loop prompts,
in light of Grice's worries, certain further observations our theory must
heed.

(a) If the subject's desire to stay dry is fulfilled, he does not need to act
repeatedly to fulfill it — if dry, he does not go out into the rain in order
to act again to get dry, unless he *desires* to do this. (b) His having desires and
beliefs and acting thereupon during a given time interval is a system closed
off from other parts of his on-going life and is *stable* until perturbed either
by the environment or by new desires springing up. (c) The story presupposes
that the individual's *attention* is focused on rain, being dry, and acting in
certain ways. The subject's larger repertoire of beliefs, desires, and the like
are latent or their on-goingness is attentuated during the episode, unless the
system is perturbed. If these propositions are correct, and they appear to get
support from psychological theories of attention and from experience itself,
then Grice's point has no peculiar significance for the explicit-implicit definition issue, and hence we quite safely drop it. Instead of adding his proviso

to every definition, we embody (a)–(c) in a principle that acknowledges the competition amongst desires yet does not make that relation a part of the meaning of desire (and *mutatis mutandis* for other intentional attitudes).

> *Stability Principle*: If a subject's desires or wants *W* are satisfied at a certain time, then the subject does not act to satisfy *W* again unless he is perturbed. If other desires take command, then the subject does not act to satisfy *W*, and *vice versa*. (5)

The idea of taking command will be made acceptably clear in analogy to program subroutines or circuit gating in computer technology – but one thing at a time. The stability principle is a *ceteris paribus* clause, in effect, underlying the law-like conditions to be set forth below.

In pursuit of conditions, if we break Dennett's (4) up into two parts we shall see that some modifications are needed.

> The man believes it is raining implies that if he desires to stay dry, then he will act to get under a tree. (6a)
> The man desires to stay implies that if he believes it is raining, then he will act to get under a tree. (6b)

(6a) and (6b) are elliptical: they rest on an underlying presupposition that the man believes some relation between raining and getting wet and between a certain act and getting dry. According to Grice, the man desires to stay dry just in case he is disposed to act in ways he believes will realize getting dry and not in ways that will not (Grice, 1974–75, p. 24). This way of putting the matter does not mention rain, but does relate the act of getting dry to a certain belief that he will get dry. We might interpret Grice in two ways. The first is essentially the same, incidentally, as Scheffler's way (Scheffler, 1963, p. 93):

> If one desires something, then if he believes there is a relationship between what he believes and a certain act, then he acts.

Or, in the example,

> The man desires to stay dry implies that if he believes getting under a tree will enable him to stay dry, then he will act to get under the tree.

Here 'he believes, etc.' expresses belief in a *relation* between the act and the outcome. The second interpretation of Grice, which is more literal, says

The man desires to stay dry if and only if he believes he will
stay dry if and only if he acts to get under the tree.

But I don't think this is what we want. For, if x believes he will stay dry (or
is dry), there is no implication that he will further act to stay dry, although
his belief might be a disposition to do something else, like to go home. The
other half of the trial definiens says that if the man acts to stay dry he
believes he will stay dry. This seems to be correct as the act is intentional
– 'goal-directed'. In my model 'he believes he will stay dry' is more stuiably
expressed 'expects he will stay dry', as it is certainly false that his desire
will be satisfied in all cases. Acts get aborted.

If we modify Grice to read "the man desires to stay dry just in case, if
he acts to get under the tree, then he expects to stay dry," then we also
square with Scheffler's scheme, now to be expressed in this way:

The man desires to stay dry implies if he believes getting under
the tree will enable him to stay dry, then if he acts to stay dry
by getting under the tree, then he expects to stay dry.

The modified Grice, however, is just Dennett (rendered as in (6a) and (6b))
with the underlying attitudes made more explicit. We will adopt it as it is
stronger than Scheffler's version; but we add the condition of the man
believing it is raining in order to retain our intuitive insights about the symmetrical interrelationships of belief and desire expressed in Dennett's (4).
The upshot is a pair of adequacy conditions that accommodate all three
thinkers and my own views as well. Unlike the Grice and Dennett examples,
(7a) and (7b) state conditions, not tentative implicit definitions.[11] If one
requires consensus of more than the four of us let him beat his way through
the literature or conduct a poll.[12] Here they are.

$\mathscr{S}$ *believes* q implies that if $\mathscr{S}$ desires p, then if $\mathscr{S}$ acts in a
way depending on q, then $\mathscr{S}$ expects p.   (7a)
$\mathscr{S}$ *desires* p implies that if $\mathscr{S}$ believes q, then if $\mathscr{S}$ acts in a
way depending on q, then $\mathscr{S}$ expects p.   (7b)

'Belief' and 'desire' should be understood to mean 'perceptual belief' and
'desire for immediately perceivable things' respectively. Both belief and desire
are propositional (whatever that turns out to mean), and expressions such
as 'desires x of a certain kind τ' are rewritten 'desires that x is τ', although
we don't ordinarily talk that way. The idea is that all mental intentions

are Russell's 'propositional attitudes'. The ontologically conservative reader
may take 'p' and 'q' in the statement of conditions as blanks for sentential
clauses of the form 'that u is r at t' with the usual uniformity constraints.

3. A MODEL OF DESIRE

In order to define 'desire' we just need a prior analysis of 'acts' of the right
sort since we already have (1) for 'perceptual belief'. It turns out that the
definition is essentially (7b) itself so that that condition follows immediately.
Then (7a) follows from (7b) directly as they are equivalent.

To introduce the ensuing somewhat complicated proceedings let us turn
to Figure 1. In this diagram, T_τ is an automaton that combines an acceptor
(FSA) and a complete finite automaton with output (FA). $T_{\tau'}$ is again an
acceptor that might be a part of some more complex automaton. We assume
that both T_τ and $T_{\tau'}$ are embedded in super-automata (perhaps one will
do — there is no need to decide) that are able to recognize vague symbols
(B), detect winners, carry out the computation of the taking function, and
determine present states — they have all the capabilities of T' of Section
VI.3.

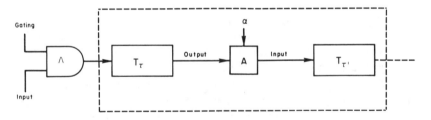

Fig. 1. Serial automaton with gating.

The output of T_τ is related to the input of $T_{\tau'}$ by A which is depicted by a
box with two inputs — the output of T_τ and α, which is an environmental
contribution of some sort, something to act on to produce input — and an
output which is input to $T_{\tau'}$. The box itself might be thought of as a 'grasping
function'.

Let us first examine $T_{\tau'}$. Suppose McGuire desires to hear a Bach piece
(I'm hereby dismissing the man under the tree in favor of McGuire and
music, which combined provide paradigm examples). To be satisfied, McGuire
must hear what she believes to be Bach. Similarly, to satisfy hunger for food

she must taste, smell, chew etc. certain inputs that she *believes* are food items. Thus satisfaction of desire implies belief; and likewise frustration implies nonbelief. Satisfaction (frustration) of desire is fulfillment (disruption) of a certain automaton acceptor. This acceptor is $T_{\tau'}$.

Next let me explain T_τ. T_τ represents the belief that supports an act that is meant to satisfy a desire. If the subject believes an input x is the right kind, she goes into a final state. This state generates an output that in turn yields input for $T_{\tau'}$ via the A-box. This production of input for $T_{\tau'}$ is an *act*. T_τ thus produces input to $T_{\tau'}$ that possibly satisfies the subject's desire as just described. McGuire desires Bach. She sees what she believes to be a sound system (T_τ goes into a perceptual state). She grasps a knob or pushes buttons with her hand and listens for Bach. (The perceptual state generates output which by way of efferent transducers moves her fingers and hands. In contact with the sound system control α she produces via A and her *Rep* function auditory stimulus patterns for reception and possible acceptance by $T_{\tau'}$.)

Evidently the crucial difference between belief *qua* belief and belief as a component of desire satisfaction, if the model is near reality, is that in the latter the subject herself participates in the fashioning of stimulus patterns. What makes the total movement ending in manipulation of some kind an *act* is its stemming from a perceptual state, or indeed from any *winner*. Any bodily movement (in a relevant context such as depicted in Figure 1) is *not* an act if it stems from a nonwinning state. However a final state is only a necessary condition for action. To be an act a movement must also produce, through A, a stimulus that is *expected*.

One of the inputs to the automaton system of Figure 1 is labelled 'Gating'. A signal of True or 1 on *gating* in our model is the counterpart of attention getting. If the signal = 1, both T_τ and $T_{\tau'}$ are reset to their initial states which, as they are winners, means the subject expects to perceive a sound system and to hear Bach. Of course it is quite possible that she be disappointed in either or both regards, that she take the right things the wrong way or take nonsound systems to be sound systems, nonBach to be Bach, etc. As the behaviorist might say if he allowed himself internal state concepts the subject's disposition to respond is being activitated; she is in a 'mental set'.

The presence of a structure such as this in McGuire's anatomical make-up means she *likes* Bach or has a disposition to listen to it under certain circumstances. If she were presented with a sound source and she acted in a certain way and listened, given that gating were activated at the appropriate time, then at that time she would *desire* Bach. Here once more I am drawing a distinction between a disposition (a 'place-holder' realized by a definite structure and expressible in a subjunctive conditional) and an explicit act, by way of a mathematical description of T_τ and $T_{\tau'}$ and their interconnections in contrast with an historical description of a computation starting at t.

Let us back-up to the action relation A. One of its relata is an output from T_τ and the other is α. Since T is an FA it has outputs that proceed both from final (always winning) states and nonfinal or disrupting states. In the latter instance there is no appropriate act to be directed to satisfying desire — button pushing on the sound system — as the subject does not *believe* that thing is a τ, i.e., is suitable to act to produce a stimulus pattern for $T_{\tau'}$. In such cases the subject either moves away more or less randomly or some other motive takes command; some other system is gated in, by the stability principle (5).

The business being conducted at the A-box is undoubtedly extremely complex and may involve other subsidiary automata and certainly neuro-muscular phenomena below the psychologist's level of scientific concern. If the control of the knob is consciously executed and intentional, then some smaller belief-to-belief loop must be involved that might be so complex as to include taking and the rest. Or it might be automatic — on the cerebellar level, one might guess. Thus Figure 1, in this respect at least, abstracts away from an extremely intricate process that no doubt has its own logic.

Since A might itself realize a taking function or lapses might occur in any of the representations intrinsic to A, it is a relation, not a function. So an output from a final state of T_τ does not uniquely produce acceptable input for $T_{\tau'}$. The object x input to T_τ could indeed be a sound system with Bach on deck; T_τ could be in a winning state and yet the action at A fail to yield Bach. Moreover McGuire could take x to be a sound system and an input z generated at A while it is false that x is a sound system or that z is Bach or both. But such eventualities are consequences of the theory, as they should be. What is believed at either T_τ or $T_{\tau'}$ depends in part on the subject and her expectations.

Duty now beckons us from this relatively straight forward expository exercise to the perils of hard, careful work. Figure 1 is a *cascade* or *serially-connected* automaton written $T_\tau \otimes T_{\tau'}$ plus the A relation. I will not go into much technical detail about the structure as it is fortunately not needed for our purposes here. A few details appear in Notes.[13] T_τ is a new kind of automaton structure consisting as usual of nonempty, finite sets S, Q, and an output set O, a transition function M, and an output function N.

So far the structure is a model of the same type as Peter the Sleeper, pp. 61–63, with one exception. Whereas Peter's N-function is a map from pairs of states and inputs, our new function N is a map from states only. Thus N is a function on Q to outputs O. The table for some specific T might give $N(q) = o$ for some q. The transition function M operates the same as in conventional FA. Suppose T is in state q and gets input s. Then q goes to some state q', i.e., $M(q, s) = q'$, and $N(q')$ is output. Note that in our new machine, called a 'Moore machine' after its inventor, the output depends only on the *next* state q' after transition from q.[14] Strings x of symbols S are computed as follows using III(1a), here (8), (but replacing III.(1b) by (9))

$$M(q, \Lambda) = q$$
$$M(q, xs) = M(M(q, x), s) \tag{8}$$
$$N(q) = o \quad \text{(from the defining table)}$$
$$N(q, x) = N(M(q, x))^{15} \tag{9}$$

where $o \in O$ and the other symbols have the usual significance. We shall also need a new complete output function to replace III(1c) for mapping input strings to output strings. Such a function is given by:

$$\mathcal{N}(q, x) = N(q)N(q, s_1)N(q, s_1 s_2) \ldots N(q, s_1 s_2 \ldots s_k)$$
$$= o_0 o_1 o_2 \ldots o_k. \tag{10}$$

where $x = s_1 s_2 \ldots s_k$ for some k.

Moore machines differ from FA in that the first output o_0 is entirely independent of x. In effect the output computed from input begins at the *second* symbol time (at time 1) and in comparison to standard FA, there is, therefore, a unit delay before computed output. $N(q)$ is often regarded as 'spurious' and is 'thrown away'. We want the Moore model because it just fits the bill in the analysis of 'desire': output depends only on the state (although of course the state has an earlier input history). In the application to desire, if T accepts x, then $M(q_0, x) = q_F$, a final state, and $N(q_F)$ feeds into the A box.

The automaton T_τ also has a component subset Q_F of final states and an initial state q_0 as already declared just above. So T_τ combines the conventional Moore machine concept with that of an FSA. The reason we have incorporated this property is that we want the system to *accept* a string as a type and then to *produce* output and perhaps *act*, as informally described, on the basis of its having accepted (belief) or not accepted (disrupted) a string. An example might be helpful. Suppose T_τ accepts alternating strings on $\{0, 1\}$ beginning with a 0. We wish to examine what happens when a string is introduced. Consider $x = 0101$. Now $M(q_0, 0101) = q_F \in Q_F$. Also, $N(q_0, 0101) = N(M(q_0, 0101))$ by (9) and

$$\mathcal{N}(q_0, 0101)$$
$$= N(q_0)\mathcal{N}(q_0, 0)\mathcal{N}(q_0, 01)\mathcal{N}(q_0, 010)\mathcal{N}(q_0, 0101) \qquad (11)$$

by (10).[16] Suppose we discard $N(q_0)$, and that the next three elements of the output are o_1, o_2, and o_3. Then since $M(q_0, 0101) = q_F$ and $N(q_0, 0101)$ $= N(M(q_0, 0101))$, $\mathcal{N}(q_0, 0101) = o_1 o_2 o_3 N(q_F)$. On the other hand if x were 0100, M would have some nonfinal value q and the value of $\mathcal{N}(q_0, 0100)$ would be $o_1 o_2 o_3 N(q)$. In the case $x = 0101$, T_τ believes something and the *perceptual* state maps to an output; in the other case T_τ does not believe x and a *nonfinal* state maps to output, but not one intended to satisfy $T_{\tau'}$, the tandem automaton.

Throughout the following discussion $T_\tau = \langle S, Q, O, q_0, M_\tau, N_\tau, Q_F \rangle$ and $T_{\tau'} = \langle S', Q', q_0', M', Q_F' \rangle$. T_τ is a modified Moore machine as just described, and $T_{\tau'}$ is an FSA. $T_\tau \otimes T_{\tau'}$ is the serial connection (see Note 14) which for us means simply that $S' = O$, the input of T' is the output of T. To cut down on an already formidable notation I write here 'T' or 'T_τ' and 'T'' for '$T_{\tau'}$'.

Given T and T' the relation A of Figure 1 is over outputs of T (which are functions of inputs y), environmental variables α of some kind as explained, inputs to T' and times; although A is not a function, it is handy to write

(12) $A(N(o, \alpha)) = x$ at t (12)

where o is a function of inputs to T (in the case we're interested in, an output function of inputs to T as we shall see in due course).

We now need explications of 'acts' and 'desires'. Intuitively an action of a subject is grounded in some kind of belief and is aimed at an outcome that is expected. We shall understand these two conditions to be necessary and sufficient for a bodily movement to be an action, that is, to be an intentional movement. First we define the idea for the serial machine in analogy to past explications of 'takes' and the like:

> $T \otimes T'$ *acts in a way depending on* y *to produce* x *at* t if and only if for some t', t'' such that $t'' > t' > t$ and some α there is an output $f(y)$ of T at t' such that $A(f(y), \alpha) = x$ at t'' and $M'(q_0, x)$ is a winner.   (13)

We can cut out still more notational junk and dispensable juggling of quantifiers by making use of the assumption, which comes for free, that the automata in question operate synchronously so that t'' is a unit of time later than t' which is one time later than t. Hence,

> $T \otimes T'$ *acts in a way depending on y to produce x at t* if and only if there is an output $f(y)$ of T at $t + 1$ such that $A(f(y), \alpha) = x$ and $M'(q_0, x)$ is a winner. $\qquad(14)$

For the subject,

> $\mathscr{S}$ *acts in a way depending on y to produce x at t* if and only if $\mathscr{S}$ realizes a serial automaton $T \otimes T'$ that acts in such a way. $\qquad(14a)$

The explication of '$\mathscr{S}$ desires x is τ at t'' is, as is our wont, entirely in terms of mathematical concepts, that is to say in terms of automata, sets and the like all in extension.

> $\mathscr{S}$ *desires that x is τ at $t + 2$* if and only if $\mathscr{S}$ realizes $T \otimes T'$ such that for every y there exist u, v, z, α, q_F such that if $Rep(y, u, t)$, $K(u, v, t + 1)$, $M(q_0, v) = q_F$ and $\mathscr{N}(q_0, v) = zN(q_F)$ at $t + 1$, then $A(N(q_F),) = x$ at $t + 2$ and $M'(q_0', x)$ is a winner. $\qquad(15)$

In slightly plainer English this says that $\mathscr{S}$ desires x is τ if any y it virtually accepts causes an action at A that could result in fulfillment. Of course this is at least as imprecise as the "folk psychology" we are trying to replace and it is just as well to forget it.

We can next prove the *Proposition*

> For any x, y, τ, and τ', $\mathscr{S}$ desires at $t + 2$ that x is τ' implies that if $\mathscr{S}$ believes at t that y is τ, and $\mathscr{S}$ acts in a way depending on y to produce x at t then $\mathscr{S}$ expects at $t + 2$ that x is τ'. $\qquad(16)$

Proof: Assume $\mathscr{S}$ desires x is τ at $t + 2$ and $\mathscr{S}$ believes y is t. Now from VIII(1) it follows that $\mathscr{S}$ realizes T, which virtually accepts y is τ at t. This just says what the first three clauses of the antecedent of (5) says. The fourth clause follows from definitions, for if u is input to T at t, then by (8)–(10) $\mathscr{N}(q_0, v) = z(N(M(q_0, v))) = zN(q_F)$ at $t + 1$. By detachment, $A(N(q_f),$ $\alpha) = x$ and $M'(q_0', x)$ is a winner at $t + 2$. So $\mathscr{S}$ realizes $T \otimes T'$ that acts in a way depending on y to produce x, by (14) and so does $\mathscr{S}$ by (14a). Since $M'(q_0', x)$ is a winner, by VI(6a) T' expects x is τ' at $t + 2$; so by VII(10) $\mathscr{S}$ expects x is τ' at $t + 2$. This proves (16) and hence that condition (7b) is satisfied by the theory.

To show that (7a) is satisfied, assume that $\mathscr{S}$ believes at t that y is τ and that $\mathscr{S}$ desires at $t + 2$ that x is τ. Then by (15) (7a) follows immediately.

Both 'perceptual belief' and 'desire' have been defined explicitly.

According to this analysis desire does not imply fulfillment nor does it imply disruption. However by the results of the previous chapter it does imply either fulfillment or disruption since it does imply expectation. In the case of 'desire' it seems to fit ordinary language better to say 'satisfaction' for fulfillment and 'frustration' for disruption.

We now might go on with very little trouble to define the 'purpose' or 'goal' of an act as the satisfaction of desire. But as long as we seem to have the hang of it there is little point in performing the exercise. Far more weighty concerns command attention — after one elucidatory comment and payoff of a promissory note.

My theory of perceptual belief and desire is similar to cybernetical approaches to purposive behavior that use the concept of negative feedback. In order to exhibit some relevant points of contact and some divergencies let us recount the McGuire-Bach scenario in a slightly expanded version. Wanting Bach, McGuire stands before an assortment of equipment y and her inbuilt automaton system depicted in Figure 1 is gated in. She believes y is a sound system (y is τ) as the stimulus patterns caused by it satisfy her expectations. She acts — $N(q_F)$ and the sound system control(s) are A-related in a grasp — to produce x. By (7b) she expects x to be Bach (that x is τ'). McGuire either believes she hears Bach or not (her expectations are fulfilled or otherwise disrupted). If fulfilled, then by the stability principle (5) she dwells on Bach until the Bach-listening system is perturbed, in which case *gating* drops off and she turns to something else. If McGuire does not believe she hears Bach but still desires Bach and believes that y is a sound system, she further manipulates the knobs, listens for Bach, and so on again until she gets satisfaction, or by (5) is completely disrupted by some external exigency that commands her attention.

Besides the obvious differences between this McGuire-Bach situation and feedback control systems — the one being discrete state (either go Bach or no-go Bach) and the other continuously varying over a range of performance parameters — the McGuirean system incorporates the take at all stages of belief and winners or states of expectation. To have intentions there must be expectations present, *à fortiori* taking, and still more deeply, vague receptual stimuli. Ultimately taking and expectation are grounded in 'self-knowledge' or, put more neutrally, in automatic self-coding means, and no such phenomenon arises in a negative feedback system (not that it couldn't but if you add it − assuming it's possible in a continuously operation system − you've moved out beyond garden variety feedback). In short there is very little resembling belief or desire in conventional control systems. In my opinion the immediate ancestors of any adequate approach to desire, belief and the rest are von Neumann and Gödel, not Wiener.[17] I hope this theory might cheer the holist. But I fear that any attempt to explain holistic phenomena must fail to please the true believer, for she is convinced that holism is epistemically (ontologically? semantically?) necessary. The conviction is reinforced by its invincible ambiguity. Perhaps holism is the ultimate example of a stipulated analytic notion outside of pure logic.

We previously administered two-thirds of a remedy to the apparently ailing taking function. What prevents taking a cannon for a mouse squeak in our model? And why not enlarge the concept to include taking of receptually good material, if close enough to x by some measure, as x itself? Our answer appealed to evolutionism in reply to the first complaint and our desire to avoid a certain incoherency in the theory itself to the second. But now a further support for taking emerges when we consider the role of taking in the context of desire-belief loops. If expectation of an event hinges on taking and tends to an act that generates still further expectations that are mostly fulfilled, taking itself gets a kind of confirmation. Acceptance as an ingredient of perception is inferentinal, in fact abductive; and an action that proceeds from the conclusion that satisfies is confirmatory. This hardly *justifies* taking, as taking is not a deliberate method but a naturally engrained feature of intentional life. What is justified, if anything is, is my model of it not the capability itself, which must be present to account for the flexible character of acceptance of stimuli by the higher organism. I suppose that any psychologist today who has given the matter thought would agree that what is perceived and conceived is constructed but is still so right as to account for adaptations to life.

4. STANDING BELIEF − REPRESENTATION

Perceptual belief is the same thing as stimulus fulfillment of expectation that is expressible in some language. In Quine's terminology the sentences expressing belief are 'occasion' sentences, i.e., sentences which "command assent or dissent only if queried after an appropriate prompting stimulation" (Quine, 1960, p. 36). Unlike observation sentences perceptual sentences involve "collateral information" in order to command assent, which here means taking and even contexts. But they express belief over a short time interval at t, the specious present. All other sentences are 'standing' sentences and they 'grade-off' from the perceptual to nearby items such as 'that was a plane that went by' and further on to 'some real functions are nondifferentiable' and 'Carnap said "being is nothing" is nonsense'. 'Standing' is Quine's term, and I shall borrow it to identify beliefs other than the perceptual; standing beliefs are those the speaker knows how to express in standing sentences.

Perceptual belief might just as well be identified outright with automaton computations and the automaton itself with belief that there are things of the type perceived. They are not states or representations although they involve both a sequencing through states and stimulus patterns *cum* input strings. But at the present time any general theory of standing beliefs (and à fortiori of intentional attitudes except those relating to immediate experience) seems to be out of the question. What I have to offer are a few remarks on issues that sooner or later have to be faced by anyone seeking a functionalist or cognitivist account of the psychology of features. I shall take my theory of perceptual belief and desire or something like it as a starting point.

The notion that belief is a kind of mental representation is attractive in explaining in principle how organisms use their heads in getting along more or less successfully. One's beliefs represent reality and are instruments for intelligent lining-up of preferences, tracing act-outcome patterns, and planning of actions. They are the stuff of 'cognitive maps' and 'models of the world'. However the aim of propounding any more than a bare sketch of belief in general, including standing beliefs, seems to me to be nearly incredible until concepts have been further clarified and more has been established about the credibility of mechanism or any other protophypothesis. Here is an attempt at limning some of the central issues.

Representation is not a clear concept, to begin with. It is not uncommon to read of propositions representing reality, beliefs representing sentences, sentences representing beliefs, sentences in some nonlinguistic code in the head representing regular garden variety sentences in the air representing propositions, and me to you and you to me, and mathematical models representing reality, descriptions of models representing theories; and all the while representatives representing in Congress and agents representing writers and permutation groups representing abstract groups and the linguists' grammar representing what you know and your linguistic competence representing the grammar. It is quite beyond belief that anyone would go out to construct a theory of mind without kicking the habit and the word itself — especially if the relationship between representation and belief is still the old intentional one, untouched. All that has happened is to push the intentional from the behaviorist's surface movement back into the head. But it is an 'in' word, and the best that can be done is tame it.

In this mix of usages there appear to be two main categories of meaning of 'represent', a *referential* sense and a *stand in* or *stand for* or *surrogational* sense. In folk philosophy sentences have propositional objects, and for Frege a referent, Truth. A sentence represents referentially. On the other hand a sentence represents a belief either couched in mentalese or an accepting automaton as a *surrogate* or agent for purposes of communication. Sentences that represent in this sense of the expression are not *about* beliefs; they are *for* beliefs. In my theory stimulus patterns x represent in the stand-in sense as effects of real causes, *ceteris paribus*. This is not a semantical kind of representation; and beyond being an effect, the surrogational property of x derives solely from its functional role in an automaton.

On the other hand final states are not elements of a language; but they are, like Fodor's MR's, "semantical." Final states might be said to be intentional or object-directed, but only because they are products of mental acts such as accepting and taking that are intentional, not because they bear a direct semantical relation to things.

I don't see how any theory of attitudes is going to get off the ground without heeding such distinctions throughout. In the sequel 'represents' used in contexts about inputs should be taken in the sense of surrogation, and represents used in contexts about winning or final states or systems of rules should be understood in the sense of intention.

Perceptual belief is the outcome of a kind of matching or inferential process wherein representations match-up or satisfy in some way. Perception can not be exclusively template matching, for reasons I shall not repeat here. It appears likely that verification of representation is some kind of computation, which it most certainly is in the case of perceptual belief, if I am right; it is bound up with actions and desires that are again computational processes as described in the previous section. According to the model, representations are strings (in the range of K for some t) that are surrogates for perceptual objects, if they compute to perceptual or, in general, to winning states, which latter represent in the referential sense. The question is whether this scheme can be extended from perceptual belief to standing belief, which also entails representations of some kind. If we could extend the model, then a reasonably good theory of the cognitive would be within reach. Unfortunately the programme breaks down in the face of the extremely recalcitrant problem of the relationship of belief to language.

In order to make a beginning along the lines proposed, let us emulate the typical empiricist position on the epistemic primacy of perception in order to see how higher level attitudes might be built on the lower, in analogy to knowledge building on sense experience by inductive and abductive extrapolation. A way of attempting this is to build beliefs up using quantifiers and connectives in a manner reminiscent of inductive definitions in formal syntactical systems. What I shall sketch is a bare outline of a kind of belief calculus, unfortunately without much precision as I have but a dim idea about how things should work out.

There is a strong presupposition underlying the approach. When McGuire desires Bach she believes in some kind of connection between turning on the sound system and getting Bach. But the statement of the believed connection turns out to be ambiguous if we examine the matter with care. For consider '$\mathscr{S}$ believes that if P then Q' and 'if $\mathscr{S}$ believes P then $\mathscr{S}$ believes Q'. Using the doxastic operator 'B' and an arrow for 'if-then' these assertions about $\mathscr{S}$'s belief may be rendered thus:

$$B(P \to Q) \tag{17}$$

and

$$BP \to BQ. \tag{18}$$

Assuming that we restrict B to $\mathscr{S}$, the one says that $\mathscr{S}$ believes if P then Q and the other that if $\mathscr{S}$ believes P then $\mathscr{S}$ believes Q. It is not clear to me (or perhaps to anyone) whether (17) and (18) mean the same.[19] Indeed the arrow tokens of the two might be different connectives. Same or not, I used an interpretation much like that of (18) for the analysis of believing in a connection between a sound system and Bach. An advantage of (18) is that it enabled me to define 'desire' in terms of *relations among* beliefs, acts, and expectations rather than in terms of *believed relations among* propositions (or whatever). This makes all the difference in the world! I have very little idea how an explicit definition of belief as in (17) would go, and in particular any unsuccessful attempt would tend to vindicate Brentano unless of course (17) and (18) turn out be be equivalent in some appropriately strong sense. It seems to me there is a lode here to be mined;

but this is no place to start digging. The success of a mechanist philosophy in completely analyzing the intentional might well depend on a strong relation, at any rate of well-understood one, between (17) and (18) with, no doubt, similar connections understanding of them among the companion construals of other mental features.

Is there any independent support for choosing (18) over (17)? Not much. They are not logically equivalent except under assumptions that are unrealistically strong. For instance, if '$\rightarrow$' in both (17) and (18) is truth functional and if $B(P \rightarrow Q)$ implies $B(\sim P \lor Q)$, then one can get (17) from (18) by assuming (entirely gratuitously) the presence of a certain complex automaton in the subject. The belief implication indicated is not reasonable (think of the freshman logic student!) and the assumption really assumes what is to be proved. Likewise going the other way is hard, but the details are not worth reviewing as that would amount to a listing of most unlikely assumptions, so far as I know. However there are several mildly interesting direct arguments for (18) as long as we restrict P and Q to expressions like 'x is τ' where τ is a sensible recursive predicate, i.e., where $\mathscr{S}$ believes P is perceptual in our sense.

If perceptual beliefs are dispositions to act it is much more appealing to intuition (mine anyway) to entertaining the possibility of one disposition implying another than of a disposition *to act conditionally*. Let me explain. $\mathscr{S}$'s belief that P *qua* disposition to act might imply her belief that Q *qua* disposition to act. On the other reading $\mathscr{S}$ might believe that if P then Q *qua* disposition to act. On the first version $\mathscr{S}$'s disposition to act in a certain way implies her disposition to act in some other. On the second the disposition is to act hypothetically, and I don't even know what *that* means. (I am not arguing that there are no cases $B(P \rightarrow Q)$, but only that they are not dispositions to act.) Action is subject to control, and so is related in some way to perception; but one does not perceive such things as if P then Q. However, the expressing sentence in $\mathscr{S}$'s language might well be 'if P then Q' while the underlying belief structure is $BP \rightarrow BQ$ (which means one acceptor computation implies another via some kind of complex interrelationship among automata). I am jogging down the street and see movement behind a bush which I attribute to a dog being there and actually say to my companion "if that is a dog it is going to bite!" (I wouldn't usually say "I believe that if that is a dog, then it will bite", although I might). But the sentence could be the expression of an underlying $BP \rightarrow BQ$ structure involving tacit expectations, takings, and so forth. The point is that acceptance of (18), on grounds that disposition to X implies disposition to Y is intuitively more appealing than disposition to X implies Y, does not rule out that the correlated linguistic expression of belief be an ordinary conditional.

This intuition, shaky though it is, gets further encouragement from other quarters supposing that the arrows in (17) and (18) have the same sense. Consider '$\mathscr{S}$ does not believe at t that x is τ' and '$\mathscr{S}$ believes at t that x is not τ'. If the latter is true, there is an acceptor $T_{\bar{\tau}}$ (whose set of perceptual states is the complement of that of T_τ) $\mathscr{S}$ realizes that accepts x. On the other hand '$\mathscr{S}$ does not believe at t that x is τ' could mean either '$\mathscr{S}$ believes at t that x is not τ' or that $\mathscr{S}$ has no belief one way or the other about x at t. Perhaps she is asleep or her attention is directed elsewhere. Thus if $\mathscr{S}$'s attention is on the matter ('gated in'),

$$B \sim P \quad \text{if and only if} \quad \sim\!BP \tag{19}$$

(19) says, in effect, that B is a linear operator with respect to the logical particle $\sim$. The punch line is that if $\mathscr{S}$'s belief system is gated in (in analogy to Figure 1) and if B is linear with respect to one logical particle it is also linear (ought to be regarded) for all the others including '$\rightarrow$' under any construal, material conditional, strict implication, etc. Thus for binary connectives L, if $\mathscr{S}$'s attention is on the x of the perceptual experience at time t and P is about x, a general linearity hypothesis says

$$B(P \, L \, Q) \quad \text{if and only if} \quad BP \, L \, BQ \tag{19a}$$

Although I will appeal to this on a few occasions I give it no blanket warrant other than that it seems true when the connective is negation. Hence (17) and (18) given these somewhat fanciful considerations are equivalent as are belief statements using other logical particles, assuming companion occurrences have uniform senses.

There is an additional argument which is based on methodological considerations. If McGuire believes the box is a sound system, then if she acts in a certain way (under the hypothesis that she desires to hear Bach), she expects to hear Bach. If this lawful condition holds, then under the same hypothesis if she does not expect Bach (ask her, or probe her head) then on the preferred interpretation (18) she does not believe the things is a sound system, or otherwise here action must have gone astray. We conclude that the 'if-then' in version (18) has the sense of some ordinary illative relation in the science of psychology that enjoys the contrapositive property. On the other hand one may not conclude from 'McGuire believes if this is a sound system, then she will hear Bach if she turns it on' that 'McGuire believes if she does not hear Bach, then either the thing is not a sound system or she did not turn it on'. Goodness only knows whether McGuire's arrow in (17) has a contrapositive (for this reason '$\rightarrow$' in (17) might better be replaced by another symbol). In brief, the relations among the BP's and BQ's are those of the ordinary logic of scientific reasoning, and all such relations can be instantiated in complex automata as I shall now briefly indicate.

The family of recursive sets or predicates is closed under set complement, union, and intersection. So if sets $\mathscr{U}_\tau$ and $\mathscr{U}_{\tau'}$, for example, are recursive so are $\mathscr{U}_\tau \cup \mathscr{U}_{\tau'}$, $\mathscr{U}_\tau \cap \mathscr{U}_{\tau'}$, and $\bar{\mathscr{U}}_\tau$. Now suppose that $\mathscr{U}_\tau$ is accepted by T_τ and $\mathscr{U}_{\tau'}$ by $T_{\tau'}$; then there is an FSA (or, in general, a Turing machine) that accepts $\mathscr{U}_\tau \cup \mathscr{U}_{\tau'}$, one that accepts $\bar{\mathscr{U}}_\tau$ and one that accepts $\mathscr{U}_\tau \cap \mathscr{U}_{\tau'}$.[20] Now let us attend to some $\mathscr{S}$ who perceptually believes at t that x is τ or x is τ' (x is τ or τ'). By (18) we take this to mean $\mathscr{S}$ believes at t that x is τ or believes at t that x is τ'. Hence she realizes a T_τ that accepts $\mathscr{U}_\tau$ or she realizes a $T_{\tau'}$ that accepts $\mathscr{U}_{\tau'}$. If she is presented with an object x she represents it by the stimulus pattern y which is either in (or taken to be $\mathscr{U}_\tau$ or $\mathscr{U}_{\tau'}$. We now *explain* the compound belief by hypothesizing an automaton $T = T_\tau \cup T_{\tau'}$ of the kind of note 20 for accepting the union of sets. Similarly for the cases $\mathscr{S}$ believes at t x is not τ and $\mathscr{S}$ believes at t that x is τ and believes at t x is τ'.

More generally, there is a Turing machine construction of cases wherein the $\mathscr{U}$ are not just FSA acceptable, but recursive, that might be hypothesized. For reasons that I have presented at some length in earlier sections, there is no cause to think that these automata are separate or separable entities in an organismic embodiment, nor that they are restricted to binary ON–OFF form, etc. Moreover they might actually be of program-like structure having many subroutines linked in a way that computes the logic of sets; or they might be of some yet unknown category of recursive structure.

These suggestions apply to sensible recursive predicates only, and show how other perceptual belief predicates can be built up and accounted for in terms of systems of rules, all at a pre-linguistic or sublinguistic level. Which structures are built-in, which learned, and whether biasing patterns are learned, no one knows. By 'biasing patterns' I mean complexes of signals that operate to gate automaton processes in or out of a relatively fixed systems.[21] In effect ever more complex predicates are built up during the subject's learning life that embody new perceptual beliefs or disenable old ones; we can account for them in some such way as the model indicates, but so far not the acquisition of them.

In order to emulate a first order monadic logic we need to incorporate quantifiers and singular terms into the scheme. Theoretically there is no difficulty in hypothesizing further recursive structures to account for quantified representations (surrogate), as quantified recursive predicates are still recursive provided that the quantifiers be bounded (Davis, 1958, p. 52). Whereas all the truth functional beliefs based on sensible predicates are accounted for in the model in terms of realization of complex embodied automaton interconnections, presumably in neuronal networks, quantification and naming seem to require *memory* together with built-in dispositions. This is suggested by the following considerations.

I have frequently urged the reader to think of realized rules as dispositions, a clearer and more credible version of the functionalist teaching that states are or are somehow related to dispositions. Now a disposition *qua* realized automaton in $\mathscr{S}$ is sufficient for perceptual belief if $\mathscr{S}$ is sophisticated enough to have expectations that can be satisfied on the basis of takings. Then it is quite tempting to say that the unexercised disposition is non-perceptual, i.e., standing belief. However this idea can not be right because it is axiomatic that no one *believes* whatever it is that is expressed in *open* sentences. If the rule system underlying the disposition is wired in or a permanent subroutine, then I would not be inclined to think a subject believes anything unless at some time in the past there had been an occasion during which it got input that drove it into a perceptual state. If you have a disposition to recognize hammers owing to wired in or biased rules or a compiled subroutine, you don't necessarily believe there are hammers unless you have been told (which is beyond our present stage of the analysis) or are, say, hit over the head with one just lightly enough to retain consciousness. If such an unfortunate event occurred you would quite possibly believe there are hammers for the rest of your life. However, one more condition is required. You must *remember* the event (which does not necessarily mean be able to recollect it). Standing belief, I am saying, depends on at least 'one-shot' learning that extends beyond reception of stimuli and perception, even of the sophisticated sort. You can *see* without believing; but you can't *perceive* without perceptually believing, although you can perceive without believing *there is* such a thing as is perceived. This further step lands us in standing beliefs, and to have them there must be storage of representations (or some item mapped into from the stimulus pattern). Perceptual beliefs are fleeting; they are time bound. Standing beliefs are relatively free.

Somewhat more exactly, if $\mathscr{S}$ perceptually believes at t that x is τ, then by definition $\mathscr{S}$ realizes some T_τ such that T_τ accepts x at t; hence the predicate 'x is τ' is recursive and so is 'there is an x such that x is τ' provided that the quantifier 'there is an x' is bounded (which means, essentially, that the range of the variable x can be arranged in a finite sequence). It follows that there is some Turing machine T such that T accepts *there is an x*. So if $\mathscr{S}$ believes at t there is an x that is τ, we account for her belief by ascribing realization of T (or some equivalent). By the linearity principle, there is an x such that $\mathscr{S}$ believes at t that x is τ (unless $\mathscr{S}$ hallucinates, which will be considered in the next chapter).

Throughout our discussion of perceptual belief up to this point belief implies the realization in $\mathscr{S}$ of an acceptor which computes to a perceptual state in real time, i.e., historically, at t; and moreover x causes some stimulus pattern y at t (i.e., $Rep(x, y, t)$). In order to advance to standing belief that some x is τ, the representation y must be stored, or it must map to some entity z, perhaps via the taking function, that is stored. Storing need not occur, of course, as organisms having memory do not necessarily remember everything they experience. So if there is to be standing belief even of the immediately experienceable we must assume that z is gated to memory by some mechanism (which is easily accounted for by recursive rule concepts); and if it is, then we say that $\mathscr{S}$ (nonperceptually) believes x is τ, where τ is still quite sensible (see Note VIII.2):

> $\mathscr{S}$ *believes* at t that some x is τ if and only if there is an earlier time t' and a y such that $\mathscr{S}$ perceptually believes that y is τ at t, and y is remembered (via Rep and K) by $\mathscr{S}$.   (20)

If $\mathscr{S}$ has standing beliefs in this very primitive way, then she has a disposition that consists of an automaton T and a stored representation of an accepted or believed event. In a neuronal system the stored representation might be adequately modeled by a single neuron associated with the net embodiment of T that feeds back to itself and has threshold $\theta = 1$ (cf. p. 38). If $\mathscr{S}$ is queried as to its belief in a τ, it samples the cell.

Beliefs that ascribe a sensible predicate to something having a proper name such as '$\mathscr{S}$ believes that Steve is Blond' do not seem to me to be perceptual but rather the result of inference. Perceptual recognition of Steve is best thought of as acceptance of x as being Steve: i.e., there is an automaton associated with a certain person named Steve ($\mathscr{S}$ might be a dog and not know 'Steve'), and on the proper occasion that automaton, realized in $\mathscr{S}$, accepts some representation of x as an element of $\mathscr{U}_{\text{Steve}}$, which is a *unit* set. On that same occasion, nearly, $\mathscr{S}$ also believes x is blond. $\mathscr{S}$'s built in logic (provided on request) construes $x \in \{\text{Steve}\}$ as the same as $x = \text{Steve}$

$[x \in x | x =$ Steve if and only if $x =$ Steve] and tacitly *infers* that Steve is Blond. If $\mathscr{S}$ has no such minimal deductive capability, then it never makes the connection that allows belief that Steve is blond but is stuck with believing something is Steve and believing that this something is blond. If it *does* have this capability, I'll say it can *ascribe to individuals*.

My fundamental presupposition here is that all of the x's of the theory of perception and belief — or more properly the inner representations y or z that are the result of *Rep* and taking — are *immediately demonstrative* or *deictic*. 'Steve' in $\mathscr{S}$'s language, if she knows one, is a proper name, though not a logically proper name (in Russell's sense); but Steve is a *type* to $\mathscr{S}$'s perceptual apparatus and co-designates with a deictic x. But now I am encroaching on semantical territory, which is the proper realm of exploration in the next chapter.

All beliefs, built up from perceptual beliefs by use of logic connectives, quantifiers, memory traces, and inferences using substitutivity of identity in perceptual contexts constitute what I will can *core* beliefs.[22] What about relations? Everything introduced so far into the construction of the core depends on monadic physical properties; they are the supports of the entire network of core beliefs. Relations present a perennial problem for empiricism which in the past has been approached in various ways ranging from Locke's atomism to James' radical empiricism. According to Locke's classical position relations consist "in the referring or comparing two things one to another," but are not "contained in the real existence of things but something extraneous and super-induced. ... " (Locke, 1690, p. 73, 74). On the opposite side James says relations are themselves part of experience, and "no extraneous trans-empirical connective support" is needed to account for concatenation and continuity in the universe (James, 1909, p. 310 f). Discounting the differences in epistemic emphasis (Locke seems to be speaking of things and James of experience of things), these represent incompatible views: relations depending on mental acts of association or comparison *versus* relations subsisting in the world of direct experience. Within our framework, are relations among sensible things perceived or are they the products of mental synthesis? The answer lies in the fact, for the logic of mind model, that relations are individuated by the same principle as properties are.

There are abstract automata that recognize or accept relations; and, furthermore, a distinction can be drawn between relations in extension and relations in intension along much the same lines as in our treatment of Condition II in Section V. Two *relational types* are different if and only

if their common extension is the domain of two different partial word
functions of two or more variables. There is the same general restriction
of this principle to the sensible as in monadic acceptance; relations must
be sensible in that they must fall among perceptual objects for the principle
to apply although a subject need not have perceptual beliefs about these
objects singly to have relational belief. One might in some cases, that is to
say, believe x to be longer than y without accepting either x or y as sensible
types. In a way this *seems* to place my kind of mechanism on the side of
James. Or, at any rate, if Lockean simple ideas correspond to perceptual
states and hence to types, then there are direct perceptions of relation-types
while there are none of the *types* of the relata — which is not to say they
are not sensed or received. Hence there are relations which are perceived
while the relata are not. On the other hand some relations like *mother of*
do not seem to be of this immediate kind, but do depend on some sharing
of types of the relata. Even at actual birth sites the relation *mother of* is
not direct and depends on inferences from types, among other things, owing
to the differences of delivery among, say, turtle births, kitten births, oak
tree births and frog births. Beliefs in relations of this kind rest on collateral
information, to use another happy Quinean locution, and hence might
not occur in the core. So I am tempted to place only those relations whose
acceptance is independent of types in the primitive class; whether or not
mother of goes in depends on the possibility of building the appropriate
complex automata up using the basic set-theoretic relations, quantification
and nontypal primitive relational beliefs. Such a project would be not unrelated to Freshman exercises such as to define 'mother of' from 'parent'
and 'female'. An example of a relational FSA is given in the Notes.[23]

The core may now be extended by adding primitive relational beliefs
and whatever other beliefs the subject has acquired that derive from the
relational by set-theoretic combinations, quantification, and ascription to
individuals. It then includes a sizeable component of standing beliefs derived
as indicated. From there on other beliefs are built up by means of transformations presumably of some illative character concerning which we have very
little idea. The system is open with respect to inductive or abductive illations,
certainly, and is not even deductively closed except under very unrealistic
attributions of rationality to the subject; and for most $\mathscr{S}$'s anything beyond
the core itself is inconsistent.

The complete definition of 'perceptual belief' specifies that belief be
expressible in some language known to the subject. Supposing the language
is English and $\mathscr{S}$ believes at t that x is τ or she believes that there are τ's,

then the respective sentences might be 'this is a τ' or 'something is a τ'. Such sentences are generated on appropriate belief occasions upon fulfillment of two logical conditions: T_τ which $\mathscr{S}$ realizes, must be in a perceptual state q_F; and $\mathscr{S}$ must *desire* to communicate her belief to someone $\mathscr{T}$ (possibly herself). Now her desires, by VIII(16), entail that she realize some automaton $T_{\tau'}$ that expects a perceivable response of some sort on the part of a listener $\mathscr{T}$. Thus necessary conditions for the speech act in direct contexts including a co-communicator are being in a perceptual state q_F of T_τ and at the same time a winning state q of $T_{\tau'}$. Given the presence of these conditions, then other things being equal $\mathscr{S}$ generates a sentence that is uniquely associated to q_F. Generation entails use of a grammar (for core belief it might conceivably be a context-free collection of rules, namely of the type illustrated in Table II.II) plus an algorithm that is called out by q_F that governs the sequence of rule applications; the generation also combines with application of phonological rules to produce speech. None of this appears to involve any insurmountable conceptual difficulties, although the actual mechanism is a task beyond anyone's present powers.

The listener $\mathscr{T}$ in the communicational situation must realize some kind of reverse process that accepts the sentence and associates it with the underlying belief, embodied in an automaton behaviorally equivalent to T_τ of $\mathscr{S}$ provided again that $\mathscr{T}$ *desires to understand*, and this latter attitude must manifest itself in some act that satisfies $\mathscr{S}$'s, the speakers, expectation of a response from $\mathscr{T}$. Numerous interesting conjectures about speech production and recognition together with reports on experimental work in the area appear in the literature and have been surveyed by Fodor and others (Fodor *et al.*, 1974, esp. Chapters 6 and 7). The dynamics of the simple communication system as just sketched seems to me, however, to be essential in understanding generation and acceptance of sentences. They depend intrinsically on beliefs, expectations and desires of the participants. It is very hard for me to see how a speech situation could be accounted for with *less* machinery.

This sort of story reveals a way of getting at the semantics of language and the place of desire in the communication loop. The semantics of sentences in the core is perhaps to be found in the underlying belief-desire structures that the sentences express. In a way this scheme proposes a basis for the semantics of natural language in pragmatics, the theory of the language user and his mental features. Semantics, or part of it, would then rest on the logic of mind. The presence of desire in the speaker-listener accounts for the sentential expression of belief, and the absence of it for tacit belief. In principle the manifold uses of language, then, might very well depend on just what is desired; e.g., assertion, exemplification, exhortation, and so forth would be distinguished by their ends. This is no deep observation; but when we see how belief and desire might be related in sentential expression in the life of a listener we begin to get a glimpse of their roles in the speech act.

I want to make some further comments about semantics, assuming a division between the place of representations in the anatomy of cognition and representation, including language, as *referential* and *meaningful*. This is just to observe very much the same distinction we set out with at the opening of this chapter between the psychology and semantics of belief. The referential aspect comes in Chapter IX.

I agree with cognitivists that there are inner mental systems that mediate between language and the world (to speak metaphorically) that are pre-linguistic and constitute the ground of the semantics of natural language. But for reasons I shall review shortly this picture must be confined to the core, at least in my version. Fodor, Bever and Garrett have summarized the principal parts of a semantic theory as consisting of

(1)   A system of semantic representations
(2)   A set of rules which carry natural language sentences into their semantic representations
(3)   A set of inference rules which apply mechanistically to semantic representations (Fodor *et al.*, 1974, p. 184).[24]

If we interpret recursive rules underlying expectations, etc. as 'semantic representations' then my theory accords with (1). In the outline of a theory connecting linguistic utterance with acceptance I identified two conditions that appear to be necessary for expressing perceptual belief: realization of a perceptual state and desire to communicate. In addition sentence generation depends on an algorithm, called by the perceptual state, that governs application of grammatical rules. For nonperceptual belief there must also be present a desire to assert, exhort, etc.; but the algorithm controlling generation in such cases is certainly not kicked off by being in a perceptual state. There must, I therefore hypothesize, be some other impulse (certainly not an environmental stimulus either!) that initiates the expression of standing beliefs, given a desire to express. Gathering these conditions into a quick and dirty summary, the 'rules of assignment' of Fodor's item (2) in the list quoted consists of

(a)   A perceptual state q_F, or, in the case of nonperceptual belief some other state or internal input, that calls out

(b)   An algorithm for sequencing the applications of grammatical, phonological, etc. rules, in sentence generation.

(c)   A desire to express.

As to item (3) in the list, in our logic of core belief the inference rules are embodied in the structure of complex automata via set-theoretic operations, quantification and individual ascription (identity substitutions). For instance if $\mathscr{S}$ believes x is τ and has acquired set union, then either $\mathscr{S}$ believes x is τ or $\mathscr{S}$ believes x is τ'; she learns the inferential connection along with learning the union. These acquired interconnections might have no very great resemblance to the school logic she later learns on a verbal level, and may be irrational.

This semantical scheme also agrees pretty well with the Fodor *et al.* (1974) summary comments on sentences of natural languages as the fundamental semantical units. In particular on their account and mine as well sentences are used to perform speech acts; and sentences and speech acts must be associated by some recursive procedures (Fodor *et al.,* 1974, pp. 218–219). However if it be insisted that internal representations consist in some kind of language like Mentalese (Fodor, 1975, 1982) that has semantical enterpretations independent of computation in order to be fit for computation, we part company, roughly for the reasons I gave at the end of Section V.4. The model of semantically endowed data operated on by a free program is simply wrong, it seems to me. In the theory developed here there is no string language that expresses proposition that are in turn the objects of belief; more nearly, realized belief structures in themselves directly are 'about' the world. This does not exclude possible worlds, in a sense, fictions, hallucinations, and the like, as we shall soon see.

My theory has the advantage of being quite specific (and therefore the disadvantage of being extremely risky) in its detailing of perception, acceptance and the rest as involved in mental representation. Mental representation has at least five components or, better, aspects, four of which are not remotely like 'brain writing' or other suggested linguiform entities (Dennett, 1978, pp. 39 ff); and the only entites in the scheme that have out-and-out linguistic properties are the stimulus patterns, which are degenerate forms at that. In the linear form (which is by no means essential) in which we take them in the abstract theory the pattern x's are syntactical components of finite state languages (they comprise, for any type τ, the Kleene regular sets — see above p. 43), if they are inputs to acceptors, and are perhaps richer systems for the more powerful rule structures that emerge in the acquisition of nonperceptual beliefs in the core. The pattern x's are representations indeed, and in a certain sense, I suppose, 'refer' to perceptual objects, if a causal theory can be said to be representational. They are *deictic* in virtue of their direct causal linkages to the perceptual objects but surrogational.

The perceptual state represents the object as an instance of a type but only in the sense adumbrated earlier. This is a second component of representation. If the mind-brain identity theory is true and if perceptual (final) states are embodied in nerve activity, they are presumably the images, ideas, impressions, or "sense data". A third component is the M function, which we shall see plays a role in determining the reference of a name much like a Fregean *Sinn* (more details anon). In nonperceptual belief memory marks paired with automata in order to account for beliefs that such and such is the case for *some x* (20) represent in a way that supports truth of quantified sentences in a language corresponding to the core (Chapter IX). This is a fourth component. Finally, a belief sentence (in our psychological reports, not in the language corresponding to the core, which is a first order language and has no means for expressing reports of attitudes) can be read to be *de dicto* when its explication in our theory has certain properties corresponding to the intensional sentences they explicate (more in Chapters IX and X). This is a fifth component of mental representation in this type of mechanist theory. Note that in none of this is there any notion of a little referring substantial mind or homunculus nor any idea of representations as picturing or imaging. Only in one case, the perceptual state given the identity theory, is there anything remotely like pictured or iconic representation; and as argued at length in VII.2, even perception can not be wholly matching template-fitting in the light of Conditions I–IV; and resemblance, you will recall, is best analyzed in terms of *taking* (VI.2). These points in great measure lend credibility to a *symbolic,* i.e., rule-processing, type of theory. Yet, despite the wide-spread agreement among many cognitivists and functionalists on the score of the computational character of mental features and therefore of representations, criticism of the approach, especially as regards the infinitary nature of recursive rules, are common. These criticisms are, it seems to me, seriously mistaken for some reasons already noted in Section VII.2, among others I shall relegate to Notes.[25]

I wish to emphasize that underlying automata structures are to provide the semantics, as roughly indicated, for natural language, not that they themselves are to have a semantics in any conventional sense. Thus my theory contrasts sharply with that of Field who advocates a relational theory of belief. Belief, for him, is a relation between a person and an internalized sentence, and the latter has its own Tarski-type semantics (Field, 1978, pp.

40 ff). This may be a way of handling Brentano (reference is to get reduced to a purely physical relation) but it departs from mine, for although I think that nonexpressed belief in the dumb or momentarily dumb is intentional — it involves taking, expectations, relations to desire, and so forth — it is not itself literally subject to a theory of reference and meaning. This I limit to language, although the 'seeds' of reference are internal, at least in the core.

Beyond the core, if you care to venture into the misty barrens with me, the prospects for illuminating inspiration within the foreseeable future are dim indeed. Although I do claim that the model of expectation, etc. has some merit especially as a lever for unseating Brentano, I have had little or nothing to say about thought (which is some kind of computational process, mainly unconscious), memory, hope, ambitions, seeking, emotions, and so on. However I am comforted by the understanding that I am not alone in my bewilderment and that much might be gained by just pursuing belief. Belief, act and expectation underlie desire and are probably essential ingredients of other intentional phenomena. But even if one were to focus on belief alone the situation as regards standing belief and language is particularly bewildering. Standing beliefs in the core might turn out to provide the semantics for associated sentences in some such way as I have tried to indicate. But I fear that most of our beliefs are a function of *verbalization* — our knowledge of language as such — and have little relation to situational contexts including speech and other human acts. Indeed beliefs far from the perceptual level seem to get such referential force as they have through the expressing sentences, if any, and not the other way around. In the conventional wisdom not even perceptual beliefs are *about* anything except perceptual objects, if they be true, while they are *of* propostions. Even if $\mathscr{S}$ believes at t that x is τ x does not strictly refer (although it is referential) and it does not 'mean' τ (cf. Harman, 1973, p. 59). And the case is even dimmer with standing belief. The semantics of immediate reference, even if we had one, would not take us very far. Most of what I know and believe I never experienced but acquired indirectly and vicariously. It is almost, but not quite, inconceivable that most of the things I truly believe can be traced to direct experience, although it is conceivable that they can be traced to someone's experience. Even exact science, reconstruct as we will, resists orderly reduction to the observable (a short history of the demise of logical empiricism). The meanings, allusions and guesses that fill my mind are not rooted in primitive belief, it seems, but in language itself, in communicational interaction with others.

Semantics when so broadly conceived as to include contextual understanding has dimensions extending way beyond what is currently of concern to psycholinguists. Miller lists six levels of understanding of language ranging from hearing auditory sequences and matching such to phonemic patterns, to accepting sequences as sentences of a language, interpreting them as meaningful utterances, understanding significance in context, and finally believing (Miller, 1964, pp. 72–74). Our theory, restricted as it is to the perceptual or to core standing sentences, has belief at about the fourth stage, while significance, which depends on some association with a network of standing belief sentences comprises an intervening stage that theory is no where near capturing. 'Signficance' comprehends at times extremely refined social distinctions and practices that are in no way related to such things as grammatical complexity or lexical diversity. Consider the following: Peter believes that

(a)   Steve is a pianist.
(b)   Steve plays the piano.
(c)   Steve plays jazz piano.
(d)   Steve plays piano.

(a) connotes that Steve is an accomplished pianist, perhaps a professional, and can do a listenable performance of a Chopin *Ballade*. (b) means that he plays for his own enjoyment or for Sunday School and maybe even teaches beginners or plays in cocktail lounges. (c) means Steve plays anything from rag-time and stride to contemporary Oscar Peterson-type jazz in an accomplished way. (d) means he plays with small dixieland or Chicago-style pick-up-groups and can improvise and fill in for any one at any time or any place in almost any style, and probably can not read notes.

(a)–(d) are somewhere close to the core but probably not in it as they are loaded with other implicitly held beliefs about musical institutions and customs which in turn are not direct. One can imagine a spectrum of beliefs ranging from those saturated with imagery and retained direct experience but yet hardly in the core, all the way up to philosophical beliefs. The former are not immersed in beliefs about customs or institutions but rather have a sense that shines forth only for she who strips off all high-level cognitive meanings. Chomsky's notorious 'colorless green ideas sleep furiously' takes on immediate esthetic value in just this way in the context of John Hollander's delightful piece *Coiled Alizarine*. This poem is charming precisely for its expressing *no* beliefs of a cognitive sort whatever; yet is not 'understandable', to anyone lacking knowledge of language at a high level transcending a core belief structure.

At the other end of the figurative spectrum are beliefs that evince the remarkable expressibility of language even when the sensible and the grammatical nearly vanish and the referential thrust is weak and blunted as exhibited paradigmatically in this sentence itself. Our quotation of others, such as 'Carnap wrote "Frege's use of the null object in his treatment of definite descriptions such as 'the 1981 model Dusenberg sports car has sixteen cylinders' is an alternative to Russell's theory of descriptions" on page of α *Meaning and Necessity*' are enough to blow the normal mind; yet philosophers thrive on them.

Many beliefs, Harman remarks, are probably impicit in that they are not close to the causal order as in the case of perceptual belief; nor are their representations stored some place for occasional retrieval.

One reason we take an average person to believe that $104 + 3 = 107$ is that, if we ask him what the sum of $104 + 3$ he will say that it is 107, and he will say this immediately without laborious calculation. He can give this answer immediately even though he has no prior explicit mental representation of this sum. But then maybe all beliefs are like this – involving no explicit mental representation but only the ability to respond appropriately if one is asked certain questions or if one is put in certain other situations (Harman, 1978, p. 60).

Such belief might be grounded in computational structures that are on all fours with linguistic rules themselves. Addition is a nice, easy example. There is a belief automaton, an adder realized somewhere. If the subject is asked at t whether $104 + 3 = 107$, the arguments decoded in some kind of signals token identical to neuroal events of some sort are computed to a YES state associated in some way we have been speculating about with 'yes, $104 + 3 = 107$'. However for all that is known, some standing beliefs might be individuated by the generative rules themselves in holistic commerce with desire, others believes in the core, etc.

Some intelligence artificers might be anxious to argue that computer studies already point the way to the semantical in their natural language understanding experiments. However I doubt this, even in the face of my admiration of much of that work. It is true that some programs 'understand sentences' by interpreting strings in the light of lists of data and 'models of the world' and even using past communicational 'experience' with, say, interactive computer users. But there is nothing like reference or perception – all of their 'beliefs are false' (Fodor, 1980); or, perhaps better, they don't *mean* anything. The computer 'belief' network does not connect up with the real world anywhere. There's nothing like a core (as I understand it); and until such programs are installed in robots that move and react and find their way among their kind, there is not much that is even remotely like the semantics of natural human language. When this has been done, then the higher level standing 'belief' structures will have gained credentials as models for psychology and mental philosophy.

Enough of recreation. We must now turn to the formidable business of deplatonizing 'reference' and 'meaning' as it arises in the core, in so far as possible. Until some clues as to the interdependencies of natural language sentences beyond the core with higher level conceptualization and with the core itself is found it is well to cultivate what little there is at hand in a more thorough-going way. Programmatic talk about representations and the intentional has gone as far as is possible without working on detailed and in principle falsifiable models.

CHAPTER IX

REFERENCE AND TRUTH

1. PURE SEMANTICS VERSUS USER SEMANTICS

Although I have been trying to maintain a division between the psychology and the semantics of mental attitudes the two have already tended to blur in the discussion of representations. There is a similar distinction that is much neater, one between intentional traits and behaviors on the one hand and linguistic reference and meaning on the other. On one opinion intentions can be ascribed to the dumb but meanings to the speech of language users only. A different view, which was at one time proposed by Davidson, is that only a creature that can interpret speech can have beliefs. For beliefs, he says, can be mistaken, and to understand the "possibility of being mistaken . . . requires grasping the contrast between truth and error" (Davidson, 1975, pp. 22–23). My theory already belies such a proposal, and theory aside, dumb animals do seem to have mistaken beliefs and are able to correct them on the spot. Any dog tracking by a spoor and losing it is able to back-track and start anew once he gets on it. He can have mistaken beliefs and correct them. Moreover, a theory of truth, say, that seeks a truth definition for a language by abstracting from use, attitude, and the context of use may be doomed to commitment to abstract entities or to reliance on other unanalyzed semantic terms (Field, 1972), possibilities that I wish to avoid as a matter of strictly naturalist policy. The view I am rejecting may be correct (Davidson does not claim that it is), but I want to be clear about my own presuppositions.

They comport pretty well with Dummett. His standpoint, which would be somewhat aside from our present purposes to review in much detail, is that a theory of meaning must be an account of how a language works, "that is, of how speakers communicate by means of it". A theory of meaning is a theory of understanding (Dummett, 1975, p. 99). By contrast with the view tentatively proposed by Davidson, Dummett requires that a semantics not stop at giving the meaning of words or sentences, but must go on to characterize what it is to know the meaning of words or sentences. A theory of synonymy of sentences that did not rely on an account of what it is to *know* the meaning of expressions would fail to reveal anything about how language works (Dummett, 1975, p. 100 ff.). A "modest" theory of truth, to make a point related to Field's just alluded to, would be one that entailed a sentence of the form '*S* is true if and only if *P*' where '*S*' is a name of *P* and the condition *P* is that under which a speaker holds *S* true. "Such a theory would be intelligible only to someone who had already grasped the concept [of truth]" in the language in which a theory of *S* is being framed, and would in no way account for the workings of language as required by a 'fullblooded theory' (Dummett, 1975, pp. 103—104). A modest theory of truth such as has been proposed by Davidson for natural languages would of course depend on that of a communally shared language, but would not be based on a theory of how language and meaning are understood; for this, Davidson thinks, presupposes a theory of *true* belief. Using the jargon of semiotic, Davidson wants a purely semantical theory while Dummett a pragmatical theory that appeals to the user in an essential way.[1]

I would like to suggest that these views conflict because their authors are caught up in Brentano's circle. Davidson is suspicious of any antecedent theory of belief because belief presupposes a concept of truth, and Dummett rejects a pure semantical theory because it presupposes only that which can be made explicit, if at all, in a theory of the understanding of language (which, I submit, calls for some kind of theory of belief). A possible way to relieve the opposition is to identify thought with language, or, if not with the ordinary spoken language of social communication, with some linguiform internal representations (Harman, 1973, p. 94 ff.). But even then if thoughts, like beliefs, are truth-bearing the workings of thoughts themselves have to be understood in some still deeper way.

I do not have very much of an idea how this puzzle might be resolved for noncore standing beliefs and whatever mental apparatuses underlie them. But for the core we might hope to make some progress. We have a glimpse of the probable dynamics of an extremely primitive communicational context including $\mathscr{S}$, $\mathscr{S}$'s beliefs, her expressing sentences, her desire to communicate her belief to $\mathscr{T}$, her speech act, $\mathscr{T}$'s response, induced belief, and so forth, all of which depends, as we well know, on takings and expectations of ·one kind or another. What I propose now is to abstract away from this rich context and examine just the relation between beliefs and expressing sentences in order to see what can be done in the way of a theory of meaning and reference that uses no unidentified or unanalyzed bits of intentionality in its explications.[2] This is intended to be in the spirit of Dummett's requirement of enquiring into the *understanding* of language. One of the aims is to break out of the circle of belief and truth by appeal to the strictly nonsemantical mechanist notion of acceptance. On the way I hope to be able to draw out of the basic model some observations about names, reference, intensionality and synonymy.

The best way to approach this tangled skein of concepts is to complete the account of the adequacy of my handling of belief.

2. BELIEF SENTENCES.[3]

The definitions of 'expectation' and 'belief' that I previously wrote meet certain requirements that I believe any philosopher would impose on any suggested analysis of the intentional. 'Expectation' entails as it should a condition (VII(2)) that we put together from some of Chisholm's observations about perceptual *expectation, fulfillment,* and *disruption,* where all of these latter concepts were broken down in terms of accepting and taking automata. Moreover our analysis of 'acceptance' was shown to satisfy certain conditions suggested by the facts of gestalt perception. Then 'belief' and 'perception' were defined in terms of acceptance, 'act' in terms of 'belief', and 'desires' in terms of these latter two concepts together with 'expectation'. As a group these logical constructions entail a pair of conditions (VIII(7a) and (7b)) on belief and desire that I extracted from current thinking on the topic of the intentional — from sources that agree on the conditions but probably are rather far apart in respect to their several philosophical stances. In effect, the conditions I have tried to meet characterize intentionality and serve to formulate what Brentano's problem is about, at least in part. What is needed in addition and what, it turns out, also forms a bridge for a transition to properly semantical concerns is a study of intentional sentences. The fundamental idea of Brentano that intentional acts of the mind are directed to inexistent objects is reflected, in a formal mode so to speak, in certain properties of intensional sentences. Belief sentences, for example, are declarative, meaningful, and compound; but the truth value does not depend on that of component parts, in particular of subordinate clauses. Our next project, then, is to review these properties and then argue that the purely *extensional* sentences that constitute our *analyses* of belief sentences have the same properties as the full, unanalyzed attitudinal sentences. In effect, the properties of belief sentences we now discuss amount to further adequacy conditions on any proposed analysis or definition of intentional terms.[4]

There are three conditions which collectively characterize intentional sentences. The first says a sentence has this property if it "uses a substantival expression . . . in such a way the neither the sentence nor its contradictory implies that there is or there is not anything to which the substantival expression truly applies" (Chisholm, 1957, p. 170). Neither 'Diogenes looked for an honest man' nor its negation implies either that there is or is not an honest man. Sentences of this kind must not be confused with items such as 'Charon transports souls' in which 'Charon' either has no reference or a deviant reference of some kind. Roughly, in the case of the intentional the characteristic has to do with the logic or sense of the sentence and not with one's metaphysics or theory of fictions. Of course you might not think this distinction is very clear either; so it is perhaps safer to say simply that 'Charon . . . ' does not satisfy other intentionality conditions.

Second, any non-truth functional sentence containing a propositional clause is intentional provided that neither the sentence nor its negation implies the truth or falsity of the clause (Chisholm, 1957, p. 171). 'Peter believes that Sagan believes the world will come to an end' implies neither that Sagan believes any such thing nor that the world will or will not come to an end.

Third, suppose that 'a' and 'b' are proper names or descriptions and that '$a = b$' is true. Let A be a sentence in which name 'a' occurs and B be a sentence exactly like A except that 'b' occurs instead of 'a'. Then A is intentional if A and '$a = b$' together do not imply B. Although Steve believes that the thing is McGuire's shoe and 'McGuire's shoe is the shoe that McGuire threw at Jones' cat' is true, it does not follow that Steve believes that the thing is the shoe that McGuire threw at Jones' cat. However, 'Charon transports souls' together with 'Charon was the son of Erebus' does imply 'the son of Erebus transports souls'; the substitution does not fail here and thus the sentence in question is not intentional.[5]

Perceptual belief sentences, and à fortiori sentences expressing core beliefs satisfy all three of these conditions. What I will argue is that my analysis of belief shows why.

As to the first, consider Scrooge's belief that he saw Marley's ghost. The Christmas Carol allows several interpretations: Scrooge was awake; Scrooge was awake and hallucinating; Scrooge was asleep and dreaming; none of the above. The latter is a sop to mystics and children and I shall not consider it further (of course it is my own reading at Christmas). Scrooge was not asleep during the Marley episode as Dickens has him going to sleep later. So there are two interesting cases for us: there was a perceptual object, a, ($a \neq$ Marley as Marley was dead and buried) and Scrooge took a to be

Marley; or there was none. In the perceptual case Scrooge realized a Marley recognizer left over from better days. So

$$\text{Scrooge (virtually) believes at } t \text{ that } a \text{ is Marley's Ghost} \qquad (1)$$

analyzes out to

Scrooge realizes some T_M such that there are y, z, and $t' > t$ and $Rep\,(a, y), K(y, z, t')$ and $z \in \mathcal{U}_M$. $\qquad (2)$

'a' is an abbreviation of the demonstrative 'that thing', T_M is a Marley acceptor, and $\mathcal{U}_M$ is a set of Marley strings such that, as usual, $z \in \mathcal{U}_M$ if and only if $M_M(q_0, z) = q_F$, final. (2) does not imply there is or is not anything, Marley, and neither does the negation of (2). Therefore (1) has no such consequences.

This is not a particularly subtle result, but it does illustrate my manner of proceeding. The moves above can be made more precisely (what does it mean, as in Chisholm's first condition above, to *imply* an individual does or does not exist?) (2) being a purely extensional sentence is open to existential quantification in the usual way. Consequently from (2)

There is an x such that Scrooge realizes some T_M such that there are y, z, and $t' > t$ and $Rep\,(x, y), K(y, z, t')$, and $z \in \mathcal{U}_M$, $\qquad (3)$

and from (1)

There is an x such that Scrooge believes at t that x is Marley's Ghost. $\qquad (4)$

Thus perceptual beliefs in those cases where the subject takes something, wrongly or rightly, to be of some kind are *de re*, that is, they are beliefs *about* real things although they do not imply anything one way or the other about what is ascribed (here Marley). One can not infer from (2)

There is an x such that x is Marley's Ghost and Scrooge believes at t that x is Marley's Ghost. $\qquad (5)$

Of course we already know there is no contradiction in x being Marley's Ghost and Scrooge not believing it (cf. the Gettier Table VIII.I). (3) might not at first glance seem to accord with Chisholm, whom we quoted as saying that the sentence does not imply there is a thing. But this is not clear. It does imply there is an x, but not an x that is Marley. I will call this sort of case '*weak de re*'. Of course failure to get (5) *does* conform to Chisholm's second condition above about lack of entailment of subordinate clauses.

If our interpretation is that Scrooge was hallucinating; then (1) is not even weakly *de re*. In that case, Scrooge realizes T_M as before, but there is no objectual x. Dickens has placed him in an atmosphere charged with Scrooge's own bitterness, and unbeknownst to himself Scrooge is peculiarly susceptible to certain inner occurrences traceable to some combination of his realizing T_M, the irritating confrontation with his nephew and clerk, the ambience of the Christmas eve, and so on. We may assume that T_M is gated in and in an initial state, for Marley was definitely on Scrooge's mind — he had been mistaken for Marley, nearly, earlier in the day. His inner system of stimulus representations is alive with strings totally outside of the receptual category of those elements that are accepted as Marley strings. However, as q_0 is a winner, Scrooge takes some string $y = a_1 a_2 \ldots a_n$, where none of the a_i are in S_M, to be in $\mathcal{U}_M$.[6] In all strictness we are supposing that Scrooge's hallucinatory belief is not perceptual, as by hypothesis there is no object, and that the perceptual state is caused by the autohallucigen y. An appropriate formalization of the case might therefore be

$$\text{Scrooge believes at } t \text{ that } a \text{ is Marley's Ghost if and if if there}$$
$$\text{are } y, z, t' > t \text{ such that } K(y, z, t') \text{ and } z \in \mathcal{U}_M. \tag{6}$$

This analysis, it seems to me, accords with our way of talking about hallucinations, dreams or other deceptions wherein there is no thing. So here belief not only does not imply the existence of Marley, but it does not 'imply' a thing. The belief is not *de re* in the weak or in any other sense, and existential quantification into the right side of (6) does not commit us to anything as it is quite vacuuous. And again, the second intentionality property is satisfied as 'a is Marley's Ghost' does not follow from (6).

Counting hallucinations, then, there are two cases of perceptual belief, no perceptual object (6) and weak *de re* in which there is an unspecified x (4). No perceptual belief implies either the truth or falsity of the subordinate clause and therefore is not *de re* in the strong sense expressed by (5). The same is true of other beliefs in the core. We have already seen that the negation of (2) does not imply either that a is Marley's Ghost or that a is not Marley's Ghost and assuming that Scrooge does realize T_M and that his attention to the scene is the same as before, then by the linearity principle VIII(19) 'Scrooge believes that a is not Marley's ghost' does not imply either either. Likewise it is true by inspection that '$\mathcal{S}$ believes at t that either x is τ or x is τ'' does not imply 'either x is τ or x is τ'' or its negation (use Note VIII.20). Or alternatively, if the linearity principle (VIII(19a)) turns out to be true for alternation, then if '$\mathscr{S}$ believes at t that either x is τ or x is τ'' implies either of the two sentences, so does 'either $\mathscr{S}$ believes at t that x is τ or $\mathscr{S}$ believes at t that x is τ''. But whatever the latter imples, '$\mathscr{S}$ believes at t that x is τ' also implies; but this sentence does not imply its subordinate clause as we have already seen. Finally '$\mathscr{S}$ believes that some x is τ' implies at some time t $\mathscr{S}$ believes that x is τ' and that a representation of x is remembered by $\mathscr{S}$ (VIII(20)). But from this the subordinate clause does not follow, although as the quantified belief is weakly *de re* it does imply 'there is something x such that $\mathscr{S}$ believes x is τ''. Core beliefs are not *about* anything (except in the weak sense) while they are *of* propositions or sentences or something or other we have to try to get clear on — they are *de dicto*. but before discussing the *de dicto* character of perceptual belief I should like to comment on Quine's handling of propositional attitudes (Quine, 1956, 1977).

Unlike functionalists who seem to think science is stuck with role-playing psychological states and Brentano's problem, Quine is wary of intentions, purposes, intensions, and other nonidentifiable items. In the end Quine advocates *elimination* of nonextensional talk in science, including psychology, altogether. As remarked earlier (Note VIII.9) this is his way around Brentano. But being unable to eradicate ordinary speech he recommends various surface semantical *cum* syntactical devices that might enable one as ontologically conservative as he to express propositional attitudes with minimal commitment to intensions, essences, and the like. He puts himself "in the position of a Jewish chef preparing ham for a gentile clientele" (Quine, 1977, p. 7) — which alone is worth more than some entire essays. Let us consider his position *via* Ralph. Quine's Ralph believes that Ortcutt is a spy. This can be read *de dicto* — namely, that Ralph has belief of a certain 'proposition'; and on this reading it does not follow that Ortcutt is a spy, which just illustrates Chisholm's second property. But it can also be read *de re*: Ralph believes 'spy' of Ortcutt. Here 'Ortcutt' refers, and one can existentially quantify into the belief context as we did in (2) above. Otherwise, it can be read 'Ralph believes spyhood of Ortcutt' which is meant to express a triadic relation among Ralph, Ortcutt and spyhood. Although this has the advantage of "putting 'Ortcutt' in referential position" for the *de re* case, it commits one to an intension, *spyhood*, which is just as objectionable to Quine as unanalyzed intentions are to me. Quine does not consider hallucinatory cases, and of course I have little to say about the general case of standing beliefs. Evidently our positions agree that what is *de re* and what not depends on the 'situation at hand', but there is a difference in treatment. Quine objects to use of intentional modes in psychology, but in informal cases decides what a proper reading of an intentional sentence shall be and then employs some kind of semantical paraphrase to make the right terms referential or not. What I do is attempt to define belief contexts away and then interpret the situation (such as a hallucinatory belief) in terms of logical concepts which are all set-theoretic and first order.

All beliefs including perceptual beliefs are *de dicto*; they are all *of* intended objects, either propositions or sentences even though some of them, as just seen, are *about res*. I will consider the nature of propositional objects in the next chapter. In the present context to be *de dicto* is just to have Chisholm's three properties and in particular is to be a belief (or desire, etc.) sentence in which substitutivity of identity fails. Sentences such as 'Scrooge believes at *t* that *a* is Marley's Ghost' and 'Ralph believes that Ortcutt is a spy' in the reading 'Ralph believes spyhood of Ortcutt' are both also weakly *de re* as in the one example '*a*' refers and in the other 'Ortcutt' does (as do, of course 'Scrooge' and 'Ralph' unless our sentences are themselves parts of larger intentional contexts).

However in strictly *de dicto* readings these names do not refer, as is borne out by the effect of substituting one for the other. In Quine's story, Ralph knows Ortcutt as a pillar of the community, and there is a certain man in a brown hat whom Ralph suspects is a spy (Quine, 1956). Let us modify the tale slightly for the case of perceptual belief. In the new story the man in the brown hat is a spy, and 'the spy in the brown hat' describes him. In fact that man is Ortcutt, but Ralph doesn't believe it. So we have

$$\text{Ralph believes at } t \text{ that } a \text{ is Ortcutt} \tag{7}$$

and

$$\text{Ortcutt} = \text{the spy in the brown that} \tag{8}$$

where '*a*' is the demonstrative 'that'. It is up to us to explain why it is that

$$\text{Ralph believes at } t \text{ that } a \text{ is the spy in the brown hat} \tag{9}$$

does not follow from (7) and (8). (I am assuming that in (9) the spy in the brown hat does not have his hat on, or the story fails to be of any interest.) Of course our intuitions tell us why: (7) and (8) could be true while (9) false. But our wont is not to assert intuitions but to examine the logic of the case and lay down reasonable analytic criteria.

The basic idea is that Ralph realizes both Ortcutt and spy-in-the-brown-hat recognizers, but they compute differently. Substitution is to be allowable only when the relevant acceptors compute the same. The justification for the approach is Frege deplatonized and is therefore an argument from authority plus an appeal to what I take it are shared intuitions about the relevant kinds of inference in psychological languages.

I will follow Frege's distinction between the *sense* and the *reference* of proper names like 'Ortcutt', but in spirit, not the letter. The reference of a name 'a' is the object a and the sense is, roughly, the 'meaning'. In fact in Frege, 'sense' is ambiguous, and our use will be of just one of the disambiguates. What I take to be the primary sense of 'sense' in Frege is this. The sense of a name 'a' differs from that of a name 'b' in '$a = b$' when there is "a difference in the mode of presentation of that which is designated" (Frege, 1892, p. 57). In this sense 'sense' has a kind of steering virtue, and two unlike senses steer one to the referent of the name, if there is an object, in differing ways.[7] The other meaning of 'sense' is that of an object that is grasped by the mind when one talks about the meanings of words or uses words in 'oblique contexts' such as the subordinate clauses of belief sentences. In (7), for instance, 'Ortcutt' is a name occurring in an oblique (a *de dicto*) environment. Frege would say that 'Ortcutt' has *indirect reference*, and that the indirect referent is the 'customary sense' (Frege, 1892, p. 59). That is to say, the word refers to its own sense in the second or objectual sense of 'sense'. It does not refer to 'Ortcutt' except indirectly.

Now as is very well known, Frege taught that inferences involving oblique contexts (moves such as from (7) and (8) to (9)) *salve veritate* hold only when the indirect references of the interchanging names are the same (Frege, 1892, pp. 65 ff.): the customary senses, which are the objects of indirect reference, are one.

My way is to shift this doctrine over to the other sense of 'sense'. I shall say that identity substitutions can be made in *de dicto* contexts only if the names to be swapped have the same sense in the primary version "same mode of presentation of that which is designated". (Here and in later developments the other sense of 'sense' *qua* abstract entity of some kind grasped by the mind will be dropped altogether.) You don't have to be particularly discerning to suspect that this 'same mode' reduces, in my theory to 'some way of accepting'. I regard my appeal to Frege as producing sufficient justification for a certain 'intensional substitutivity principle' for names in perceptual belief contexts. In the remaining part of this section I will present some of the necessary details for naturalizing the Fregean notion of sense in the primary version.

Frege's underlying idea was to examine the conditions under which sentences containing subordinate clauses have the same truth value. Framed in a formal rather than semantical mode (involving the concept True), we say that name substitutions are allowable just when the resulting beliefs are the same: '$a = b$ and believes at t that x is a' implies 'believes at t that x is b' if and only if the two beliefs are the *same*. Now by VIII(2), this is equivalent to

> '$a = b$ and $\mathscr{S}$ believes at t that x is a' implies '$\mathscr{S}$ believes at t that x is b' if and only if $\mathscr{S}$ realizes T_a, realizes T_b, and the base Turing machines of the acceptors T_a and T_b compute the same partial function on the common domain $\mathscr{U}_a = \mathscr{U}_b$.   (10)

As noted just before VIII(2) the idea of a base Turing machine was introduced in discussing Condition II of Section VI.2. In neither Chapter VIII nor in VI did I develop the idea in detail because I wanted to spare the reader needless pain: in VI I only wanted to indicate the plausibility of a purely mechanical analysis of the gestalt phenomenon accepting a single set of strings to be of two different types; and in VIII I wanted, just once more, to attack the hopelessly inadequate notion that mental features such as beliefs are machine states and can be individuated in state terms. But now the work has to be done, and we'll do it in terms of answers to three question: (1) just what is the connection between a computation of a *partial* recursive function and acceptance by an acceptor? (2) to what kinds of automata do the idea of different computation apply (we shall have to require systems more complex than FSA)? (3) since our problem is concerned with acceptance of objects as *identical to individuals* (e.g., acceptance of a in 'a = Ortcutt'), in what sense is there a computation? — functions on unit sets would appear to be too trivial to support any kind of notion of computing in the same way or of Fregean 'mode of designation'.

(1) The question concerns the precise connection between acceptors T and base machines. The fundamental facts are: that every recursive set is the domain of a partial function; that in general there are many functions on the same domain; that Turing machines for computing different functions compute in different ways ('computing a different function' being an explication of 'computing in a different way'); and that the way of computing of a Turing machine is captured in the structure of an acceptor that is constructed

from it. So let T be an acceptor that accepts a set $\mathcal{U}$. $\mathcal{U}$ is a subset of S^*, which latter is the domain of a *characteristic function* that the acceptor computes, strictly speaking. (A characteristic function of a set has value 'yes' when an element is in that set and value 'no' otherwise; and such is of course exactly what an acceptor computes). But $\mathcal{U}$, as it is recursive, is the domain of some partial function f (the function is said to be 'partial since its domain is not the whole of S^* — it is 'undefined' outside of $\mathcal{U}$) computed by the *base* Turing machine. Since $\mathcal{U}$ is recursive, the function is defined for all its elements, but not for those elements of S^* not in $\mathcal{U}$. Finally the constructed acceptor T results from throwing output of the base machine away (by treating computed values of f indifferently); then the final states Q' of T are just those that yielded function values in the base Turing machine, and $Q - Q'$ are all those that did not. Thus in effect a characteristic function on S^* is constructed from a partial function of domain $\mathcal{U}$. Derivatively, we say that two acceptors compute in the same way when their base machines from which they are formed compute the same partial recursive string functions. In effect they are internally responding differently to input, although they might have exactly the same domains.

(2) Throughout this book I have used finite automata, especially FSA's, in analyzing belief, etc. although in the general case certainly the recursive rules underlying cognitive activity are more complex. In these remarks on substitution and later on meaning it turns out the acceptors must be Turing acceptors up to arbitrary recursive sets. However I am still not going to formulate the general definitions but will adhere to use of the simple models. So I ask the reader to imagine that FSA are more powerful than they are in order to proceed with the theory and yet keep the complexity low enough so that the argument can be followed without undue misery.[8]

(3) The set recognized by an Ortcutt or Marley's Ghost acceptor are unit sets. One question is, what sense can be made of different computations on one element? Well, of course, there *could* be such functions: consider the functions whose values are x^2 and the 10th root of x on the common domain 2. However the point that needs making is that the relevant functions are on subsets of *strings*, not of perceptual objects. The strings representing objects (which in turn might be taken to be other than what they are) will always comprise a nonunit and in general infinite set of representations, for individuals appear in different ways. Different presentations of any object x are represented by different stimulus patterns y in $\mathcal{U}$ or taken to be in $\mathcal{U}$. Jones full on in the morning does not appear the same as Jones in a smoky haze at night. So a single individual present in diverse acceptance events

causes different stimulus patterns. These patterns as representations form an equivalence class, so that one might in this sense think of $\mathcal{U}_{Ortcutt}$, for instance, as a unit set (as we did in VIII.4) consisting of that class or of a *leader* or *representative* of that class (in a yet another meaning of 'representative' taken from modern algebra). But for present purposes $\mathcal{U}$ is the domain of a string function.

Thus the reason we may not conclude that Ralph believes that the thing a is the spy in the brown hat is that the acceptors corresponding to the spy and to Ortcutt do not compute the same. In all of this I am of course assuming that the spy acceptor is a composition of spy and brown hat acceptors, both of the types involved being sensible, and the extension being a unique individual. It is worth emphasizing that just as the reading of a belief sentence in a *de re* mode depends on context or collateral information, so does the determination that the Ortcutt and the spy acceptors compute differently. We base the finding that an inference based on substitution of identities won't go through on empirical information. Logic, at least in psychology and *à fortiori* in pragmatics, is not only formal or semantical but in part relies on empirical considerations concerning the user.

It is a straightforward matter now to show that the same treatment of substitutivity recommends itself for desire contexts and for other beliefs in the core. All one need do is observe that desire (and I suspect all other features such as liking, hoping, seeking, looking for, etc.) reduce to belief, action, and expectation (VIII.(12)–(15)) while all core beliefs amount to set-theoretic operations on acceptors; 'same computation' resolves down to questions of the computations of component automata.

I also included in the belief core what I called 'ascription to individuals' (see pp. 240–241), which is an inferred consequence of perceptual beliefs. McGuire believes at t that Steve is blond and if so, I said, her belief is a consequence of her belief at t that a is Steve (a = Steve) and that a is blond. Now Steve is director of the X group. From this identity statement it does not follow that McGuire believes the director of the X group is blond. But the reason is not the possibility of failure of substitutivity in 'Steve is blond' but rather of inferring 'that is the director of the X group' from 'that is Steve'. Substitutivity *depends on sameness of computation in Steve and director acceptors*. When one ascribes to individuals as an inference from perceptual beliefs, substitution is allowable only if it is allowable in the *premises* in the first instance. However since 'Steve is blond' is nonperceptual on my reckoning, although it is in the core, McGuire might directly make the substitution on grounds of her standing beliefs acquired in the English speaking community. The two cases of 'Steve is blond' are radically different, the one being an inference from perception, as just reviewed, and the other a recollection of standing belief.

3. DENOTATION

My approach to reference and meaning is founded on the notion that linguistic signs *qua* signifying involve the signs themselves, objects of various kinds (truth, extensions, objects, propositions, intensions, properties or whatever) and computational rules realized by the language user. In the case of sentences expressing underlying beliefs in one's core, there is a relation among the user, a realized automaton, a perceptual object and perhaps other entities. Reference, therefore, is not a dyadic, but at least a *triadic* relation. The same is true of other semantical relations.

Our object language is the core fragment of English, which I shall review in a moment; and our metalanguage is English including the apparatuses for talking about the core language, C, and all of the mathematical machinery we are accustomed to using from the relevant parts of automata theory. Since the study of semantical relations involves the user, the metalanguage might be termed 'pragmatical'.[9]

There is a contrast of some importance between our treatment of belief sentences whose relationship to the core is at the present time a mystery, and those of the core itself. In Sections VIII.3 and IX.2 our attitude was that of the philosopher setting out a theory of belief and attempting to justify it in the light of psychological facts and of logical features of belief sentences '$\mathscr{S}$ believes ...'. There we ourselves as the users of certain expressions in the psychology of belief attempted to give a reduced account in the logic of mind. The beliefs we attributed to $\mathscr{S}$ took no account of $\mathscr{S}$'s *own* ability to express belief: $\mathscr{S}$ could have been dumb. In effect our treatment was 'first person'.

In this section and the next, by contrast, our aim is a semantical theory of $\mathscr{S}$'s language, assuming she has one; the idea is to ground semantics, for the core, in belief, in particular in *acceptance*. In effect, our attitude is to be that of a 'third person' examining another's language and semantics. If enough were known, this second stage of the theory could deal with belief sentences; but they are hardly in $\mathscr{S}$'s or our own *core*. I will have something further, though by no means final, to say about this situation in the last chapter.

There are two steps preliminary to reference proper. The first is the definition of the core language C, and the second is the definition of an *idealized user*, $\mathscr{S}$, various descriptions of whom will occur in our pragmatical metalanguage. C is a fragment of English that $\mathscr{S}$ *knows*. To say that $\mathscr{S}$ knows C means that (a) $\mathscr{S}$ is able to accept every sentence of C — she realizes a complex automaton such that for every sentence p in C, if p is presented to her, the automaton assumes a state that means that p is a sentence of English.[10] On the basis of Chomsky's work plus the mechanist hypothesis that grammatical transformations, if any, are effective, this implies just that the acceptor involved is a Turing acceptor (cf. Sections II.3 and VI.2): this requirement is essentially *syntactical*; (b) if $\mathscr{S}$ believes that P, then there is a sentence p acceptable to her that is correlated to the final state of the acceptor underlying her belief such that if she desires to express that P, there is an algorithm that generates p via some system of grammatical rules (Section VIII.4). I also add the simplifying assumption that if P is believed, then the expressing sentence is just 'P', i.e., 'P' $= p$.

Now for C itself. As you already know, the core is a pretty stereotyped part of English, and in fact is a formalizable first order language (and, I think, context-free although this point is relative only in regard to the complexity of the acceptor that tells which sentences are the sentences of C). But our intention is that a semantical theory of C be the initiation of a more complete treatment of natural languages in a pragmatical way. C is tenseless and third person: neither 'I' nor 'you' occur in C, and 'he', 'she', and 'it', are to be identified with 'this' or with proper names such as 'Steve'; it contains no pronouns other than 'this'; it contains proper names such as 'Steve', 'Cleveland', etc.; it has predicates, including relational predicates, including, again, identity, all of which are *sensible* (for the significance of 'sensible relational predicate' see Section VIII.4) or *observable*, which means they correspond to automata that underlie perceptual belief. In addition the core includes certain truth functional sentences and quantified sentences provided that the quantifiers be bounded. All of these ideas were introduced in a preliminary way in Section VIII.4 and will be formalized to some extent in connection with a theory of truth for C.

We need an *idealized* user of C for two reasons. It would be impossible to formulate any kind of pragmatic theory of reference for every user taking into account her distinctive linguistic idiosyncrasies; and, indeed, each user of English, including C of course, has her *own language* up to within a kind of near equivalence to every other user. So just as Chomsky needs an ideal speaker who has an ideal competence in order to achieve any hope at all of doing scientific syntax of natural language (see Chomsky, 1965; Nelson, 1978a) we need an ideal speaker for semantics. So along with C we presuppose a fixed user $\mathscr{S}$ who knows C in the sense just reviewed. $\mathscr{S}$ is an *exemplar* of English speakers.[11]

The second reason for an idealized user is that we want to advance certain *definitions* of 'denotation', truth, etc. that are *objective*, that is to say, are not dependent on individual perceptual belief. *Scrooge* thought that 'Marley's Ghost' denoted something even if *we* were right in interpreting the relevant episode in *A Christmas Carol* as hallucinatory. He thought the name denoted and we didn't. But any serious theory of reference must seek to understand 'denote' and other terms even though a name to which the analysis is to apply be used incorrectly or nondenotatively more often than not. There appear to be only a relatively few sources of variation in sensible denotation and belief. One source could be that the acceptor systems that speakers realize are not *equivalent*. To say that any distinct $\mathscr{S}$ and $\mathscr{S}'$ have equivalent perceptual beliefs is just to say that if $\mathscr{S}$ believes that x is τ then so does $\mathscr{S}'$ and vice versa for any x and any τ. Now if all $\mathscr{S}$ are behaviorally equivalent in this sense it suffices to choose one to stand for all in our theory of denotation and truth; for a necessary condition of a theory independent of individual variation is unanimity. So we require not only one language but one set of beliefs. Any one subject who is representative of this equivalent lot is an *exemplar*.

Next I will assume that in all cases of acceptance (VII(6), (7)), if there is a computation of z from y, $K(y, z, t)$ for some t, then $y = z$: taking reduces to acceptance in the ideal case (which precludes the discrepancy between Scrooge and ourselves). For we know things not τ can be taken to be so and things τ taken not to be so (see the Gettier discussion, especially (4) and (7) of Table VIII.I). This stipulation is obviously necessary to ensure behavioral equivalence and to support a step toward verdical acceptance.

I will require that the *Rep* relation be a $1-1$ function: for all cases wherein $Rep(x, y, t)$ and $Rep(x, z, t)$ for any t, $y = z$; and if $Rep(x, y, t)$ and $Rep(w, y, t)$ for any t, then $x = w$. Limited in this way, '$Rep(x, y, t)$' means that x is a *cause* of y (cf. VII.1 where we introduced *Rep* as a causal relation); all stimulus patterns are unique 'images' of objects and there are no 'lapses'.

Finally let me explain what I mean by saying C is tenseless. According to Note VIII.2 there are two distinct time parameters that attach to perceptual belief: the time of the belief, expressed by us as '$\mathscr{S}$ believes at t . . . ' and tense proper, as in 'A was a student'. But in perceptual belief, we said, they may be identified; and in deciding to identify we in effect just advocate using a tenseless mode '$\mathscr{S}$ believes at t that x is τ' means both that there is a belief held at t and that x has the property τ at t.

The core also includes nonperceptual (elementary standing) beliefs such as *ascriptions to individuals* as in 'Steve is blond', and beliefs expressed by quantified expressions. All such sentences could be treated epochally after Quine's (1960a).[12] However in order to side step yet an additional detail in what is already going to be quite a complicated exercise, I will ask the reader to take beliefs and the expressing sentences of them neutrally. 'is' is the copula throughout, and is to be regarded tenselessly. It is as if I asked of a student in Logic I to phrase 'x is τ' or 'x is a τ' as 'τx' or 'x be τ'.

A theory of reference is essentially timeless; it is dispositional – for us, mathematical – although the referential *use* of any sign is temporal. For this reason when we speak of $\mathscr{S}$ believing (or now *accepting* or *fulfilling expectations*) something, we are to be concerned only with the question whether or not something is *acceptable*. Thus in the next paragraph I will write a new definition of 'acceptable' for our use in reference theory, modeled after VII(8) but incorporating our recent structures about the functionality of *Rep* and the effective elimination of the taking function K (or since we are now speaking dispositionally, the resemblance function R). In (11), unlike VII(8), acceptability is to be a trait of $\mathscr{S}$; and as acceptability is a species of belief I will express its definition as a propositional attitude.

> x is τ is *acceptable* to $\mathscr{S}$ if and only if $\mathscr{S}$ realizes some T_τ and there exists some y such that $Rep(x, y)$ and $y \in \mathscr{U}_\tau$ and $\mathscr{S}$ knows 'x is τ'.   (11)

This is like VII(8) save we have omitted reference to taking (the resemblance relation R), have ruled that *Rep* is to be function, and have detemporalized it. Also, following the style of VII(10) we attribute acceptability to $\mathscr{S}$, who realizes T_τ, not to T_τ itself.

I will now specify what it means for 'this' and for proper names like 'Jones' to denote.

> 'this' denotes this thing (the physical object a) if and only if there is some τ such that a is τ is acceptable to $\mathscr{S}$ and $\mathscr{S}$ knows 'this is τ'.   (12)

Here and in other sections of the theory I will frequently add "$\mathscr{S}$ knows 'this is τ'" for emphasis, although the phrase is officially a part of the concept of acceptability as in (11). The *deictic* or *logically proper* 'this' denotes any object that has some sensible property or other and that $\mathscr{S}$ would accept if she were presented with it and such that $\mathscr{S}$ could utter the sentence, 'this is τ'. I use a subjective mode of reading of (12) because of its reliance on acceptability — presence of a specific structure in the exemplar. Running back through the definitions VII(5) and VII(11) we see that denotation in the immediate case of the logically proper name entails fulfillment of expectation; it does not, however, involve taking as taking could possibly occur in a hallucinatory situation wherein 'this' is nondenotative.

It might strike one that there is no very tight coupling of 'this' to a. One could argue that although a would 1–1 cause T_τ to assume a final state in an actual computation of T_τ (implying $\mathscr{S}$'s attention is on τ as T_τ is 'gated in') and to utter 'this is τ', nevertheless $\mathscr{S}$ might be using 'this' to refer to something other than a. If Peter faced with a basketful of kittens says to you 'this is a kitten' you might be at a loss as to the referent. But it seems to me the vagueness here would obtain on *any* theory of reference unless 'this' or any other logically proper name be tied to the object by pointing or touching.[13] Such an act associated with 'this' would almost certainly mean the presence of an intention or desire on the part of $\mathscr{S}$ to communicate information about a particular individual. I can see no reason, in principle, why referential situations in all the implied complexity could not be reduced in our terms. In fact we sketched such an account (pp. 242–243); and the interchange with a listener $\mathscr{T}$ would, I believe, suggest a complicated theory of the immediately demonstrative. So I deny, in anticipation of a likely charge, that (12) slips in an unnoticed bit of intentionality. For our momentary purposes I am going to assume that 'this' is indexical in the direct physical way, incorporating as part of a touching, pointing, or a pointing at an iconic representation (e.g., a view through a telescope, a microscope, a mirror, etc.). I am aware of the complications here, but even more keenly so of the impossibility of tracking every conceivably relevant issue to its lair in an exploratory account such as this.

Those names that the linguistic tradition terms 'proper names' function in the core sentences either as *grammatically proper names* or as *grammatical predicates*. What makes an expression a proper name is not anything intrinsic to the expression itself but its place in use in a sentence. Consider again 'this is Steve' and 'Steve is blond'. In the first, 'Steve' is a predicate (of course it is one of two *logical* subjects according to the way contemporary logicians reckon syntax), and in the second it is a subject and as such, in that occurrence, is a proper name. In my theory the predicative use is primary and the second is derived. Any sentence of C in which a name is used as a proper name is a product of inference from sentences in which the name as employed is a predicate. I came to this conclusion from no *a prioristic* reflections on logic and language reminiscent of the recent 'linguistic turn' in Western analytic philosophy, but rather from an examination of the psychology of acceptance and the use of it as a vantage-point from which to attack reference. Our psychological subjects accept (recognize — fulfill expectations of) objects as individual things according to the same logical processes as they accept objects as instantiating sensible types.[14] As we have seen in the foregoing sections identification of an object as an individual requires the realization of automata just as acceptance of a thing as of a sensible quality or natural kind. And identification of a thing perceptually as Ortcutt or whatever is therefore logically antecedent to predicating anything of Ortcutt as an individual. Thus what I have been calling 'ascription to an individual', which is a label for beliefs in which sensible predicates are applied to properly named things like Steve or Ortcutt, is a conclusion to an inference. To spell it out in a little more detail than heretofore (cf. Section VIII.4): if τ is an individual and $\mathscr{S}$ believes at t that a is τ, she also can express 'a is τ'. In the quoted sentence (of C) 'is' is the 'is' of identity, while, as I just argued, that 'is' in the belief sentence itself is part of an entire complex (that belief sentence itself) that analyzes out to '$Rep\,(a,\,x)$ and $x \in \mathscr{U}_\tau$' $\mathscr{U}_\tau$ being a unit set. As $\mathscr{U}_\tau$ is unit, the analysans is equivalent to '$Rep\,(a,\,x)$ and $x = \tau$'. Consequently if τ' is a property, and if $\mathscr{S}$ believes at approximately the same t that a is τ', and she *tacitly infers* to τ is τ', then i.e., $\mathscr{S}$ believes at t that τ is τ'.[15] So acceptance that τ is τ' is an inference, and our placing of 'τ' in the position of a grammatical subject renders it denotative *qua* proper name. In this manner the naming power of 'Ortcutt', etc. is derivative. (Caution: in this situation $\mathscr{S}$ knows the sentences (i) 'a is τ'. (ii) 'a is τ'', and (iii) 'τ is τ'', but the question of the deduction of (iii) from (i) and (ii) does not arise here. Whether (iii) is indeed a consequence is a matter of a theory of truth for C which we do not have as yet. The inference referred to above is 'tacit'; $\mathscr{S}$ believes that 'τ is τ'' as a result of underlying recursive processes in her mind, not as a result of conscious inference from expressing sentences (i) and (ii)).[16]

Building on this background we arrive at a definition of 'denotation' for proper names of C. Let τ be an individual and 'τ' the corresponding name in C (see Note 17).

> 'τ' *denotes* τ if and only if there is an a and a τ' such that a (this) is τ is acceptable to $\mathscr{S}$ and a (this) is τ' is acceptable to $\mathscr{S}$ and $\mathscr{S}$ knows the sentence 'τ is τ''.   (13)

In both (12) and (13) denotation depends upon there being acceptance of a thing denoted subject to predication. There is no such thing as a purely denotative term, that is to say, a pure index without implicit attribution or *intention* — expectation of a thing *qua* type. However it does not follow from this consequence of my theory that the logically proper, purely deictic 'this' has a *meaning*. By contrast, however, a derivative or anaphoric name like 'Ortcutt' does have meaning in the sense that it is not accessible to substitution of 'the spy in the brown hat' in belief contexts (cf. Section X.3). On this theory both logically proper names such as 'this' or derived names such as 'Ortcutt' denote via a causal connection with the object; and if this causal tie were propogated up into noncore sentences and throughout the English speaking community, we would have, in so far forth, something similar to the Kripkean picture of naming (Kripke, 1972). But only remotely. In the case of a name 'τ' there is a crypto-inferential underlay involving two immediately demonstrative acceptances (of a is τ and a is τ'). There are several kinds of possible situations. In a perceptual encounter 'Steve is blond' has the causal and inferential springs just uncovered. At the time 'Steve' is learned, however, one of three things must have happened: (i) there was a simultaneous acquisition of an acceptor T_{Steve} by $\mathscr{S}$, and some kind of association of 'Steve' with it; (ii) there was *a priori* internalization of T_{Steve} ($\mathscr{S}$ got to know him before she knew his name) and then later an association of 'Steve' thereto; or (iii) $\mathscr{S}$ learned about Steve and learned his name via the speech community without ever having met him face-to-face, and she might *never* acquire T_{Steve}. For some one in the community, the theory goes, either (i) or (ii) must have been the case; the learning of 'Steve' was propagated community-wide later. My point in emphasizing the qualifier 'remotely' in comparison with Kripke is that for me even at a naming T_{Steve} is acquired by the namer (the local pastor, say) — case (i) — and only 'this' is logically proper. Any utterance of English speakers using 'Steve' even at that moment is partly inferential.

A more important observation is that neither (12) nor (13) are mere lists enumerating the extension of 'denotation' (i.e., an enumeration of pairs like ('τ', τ)), but are reductions to nonsemantical concepts in the spirit required by Field (1972). He has argued, correctly I believe, that Tarksi's theory of truth does not offer a truly primitive theory of reference as it ultimately relies on a definition of denotation which, although an extensional equivalence, does not really achieve a reduction to nonsemantical terms. I think that my definition does achieve reduction, for C anyway, although there would seem to be no call to defend the claim now beyond what I have already written in the previous pages. The theory ultimately depends on no concepts other than *Rep*, acceptance, and a kind of tacit identity inference. And acceptance, in turn, is intentional but can be analyzed back down to sets and mappings.

4. A THEORY OF TRUTH

It is now a relatively straight-forward task to formulate a definition of 'truth' for *C*. Following the usual approach, I first give the syntax of *C* as if regularized in a standard first order way (see Note 11). I shall present this pretty much with unrelieved technicality and then summarize the result as simply as possible. Following is the syntax of *C*:

Names:	this, Jack, Jones, McGuire, Cleveland, ...
Variables:	v_1, v_2, v_3.
Predicates:	blond, red, apple, man, longer than, identical to, ...
Connectives:	~ (not), $\wedge$ (and).
Quantifier:	($\exists$ . . .) (there exists such and such).
Parentheses:	(,).

The list of predicates is meant to include relational predicates of arbitrary *n*-arity as well as monadic predicates, but I distinguish among them by no specific notation. All of the predicates are sensible. The quantifier is bounded, which means that it always ranges over finite sets of objects. This is, of course, a matter of interpretation, which is in a way built in because all we shall be concerned with are physical objects and their sensible properties.

An *expression* is any sequence of symbols from the above lists. Let '$\mathscr{A}$' range over expressions. If $\mathscr{A}$ is a variable or a name, it is a *term*. Let '*t*' vary over terms. Let '*v*' vary over variables. Let, II_n, vary over *n*-ary predicates.

If Π is an *n*-ary predicate letter and $t_1, \ldots, t_n$ are terms, then $\ulcorner \Pi(t_1, \ldots, t_n) \urcorner$ is an *atomic sentence.*

'Sentence' is defined in the usual way:

(i)   Every atomic sentence is a *sentence*;

(ii)   If $\mathscr{A}$ is a *sentence*, so is $\ulcorner \sim\mathscr{A} \urcorner$;

(iii)   If $\mathscr{A}$ and $\mathscr{A}'$ are *sentences*, so is $\ulcorner \mathscr{A} \wedge \mathscr{A}' \urcorner$;

(iv)   If $\mathscr{A}$ is a *sentence*, so is $\ulcorner (\exists v)\mathscr{A} \urcorner$, where *v* is any variable;

(v)   Nothing else is a *sentence*.

We next introduce the idea of sequences of objects $(a_1, a_2, a_3, \ldots)$, where each a is a physical, perceptual object of some sort, in preparation for the definition of 'satisfies'. Following Tarski (1936) we want to obtain an exact version of the intuitive idea of an object satisfying sentences (as in "2 satisfies the equation '$x^2 = 4$'"); but inasmuch as we shall have sentences with any finite number of distinct free variables we need to provide for satisfaction not only by single entities such as o or 2 but by large arrays. This is accomplished by associating to each sequence σ a function $\bar{\sigma}$ from terms of C to objects o. At this point the idea of denotation we introduced in (12) and (13) plays a crucial part. The definition of $\bar{\sigma}$ is as follows. Let $\sigma = (a_1, a_2, a_3, \ldots)$; then

$$\bar{\sigma}(t) = \begin{cases} \text{whatever } t \text{ denotes, if } t \text{ is a } name \text{ of } C \\ \\ a_i, \text{ if } t \text{ is a variable } v_i \text{ of } C \end{cases}$$

I will give two definitions of 'satisfies'. The first harks back to Tarski and is *inductive*. The second is *explicit* and depends on several pragmatic assumptions about $\mathscr{S}$.

(i′) σ *satisfies* $\ulcorner \Pi_n(t_1, \ldots, t_n) \urcorner$ if and only if $(\bar{\sigma}(t_1), \ldots, \bar{\sigma}(t_n))$ is τ is acceptable to $\mathscr{S}$, where 'τ' is a translation of Π_n into the metalanguage:

The definiens of this clause entails that $\mathscr{S}$ realizes an appropriate relational acceptor and that $\mathscr{S}$ knows the sentence $\ulcorner \Pi_n(t_1, \ldots, t_n) \urcorner$. Thus for a 1-ary predicate, (i′) reads "σ satisfies 'Steve is blond' if and only if σ('Steve') is blond is accepted by some T_{blond} that $\mathscr{S}$ realizes and $\mathscr{S}$ knows 'Steve is blond'". Let p be $\mathscr{A}$ restricted to sentences.

(ii′) σ *satisfies* $\ulcorner \sim p \urcorner$ if and only if σ does not satisfy p;

(iii′) σ *satisfies* $\ulcorner p \wedge p' \urcorner$ if and only if σ satisfies p and σ satisfies p';

(iv′) σ *satisfies* $\ulcorner (\exists v_i) p \urcorner$ if and only if some sequence σ' differing from σ in at most the i-th place satisfies p.

The second definition arises from the observation, duly noted in our introduction of the idea of core belief in Section VIII.4, that the family of recursive sets is closed under set-theoretic operations of complement, intersection, and union. Thus if $\mathscr{U}_\tau$ and $\mathscr{U}_{\tau'}$ are both accepted sets and if $\mathscr{S}$ believes x is τ and x is τ', then she must realize an automaton for the intersection; and of course similarly for the complement and the union. Likewise if she believes something x is τ, then she must at one time have stored a thing *a* that is τ (cf. VIII(20)). Sentences in the core correspond to automaton structures; in particular they are associated to final states, as summarized a few pages back. So if *T* corresponds to *P* or *Q*, for instance, then the exemplar $\mathscr{S}$ realizes *T* entails that $\ulcorner p \vee q \urcorner$ is expressible.[17]

In order to justify the second definition I shall derive it as a conclusion, assuming as premises the first definition of 'satisfies' and the principles of linearity (VIII(19), (19a)) which express that $\mathscr{S}$ believes *P(L)Q* if and only if ($\mathscr{S}$ believes *P*) *L* ($\mathscr{S}$ believes *Q*) where *L* is any connective 'and', or, etc. in the metalanguage, provided that $\mathscr{S}$'s attention be aroused (technically, that the subject automata are activated). However, since we wish to rephrase VIII(19), (19a) for acceptability (believability less taking, *Rep* 1–1, etc.) we need not heed this latter proviso. The subjunctive nature of descriptions about *T* in $\mathscr{S}$ already include attention: "if *T* were given input, then *T* would go into a final state, etc."; we shall be talking about acceptability, not acceptance or belief at *t*. For easy reference, revised for acceptance, VIII(19) says

> *P* is not acceptable to $\mathscr{S}$ if and only if not-*P* (the negation) is
> acceptable to $\mathscr{S}$. (14)

Similarly, VIII(19a) revises over to

> *P* is acceptable to $\mathscr{S}$ and *Q* is acceptable to $\mathscr{S}$ if and only if *P*
> and *Q* is acceptable to $\mathscr{S}$. (15)

$\mathscr{S}$ also believes certain existentially quantified statements that reside in her core; and in Section IX.1 we have seen that quantified statements in which sensible property types figure and in which belief is nonhallucinatory are weakly *de re*. This again amounts to a kind of linearity principle which I will write for acceptability, not belief, with the usual deletions of taking, etc. in mind.

> *x* is τ is acceptable to $\mathscr{S}$ for some *x* is and only if some *x* is τ
> is acceptable to $\mathscr{S}$.[18] (16)

Now if σ is a sequence of objects that satisfies *p* according to the first definition, let '*P($\bar{\sigma}$)*' be the translation of *p* into the metalanguage.

> *Proposition*: σ satisfies *p* if and only if *P($\bar{\sigma}$)* is acceptable to
> $\mathscr{S}$ (17)

The proof is by induction on the number *m* of symbols $\sim$, $\wedge$, and $\exists$ occurring in *p*. If *m* = 0, *p* is atomic and the proposition follows from clause (i') of the first definition where 'p' is '$\ulcorner \Pi_n(t_1, \ldots, t_n)\urcorner$' and '$P(\bar{\sigma})$' is '($\bar{\sigma}(t_1)$, $\ldots, \bar{\sigma}(t_n)$ is τ', and where 'τ' is a translation of Π into the metalanguage.

If p is $\ulcorner \sim q \urcorner$ and if σ satisfies p then by (ii') and only then σ does not satisfy q. By the induction hypothesis, σ satisfies q if and only if $Q(\bar{\sigma})$ is acceptable to $\mathscr{S}$. Hence σ does not satisfy q if and only if $Q(\bar{\sigma})$ is not acceptable to $\mathscr{S}$. By linearity, (14), σ does not satisfy q if and only if not-$Q(\bar{\sigma})$ is acceptable to $\mathscr{S}$. Therefore σ satisfies $\ulcorner \sim q \urcorner$ if and only if not $Q(\bar{\sigma})$ is acceptable to $\mathscr{S}$.

If p is $\ulcorner q \wedge r \urcorner$ then and only then by (iii') σ satisfies q and σ satisfies r. By the induction hypothesis σ satisfies $\ulcorner q \wedge r \urcorner$ if and only if $Q(\bar{\sigma})$ is acceptable to $\mathscr{S}$ and $R(\bar{\sigma})$ is acceptable. So by linearity (15) σ satisfies $\ulcorner q \wedge r \urcorner$ if and only if $Q(\bar{\sigma})$ and $R(\bar{\sigma})$ is acceptable to $\mathscr{S}$.

Similarly for the case when p is $\ulcorner (\exists v_i) q \urcorner$ using (iv') of the first definition, and (16).

This proves the proposition.

Finally, the definition of 'true', still following in the wake of Tarski:

$$p \text{ is true if and only if every sequence } \sigma \text{ satisfies } p; \qquad (18)$$

and

$$p \text{ is false if and only if no sequence } \sigma \text{ satisfies } p.\,[19]$$

It is easy to see that under the given assumptions about $\mathscr{S}$ and the linearity assumption the *Proposition* also implies each of the clauses of the first definition by a kind of reverse argument; and for this reason we can take the *Proposition* as an explicit definition of truth in C.

5. ADEQUACY

Is this treatment of 'truth' satisfactory? There are plenty of comments that could be made, but I am going to pay attention more to those that apply to my treatment here – its virtues and shortcomings – than to the place of Tarski-type definitions in logic and epistemology. I am less concerned with the philosophical problem of truth, which is a several-lifetime project of study in itself, than to the plausibility of mechanism's scaffolding for a typical theory.

First, I have entered the claim and attempted to demonstrate, that truth, at least for the simple language C, can be explicitly defined in strictly syntactical-pragmatical terms with no covert appeal to semantical notions. I am the first to acknowledge, however, that it applies only to a physical domain and that it involves a lot of material assumptions, among them of a 1−1 causal relation between objects in the domain and stimulus patterns, an exemplary acceptor, linearity of belief, and a good dose of evolutionism.[20] Setting aside everything save the linearity question for the moment, (14), (15), and (16) are indeed disputable. Recalling, however, that in the full form each statement must be accompanied by the proviso that the subject's attention is directed to the relevant phenomenon, *viz*. that if the question is whether x is τ then T_τ is gated in, the principles become at least plausible and are of empirical significance, although I would not know how to set up a decisive test. On strictly *a priori* grounds, if $\mathscr{S}$ realizes automata for τ, τ' and for τ and τ' (intersection); if she believes τ of x and also believes τ' of x where both are perceptual; and if the intersection $T_\tau \cap T_{\tau'}$ is open to input it seems she must believe x is τ and x is τ'; and similarly for the other connectives. The real question boils down to whether the conditional connection between attention and belief is as strong as I am inclined to think it is. And this is surely an empirical question.

Neither definition satisfies Tarski's *material adequacy* condition for a definition of the truth predicate, even though in my first definition I have followed the usual presentation of the definition clause by clause.[21] This condition, which I suppose the reader to be familiar with, says that any definition of truth for a language such as C should have as consequences all sentences of the metalanguage:

the sentence p is true if and only if P

where P is any sentence of C expressed in the metalanguage and p is its name. Thus sentences of the metalanguage such as

'Steve is blond' is true if and only if Steve is blond

and

'this is longer than that' is true if and only if this longer than that

would be consequences of (18), if that definition were adequate.

Now a classical, Tarskian, definition of truth applied to C would differ from our first definition only in clause (i'). For him, this clause perhaps would read as follows:

(i')* σ satisfies $\ulcorner\Pi_n(t_1, \ldots, t_n)\urcorner$ if and only if $(\bar{\sigma}(t_1), \ldots, \bar{\sigma}(t_n))$ is τ, where 'Π' and 'τ' correspond as in my (i'). If it is possible to argue from P being acceptable to $\mathcal{S}$, to P, P atomic, then if Tarski's definition satisfies the adequacy condition, so does mine.

I think it *is* possible to give an argument in support of acceptance of P implies P, but not of its converse. I will sketch the favorable part in terms of three relevant points, one of which hinges on evolutionism, the second on taking, and the third on the distinction between a truth *definition* and a *criterion*.

As to the first, about the best I can do is embellish the argument of Section VIII.1, that is meant to support *same* computation from an argument x by the base machines of T_τ and $T_{\tau'}$ as a necessary and sufficient condition for the sameness of *sensible* types τ and τ'.[22] If *types are so individuated* by internalized automata, then it is true that if x is τ is acceptable to $\mathcal{S}$ then x is τ. There is obviously a gap here, even if we limit outselves to naturalistic grounds (not to say to Cartesian grounds, on which what is accepted as true and expressed might be a deception). But, again, I see no reason why the position should strike one as implausible, given evolutionism. If evolutionism is a true theory of the growth and adaptation of organisms, then it is simply *not* credible that organisms could adapt and survive if their response repertoires were adjusted to a world other than the real physical one. Moreover the plausibility of a connection between acceptance and reality is further secured by the 1−1 assumption concerning *Rep* in the idealized case. The object 1−1 causes the stimulus pattern, discounting lapses. No other kind of thing could cause the stimulus. And combined with the selectiveness of evolution, 1−1 causality should steer acceptance aright.

Second, we have limited the resemblance relation R to an identity relation, which entails that all patterns come from clean receptual classes. We invoked this assumption in order to set up $\mathcal{S}$ as an exemplar; but it serves extended duty here. $\mathcal{S}$ takes the stimulus only as it is, and not as another thing. Combined with the evolutionist point, the point of pristine stimuli seems to assure that acceptance accord with reality ('accord' does not mean 'match' or 'picture' in *any* sense!).

Third, as to the perfect observer $\mathcal{S}$, we are seeking a definition of 'truth' that is adequate, not a criterion for application of the predicate, which in some sense involves inductive logic and perhaps a closer psychology and epistemology of perception involving taking, confirmation, estimation, error reduction, and the like. A definitional standard in such a case as 'truth' where we are far from some entrenched linguistic usage to report is essentially an *explication* in Carnap's sense; and any conceptual instruments, already a coherent part of an overall theoretical approach, that lend precision to the construction of the explication are legitimate provided that they do not smuggle in synonyms for the term in question. Logic itself, and in particular the purely semantical theory of truth, already abstracts and idealizes for its own good purposes in similar ways. $\mathcal{S}$, under the restriction to 'cofinal' causes and identity takings, plays just such a standard-setting role and it is for this reason we call her an 'exemplar'.

Although these points have some force, they only support half of the equivalence needed. They allow some confidence in asserting that if x is τ is acceptable to a perfect $\mathcal{S}$, then x is τ, but hardly in asserting the converse. Presumably there are at least a denumerable number of facts x is τ on the immediate perceptual level that could be expressed in the metalanguage; but since each one requires an automaton for acceptance and since the neural resources for embodying automata are finite, some of them will never be perceived. There is no problem with the expressing of *sentences* in C, which are denumerable and which are generable by a Chomskian grammar (which, incidentally, would provide us with an alternative definition of 'sentence' for the core). Perhaps this aspect of finitude should count as a failing of the theory — too rigid an insistence for the core part of English on 1—1 associations of sentences with acceptor final states as a condition of assertability.[23] But I can not see any other way, at the moment, to tackle reference in a sufficiently rich model to get a semantical theory. However, this might be, if you want to make an outright assumption that P is acceptable if and only if P for atomic sentences, then our first definition is equivalent to Tarski's. You might then go on to ask: why not be content (except for the theory of denotation) with the classical approach?

One reason why not is that, the theory exemplifies for C what a 'full blooded' concept of truth as required by Dummett and as contrasted with Davidson (and now Tarski) might be like. In his article on 'Truth' Dummett suggests that one feature of that concept, among others he discusses, that a sentence p must have to be true, is effective decidability:

We are entitiled to say that a statement p must be true or false, that there must be something *in virtue* of which either it is true or false only when p is a statement of such a kind that we could in a finite time bring ourselves into a position in which we were justified either in asserting or denying p; that is when p is an *effectively decidable* statement (Dummett, 1958—59, p. 66, *ital.* mine).

This sentiment, I take it, is of a piece with what is expressed in his later work to the effect that semantics must characterize what it is to know or understand, since obviously understanding or knowing sentences is required for deciding truth or falsity (see Dummett, 1975; also above pp. 251–252). So one reason you don't just take Tarski and adapt his theory to ordinary language (which he was skeptical about in any case) on either Dummett's grounds or mine is that you need *deciders* – even in the abstract definition, if truth is going to have anything to do with actual language in communication. And you can't have semantics based on use and a Tarski adequacy condition since there is only a finite number of deciders in any one individual's head.

An objection could be raised if my quoting of Dummett is meant to establish some connection between his philosophy of truth and my theory for C. *Understanding* is not required for effective decidability of a sentence as an effective procedure operates mechanically on sentences. Further, acceptability in the logic of mind is a relational trait between objects and rules in the mind not a relation between sentences, except derivatively via association with automaton states.

Lightweight as this objection is, it does deserve comment. Dummett means by 'effective decidability' something like 'intuitionistic justification', which is a matter of creative construction, or a method of establishing truth in some step-by-step manner. This, he says, is an adaptation of intuitionism in mathematics to ordinary statements in general (Dummett, 1958–59, p. 66). As such 'effective decidability' is a notion that applies to mental processes – as does our own notion of acceptability – and applies (sticking strictly to the intuitionistic antecedents of the position) to sentences only as written reports, so to speak, of underlying intellection (i.e., the logic of a mathematically language is a reconstruction of mathematical *thought*).[24]

I claim acceptability by $\mathscr{S}$ of x is τ is the same as effective decidability, in the core case.[25] Surely the computation of $M(q_0, y)$, where $Rep(x, y)$, is effective as it is done by a Turing machine (i.e., an acceptor of some kind). However *Rep* does span things and representations (patterns) of them; and ordinarily we do apply 'decidability' only to numbers or to linguistic entities, not perceivable things. But any similar view, e.g., Dummett's or Putnam's, has to face the issue as indeed must any *causal* theory of acceptance and perception. After all, the cause is *efficient*, which I take it connotes an exact counterpart of what we mean in logic by 'effective'. The cause has whatever it takes to yield the effect. Indeed, to press the opposite would be simply silly. So I maintain that effective decidability can be replaced in Dummett's thinking by acceptability in the full sense we attribute to $\mathscr{S}$ in accepting objects.

These developments contribute to a correspondence approach to truth although the correspondence is triadic, not dyadic. The correspondence between a sentence and reality is indirect, via a causal connection between an object and a stimulus which is accepted as a type in terms of a state that the sentence about the object is tied to. Here there is no ineffable Wittgensteinian 'picture' of atomic facts nor direct coupling of a sentence to a realm of sense data in the manner of one stage of Bertrand Russell's philosophy. Nor is there a correspondence of internal sentence in some brain script to the real world, as seems to be proposed by some functionalists. One might say that the role of a true sentence is to express acceptance, which might then induce a like acceptance in a listener for her own needs in grappling with the perceptually experienced. True perceptual belief is *real*; it either is or was caused by real things that are construed by human organisms in ways that enable them to adapt successfully to the world in concert with their fellows. Although so far limited to a sadly inadequate fragment of English, the theory is in the line of development of the naturalism of Dewey but with a realist rather than instrumentalist cast to it.

In VII(12) I defined 'perceives' in terms of *virtual* acceptance, which you will recall is fulfillment involving the full take and possible lapses in *Rep*, plus verdiciality: $\mathscr{S}$ perceives that x is τ at t if and only if x is τ and $\mathscr{S}$ virtually accepts x is τ. At a first glance back this analysis of perception mixed in with the treatment of truth in the present section seems to cook down to an odd concoction. For at the moment the true is the acceptable, in a sense, and yet in VII(12) the truth of x is τ added to the concept of acceptance to get perception. Why not simply cut out taking, lapses, and the like and simply define pure perception or knowledge as acceptance – in the restricted sense of this present section – and have done with it? There are two reasons. First perception is a skill of an organism, is not a sentence and is hence neither true nor false. It's not the right category. The occurrence of the condition 'x is τ' in the definition of 'perceives' guarantees rightness or veridicality of a virtual acceptance, and this has nothing to do with the truth of sentences in a language spoken by the subject organism, if any. Nevertheless, you might point out, acceptance in the pure, not the virtual, sense is necessary and sufficient for the truth of sentences about the condition x is τ. This brings me to the second reason. Acceptance without taking and lapses in *Rep* is too pure. I think that we do want to be able to say that organisms *take* things right in their acceptances and therefore perceive, even if what they accept is in part a construction under their own recursive processes (like in the use of the super automaton T' in taking, pp. 88ff). Besides there is no exemplar $\mathscr{S}$, really, and pure acceptance is too rare to be used to account for perception. Now to *test* for perception in an organism requires a concept of truth for the clause x is τ. But that is a concept for a scientific section of English far from the core. So at the present time we have to live with a distinction, noted earlier in this chapter, between a psychology of perception, acceptance and belief, and a semantical theory of sentences expressing acceptance. The first study, too, has a language which we would dearly love to have a semantics and theory of truth for; in the second we win some ground by focusing on a simple language and a simplified, idealized model of ourselves.

There is, however, no incompatibility between the theory of truth and the definition of 'knows' in the case of perceptual belief given in VIII(3). In that definition simply drop the clause 'x is τ', restrict K to the identity relation on the first two components, and impose the $1-1$ requirement on *Rep*. The automaton of the definiens is part of the exemplar as here described, and the residual condition plus the expressibility proviso yields a characterization of knowledge. This works, however, only if we have sufficient grounds (I have just argued that we do) for asserting that if P is acceptable to the exemplar, then P. The surviving clause in the Gettier-type analysis of Table VIII.I is (1) alone. This accord between the concept of truth implicit in VIII(3) and that of this chapter is no accident. The psychological theory and the semantical theory (of truth), again distinguished between in the last paragraph, fall into one theory in the area of perceptual knowledge as well as of perceptual belief; neither goes beyond the core language C and its truth predicate.

CHAPTER X

TOWARD MEANING

1. LINGUISTIC MEANING

The subject of meaning is notoriously foggy and undeveloped; according to some thinkers, not a subject at all. Yet, no meaning, no language; and failure to understand meaning is failure to understand the human being himself. I do not have very much of an orderly nature to say about meaning or intension, for I am convinced that any thing remotely resembling a *theory* of meaning, given our present limited insights in linguistics and psychology, is risky and presumptuous. If ever there was a place from which to launch the most irresponsible metaphysics, this is it. So I am somewhat hesitant about putting forth the position that the path to it is by way of intentionality. Yet we can make sense of mental attitudes and purpose to some extent in terms of expectations and so back to computational systems. What I hope to do is indicate (not even *sketch*) a kind of theory based on acceptance, in a manner parallel to the treatment of truth in the previous chapter.

When a person utters a sentence in order to inform another or to induce another to action, she has expectations about verbal responses or actions on the part of her audience, and fulfillment or disruption provides a check on the efficacy of her performance. Such situations embody meaning in a fundamental social sense of that concept, and in our theory can be described in terms of the subject $\mathscr{S}$, her desires and expectations, and the responder $\mathscr{T}$, her desires, responses, expectations of being understood, and so forth. There are philosophers who think that meaning emerges only in such situations (Grice, 1975, p. 45): for a sentence p to mean something one who utters it must intend to induce belief: inducing is a necessary condition for meaning. Certainly a social picture of meaning suggests some underlying psychology, although Grice disclaims "any intention of peopling all our talking life with armies of psychological occurrences" (Grice, 1975, p. 47). However, the social content can not be all there is to it. As both our intuitions and our theory tell us, inducing belief in a communicational setting entails various intelligent processes that are *intentional* in some sense that is basic to meaning *qua* belief-inducement. If this were not so, Grice's position would be circular (Harman, 1968, p. 591) and of a piece with his contextual stance regarding belief and desire (cf. above Section VIII.2 and Grice, 1974–75). A way out of the circle (which is just another manifestation of Brentano's problem) lies in a theory of meaning of linguistic expressions as such; and this end can be approached without disacknowledging any of the fundamental observations about the psychology of communicational interplay.

There are a number of approaches to linguistic meaning: that of the psycholinguist, the philosopher, the sociologist, the logician, the computer scientist, the literary analyst, the psychiatrist and the speech specialist, to mention some. Within each discipline there are again many schools, nearly as many as there are scholars. This is not very comforting to anyone looking for a hook to hang an idea or two on.

As a starter, no matter what attitudes or presuppositions are taken, a philosopher must initially distinguish *at least* between a psychology of meaning and a logic even though in the end they might form a combined semantics. For consider a relatively simple problem about *extension*. In the logical part of semantics the extension of a term is closely affiliated with the concept of *truth*. Fido is in the extension of 'dog' if and only if 'Fido is a dog' is true. On the other hand your average four year old child often calls things 'dogs' that are not and calls dogs something else. So there is a difference between logical or psychological extensions. What is the relation? However the details might turn out, it is akin to the relation of truth to belief.

A less trivial example concerns intension. A consequence of possible world semantics (which I shall describe in a moment) is that all logically true or necessary statements have the same intension. This might be tolerable for purposes of strict logic, but it certainly is not for psychological semantics, which must be concerned with grammatical meaning in some sense distinct from mere syntax, nor for philosophy of science.

Generally speaking philosophies of meaning these days either proceed from an essentially *logical* stance, as do the several varieties of possible world semantics, and then somehow coax certain psychological aspects of meaning into that logical framework; or they work the other way around, from an essentially psychological or sociological stance, and view even logic itself and formal semantics (model theory) from within the empirical framework. Both groups, however, tend toward theories of meaning that in one way or another reduce meaning to reference and extension. My own view also is to seek for an account ultimately in extensional, mathematical terms; and this it shares with both. But since semantics for me is part of a logic of mind I obviously fall in with the psychological movement.

In the following brief sections I am going to introduce several concepts of meaning which do not comprise a systematic theory. I will treat more or less isolated topics on a common theme of reducing questions of meaning to those of intention. For various comparisons, criticism and contrasts I will relate the discussion to two schools of meaning represented by possible world theorists (more or less as a group) on the one hand and Hilary Putnam on the other — not that they are by any means of disjoint opinion on all topics. First I shall address the problem of propositions — what are they? — objects of belief; this is a branch of psychological semantics. And then I shall turn to intensions of names and predicates from a point of view that addresses both *logical* and *psychological* aspects. The job is a bit of a botch, I am afraid, but I don't know any better.

2. PROPOSITIONS [1]

In recent years there has been a flood of proposals for semantics of ordinary language that are essentially reductive: reduce meaning to reference, somehow (Lewis, 1972; Hintikka, 1969; Montague, 1970). Philosophers who take this line, which originated with some of Carnap's ideas (Carnap, 1956a), fall into a territory somewhere between Quine, who wants to rid science and philosophy of mysterious entities such as meanings and intensions altogether (except for 'stimulus meanings' — essentially our $\mathcal{U}$ — which are indispensable and becomingly empirical), and the out-and-out platonist such as Frege. Reductive semantics, by which I mean efforts to capture *meaning, intension*, and *proposition* in terms of the mathematical ideas of sets and functions (presumably in extension), is beset with its own difficulties. It wishes to avoid ontological prodigality beyond the requirements of logic and mathematics — roughly sets at various levels, and no more — but yet requires certain primitives, especially *possible worlds*, that other philosophies are inhospitable to. Let me try to illustrate the advantages of this reductive approach and at the same time lay the ground for later criticism.

The philosophical tradition has long distinguished between *propositions*, and the *sentences* that express them. Thus, the tradition says, sentences of different languages can express exactly the same propositions or meanings; — for instance, 'shapka no golovy Ivana' and 'the hat is on Ivan's head' mean the same. For the possible world semanticist that proposition is the set of all possible worlds in which 'the hat is on Ivan's head' (presuming that we know who Ivan is, etc.) is true, and is the same set of worlds for the

Russian. Likewise 'Ronald Reagan is a Stalinist' though most likely false expresses a certain proposition that is, on this view, just the set of all possible worlds in which the sentence is true. The approach has a certain intuitive appeal to it, especially if one thinks of a proposition as just the circumstances that would make a sentence true, if it were true. And sure enough, the characterization of 'proposition' is extensional. But what about the intelligibility (as a starter) of 'possible world'? *Are* there such things? Where? Can you always tell one from another? Is the Ronald Reagan who is a Stalinist in some other world the same person as the Ronald Reagan who is President of the United States? And so on.[2] I am not going to come anywhere near a satisfactory discussion of all of these questions in this book, except for perceptual sentences.

Suppose $\mathcal{S}^+$ is a fixed believer, but not necessarily identical to the exemplar; she takes, and her *Rep* relation is not necessarily functional. In VIII(2) two beliefs were said to be the same if the underlying acceptance computations are the same. For our purposes there I wanted to indicate a condition of sameness of belief for two perceptual beliefs at some time t. But here, as in reference theory, I will use the dispositional concept of *acceptability,* now generalized back to the form of VII(8), which I repeat for our equally generalized $\mathcal{S}^+$:

> x is τ is (virtually) *acceptable* to $\mathcal{S}^+$ if and only if $\mathcal{S}^+$ realizes T_τ and there is a y and z such that $Rep\,(x, y)$, $R(y, z)$ and $z \in \mathcal{U}_\tau$ (i.e., $M(q_0, z) = q_F$) and $\mathcal{S}^+$ knows an expressing sentence. (1)

For core belief I did not spell out (didn't have to for a theory of truth) the details of T_τ which might be an extremely complex automaton corresponding to the result of various set-theoretic operations on recursive sets of stimulus patterns, and quantification into acceptance contexts. We still do not need to go into this matter; but to make (1) more perspicuous, I will generalize it for artibrary p in C, and in the analysans simply remind you of the computational etiology underlying acceptability.

> P is acceptable to $\mathcal{S}^+$ if and only if she realizes an automaton and relations *Rep* and R, goes to a final state, and knows the sentence p that expresses P (1a)

Now for 'same belief':

> Belief that P and belief that Q are the same for $\mathcal{S}^+$ if and only if P is acceptable to $\mathcal{S}^+$ if and only if Q is acceptable to $\mathcal{S}^+$

and the functions underlying the realized automata are the same.[3]   (2)

Intuitively, this means the same objects satisfy the beliefs in the 'same way' (Section VI.2). As heretofore, let 'p' express 'P' and 'q', 'Q'. Then

p and q of C are *synonymous* if and only if belief that P and belief that Q are the same for $\mathscr{S}^+$.   (3)

Alternatively we might say that p and q express the *same proposition*. These definitions relativize propositions to the user, a fixed $\mathscr{S}^+$, in a manner recalling the definition of truth, especially the second. I will have more to say about this shortly.

As it stands this analysis does not satisfy any demand you might have about just *what it is* that is believed and that can either be or not be identical with another belief. The classical method of manufacturing an equivalence class out of equivalences (the Frege-Russell method of making the cardinal number of a set A — just the class of sets equipollent to A) is not applicable here. If a proposition were a set of synonymous sentences, then propositions would be relativized to C. But one of the (somewhat dubious) reasons for wanting propositions is to have a same meaning to give sentences of more than one tongue. A better reason for wanting propositions is to have an *object* of belief, even for the dumb; it might be claimed they believe something which can not be the facts, as beliefs, indeed all of them, might very well be false. For perceptual belief there is the perceptual object, even for false but nonhallucinatory beliefs; and beliefs are *about* them since beliefs are weakly *de re*. However even in the absence of objects there can be belief of something. They are *de dicto*.

So there is again an ambiguity in 'proposition' reminiscent of the ambiguity in Frege's 'sense'. It divides along the same line as 'primary sense' and 'seconary sense', as I called them in Frege's semantics. The meaning of 'proposition' captured in 'synonymous' in my analysis (1)–(3) is literally 'guide the same way', just as acceptance guides to a state if a sentence is true.[4] The other part of meaning of 'proposition' is that of an object of some kind. In principle, I think a theory of language and mind can get along nicely without propositions or senses in this latter sense. But it is comforting to the mechanist to see that he can get a credible theory of objects, here intentional objects, in a naturalistic way.[5] I am going to emulate Quine's Jewish chef, although I am willing to partake sparingly at the board myself.

The proposition as intensional object of a core sentence p is **U**. **U** is the set of all stimulus patterns that lead to acceptance by T. It is the subset of good stimulus patterns and bad, $U \subseteq (S \cup B)^*$, such that $y \in U$ if and only if there is a z such that $R(y, z)$ and $M(q_0, z) = q_F$. Another way of putting it: U is the set of all stimulus patterns that fulfill $\mathscr{S}^+$'s expectations. Except for hallucination there is also a perceptual object x such that $Rep\,(x, y)$ which is the *actual object*; but it does not figure in U. The important point is that U is an *intentional object*. This intentional object of expectation we take to be the intension of the associated sentence. It is interesting to note that this semantics makes the proposition the set of things, MR's, that *have* a reference in Fodor's theory via some putative causal relation to physical things. In the language of Chapter VIII they, as surrogate representations, are simply automaton strings.

At this point we have propositional objects as well as propositions in the sense of same rules of acceptance, (1)–(3) above. To get a single entity, one might think of a proposition as a *pair* consisting of an object U and the function that T computes. This might at first strike one as quite an *ad hoc* construction, but I think not, although I have no idea what an adequacy condition for an analysis of 'proposition' might be. In principle, however, U is a tractable natural entity – a set of stimulus patterns – although at the present time I see no conclusive way how to tell one from another. That is a question for science and instrumentation eventually and not of philosophy. The rules that compute are real network configurations of some sort as discussed at some length in various passages in connection with my overall realistic stance regarding recursive rules, and in connection with questions of complexity and automaton compositions in various passages. Moreover it pretty well satisfies one's feelings about an intentional object, at least. The object of a perceptual belief would seem to be anything that fulfills – puts one in a perceiving state – and different beliefs about the same or different objects do seem to be individuated by how and what one perceives – the way you take things.

But we can do better. My conception of an intentional object plays very much the same conceptual role as classes of possible worlds in semantics, with some added advantages in its application to the perceptual. The elements of U are finite sequences of symbols from the union of a basic automaton alphabet and degraded symbols, and under the psychological interpretation are stimulus patterns. Each pattern y, before or after taking, (cf. Section VII.1), is a *possible world*, and U is a *class* of possible worlds; or, if you prefer, it is *analogous* to the possible world in a very tight sense as the following considerations show.[6]

Suppose that any world, including our actual world, has an underlying four-dimensional Euclidean geometry with one time and three space coordinates. Each point in this space is represented by a quadruple of real numbers in a system with origin $\langle 0, 0, 0, 0 \rangle$, some place in the universe. Also let us suppose that matter is homogeneous and that there are no fields. Now each point is occupied by matter or not. Taking the subset of all points such that each is occupied by matter, we have a possible world, indeed the actual one. Thus we can identify the possible worlds with subsets A of the space of points; the subsets might well be regions that are disconnected, noncompact, etc. To make the model more realistic, we suppose in addition that each subset A is replaced by a family of subsets such that each set of the family is the result of changing A by a rotational or translational transformation of the axes from the system with origin $\langle 0, 0, 0, 0 \rangle$.[7] Constructed in this way the class of possible worlds corresponds $1-1$ to the class of worlds in the ordinary sense as alternative arrangements to our very own actual world. What Quine's construction does is carry out the promise that intensional entities be manageable in purely extensional, mathematically respectable terms. In addition, his world theory affords answers to questions raised earlier, such as the ontological nature of worlds (levels of levels of sets), how individuate them, etc.

A question does arise, however, as to whether the off-hand notion of a possible world as an alternative to this one we live in, or as this one with certain changes, is adequately grasped by the model. Some proponents of possible world semantics think not; Lewis, for one, does not believe that our own world is a purely mathematical entity (Lewis, 1973, p. 90). But this question need not trouble us: we can have the mathematical exactness and the material reality all once. We shall have to pay something for the next step; but let us issue a note forthwith and proceed.

The next step still follows Quine and takes candidate U, waiting in the wings, as the intentional object *simpliciter*. We take as propositional object just that part of the world that impinges on $\mathscr{S}^+$, in fact just the stimulation impingements themselves.

If the human . . . animal under consideration is attitudinizing strictly about what might hit him, then, instead of taking account of all the possibilities of occupiedness and empness on the part of all the points of space-time, we could just as well limit our attention to the surface of . . . our animal and take account merely of the possibilities of activation and inactivation of its several nerve endings. . . . instead therefore of a cosmic distribution of binary choices (occupied vs empty) over the points of space time, what we have to consider is a distribution of binary choices (activated vs quiescent) over sensory receptors. . . . (Quine, 1969b, p. 155).

These stimulation patterns are interpretations of our abstract symbols s, or sequences of them, x; and you might think of each occurrence of a stimulus element (Section II.4 and V.1) as a set of occupied points, and an array of the m as stimulus patterns in both Quine's sense and mine. Each organism has its own point of origin and thus its own identity in all possible worlds. Its belief attitudes are now focused on and restricted to its own stimulations; but for perceptual belief and the rest of the core, which builds on it, this is enough. One point of difference with Quine is that the identification of strings with regions of points discretizes the domain and hence the geometry of U is discrete, while Quine's and that of the possible world theorist's is continuous. However, this probably does not come down to anything very significant as the field of stimuli to which an organism responds is discrete anyway. Quine's space would have to be thinned out in some way to effect the correspondence of stimulations to just noticeably different inputs.

So far I have argued that U has the merit of being a good intentional object in that its elements are precisely the entities that fulfill expectations and hence establish belief, and in that U is very close in spirit to the popular semanticist notion of a proposition, which can be seen in terms of Quine's construction of a Democritean realm as a way of giving identity to possible worlds. The only thing still to be added is the paired recursive rule, for a region of points as such fulfills expectations that lie behind rather different beliefs, e.g., that a is both Ortcutt and the spy-in-the brown-hat. U alone (or for that matter a full set of occupied points that are not contracted to the organism) is not enough to distinguish types τ and τ' as we saw long ago, and thus does not succeed in grasping the intension in Frege's sense of differences in the mode of presentation of what is designated (for Frege, (T and F); 'proposition', too, is two-edged and we are out to get the whole idea. Quine's does not, even for the directly experienced cases of belief. So we take the *pair* of U and a rule system.

An advantage of this theory is that it does not need possible worlds with ghosts or centaurs in them to give meaning to certain beliefs. Scrooge, we saw, could believe he saw Marley's Ghost in the absence of any perceptual object; that belief, if it's the one he had, could issue just from the taking of a degraded stimulus in U as a stimulus in $\mathcal{U}_{\text{Marley}}$. Belief in ghosts is accounted for by the presence of ghost recognizers in subjects; and such a belief is about actual things (except for dreams and hallucinations) in *this* world. We can also accommodate the dreams without getting into funny kinds of being, although I do not claim to have much of anything to say about sensuous images in dreams at this point.

Sometimes semanticists justify their traffic in possible worlds on the grounds that ordinary human planning and decision making rest on tracing out possible courses of events. According to Hintikka, " . . . there is a sense in which others than the actual world . . . are merely 'possible courses of events', and this is the sense on which I shall try to capitalize" (Hintikka, 1969, p. 49). Similarly, David Lewis points out that we already have naive beliefs that tables and chairs might have been arranged in ways other than they actually are (Lewis, 1973, p. 88). I can hardly object to this view because my own includes strings having arrangements of parts other than the way they are in any particular recognition event. I agree with Hintikka that "the consideration of different possibilities is precisely what makes propositional attitudes propositional . . . " (Hintikka, 1969, p. 149). However possible world philosophers also need worlds which are not alternatives to actual ones, but which cater to ghosts besides, while mine do not. All I need is a recognizer that can *take* a thing to be a ghost. Indeed the taking feature of intentionality seems to have been missed in construing propositional attitudes *only* as 'consideration of different possibilities'.

This brings me to a possible objection that intentional objects are 'subjective': (1) they are inner mental occurrences, and (2) they are individual, not communal. Some semanticists might argue that a proposition or other intension is objective and the same for all minds that understand the sentences or terms expressing them (cf. Frege, 1892, p. 59). It might also be charged that strings and automaton states are just traditional percepts and concepts fancied up almost beyond recognition. Although I am far from clear on what 'percepts' and 'concepts' are, if some one sees that they are the same as my theoretical entities I am made happy by it, noting that these psychological entities have then been naturalized.

(1) As argued at quite some length in Chapter VII, in order for there to be taking (and there must be if one is moved to model the psychological facts of acceptance and perception as reviewed in VI) a distinction has to be made between the outer thing *res* and an inner thing, the pattern, from which computation proceeds. And so it comes to be that the entities which both *represent* the perceptual object and are *taken to be* in the set of accepted things – virtually accepted in the precise sense of VII(8b) – are most naturally construed as the states of affairs that fulfill expectations. One might consider the 'pure' stuff $\mathcal{U}$ as the intentional object. Making the assumption that *Rep* is some kind of structure-preserving map (an even *stronger* assumption than the one I made in defining 'truth'), we could move back and forth between the $\mathcal{U}$'s as representations and real things, as does Quine in settling for pattern stimulations as possible worlds rather than real points (Quine,

1969b, p. 117). Take the inverse image of the *Rep* map as the intentional object. But if we make this move we lose the take altogether and ghosts and dreams with it.

Now there is a counterargument saying that what a subject expects and what fulfills expectations are not necessarily the same. Keep your set **U**, but do not count it as the propositional object. What $\mathscr{S}^+$ expects is that x is τ, and just those states of affairs in which x is τ is true should count as the object. Or under the real-to-stimulus-or-inner-thing map take $\mathscr{U}$ as the object if you will, it being the set of strings that really, not virtually, fulfill.

But if we follow this advice we shall again have lost dreams and ghosts — unless we revert to a possible world theory that welcomes them — and the elusive quality of intentionality as well. On my view whatever satisfies a seeking, hunting, wanting, or expecting must count as being in the intentional object. otherwise all takes would be *mis*takes. But subjects who take flat singing to be the song (recall Jones), or illegible writing to convey what is intended by the writer are not always wrong. Sometimes a take is right, and sometimes wrong, but which is which is a question of evidence and fact, surely, and not merely one of attitude. The whole game of intentional attitudes is lost if one fails to distinguish what is taken from what is, as is the *de re*/*de dicto* distinction in perceptual belief, the puzzles of inreferential context, and the rest.

If I am right, then any coventional possible world theory misses the boat. Although a theory of perceptual belief or acceptance does not cover all cases of belief by a long shot, only the core, a general theory must of course account for taking. But in that special case if $\mathscr{S}^+$ believes P if and only if 'p' is true in all possible worlds that satisfy that belief (or in Hintikka's terms is true in all aternative worlds), then and only then a certain string z is in $\mathscr{U}$ (in my terms). But I am claiming that a z not in $\mathscr{U}$, not even in $\mathscr{S}^+$'s repertoire of good strings, could fulfill; and if not, our theories must be confusing epistemic questions and questions of evidence with questions of attitude. I conclude that all such semantical approaches to intentional attitudes, particularly propositions in the perceptual case at any rate, are inadequate.

I admit that mine is too, as it says nothing about belief or other attitudes beyond the core language. We do have beliefs, perhaps all the important ones, that stretch out to the world beyond direct experiences. However I find some comfort in noting that the way of understanding the intentional in this kind of logic of mind has advantages: it does not ignore the taking feature of intentionality and can in principle, so far as I can see, eventually be extended to more general cases of mental attitudes. The conventional view has many difficulties just in the easy cases.

(2) If all of us were like $\mathscr{S}+$ and realized automata that divide types the same way and compute the same functions, then propositional objects would be communal. I strongly suspect that even in the realm of the perceptual and core languages there are wide differences, not only in *what* we believe but in *how* we believe — both in the sets of stimulation and the determining rule systems. We learn to perceive and identify things by acquiring acceptance rules, somehow; and thus meanings arise through experience (as does our knowledge of rules of the syntax of a language in Chomsky's theories). That these rule systems are the same among the members of the species of dumb animals is likely at one level quite unlikely at another. There seems to be more built-in readiness to cope, and less plasticity of response, in lower organisms; hence sameness of structure is likely; and there seems to be no taking (recall the frog, Section VI.1). On the other hand in the case of complex enough organisms that lack speech and therefore undergo little virtual or vicarious learning, it seems unlikely that there would be tight perceptual uniformity. However, for humans, without positing *a priori* or native common rules (which does not exclude hypothesizing a lot of common in-born structure for learning to perceive, learning language, cognition, etc.) sufficient uniformity of meanings and sense across individuals can be explained by the fact that most of what we learn we learn in well-knit social groups. Communication requires common perception of objects to a great degree, while further uniformities in our mental ways are rooted in communication itself. Development of communication is a boot-strapping societal operation. In philosophy of mind we account for nothing by positing abstract objects and senses for all to grasp, even though complete empirical grounds for understanding how meanings get to be relatively uniform still eludes our command. To say that I understand you because my mind latches onto the same abstract object that determines your talk is not one whit different than explaining the efficacy of opium by a dormative virtue or jealous behavior by jealousy.[8] And I am afraid classes of possible worlds are in the same case. None of the problems of uniformity of meaning are peculiar to my approach. They are the very stuff of the disputes surrounding Chomsky's teachings about the acquisition of language and universal grammar, and the issues are about the same here, *mutatis mutandis*. I have already said most of what I have to say on this question in Chapter V.

The other half of my comments on the uniformity of meaning in the presence of diverse individuals goes back to the distinction between behavior and structure discussed in Section III.1. Organisms might share behaviors including the computational behaviors of base automata (which underly our treatment of gestalt phenomena in Section VI.2 as well as of substitution in *de dicto* contexts in Section IX.1), and be vastly different structurally. The rule systems incorporated in acceptors in general need not be homomorphic nor even categorically the same. And the embodying networks in nervous systems, or wherever they are, might be grossly unlike one another, as we illustrated in the operation of a simple binary adder. Moreover, since rule systems need not be isolated chunks but rather unidentifiably intermingled in composite structures on the automaton and network levels, we need not expect meanings to be dangling in the head like so many berries. For these and possibly other reasons I conclude that there is no loss of uniformity or 'objectivity' in taking $\mathscr{S}$'s sets of stimulus patterns with paired rules as propositions.

Even though we might choose to adopt propositions in this secondary sense, I do not believe any philosophers, except for oddly gifted ones, have a pre-analytic, reasonably precise notion of what a propositional entity is anyway. A concept that allows us to say when sentences are synonmous and when not is enough without our grasping for some kind of entity for sentences to be about, other than ordinary material objects. We can account for intentionality, and I believe I have shown a plausible way to do so in terms of automata and states without populating a transcendental universe of some sort. Logic books introduce propositions for various reasons, among them to provide a pivot for translations and to have something for sentences to convey. It is enough that they convey belief or desire; and that we can explain. The translation notion seems to be that to go from English to Russian, say, first extract the meaning of an English sentence and then insert it into a Russian sentence; and since meaning is preserved the sentences are synonymous. I doubt that anything even remotely like that happens, and my reasons are roughly Quine's (Quine, 1960, Chapter II). On our account synonymous sentences of two differing languages (core sentences, at least) have common underlying acceptance processes – which is all a proposition is. Synonymy is no simple-minded matching up of abstract entities.

Other than omitting considerations of intentionality in intensions, popular possible world theories have further drawbacks when we turn from the *psychology* to the *logic* of intensions. The principal issue I have in mind is logical truth. Suppose, to engage in a bit of harmless fancy, we drop our strictly materialist definition of truth of the previous chapter in favor of a model-theoretic approach and loosen up the core as needed to express first order set theory in some axiomatization; that is to say, let us allow mathematical interpretations as well as this physical one. I do not want to delve into the technicalities involved here. Just suffice it to say a sentence of the broadened language is *logically true* if and only if it is true in every interpetation. According to possible world theory any two logically true sentences have the same meaning because they are true in all possible worlds. But this is absurd, as all philosophers of logic know − this is nothing new − because it entails that two theorems of analysis, say, the Heine-Borel Theorem and Jordan Decomposition Theorem mean the same.

On the other hand if mathematical thought processes are computational − in some way extending acceptance and the tacit logic of the core − then, even if it should turn out the underlying mental computations are of the same function so that by our definition they have the same meaning, which is highly unlikely, they might be computed differently or run through different algorithms. Simply put, a mechanist theory of meaning is capable of *refinement* at various levels. It is not entirely implausible, it seems to me, that all logical or analytical truths, if there are any of the latter, have the same meaning in that they hold true *no matter what*, while they at the same time have objectively different meanings in some refined sense that accords with our intuitions about the differences in grasping Heine-Borel *versus* Jordan. This is not only a question of subjective psychology but of the use of mathematics as a scientific tool. Anyone who has thought seriously about the matter knows analyticity is a question of pure logic while scientific insight and novelty are not. We are, of course, still far from understanding language and meaning in such recondite affairs; but a mechanist view does not foreclose a theory of meaning in mathematics while possible world theory does in the bald form that claims that a proposition is a set of possible worlds in which a sentence, that expresses the proposition, is true.

3. INTENSIONS OF NAMES AND PREDICATES

Names such as 'Morley' and 'Ortcutt' are primarily *predicates* and become proper names in virtue of coreferentiality with the deictic 'this'. In sentences that I call 'ascriptions to individuals' (which are the result of tacit inference) names *denote* (cf. IX(13)). On the other hand if 'this is Ortcutt' expresses at t the belief that this is Ortcutt, which means $T_{Ortcutt}$ computes some z to be in the unit set $\mathcal{U}_{Ortcutt}$, then the 'is' of the expressing sentence should be read as the copula, not the identity 'is'. If so , it is reasonable to say that

'Ortcutt' now conceived as a logical predicate *applies* to the unit set of Ortcutt or has that set as its *extension* Hence there is no essential difference in talking about extensions of proper names and common names, or in general of predicates, depending, of course on the use of the expression in sentences.[9] I am inclined to think the same is true of *denotation* or *reference*: that is to say, otherwise general terms such as 'red' are sometimes used referentially or as abstract terms. At a textile fair you point at a Uzbek shawl and declare to me both 'this is almandine red' and 'this is my favorite color' from which you should not object to infer 'almandine red is my favorite color'. In the first sentence 'this' denotes the same thing as 'almandine red' does, otherwise the inference does not go. However I do not wish to promote this idea any more presistently. I am just establishing a tentative and probably not very secure basis for treating all names, 'proper' and well as 'common', and adjectives too, on an equal footing with regard both the extension and intension. In the following I shall call all names 'predicates' keeping in mind, of course, that some and maybe all of them can be used denotatively.[10]

According to the logic books the extension of a predicate such as 'red' is the set of all red things, or equivalently the set of all objects x such that 'x is red' is true or satisfies 'is red'; and the extension of 'between' is the set of all ordered triples x, y, z such that x is between y and z; and so forth. Given the present approach to these matters we can obtain an analysis of the conventional idea in terms of the exemplar $\mathscr{S}$ of Chapter IX. Let Π be any predicate in C and 'τ' its translation into the metalanguage as heretofore. Then the extension of Π is all of the real perceptual objects that $\mathscr{S}$ accepts as τ:

> The *extension*$_1$ of Π is the set of x such that there is a T_τ that $\mathscr{S}$ realizes and a y such that $Rep\,(x, y)\; y \in \mathscr{U}_\tau$ and $\mathscr{S}$ knows 'x is Π'.[11] $\qquad\qquad\qquad$ (4)

I call this 'extension$_1$' for contrast with a related notion. At the moment, however, keep in mind that in this standard notion *Rep* is to be 1–1 and there is no taking function. That this captures the textbook idea is easily seen by picking an x that meets the conditions of (4); then by the definition of satisfaction, IX(17), x is in the extension of Π in the usual sense. According to the definition, only things of type τ as strictly processed by T_τ are in the extension of Π. But for various reasons we shall want a broader notion that allows items in the extension that are just vaguely or fuzzily (or for us; *virtually*) τ. The new concept that fits this bill is extension$_2$, and its definition uses $\mathscr{S}^+$ (p. 283):

The *extension*$_2$ of Π is the set of all x such $\mathscr{S}^+$ virtually accepts
x is τ and $\mathscr{S}^+$ knows 'x is Π'.   (5)

If written out, the definiens is like (4) except no restriction is placed on *Rep*
and taking and the R relation is allowed (if you want a reminder, see X(1),
which goes back to VII(6), (11) which reemphasize all of the components
buried in 'acceptability'). Under (5) the extension$_2$ of an expression could be
very broad; a black thing could be in the extension$_2$ of 'red' if it were so
takeable by $\mathscr{S}^+$ in the R of stimulus to stimulus. By contrast extension$_1$
represents, as $\mathscr{S}$ does for truth, the ideal case.

Both (4) and (5) are meant to comprehend relational predicates in the
core, although for our present purposes there is no point in writing out
the definitions in full n-tuples and n-ary predicates notation. On psychological grounds there is very little reason to introduce more than about 4-ary
predicates considering that predicates in C are all sensible. At any rate we will
not lose anything by discussing only monadic predicates and the comments
we shall make are extendable to others.

Extension$_1$ is the logical concept and extension$_2$ the psychological. If we
dispense with the stereotype $\mathscr{S}^+$, there could be very many extensions$_2$
in a language community just as there are many propositional objects U.
Extensions$_2$ tend to be individual, not communal, but of course they must
be very close in the sense of enjoying a large intersection in a community
that gets along.

In the remainder of this discussion I am going to assume that all *kind*
predicates such as 'human', 'atom', 'Republican', etc. even those beyond
the sensible such as 'plum' and 'Steve' (which when used as a predicate I
reckon a kind — for reasons I'm not going to repeat again) are like my types.
Instances are accepted in analogy to our FA acceptance.[12] This decision is
consistent with other parts of the logic of mind in principal although I
disclaim any recommendation as to the details of acceptance beyond the
core. Now to 'intension' which I also ask you to think of as no longer limited
to core predicates, but as extended to natural kinds.

Before introducing objects in Chapter VII we characterized stimulus
pattern types τ and τ' to be the same just in case the base machines from
which T_τ and $T_{\tau'}$ compute the same partial functions. Then in VII.1 we
extended this idea to properties of perceptual objects themselves. Third,
in Section IX.1 we introduced a criterion of substitutivity of 'a' for 'b',
when $a = b$ in attitudinal contexts which required that the sets $\mathscr{U}_a$ and $\mathscr{U}_b$
be identical and that T_a and T_b compute the same function (in the base

machine sense). Although we had not yet introduced the core language C, we were stipulating that substitution be allowable only if the *senses* of a and b — on our version of the Fregean primary sense of 'sense' — be the same. In this same spirit we now identify the intensions of two predicates if the relevant underlying partial functions are the same. I omit explicit reference to any subject $\mathscr{S}$, the necessity for the predicates to be known to her, etc. in the following schematic formulation:

> Predicates Π and Π' have the *same intension* if and only if the partial functions of the base machine of T_τ and $T_{\tau'}$ are the same. (6)

where Π and τ, etc. correspond as before.

The *intension* of a predicate (or a name), if you like substantive entities, is thus just a function from stimuli to responses; and just as we earlier distinguished among types of one and the same set of stimuli we here also distinguish intensions of terms having the same extension by different functions computed *via* acceptors. I am myself somewhat reluctant to take this step toward hypostatization of 'intension' because of the likelihood of someone's associating intensions in my scheme of things with the *secondary* sense, that of a Fregean thing grasped by the mind. I think there *are* concepts, but they are not intensions. In fact to keep matters as straight as possible, let us characterize concepts as natural kinds and therefore corresponding to physical types. A *concept* is a final state of an automaton and thus a psychological state of some kind in the *mathematical* sense, i.e., it is a state *type*. If the mind-body identity theory, which we will briefly examine in Chapter XI, is true, a final state *token* seems to be mighty like a Lockean idea or a Humean impression. If $\mathscr{S}$ perceives an apple, then we know from VII(12) that $\mathscr{S}$ accepts a thing as an apple, which means she computes to a final state. I am suggesting that her conscious experience of the 'phenomenal' apple is that state. I am *not* saying that a concept is an intension, although the two are obviously related in perceptual cases: one is a function and the other is in a certain sense the value of the function. Concepts, we shall find, do not determine extension whereas intensions *qua* functions do.

As explained in a moment intensions are of one kind, not two as for extensions. However we may still desire to distinguish between the intension relative to an individual subject and communal or ideal intensions of the exemplar.

The present way of construing 'intension' inherits the idea of one set, now the extension of a predicate, instancing two or more types, a situation that comes up in the study of gestalt phenomena as we saw in Chapter VI. Given a common extension of two predicates in either the meaning extension$_1$ or extension$_2$, they have different intensions if and only if the property types they express are different. This follows from (6) taken together with that part of the doctrine of evolutionism discussed in VII.1 that says that sensible properties are the same if and only if their instances are responded to in the same way. Note that although the concept extension$_2$ allows all kinds of assorted items to be of a type, it is not the *type* alone, i.e., individuating function, that fixes the thing in the extension, but also the *taking*. There is an asymmetry in the theory: for a given individual, there is but *one* concept of intension that goes with *two* concepts of extension. We get different ideas of the extensional because of the phenomena of taking and forcing the fulfillment of expectations, not because of *any difference in the types or the corresponding automata* (excluding, of course, the super automaton T' that detects winners, implements that take, etc.). The overall situation is somewhat complex, though I hope not needlessly so, and is worth reviewing. For the exemplar $\mathcal{S}$ there is *one* intension of a predicate Π and one extension$_1$, although the latter might be the extension of other terms than Π. For ordinary subjects Π has an extension$_1$ (extending (4) beyond the exemplar to individual idiolects), an extension$_2$ − one of each for each subject − and *one* intension for each subject. When logicians talk of *the* extension and the intension they certainly have in mind extension$_1$. When psychologists and philosophers who take a psychological approach to language talk of these dimensions of meaning, you can not tell what they mean unless there is added comment.

Let us compare intension *qua* function with possible world intension theory. Observe that intensions *qua* determiners of extension are for us maps from extensions to perceptual states, maps that incorporate the 'way of computing' of base machine functions. As explained in subsection (1) of IX.2, acceptors compute characteristic functions of sets. In this regard the theory does not remotely resemble possible world semantics, which counts intensions of predicates as maps from possible worlds to sets (Lewis, 1972). The schemes work in opposite ways. Lewis and his ilk follow Frege rather closely, who regarded the extension or 'designation' of a predicate (name) to be a function of the intension (sense). Both Frege and the semanticists think of a function from intensions or possible worlds as picking out a set or other objects − a truth value, a denotation, or an extension. In possible world schemes, but not Frege, this general functionality principle is inspired by the extensionalist attitude already noted, and naturally yields many intensions for an extension. Many predicates having different meanings might have the same extension, i.e., 'rational animal' and 'featherless biped' or on the perceptual level, 'puce' or 'Rembrandt red' or 'Hesperus' and 'Phosphorus'. According to my theory, however, the extension (more pointedly, the set of stimuli corresponding to objects) is the domain of a function, not the range or an element of the range. An object is picked, submitted to computations, and then classified as to type.

It is not clear to me what the consequences of this might be for logic and semantics, if any; but for psychology and ontology they are evident. For me, intensions, though certainly mathematical objects as they are for possible world thinkers, are *computable* and realized by computations in the head. If we assume that intensions are common across people (as entertained by the exemplar) the position is Platonistic but no more so than computer science is Platonistic. An *explanation* of how meanings determine extensions is within scientific range. For the other position, this seems not to be the case. One can not, for instance, easily get his hands on a possible world to compute out a map whose computed value is an infinite set! In some way which I suppose could be made satisfactorily clear, the Platonism is more extreme, even though the semanticist stick to more or less ordinary objects, possibilities and maps; however, it has to be granted that the theory does not need to commit itself to still more suspect things such as Fregean senses.

My philosophy of language is in some respects similar to Putnam's in the area of questions of meaning, and somewhat more distantly related to Saul Kripke's views. Putnam, in particular, takes a psychological approach but not a logical approach (as distinguished earlier) to the subject, although not always consistently. In several papers (Putnam, 1970; 1973a; 1975) he has argued that some of the fundamental suppositions underlying meaning analysis in contemporary thought are radically wrong. In particular, (1) knowing the meaning of a term is *not* just a matter of being in a psychological state, and (2) the meaning of a term does not determine its extension. The first part is not understandable without some preliminary work, so we begin with (2).[13]

If meaning is interpreted as 'intension' in my sense, then meaning certainly *does* determine extension$_2$ for a fixed person or for $\mathcal{S}^+$ and whoever shares the stereotype; but it does *not* determine extension$_1$ except for $\mathcal{S}$. It seems to me that this is all Putnam's argument comes down to. Let us consider this is in slightly more detail. He, Putnam, can not tell an elm tree from a beech tree.[14] Yet he says the extension of 'elm' to him is the same as that of 'elm' to any other English speaking person; and similarly for the extension of 'beech'.

Since Putnam's *concepts* of *elm* and *beech* are the same (whatever that might turn out to mean) and since the extensions are different, the concept does not determine the extension. I like the conclusion, but not the argument as it is incoherent.[15] If Putnam can not tell an elm from a beech, then there must have been an occasion in which he called an elm a 'beech' or a beech an 'elm'. If so, the extension of elm in his idiolect is certainly not extension$_1$ or the extension of all English speakers, as it contains a beech. Either the extension is not extension$_1$ but rather his very own extension$_2$ — the psychological concept — or he has no understanding of 'elm' or of 'beech' in terms of experience at all. His knowledge is like mine of 'banyan'.

Putnam uses 'concept' for 'meaning' in this argument, and let us do the same using my explication of 'concept' as a final state set down a few pages back. Then there is a still stronger version of Putnam's (2), which says that *not even extension$_2$* is determined by meanings. For in general the subset of $\mathcal{U}_\tau$ determined by a final stage q_F will be different than that determined by $q_{F'}$ where both are final states of T (see Table VI.I states q_2 and q_3); and consequently the objects a will be different for different states of the same acceptor.[16] Close attention to the definition (5) unpacked according to the parenthetical remark following (5) shows, however, that intension in sense (6) does determine extension$_2$. 'Meaning' interpreted as 'concept' does not determine extension in *any* sense, while interpreted as 'intension' it determines extension$_2$.

Another meaning of 'meaning' is 'analytic definition' or 'list of essential properties'. Here again, if 'extension$_2$' is the understanding of 'extension', extension is not determined by meaning from our point of view either; and this agrees with Putnam (1970). The divergence between mechanism and trait inventory was already noted in our way of handling gestalt perception in Chapter VI. Any model that satisfies the four conditions reviewed on p. 170 hardly simulates perception by checking off items on lists.[17]

The upshot of these brief deliberations on (2) is that meaning does not determine extension$_1$ under any construal, including mine, of 'intension' while intension in that sense does determine extension$_2$ Moreover meaning interpreted as concept or list does not determine even extension$_2$. Conceivably some kind of analytic definition writ by the complete knower would determine extension$_1$, a kind of guess that suggests Putnam's point (1). But before proceeding to (1) let me say that whether or not we mutually agree on point (2) certainly depends on some kind of explicit theory of language use and underlying hypothesis of mind if the aim is to advance beyond programmatics.

According to Putnam's (1) knowing the meaning is not just a matter of being in a psychological state. It is very hard to say much about knowing what 'knowing meaning' means. If it means 'knowing enough to determine extension$_1$', then the point has already been argued. I think the force of (1), according to Putnam, is that one knows enough when he has scientific knowledge about a kind, and I agree with him. Putnam argues a sociological thesis to the effect that there is a division of labor in our linguistic expertise. The informed scientist knows what the extension of 'water' or 'aluminum' is and hence he knows the meaning of the indicated terms. We nonscientists acquire our beliefs and with them our vocabularies in part from experience and in part from scientists. In performing for society the function of obtaining knowledge they institute veridical references for our dealings with natural kinds as well.

If we are able to sustain the idea of 'sensible' predicates or types (which I think we can by characterizing such predicates as just the ones expressing the types we are fulfilled by and react toward and have desires about, ultimately to be determined by psychology, not philosophy) then most normal people, not just the scientists, have enough knowledge to get along in the world and their subjective extensions$_2$ are close to extension$_1$. For the exemplar, indeed, types or natural kinds are individuated by intensions in the realm of the perceptual; and this in turn suggests that all natural kinds are individuated by recursive relations internalized in the expert's head, an idea much too vague to have much immediate importance of any kind. Yet, if it is right it means that meanings are correlated 1–1 to physical properties or *are* physical properties represented to the complete knower by lists or analytic definitions after all. I shall return to this topic in Chapter XI.

Of a piece with the denial that meanings are lists is the denial that meanings of proper names are *definite descriptions*. This doctrine which apparently originated with Frege and was advertized and developed by Russell holds that proper names get their meanings from descriptions having the same reference. A definite description, recall, is a name that ascribes a short list of properties to a unique thing, and in English is stereotypically headed by 'the' as in 'the man on the beach'. Names such as 'Ortcutt' have no senses as they stand, according to this theory, but assimilate the sense of definite descriptions in contexts about definite objects. Thus the sense of 'Ortcutt' is given by the description 'the man on the beach', which denotes the same thing, for Quine's Ralph. Now on Putnam's reckoning a definite description is again just a list — comparable to the analytic definition for predicate expressions or common names — while for myself it is also a list and therefore subject to the same criticism if meant as a construal of intension, as a list of traits. This whole issue here is applicable to expressions such as 'Ortcutt' in the nominal, not predicative use – to the subjects of ascriptions to individuals.

A similar theory has been proposed by Saul Kripke who also denies that proper names have sense, derivative or otherwise, and *à fortiori* do not have senses indentical to those of definite descriptions or lists of some kind (Kripke, 1972). 'Ortcutt' or 'Cicero' establish their references to objects by a kind of direct, causal connection that is established at namings or baptisms. At the moment my boat was christened 'Loon' the reference was fixed; then the causal association of 'Loon' to the boat was propagated throughout part of the speech community probably via descriptions (I don't remember) such as 'the boat Nelson bought' which served to fix the reference of the name for those not at the naming (as a matter of fact the name was given to the boat *in absentia*; and through a nexus of utterances got its specific reference through something like 'this is Loon'). But definite description used to communicate namings in this way does not have the consequence that the description gives the sense, as proper names do not have senses. In the example, the description certainly doesn't list any remarkable properties of the *boat*. As Kripke himself has noted, this no sense theory of proper names is essentially that of John Stuart Mill, and for that reason is sometimes called 'Millean' as opposed to a 'Fregean' or 'Russellean' theory, of names which hangs references on descriptions (see below pp. 332–333).

Kripke's semantics of names has some remarkable philosophical consequences, some of them departing sharply from the conventional philosophical wisdom of twentieth century analytic philosophy. Proper names refer independently of contingency since reference does not get steered by descriptions or other auxiliary representations. 'Ortcutt' is Ortcutt anywhere anytime whether black-haired or grey, a pillar of the community or a spy, healthy or disease-ridden, in office or out. Proper names are thus 'rigid designators' as they refer to their objects no matter what – in all possible worlds.

One interesting consequence of this theory is that the truth of identity statements such as 'Hesperus = Phosphorus' or 'Twain = Clemens' are not *contingent*, i.e, dependent on anything in the actual world, but are *necessary*; as the names occurring in the sentence are rigid, the sentence holds true in all possible worlds. This means that some sentences that have empirical content, that is to say are synthetic, are both ncessary and *a posteriori*.

I have indicated resemblances between Putnam's theory and my own and with him have denied that concepts or lists determine extensions. On the other hand there are intensions in what I have been calling the primary or steering sense, and these things (still persisting in the hypostatization) are recursive string functions. And as proper names and common names differ for me in no absolute respect this on the face of it puts me into opposition to Putnam and also now to Kripke. But the observation is really superficial, and it may be of some interest to see wherein it seems we must agree.

I will focus on the use of certain expressions as names in sentences. Hence it is natural to delimit the discussion to the core, as names on my view are in the beginning sensible predicates in the etiology of reference (p. 240 f. Section VIII.4). At a naming, a namer, $\mathscr{S}$ (no longer an exemplar) accepts a (this baby, say) as Peter, 'Peter' here being our linguistic *predicate* for a type that $\mathscr{S}$ and others have already realized in acquired acceptors. How the latter are acquired is of course beyond us, and at any rate presents a problem not dissimilar to that of acquiring or internalizing recursive rules of language or other features of mental life. The naming itself is an utterance by $\mathscr{S}$ of 'this is Peter' or equivalently 'I name this child "Peter"'. Of course $\mathscr{S}$ could name Peter 'Charles' or 'Robert' or 'Kurt': there is a genesis of the chosen name through a social institution such as the family in discussion, thought, and agreement, we hope, prior to the naming. 'is Peter' has *intension* in my sense of the word. So far 'Peter' is not a *name* but a *predicate* that has come to be associated via the expressing sentence to a final state (a 'percept') in some T_{Peter}.

$\mathscr{S}$ and friends commence to turn out sentences which *ascribe* to Peter, such as 'Peter is a small baby', which is an inference from 'this is a small baby' and 'this is Peter' as previously discussed. At this stage 'Peter' is now being used as a name of Peter, referring in virtue of the statement 'this is Peter' and the referentiality of 'this'. This name, any name if this etiology is a close model to the real one, is essentially anaphoric. In the inference to 'Peter is a small baby' the intension of 'Peter' in predicate position in 'this is Peter' is preserved; it is the sense of 'Peter' *qua* name and is the haecceity of Peter. This whole story, as I have argued at length, is a consequence of building perceptual belief, expressed in perceptual sentences, on acceptance, fulfilled expectations, and so forth.

The 'causal connection' involved in the naming is indeed complex. Peter is *Rep* to $\mathscr{S}$ and others present, and the representation is taken in the now familiar way; an accepting state is assumed that says the gatherings' expectations of this little child's really being Peter are fulfilled. The sentence 'this is Peter' is gated out in $\mathscr{S}$'s system from the state q_{F}, communicated to others, provided that $\mathscr{S}$ so desires; the *sentence* is accepted, understood as good baptismal English, and so forth. Thus 'Peter' becomes associated with an acceptor T_{Peter} whose underlying base function gives or is the sense of the name.

The model is probably too simple but indicates what is buried in 'cause'. If one entertains the steps that lead to the model seriously, such would indeed seem to be a reasonable picture of the causal etiology of a naming.

People not on the spot at naming learn 'Peter' roughly as described for people learning 'loon'. If they never get to know Peter, they do not acquire a Peter acceptor through experience; and so the reference of the name has to be fixed possibly through definite descriptions, even a different one (even token-different) on different social occasions. But there is nonetheless an extension₁ of 'Peter' and an intension, approximately the same for all present at or near the naming or for all later in proximity to Peter.

In some such wise names do have senses in the *primary* sense, not in that of a conceptual Peter-berry one plucks in order properly to use or understand 'Peter'. If you wish, take the entire mechanism steering to referent Peter when 'Peter' is uttered as a name as the intension.

It seems to me this analysis has decent credentials as it works in the analysis of belief sentences (although I did not explicitly use 'intension' there owing to the dumbness, at that stage, of $\mathcal{S}$). The underlying recursive word or string function is the gist of our way of interpreting 'same proposition', and derives in the perceptual setting from perceptual discrimination itself. In particular the analysis expresses intentional attitudes of the mind; intensions are not *ad hoc* entities pasted on to names to aid reference, conceived as some mysterious link between name and thing.

A similar kind of analysis, though less complex as it does not require the inferential step to ascription to an individual, holds for intensions of common names. For the core, which is all I claim much about, there is 'meaning in the head' in this accepting way; but it violates nothing in Putnam's scheme of things so far as I can see. I have already registered enough guesses as to what might be the nature of meaning in scientific languages.

As to the deeper consequences of such a causal theory of reference, there is not much to be said at this time. I do not know how to begin to manage noncore belief and acceptance and their interanimation with linguistic skills, on which I suspect a lot hinges. If U is taken as a set of possible worlds according to my Quinean construction of propositional objects for perceptual belief sentences, then it is easy to see that 'Peter' refers to the same individual in all possible worlds. So it is in *this* manner, relative to *this* notion of possible worlds, a rigid designator, even though 'Peter' has a sense *qua* function. 'Peter' is a kind of universal, if you please; and all instances of him get the same name *via* the recursive process (in effect computations of a characteristic function) to a state — the 'intelligible species'. I can't see how a name could rigidly designate according to *any* theory without an idea of sameness, universality, or meaning in the head in a very fundamental psychological sense.

CHAPTER XI

PSYCHOLOGICAL THEORY AND
THE MIND-BRAIN PROBLEM

The central theme of this book is that intentional features of mind are explainable in mathematical terms, in principle. During earlier discussion a number of other issues came up which I pushed aside with the promise of doing something about them later. The mind-body problem in particular can not be avoided any longer. In the first chapter I argued *against* simply removing datable thoughts, pains, sensations, raw feels — in short, mental occurrents — from the concerns of scientific theory, as urged by eliminationists, and *for* provisionally separating mental features from occurrents and for attempting to cope with one category at a time. Mind, I said, is a system of rules, its logic, but it does not qualify as such unless the subject is able to use language and is sentient, i.e., is a living, feeling, thing. What is the relation of occurrents to automata on the one hand and to the body on the other?

Any hope of dealing with this knottiest of all metaphysical questions is to be found only within the framework of something like a logic of mind. The main reason for my claiming this is negative. Once one digs into the details of a mechanist (or certainly other serious) approach to features, the less likely it is that occurrents might also be accountable in such (roughly 'functionalist') terms. In fact a functionalist theory of feeling is plausible only if it is sufficiently vague and metaphorical, as I will show. Another philosophy that loses much of its appeal when examined in the light of a fairly detailed modeling of intentional traits is epiphenomenalism. If man's intelligent activities were reducible to brain processes at the level of classical mechanics, then I suppose one could tolerate the idea that feelings and awareness somehow got tacked on by the Deceiver; but one resists the idea if it means inefficacious sentience is sprinkled around amongst *real* intentional attitudes and actions. This is not much of a reason for rejecting epiphenomenalism, but combined with Occam's Razor it's not bad. Either feelings count or they don't; and if they don't then perhaps elmination of them is justified for scientific purposes after all. At any rate I do not intend to discuss epiphenomenalism further here. I shall, however, argue against the functionalist theory of occurrents at some length. Finally, substantial dualism in its contemporary form at least as I am aware of it, is so full of confusions as to transcend credibility (see Section XI.4) Somewhat reluctantly, then, I incline toward some kind of identity theory or even toward panpsychism as a not-too-unreasonable alternative to wielding Occam's Razor.

In the following section I shall record a few observations, some of them reviews, about empirical realism, the logic of psychological theory, and the will, before turning to the mind-body puzzle. The remarks are not very systematic and, I am afraid, will tend to be no more than tenuously connected fragments. Most of what I have to say follows quite directly from the functional aspect of the theory, namely that automata rules are realizable in a great variety of material media.

1. REALISM AND REDUCTION

The operations of the brain are guided by recursive rules. Less metaphorically and less compactly stated, the intelligent organism realizes a structure that is expressible in a formal language of automata theory. The idea is typical of functionalism: one can attribute the same input-output and state structure to diverse material things. However, that doctrine would be nominalistic if it were claimed that one and the same psychological subject could be described in irreducibly different ways, one physicalistically and the other psychologically while there would be no actual corresponding distinction in the thing itself. You could be a functionalist and at the same time deny the fitting-guiding notion, holding that there are just different descriptions both of which fit.

Or, following Dennett (1978), you could hold the view that some psychological predicates like 'belief' and 'desire' are *ascribable* to subjects; they do not really describe mental features, much less guide. But if rules of mind are real, the fit-guide distinction can be made (pp. 75–80); and using it, it makes some sense to mark a distinction between the physical and the mental in the thing, relative to theory. This suggests some topics related to classical metaphysics as well as to reduction.

The doctrine of real rules is closely related to medieval realism, the doctrine that universals are in things but do not exist prior to things except in the mind of God. The universals in this case are relational structures in the logic of mind while they are essences, properties, formalities, etc. in medieval thought. More specifically, the doctrine of real mental rules illuminates and is illuminated by Duns Scotus' *formal distinction* (Wolter, 1967), if we think of his thought as applying to psychology (none of my remarks are meant to extend to anything else). According to his teachings, certain distinctions that the philosopher makes (for reasons only remotely connected with our cares here) such as that between the 'common nature' of individuals (the humanity of Peter and Paul) and the existence of individual things are objectively in things 'prior to thought' but they are not *real* distinctions. By contrast Thomistic philosophy claims that essence and existence are really distinct, like Plato and Voltaire, although the distinction is not spatial or temporal; it is ontological. Otherwise entities that are distinguishable are distinguishable conceptually or logically only. Scotus' formal distinction is in a sense intermediate between the real and the logical distinction; there is a real basis for a distinction in the thing although that thing is an ontologically inseparable unity.

Thus there are three kinds of distinction between entities A and B: the purely logical distinction where there is no prior division in the thing (e.g., between Clemens and Twain or between definiens and definiendum); the real distinction (e.g., between Twain and Reagan, or body and soul for the dualist, or essence and existence for Aquinas); and the formal distinction. In the latter A and B form a unity and can not exist apart; yet the distinction is not only conceptual but is grounded in the thing.

Now this trio of distinctions is not blindingly clear, and there is perhaps good reason to reject it along with other sundry medieval baggage. But on the contrary, it seems to me, it does indicate pretty closely the sort of metaphysical contrast one might draw between mind and matter. In the spirit of the formal distinction there is only the individual brain. But there is actually an extra-physical structure of the brain that exists independently of your or my knowing it (of course according to empirical realism it is not independent of the ground *theory*) that can not exist apart from the brain, and that is yet not merely logically distinguishable from the brain *qua* material thing. If the distinction were merely logical then the distinction between a physical system that realizes an automaton T and one that does not (one that fits but does not guide) would also be a logical distinction. However this is not so, as the truth conditions of descriptions of nonhomomorphic structures are not the same; and since we are dealing with physical systems are in actual fact different. Therefore the distinction between the brain qua physical organ (together with other relevant parts of the body) and the mind qua system of rules is not merely conceptual. And as there is but one particular thing there is no system of disembodied, platonistic rules outside of our abstract representations (universals). The distinction is not real, but 'formal'.[1] Now I propose that we construe the Scotian formal distinction when applied to our subject as "formal" in the sense just explained.[2] This is perhaps of no great historical importance as a gloss on Scotus, yet it does follow his intentions in principle, it seems to me, and makes a rather foggy creative insight fairly clear. And it does explain what I mean when I say my theory is of a piece with moderate medieval realism and indicates my rejection of anything like a real distinction on the one hand and of fitting only (nominalism) on the other.

Empirical realism has a close affiliation to the results on meaning reached in Section X.3. Intensions, according to X(6) do not determine extensions₁ (X(4)) except in the case of the perfect knower, i.e., the scientist who is ideally in a position to possess the truth, relative, always, to his selected language systems. This ideal case is represented by something like our exemplar, $\mathscr{S}$, whose powers we now suppose are extended beyond the core to languages strong enough to express psychology, that is to say, recursive functions and automata theory. Her acceptances and beliefs will in that case have historical, social, written, and artistic inputs far beyond the immediately perceptual. The meanings then are virtually the automaton-theoretic properties of the mind which are known only if an expressing language that the mind realizes is known (cf. Section III.3, Putnam, 1977). For, extending our theory of the perceptual, properties are individuated by the recursive functions underlying automaton acceptance; and acceptance in the ideal case is the condition of truth (IX.4). In this rather curious circular fashion our theory of mind applies to ourselves and what is real to us is in part our own intellectual processes (cf. Section I.2). In any case the true and the real are relative to language, and which language to pick is a question of one's problems in the context of on-going science. If the psychologist goes the mechanist route, then, ideally, considering the terrain just surveyed, the meaning and truth of a theory in the expressing language are quite objective and apply to the enquirer herself and, indeed, to her own language (shades of Gödel!).

But why a recursive rule language? An answer to this question leads naturally to the concept of reducibility. Reduction is the *bête noire* of functionalism and mechanism. For, if functionalist languages are reducible to neuroscience and on down to biochemistry and physics, then the autonomy of psychology, which is the functionalist's favorite theme, must be given up. There are two principal reducibility theses of moment. The first says that an essentially behaviorist language that limits itself to descriptions of outer behavior – stimuli, responses, inputs, outputs, and generally to descriptions in terms of ordinary language – is sufficient for psychology. The second

claims that psychology is reducible to neuroscience, or is nothing but neuroscience when it finally becomes scientific.

Historically the motivation for behavioral reduction is mainly ontological,
and for two reasons. One is to reduce commitment to obscure entities such
as meanings, platonic ideas, forms, mental substances and the like and is
chiefly of a nominalist cast; the other is to eliminate nonobservable properties
and states of physical things. A parallel mathematical example of the first
kind of reduction is the definition of numbers as sets or properties of sets;
while an instance of the second is to define 'less than' in its arithmetic sense
in terms of '+' and '=' plus logic; or, for a more empirical example, to define
'acceleration' or 'mass' in observationally measurable terms. I am not concerned with the first as mechanism is already committed to materialism
although it is realistic in the empirical sense already discussed.

Concerning the second form of reduction, the idea is to get rid of states
as anything more than 'intervening variables' or 'dispositions' (cf. Section
V.2). But, again, if mechanism is true, there *are* states — so to eliminate
all talk of them by reduction would have a conceptual effect similar to
defining 'mother' as 'female parent'. Such a minor logical feat does not do
away with mothers but just goes to show that we can limit in rather uninteresting ways our vocabulary for talking about them. If one's reductionist
goal is to lessen ontological commitment, well and good; but if the commitment is real the exercise would seem to be idle. An equally cheering
remark can be leveled against behavioristic reduction of other functionalist
theories if they are real.

The solution of the exercise for those interested is as follows. If the table
of an FA (even an NFA) is known, then one can always eliminate expressions
for internal states in favor of a behaviorist language of animal behavior in
essentially molar or S—R terms, in principle (as already mentioned in Section
V.2).[3] Even concepts such as *belief* and *desire* are perhaps reducible, although
I would not want to be the one to try it.[4]

A far more serious challenge comes from another quarter, neuroscience.
However if mechanism or some kind of functionalism is true, there are
various arguments to the effect that reduction to neuroscience fails. Most
such arguments are roughly of the following kind.[5] If a reduction were
possible then there must be a deduction available of certain automaton
statements expressing the transition from one state to the next from some
neurophysiological language together with so-called 'bridge' or 'correlation'
laws that relate abstract automaton state expressions to neural entities of some
kind. However this can not be done. Suppose a true sentence of the theory
of some automaton were the following:

If s is input to T and T is in state q, then T goes to state q'.   (1)

Let $\mathscr{C} = \{i_1, i_2, \ldots\}$ be a class of mutually isomorphic physical systems that realize T. For simplicity let s and q' be their own correlates in the bridge laws and let x_1, x_2, etc. be physical things (nerve firings perhaps) of i_1, i_2, etc. each of which correlates *via* our laws to state q of T. Now the sentences of neuroscience about $\mathscr{C}$ from which the reductionist would like to deduce (1) are

If s is input to i_1 and i_1 is in x_1, then i_1 goes to state q'
If s is input to i_2 and i_2 is in x_2, then i_2 goes to state q'

.

.

.

etc.   (2)

Suppose that $x_1 \neq x_2 \neq \ldots$ while yet all the members of $\mathscr{C}$ realize the state q of the formal automaton T. Then a law for $\mathscr{C}$ will be

For all $i \in \mathscr{C}$ there exists a state x such that if s is input to i and i is in state x, then i goes to state q'.   (3)

One can not deduce (1) from (3), hence on this way of looking at things the theory of T is not reducible to the theory of the neural systems that realize it.

Although this argument is standard, it is shallow, and some misleading conclusions have been drawn from it. What is being assumed here is that psychology, or cognitive science anyway, can be grasped by some form of machine functionalism more or less like mine. Mental entities *qua* functional are ontologically physical, but only *token identical* to underlying brain events, which is to say one and the same functional entity q gets instantiated in different ways, x_1 and x_2. Now the laws governing these physical states might be grossly different as x_1 might be neural and x_2 a state of a sliver of silicon. In this sense there is indeed irreducibility, and – considering an analogous circumstance for functional inputs and outputs – psychology is *anomalous*. It is outside the pale of the laws of physics and biology. Laws of nerves are not anything like laws of silicon.

But look! The physical realizations described in (2) could very well be isomorphic structures, or at any rate behaviorally identical (Cf. Section III.1) in which case there is a *reduction of sorts*: Correlate structures to structures and deduce. There is hardly anything new in this observation; but applied here it takes some of the force out of the idea that psychology in a machine functionalist version is "anomalous". Yet it is autonomous for much the same reasons as logical design in the computer field is distinct from physics. I think one reason anomalous monism has been so popular is that those who espouse it apply argument's that apply convincingly to occurrent "states", to cognitive "states" (features) as well, thereby blinding themselves to the problem of reducibility of a *system,* which isn't a state at all (See my 1988 'The Mind-Machine connection, to appear).

A much more difficult question that can be raised from an essentially physicalist or neuroscience point of view has to do with error. Mechanism, in analogy to computer logic theories and also to linguistics, makes a radical competence-performance distinction. In particular there is an underlying assumption that a nerve net (say) that embodies an automaton structure neither 'fails' nor yields 'spurious' output. In computer science a distinction can be usefully made between error-free and faulty behavior because the engineer knows what the computer designer's intentions are: he knows what is to count as normal computer behavior (pretty much). However, in neuroscience the distinction between a 'normal' and 'abnormal' firing pattern for neurons can be made only relative to the theory holding the day, and certainly not to Nature or the Maker as no one knows what His intentions are. In fact the underlying nonfailure assumption has two parts. The first says that the distinction of correct and incorrect operation can be made; the second says that sciences of the mind can safely stick to normal automaton behavior that follows recursive rules (I am engaging in self-criticism and am referring just to ourselves as mechanists, not to psychiatrists or clinical psychologists). The second half of the assumption is just another way of stating the functionalist thesis, and it strongly suggests that if there is such a thing as brain processes failing, then that dysfunction is going to be the same for behaviorally equivalent and in particular for isomorphic systems.

Let's grant the first part of the assumption. Psychology, psychiatry and psycholinguistics all accept a working normal-abnormal (perhaps better 'ideal' and 'real') or competence-performance distinction. But the second part gives trouble. For, returning to the computer analogy from which the functionalist idea probably proceeded, two computer circuits realizing the same abstract automaton can be materially different (germanium rectifiers *versus* silicon transistors). But the *failure properties* might be (they are) radically different. One switching device might fail (intermittently put out a 0 for a 1 or *vice versa*) in a way that satisfies an exponential failure theory, and another a normal failure theory. Assuming that we know how to separate the normal from the abnormal in the brain operation, what conceivable right do we have if we accept the computer analogy all the way to think that every organism that realizes *T fails* to operate according to *T* in the same way? What right do we have to say that their behaviors – *all* of their behaviors now – are identical just because they realize the same abstract system? None whatever. As has often been noted, functionalism is in part normative.

However there is some comfort to be had from mechanism itself. Our claim is that we are NFA. I have used FA models, which are deterministic or monogenic, throughout earlier pages; but the basic theoretical claim is that we are NFA. And when we take 'failure' and 'abnormality' into account the automata involved in the composite NFA should most likely be taken as *probabilistic* automata, which are special cases of NFA (Cf. Note III.2). If so erratic behavior is simply that having relatively lower associated probabilities than the normal. A consequence (which I leave to the reader to reflect upon) is that functionalism becomes somewhat narrowed: two adder networks, for example, made of different hardware would no longer have quite the same behavior, but would be close enough for reliable arithmetical computation. Similarly an organism's behavior would reflect the specific properties of the material medium (brain, nervous system), but within a species would be essentially the same up to within individual differences and indeterminacies already alluded to in several parts of this book. I have not attempted to remodel the concepts of expectation and the rest in NFA terms; but I think it could be done.[6] And I know of no other way to make functionalism and in particular a logic of mind more plausible than it already is. But that suggests another book and probably not one that anyone should attempt until the more idealized treatment that assumes something like an ideal-actual or competence-performance distinction shows its theoretical power. The probabilistic automaton suggestion does entail a move away from pure functionalism toward neuroscience; but it still retains the original insight, correct I believe, that mind is largely describable in its own irreducible terms and that mental features are recursive processes. These remarks are inconclusive, and they pose problems for my own approach; but they are not devastating, only the issues are complex beyond any means for coping with them in the immediate future.

2. EXPLANATION

Psychological theory is going to include a lot more than explanations of mental features and linguistic ability, which have traditionally been the chief interests of cognitive science. Tests, measurements of responses, statistics of learning, operant conditioning, abnormalities, speech defects, motivation, and the brain itself — to mention several central areas — are not likely soon to lose their positions in psychology. But my limited subject has been the mind as intentional, and I hope I might be forgiven for restricting my discussion of the topic of explanation to just that.

There is no sharp line between scientific explanation and philosophizing about phenomena if the latter be taken in the naturalistic spirit of much of American philosophy as itself contained in empirical science. Philosophy is more speculative, less empirical, and attends more to the articulation and clarification of concepts, a concern that derives unmistakeably from age-old issues in logic and ontology. The concepts of *same* and *different* and all the plays on these, of *types* and *states*, reduction, realism, possible worlds, the meaning of 'meaning', or 'rule', and the use of basic concepts such as evolution signal some of the focal interests of much of contemporary philosophy of mind and thought. Yet ultimately philosophy must justify itself in the arena of empirical science in terms not only of its clarificatory contributions but of its material suggestiveness, not on some special grounding in the *apriori* or in common sense or ordinary language — although neither of the latter two commodities are dispensable to either philosophy or psychology. However rather than dwell on topics already worried about at some length elsewhere I will in this section focus on two fresh topics in the broad area of explanation: (1) psychological explanation of behavior assuming mechanism has been accepted as a framework; (2) explanation in artificial intelligence studies.

(1) Often philosophy of science has tended to launch its theories of explanation from a consideration of the so-called 'covering-law' model of Hempel and Oppenheim (Hempel and Oppenheim, 1948), and then to seek adjustment of that model in giving putatively adequate accounts of statistical, purposive, functional, etc. explanation. Quite briefly, explanation of a phenomenon according to the Hempelian model consists in deducing a sentence describing that phenomenon from a general statement, a lawlike or 'nomological' statement, together with a statement of the presence of contributory or side conditions. Thus if a sprinkling of salt in a pot of hot water dissolves, an explanation of the phenomenon might consist of indicating a deduction of 'the salt dissolves' from 'salt dissolves in water under certain conditions C' and 'the stuff in the pot is a salt sample under C'. An extension of the covering law idea is to explain empirical laws, which inductively summarize observable facts, by deduction from 'higher level' laws.

For instance the inductive generalization that salt dissolves in water under conditions C might itself be explained by a deduction from the theoretical premise 'materials having microstructure M, given C, dissolve in water', and 'salt has structure M'.

Purposive or functional explanations (there are differences but they are of little interest here) mean to account for phenomena in terms of ends or goals. For example, "the function of chlorophyll is to manufacture starch" would perhaps be meant to answer the answer the question "why do green plants contain chlorophyll?" Or, "the function of a machine state q is to contribute to output o from input s by marking past input" might be intended as an answer to the question why automata have internal states. There is a long history of attempts to render statements such as the chlorophyll functional explanation in nonfunctional terms – in effect to work such statements around into ordinary law-like terms. For instance one might suggest as a starter that the presence of chlorophyll in a plant is a necessary condition for the manufacture of starch (Nagel, 1961, pp. 403–406). The functionalist denies that any such translation is possible in psychology and holds that mental features (for him, states) are to be accounted for only in terms of their roles in the production of behavior; for that is what states *are*. It is of course just this approach that got them into the functional state, disposition, machine state snarls that we reviewed in Chapter V.

A third kind of explanation of the psychological is one in terms of the functional (in the mathematical sense of *abstract maps*) interrelationships of physical parts that are interpreted as corresponding to abstract mathematical structures. A special case is mechanism, including psycholinguistics in the spirit of Chomsky. One may, if she wishes, construe this type of explanation as a type of the covering law model except for some disparities to be noted later. Indeed, mechanist theories would presumably explain various phenomena in the deductive pattern. To use the same elementary example as before, one might explain behavioral output o by indicating a deduction from a hypothesized law "if $\mathscr{S}$ is in state q and suffers input s, then it produces o" and the condition "$\mathscr{S}$ is in state q, etc." This type of explanation also appeals to inner states but claims no functional roles in the purposive sense of the concept for them other than that they are elements of a state space in the ordinary mathematical sense (cf. Section V.1; Zadeh, 1964). This is old ground I do not have to secure again; my wish here is only to spotlight the picture from the viewpoint of typical concerns about the nature of scientific explanation. Roughly, mechanical explanations would depend on 'high level' theories attributing recursive structures to organisms in analogy to abstract theories that attribute subatomic structures to material things.[7]

There are two important ways in which mechanistic explanation extends or differs from the Hempel-Oppenheim model. First, all functional (in the teleological sense now) explanations reduce to the mechanical. Suppose McGuire turns on her sound system and Peter asks the enquirer 'why?' He replies, "Because she desires to hear Bach", or to abuse the language slightly, "because the function for McGuire of knob-turning is to produce Bach". A reductive mechanical explanation — assuming enough were known in mechanistic psychology to deliver one — would consist of a collection of statements about realized recursive structures and their interconnections, and an indicated deduction of statements about the subject's actions that produce twistings of sound system knobs. *None* of the explanation's parts would allude to states playing roles or to role-playing dispositions. Such is the main thesis of this work.

Second, mechanical *predictions* are not just pragmatical variations of mechanical *explanations* (Hempel and Oppenheim, 1948, pp. 322–323). This is really just to say that there are no deductive type explanations, and the reason for this is the presence of various kinds of indeterminacies. There are several cases that are relevant, all of which are suggested by the basic realist-nonreductionist thesis. First and foremost, explanation of linguistic performance does not seem to afford grounds for prediction if that explanation is based on competence models. The latter are *nondeterministic* systems of rules (cf. Section II.3). A *complete knowledge* of the rules of English, for instance, would constitute a descriptively adequate theory in Chomsky's sense, but not a predictive one. If the realization, materially, of rules were common to all speakers, if one knew the neurological details, and if the underlying neurological laws were deterministic, then one could conceivably predict $\mathscr{S}$'s utterances more accurately than by plain guessing (cf. discussion of the nondeterministic worm in Section IV.4); but the list of subjunctive conditions are enough to overwhelm any but the most earnestly vague notions of prediction. True there could be predictions in some totally uninteresting statisticial sense. To see the difference contrast the problem of ascertaining the probability that a well-understood Jones standing before the *Pieta* will utter "Michelangelo died three months after completing this work" with that of finding the probability that she will utter a sentence with a greater number of occurrences of e's than o's.

More generally, an investigator might be able to explain behavior in that she knew the complete automaton table for a mental attitude, say a desire for bananas. If $\mathscr{S}$ grabs one, behavior o let us say, an explanation derived from the table might be an alternation statement, if there is a known associated stimulus present (qs, $q's$, $q''s$, etc. might all map to o). If $\mathscr{S}$ were subjected to a stimulus stream x, the investigator would not be able to predict output, however, unless she knew the present state.[8] A parallel case could arise in physics if one ideally understood a system but had no grasp of the present state. What is distinctive in our case, however, is that there might be no way of determining the present state even though that state be an entity embodied in some indirectly observable neural network. There are three sub cases. (i) Since automaton and physical descriptions are different, one could know a complete table by abductive inference, thus have at hand a complete explanatory account, but not know the material embodiment of that table. If so, neither probes nor special brain scans would be of the slightest help in predicting from a stimulus event. This essential unpredictability does not arise because mental states are mysterious, non-physical entities, but because the abstract relations of state to state or to input-output arrays can be fully known without knowledge of the specific material realization.

(ii) Consider the catatonic table below

TABLE I
Catatonic.

	M		N	
	s_0	s_1	s_0	s_1
q_0	q_1	q_0	0	1
q_1	q_2	q_0	0	2
q_2	q_3	q_0	0	3
q_3	q_4	q_0	0	4
.	.	.	.	.
.	.	.	.	.
.	.	.	.	.
q_n	q_0	q_0	0	n

Suppose s_0 is a null input in that the subject gives the same response (a stoney stare), 0, no matter what state she is in, but with passage of time there is a state sequence $q_1, \ldots, q_n$ as indicated in the table under column M, s_0. Given s_1 a wide range of positive, even violent, behaviors $1, \ldots, n$ are possible depending on the state. There is no way of predicting response. Indeed, ponder the confused state of a Baconian inductionist attempting to conclude something or other from a Table of Agreement!

Incidentally, this table illustrates that a remote stimulus might provide one of the antecedent conditions for a response of a wholly surprising nature *at a much later time.* Furthermore it is extremely difficult to see how any conceivable S–R reenforcement theory could account for the behavior of or the acquisition of the behavior of Table I. (Admittedly, mechanism as currently understood does not help much either).

(iii) One way to attempt to detect the present state of an organism is by inference from a number of systematic input-output experiments. One might, for instance, infer the starting state of an experimental input (stimulus sequence x) from knowledge of a table and observed response z. Unfortunately there are so-called "backwards indeterministic" tables for which this is not possible (cf. Table V.III). Two states q and q', might yield identically the same reponses from inputs initiated by stimulus s (i.e., for inputs sx, for all x) and yet be *inequivalent.*

In all three cases (i)–(iii) I have used FA models. But this is no restriction. The same or similar points could be made to reveal the peculiar features of mechanistic explanation using Turing machine or even rule systems of an entirely different though equivalent category.

For those who advocate the 'place holder' theory of psychological dispositions a fruitful comparison can be made here between the view that dispositional properties are ultimately traceable to physical microstructures of some sort and my view that they are realized recursive rule systems. It seems to me that both the physicalist and mechanist (in my sense) versions of the theory must be *realistic*, although since I do not know how to define 'realism' outside of the fit-guide concept for mental traits I am willing to let the point pass. In the logic of mind a statement that $\mathscr{S}$ is disposed to behave in manner o if she is stimulated by s is equivalent to one asserting that $\mathscr{S}$ realizes an automaton such that there is in its table a q such that $M(q, s) = o$. Both statements are equivalent to 'if $\mathscr{S}$ were submitted to stimulus s while in state q, then she would respond by o'. I claim that in the psychology of features, at least, this version of the place holder view affords an effective basis for totally eliminating counterfactuals from discourse. This is a pretty limited domain; yet it does add support to the place holder idea in a way that makes a specific commitment to empirical realism. The basic idea, as we well know, is the distinction between *mathematical* descriptions of mental phenomena – which involve interpretations of formal mathematical systems of rules – and *historical* or temporal descriptions of actual events. Surely this distinction is not so clear as to obviate further analysis; but it is a common working one in science, and the effect of accepting it is just commitment to mathematical entities in a manner already required in exact science.

(2) The philosopher's explication of mentalistic terms such as 'belief'

is also empirical as it is falsifiable, and is even a kind of explanation, but of a rather different kind than the psychologist's. The main difference lies in the 'framework' character of philosophy. Neither I nor any other philosopher who is as ignorant of psychology and its methods as I am is in any position to promulgate explanatory theories of intelligent behavior. Philosophy of psychology is propadeutic, although I suppose that almost any practicing psychologist, except for one interested in theoretical foundations, can get along without it. My position, as defended and exemplified in previous pages, is that philosophy is explicative and that explication establishes the material plausibility of framework hypotheses – man is a machine.

My reason for repeating the business of philosophy as I see it is to contrast it with what Searle (1980) calls "Strong AI". Many experts in cognitive science think that computer cognition is the same as human cognition (Newell and Simon, 1963, p. 270, 293). What Strong AI-ers mean by this is that some programs are not only behaviorally equivalent to human cognitions – perform the same intellectual tasks – but *explain* them (cf. Boden, 1977; Sloman, 1978).[9] Mind the computer (machine$_2$) is no mere metaphor to these persons. Perhaps the most open expression of a not-very-Strong-AI is that *thermostats believe* (McCarthy, 1979). I am critical of this position that computer programs explain mental phenomena in the sense that they display possible algorithmic ways in which those processes might be produced. It excludes the absolutely essential step of laying down adequacy conditions which any analysis via definitions, explications and now working computer programs must satisfy (cf. Section III.2). However AI is separated from conceptual enterprises of the mechanist kind in a still more fundamental way: AI practiciners, after all, are dealing with computers that are bolted to the floor or confined to a desk.

AI as currently pursued studies intelligent processes as they occur in antiseptic, closed systems of data, treating those processes in isolation from anything corresponding to the organism's environment, inputs, and active output (I do not count printers) and from other intelligences. True, some programs are user-interactive, learn, and even interact with each other as in distributed computing systems. And many of their external behaviors manufactured by the programmer are certainly adequate to the analogical argument that humans are automata as advanced in Chapter IV. However the programmed mechanisms confined as they are to mental cages can have only limited suggestions for the prime philosophical task of accounting for the intentional.

Let me be more specific. For the most part input data, which is very clean, is externally prepared, indeed 'canned', in AI projects: the computer is not an active perceiver; there is nothing corresponding to perception or to perceptual belief or desire, and therefore no possibility of empirical meanings, i.e., meanings associated to basic observational sentences. True, 'meanings' are introduced into intelligent systems via 'models of the world' — themselves represented by data structures of various kinds — and these models are used to interpret languages such as simple fragments of English. But this is in no way empirical meaning. Indeed, the situation in AI is almost exactly the reverse of our own in regard to perceptual belief vs standing belief.[10] For us a theory of perceptual belief derives quite naturally and directly from acceptance, while nonperceptual belief presents rather deep mysteries (Section VIII.4). For AI, on the other hand, all 'belief' understood metaphorically or otherwise is nonperceptual and consists of a model of the world built up in memory either by the omniscient programmer or by learning, learning in limited interaction with human beings as in learning to play games.

A model of the world which is supposed to contain among its items items about the subject program itself as a part of that world is not anything like our self-coding automata of Chapter VI (Minsky, 1965). In my theory self-coding is the basis for taking, fulfilling of expectations and is a necessary mechanism for accepting degraded, sensory input data. A world model in an AI program on the other hand would presuppose some such mechanism, provided that computers were provided with sensors. A world model, always incomplete with respect to the modeling of the computer itself for itself, could not possibly have such powers — unless a *different* self-describing program were added (cf. Note VII.10). Self-description and world modeling are conceptually different and play different roles, the one in building up and modifying nonperceptual belief structures linked tightly to language processing, and the other in making perception in a vague, noisy world possible.

For these reasons I agree with Searle's criticism of strong AI as he characterizes it. I have doubts, however, about his example of the Chinese language translator (p. 112) being anything at all like a truly sophisticated AI program.

At any rate, Searle's argument doesn't touch mechanism. For him to maintain that a subject that realizes a system of automaton that purportedly explains perceptual belief doesn't really believe anything, he's going to have to do a lot more than whomp up a little man with his dictionaries and a rule book. He's going to have to show that a system that takes, can virtually abstract universals from particulars, can perceive resemblances by taking one thing for another without matching common properties, can hear a single melody in an indefinite number of odd keys, can perceive many disjoint property types in one set of objects, can have expectations that involve taking and imply either fulfillment or disruption in counterfactual situations, can believe false propositions, is expressible in strictly extensional sentences where substitutivity fails, etc.; in short a system that adequately satisfy properties that phenomenologists and semanticists insist characterize the intentional, is not intentional.

The automaton system is strictly syntactical, as he says, in the sense that the symbols input to it are uninterpreted; but to argue that an intentional system can not be built out of strictly extensional automaton ingredients and that a semantics of a simple language grounded in the system is not the way to do semantics he has to deny that Gödelian self-reference (see Note VI.17) has anything to do with reference, and that the semantical notions as I have tried to explicate them above won't wash.

Finally the theory of perceptual belief does not rely on the notion of a man or homunculus (or the control of a central processing unit) following a free algorithm. It's the other way around. There is an embodied algorithm that in part informs or constitutes the man. It's the realization of such rules that contributes to the constitution of a cognitive agent.

I am far from denying that the theory can be taken down, point by point. But it would take some work possibly joined along with the appealing rhetoric.

3. FREE WILL

A person has beliefs or desires if and only if she realizes certain automata; these and other mental attitudes thus seem aptly characterizable as systems. The will, on the other hand, is a *state* or collection of states which the subject might or might not be in; it exercises its will on some occasions and on others not. A characterization of the will naturally arises out of our treatment of belief and desire of Chapter VIII; but it has seemed to me better to discuss the topic in the context of explanation. In this section I will expand on the above suggested analysis but not attempt a precise definition. Then I will comment on some of the traditional metaphysical issues about will, and wind up the very brief discussion with a sketch of a psychology of morality.

A person desires x if and only if, if she believes that y and acts in a way depending on y to produce x, then she expects x (*Proposition* VIII(17)). My suggestion is that the act in question be taken as short for 'act of will', that is to say, that 'will' be explained as a link in the passage from belief to action and the expected results thereof. It might be identified with the relation A of the output from a perceptual state to an expected object (VIII(12), p.

229) If we make this move there is no such thing as *the will*, but rather *will to do this or that*; and if one must have an entity let him consider the class of willings to special ends. This is hardly a definition of 'will' but it does locate the concept in the context of desire and action where it ought to be. I think one might go on to explore a more relevantly moral 'will' in terms of higher expectations about ourselves and others; but first I wish to tender sundry comments about the psychology and metaphysics of will.

The history of the subject shows that philosophers have leaned more toward the issue of determinism *versus* freedom than toward that of the moral use of the will and the intentions behind it. This emphasis is traceable to theological concerns about choice. If you choose God, then since God commands the right, there is no moral problem past that initial choice itself. If God elects you, then there is no question of what to choose. This reduces ethics to the problem of free will: if the will is free, then it is up to you to make the right choice, i.e., God; if not, God manages the whole thing, and if you're in luck you're not doomed. This is a parody, except for a certain class of fundamentalist Protestants. Even if you follow God's command you are likely to have to decide what that is; and if you are of the elect you still have to choose to show it.

During the Enlightenment the Deists replaced God's command by causal law, and the effect was of course another type of determinism. Since Hume empiricist philosophy has included several attempts to divorce the issue of physical necessity from freedom. For Kant, although phenomena are in the grip of physical necessity, the noumenal self is not, and is subject only to the demands of practical reason. This places questions of morality and freedom outside the range of preKantian metaphysics including the mechanism of the 16th to 18th centuries. Our position is similar, superficially, as it places will in the context of mental attitude, and the sciences of the mental are autonomous. If empirical realism is accepted there is no ultimate metaphysical problem of freedom of the will, and therefore moral philosophy becomes able to concern itself with questions of content which, for the devout, does not rule out God's commands.

If truth is relative to formalized theory, and if there are real mental processes of a nondeterministic sort than determinism is wrong as a blanket metaphysical doctrine. There is no over-all metaphysics outside of empirically based philosophy; and if determinism is true at all it is so relative to some ways of constructing the world and not of others. The worm argument of Section IV.5 attempted to show that there is nothing in mechanism that precludes nondeterministic rules, and that whether a thing is nondeterministic is an empirical question within a given descriptive framework. Being an

NFA is perfectly compatible, I argued, with being a rigidly deterministic system from the point of view of another descriptive base, say neuroscience or biochemistry. Also, as lately illustrated in the catatonic character of Table XI.I, if an organism's responses are deterministically related to state-stimulus pairs, a differential response might still be distantly related in time to the stimulus kicking it off and be totally unrelated in any one-one sense to a temporally contiguous one; indeed the response, as we see from the table, might be one of a very large array related to the stimulus. And if that response proceeds from an act of will as in the suggested description above, it is terribly hard to see how one could pin down any particular event that looks like its cause at all. Of course all I am saying is that in deterministic automata the internal state plays just as much a 'causal' role in the production of actions, if not more, than any outer events. Our model allows, further, extremely elegant output, namely speech, having *no* correlated input stimuli whatsoever. This does not preclude deterministic neurophysiological descriptions at a different level. But it does show how an individual can be free as to mental processes including the will construed as relation of state to act and yet not be merely a random 'noise' generator. Acts are one's very own, and one is responsible for them.

Moral conduct does not seem to arise within the primitive context of belief and desire in which I placed the will. However the moral is certainly a part of the intentional *qua* psychological phenomenon. To get a line on it I propose that we stretch our theory of attitudes beyond the perceptual to 'higher levels'. Among our expectations are expectations of the actions of others and also *the internalization of the expectations others have of us.* We come to expect of ourselves what we perceive others to expect of us. This view might be interpreted as a naturalization of the super-ego concept of Freud, omitting the special sexual connotations. If want and desire at this higher social level are related to belief, act and expectation in some way parallel to the analysis of Chapter VIII, then it would seem reasonable to construe the will also in a parallel way. If so, I act rightly when I will to act in a way I think is expected of me by others and wrongly otherwise. This is not all there is to ethics even on the psychological level; and it is certainly guilty of 'naturalism' as it promotes the idea of defining ethical concepts in terms of the psychological. But I doubt that it is a weakness; in fact it is what I intend.

Assuming that formalism is the only cognitivist alternative to naturalism in ethics, my proposed theory still elucidates and naturalizes (now in the meaning of squaring it with natural science) classical formalism.[11] Take the *moral sense* theory as represented by Thomas Reid (Reid, 1788). Persons do have moral sense or conscience (if they do not, they are clinically psychopathic, which is subject in principle to socio-empirical test), although it is not the 18th century Protestant sense attributed to all humans absolutely. It seems to me that if any analysis is adequate one that unpacks 'moral sense' or 'conscience' or 'sense of duty' in terms of one's perception of other's expectations of him comes close to filling the bill, at least. And we do have hope of getting a strictly scientific handle on expectation and the rest of the intentional. If we were to extend the notion of the exemplar $\mathscr{S}$ in whose terms we defined 'truth' for the core language in Chapter IX to the realm of the ethical we might arrive at the idea of one who has universalized expectations of himself and others. This is not quite Kant (there is obviously no similarity to the transcendental cast of his thought); but if I were always to act in such a way as to reach the highest expectations (read 'aspirations') of the moral exemplar I would have followed an imperative; not one emanating from practical reason but from the accrued moral experience of beings who are guided by the expectations others have of them.

4. MENTAL OCCURRENTS

The separation of mental features, our analysis of which now includes the will and moral attitudes if we allow an extension of the treatment of expectation away from the perceptual, from mental occurrents is roughly that of Peirce's thirdness from secondness. An occurrent or mental event is the instantiation of a quale, the event being the second and the quale a first. In current jargon the quale is a type and the instantiation a token, while the experience of the token is a mental state.[12] We are conscious of some states and not of others. For instance if acceptance entails a sequence of states (it does according to the theory of Chapter VI), normally only the final or perceptual state (the sense datum or image) is anything we are consciously aware of. Similarly thought processes are mostly submerged, and there are but few salient states that count as 'datable' thoughts. This view might lead on to a more profound one to the effect that there is no conscious continuum or field in which we experience events when awake or in dreamful sleep, but only a stream of mental states themselves (perhaps there is no 'modulated carrier' but just free 'pulse streams', so to speak). However I do not care to tackle this question for lack of anything interesting to say about it except in the context of attention.

Questions of selection or attention (the selective conscious act of Mead (Mead, 1934, p. 28)) are mental feature questions, I think, and have been handled here in terms of 'gating' (See Figure VIII.1) or in programming jargon of calling subroutines from main programs. This device worked for Scrooge and preserved the inexistential character of his Marley experience; for the belief-desire loop, and for evading Grice's problem of the regress of definitional programmes, and for the belief operator, B (Section VIII.3, 4). Thus 'selective consciousness' comes to be an underlying mechanical process attended by experience of a mental event.[13]

Consciousness of self seems to depend on possession of language containing the appropriate designations ('I' and 'me' the object) or possibly on something akin to the super automaton T' that made use of self-description, tacit in perception, to account for acceptance of extra-categorical, receptually degenerate stimulus items (Section VI.3). But this is wild guessing. The language theory of self-consciousness is attractive as it might be used to reduce the peculiarly human, often frightening phenomenon to sequences of mental events attending speech utterances.

The selective character of attention in conscious life also accounts for the distinction between mental events as somehow 'just there' or suffered more or less dimly and those that are *intentional* (some might say 'referential', but I reserve this term for linguistic expressions). Acceptance of an event as a fragment of Bach, thinking now of perceptual states not as neutral, abstract automaton entities but as sentient events, is quite a different thing than background Bach in which one swims inattentively awash while contemplating reports of budget cuts. Here a field warp or carrier wave *cum* modulation metaphor is perhaps useful. The experience in the first case is intentional in the literal sense that uttered linguistic expressions of it are referential precisely because of an underlying acceptance computation mapping to Bach perceptual states.[14]

These ruminations suggest (and they are barely suggestions) that sentience is entirely a matter of clusters or sequences of mental occurrents. If so, one who is able to solve the ontological problem of mental events also solves the principal problems of mind-body. At any rate I shall put aside lingering concern about the conscious field – if it turns out there is totally unmarked consciousness – and deal now with the status of occurrent mental states only.[15]

Hilary Putnam, who has done as much as anyone else to bring the viewpoint of functionalism including mechanism in the version of this book to philosophical prominence, has at various times proposed that mental states (not necessarily just 'experienced mental events or occurrents' as in our present context but almost anything in the mind) are nothing but logical states – and that mentality including sentient quality derives from the 'role-playing' character of states. If we divide the mental state terrain into the features and the occurrents, he seems to be wrong on two counts, once one examines the territory closely (he never explicitly distinguishes features from occurrents). Yet the basic insight has been as fertile as anything I know of in contemporary mental philosophy.[16] He is wrong, I think, in identifying mental features with states – in the strict sense of our automaton q's – for the reasons dwelt on in Chapter V, and also for the reason that analysis bears out the general thesis that dispositions and attitudes are realized rule systems, not individual states. That he is wrong about occurrents is the burden of the following remarks. Pains, etc. are not 'functional states'.

For design reasons, in computer technology, it is customary to distinguish the physical from the logical state (as we shall see in a moment, one interpretation of this is the distinction between the physical thing that interprets the q symbol and the q symbol itself) of a computing circuit. Putnam's idea is to fill in the analogy: mental occurrent is to physical thing (i.e., neurophysiological state) as the engineer's logical state is to the physical (i.e., the electronic, solid state, relay or other state). Now engineers long ago saw (perhaps Von Neumann was the first to see it clearly) that many qualitatively different electronic or other devices can realize one and the same logical state; therefore, logical and physical states are not the same. And using the analogy this suggests that mental occurrents, like logical states, are not physical states. Using the stock example, pains (pain experiences) are not C-fiber stimulations. The identity theory is false.[17] In the paper cited (Note 15) I followed William Kalke in his explicit reformulation of this argument, which might be set down as follows:

(i)   If two systems of different physical constitution are automaton-isomorphic, then corresponding physical states realize the same logical state.

As a corollary of (i) we have

(ii)   If two different physical systems are automaton-isomorphic, the logical states are *not* identical with the physical states that realize them.

Assuming that any physical system is isomorphic to some other different physical system, it follows that

(iii)   Logical states of physical systems are not identical with the physical states that realize them.

(Kalke, 1969, pp. 83–94). Now if 'mental occurrent' is taken to mean 'logical state' by the aforementioned analogy,

(iii')   Mental occurrents of animals are never identical with the physical states that realize them.

(iii) implies that the sensation of red (a logical robot state) is not identical with flip-flop 72 being on (a physical robot state), (Putnam, 1964, p. 671); and (iii') that a sensation of red is not identical with stimulation of nerve fibers.

The concepts to have in mind here are a formal automaton language interpreted in a number of physical domains such that the latter are mutually isomorphic. Note that the elements in the one-one correspondence of the isomorphism are physical entities and that these things are assigned under the interpretation map to automaton q symbols.

The question before us now is, what are the *logical states* of the isomorphic physical systems? In Putnam's mind they can not be physical states as his whole point is that the logical and physical are nonidentical. One plausible view, perhaps, is that logical states are just the q symbols themselves, whence (iii) and (iii'). Unfortunately it is totally counterintuitive to identify symbols of a formal language (either tokens or types) with mental occurrents such as experiencings of red spots! Neither pains nor spots are conventional alphabetical symbols such as q's or arabic alif's.

Moreover given this interpretation of 'logical state' the argument (i)–(iii) is unsound as (i) is *false*. Two computer circuits can be isomorphic and yet *not* realize the same logical symbol q or even *behaviorally equivalent* q's. For consider the formalized automaton A, the theory of which we suppose to have been summarized in the Table II(a) below.

TABLE II

(a) Abstract automaton A.

	M_A		N_A	
	s_0	s_1	s_0	s_1
q_0	q_0	q_0	o_1	o_2
q_1	q_1	q_3	o_1	o_1
q_2	q_2	q_2	o_2	o_1
q_3	q_3	q_1	o_2	o_2

Table II (*continued*)

(b) Physical automaton B.

	M_B		N_B	
	0	1	0	1
a	*a*	*a*	0	1
b	*b*	*d*	0	0
c	*c*	*c*	1	0
d	*d*	*b*	1	1

(c) Physical automaton C.

	M_C		N_C	
	0	1	0	1
e	*e*	*e*	1	0
f	*f*	*h*	0	0
g	*g*	*g*	0	1
h	*h*	*j*	1	1

Tables (b) and (c) depict two isomorphic physical devices. The input and output symbols 0 and 1 are signals of some sort and the symbols *a, b, c*, etc. stand for physical states of some sort.

The interpretation map from *A* to *B* is

states	inputs	outputs
$q_0 - a$	$s_0 - 0$	$o_1 - 0$
$q_1 - b$	$s_1 - 1$	$o_2 - 1$
$q_2 - c$		
$q_3 - d$		

and from *A* to *C* is

states	inputs	outputs
$q_0 - e$	$s_0 - 0$	$o_1 - 0$
$q_1 - f$	$s_1 - 1$	$o_2 - 1$
$q_2 - g$		
$q_3 - h$		

The isomorphism from B to C is

states	inputs	outputs
$a - e$	$0 - 0$	$0 - 1$
$b - h$	$1 - 1$	$1 - 0$
$c - g$		
$d - f$		

Observe that although state a of B and e of C are associated in the isomorphism, a is the interpretation of state symbol q_0, while e is the interpretation of q_2. Moreover, q_0 and q_2 of the abstract machine A are *not even behaviorally equivalent*! For instance $N_A(q_0, s_0) = o_1$ and $N_A(q_2, s_0) = o_2$. This shows that (i) of the Putnam-Kalke argument is false and hence the whole thing is unsound. If there actually are organismic realizations of automata that manifest the phenomenon of Table II then the negative conclusion concerning (iii') for the mid-body issue is not merely a counter suggestion from analogy.

Rather than interpret symbols of q directly as physical states we might consider interposing a mathematical realm of objects as interpretations and avoid the paradoxical matter just exemplified in Table II by fiat: to be isomorphic, interpretations must satisfy the condition that corresponding states be assigned the same formal symbol. The proposal is that these new objects be the things we construe logical states as. In automata theory a usual interpretation is the domain of symbol types s, q, etc. themselves (Nelson, 1968, p. 297). But they might otherwise be new abstract entities called 'states', that are neither symbol types nor physical things; or, they might be numbers; or better yet, perhaps, the occurrent mental *types* themselves. If you choose the latter you get a platonistic realm of *pain, yellow, the transient thought* of π, etc. etc.; and with it a new type of non-modeltheoretic realization. Mental occurrents instantiate these entities while the latter are in turn interpretations of languages as numbers are of a language of arithmetic. You either get stuck with a kind of dualism under this scheme, about which I shall have some remarks in a moment; or, if you attempt some kind of ontological reduction paralleling one of the familiar eliminative definitions of numbers in favor of sets, you get entities that are no more like pains, or experienced pain states, than brain states are — perhaps sets or even numbers themselves. However it seems to me that it is simply absurd to say that a logical state (still following along with Putnam and reckoning mental states as logical states) such as pain is a symbol type (alif?), a set, or the number fifteen.

If you take unreduced thoughts or pains as ultimate in this special realm you get Popper (Popper and Eccles, 1977, Part I).

Popper's World 2, which is a real world of mental items, is a Platonic heaven much as is the interposed realm. Although he wants no truck with ontology, Popper does maintain that his World 3 (products of the human mind such as poems, symphonies, scientific theories) is Platonistic, but that World 2 is not. As I am not sure how to distinguish 2 and 3 (where are thoughts? 2? are thoughts ever propositions — 3 presumably?) let's throw them together for the time being. The physical world including the brain *interacts* with 2 and 3. An action based on belief in a proposition or a theory would be a product of interaction, for instance. That interaction could not be any kind of rule-guiding as in my theory as his paradigm mechanist is LaMettrie (Popper and Eccles, 1977, p. 206) not Hilbert or Turing. The interaction is not Cartesian as he also claims that Worlds 2 and 3 are dependent on us — one emerges and the other is created by us; so they are not Cartesian substances; besides the scheme does not seem to be nominalistic enough. If I thought I understood Popper and had the courage to come right on out with it I would tag him a 'Platonistic interactionist' and his school 'Popperian Platonism', although some scholars might demur, preferring 'triadic dualism'. If the doctrine is really Platonistic of course it does not help out at all in reaching a suitable construal of Putnam's 'logical state' as it is simply a category mistake to affirm or deny that platonic ideas are identical to the things that instantiate them. On the other hand if mental states of World 2 are just ontological danglers of some sort, then one might as well simply embrace the scientifically most conservative position that they all correlate with some kind of physical states empirically. But then to import into this eminently sound conceptual scheme the notion of interaction is simply gratuitous. *That* is where the whole problem starts, not where it should end!

Eccles, on the other hand, seems to be a straightforward Cartesian, as there are signs that he is fond of mental substances. Whether or no this is so is perhaps debatable, although he does consistently write of *the* self-conscious mind and *the* brain as things having certain interactive powers; they are categorically *the same* in Ryle's sense. Indeed, he refers explicitly to his philosophy as a 'dualistic hypothesis' (Popper and Eccles, 1977, pp. 361–365).

Perhaps by 'Popperian Platonism' and 'Cartesian Ecclesianism' we shall remember them, and for our limited ends here pass on by to a third interpretation of 'logical state'.

The interpretation I have in mind might perhaps be taken more seriously than the other two although it tends to generate its own special absurdities. The idea is to take logical states as *equivalence classes* of the physical states that correspond in an isomorphism. This move saves (i) and, let us suppose, (iii') as well. But then if mental states are logical states they are classes of physical things, or possible equivalence *properties*, namely some kind of property of physical properties. Although one might consider features to be second order properties – acceptance, for instance, is a property of an automaton which latter is an ordered quintuple $\langle Q, S, q_0, M, Q_F \rangle$ of *sets* – , it does not seem credible to me to identify a toothache with a set, and I do not know what to make of the recommendation that a pain is a second order property (cf. Putnam, 1969, p. 244 f.). I at one time thought this was wrong and obscure (Nelson, 1976a, p. 378), but now my attitude is somewhat more tolerant – not because I think that the idea is clear, credible, or plausible, but because the entire ontology of events, states, properties, experienced events and properties, and so on is in far too poor a condition to allow conclusions one way or the other.

A fourth and to me most plausible way of taking 'logical state' of a thing is this. It is just the physical thing under a state-space description; an internal state considered in abstraction from its physical properties, as an element in the interpretation of a formal system (cf. Section III.II). Physical states regarded thus indifferently (technically: in an automaton logic language rather than a neuroanatomical language) are logical states. Corresponding logical states are thus the *same* from the mental feature point of view but not as regards *material quality*. So in a way (iii') becomes true, but not in any deep ontological sense. In particular a rolling stone could be correlated to a toothache and therefore be the same logical state in a shared rule struture; but this circumstance does not make a toothache event qua *mental state* a rolling stone.

Unless some one can come up with another alternative for 'logical state' I think that the logical or 'functional' state theory of occurrents is not likely to have a very bright future.[18]

If we discount epiphenomenalism and dualism as briefly encountered earlier, then we are left with materialism or some version of idealism or panpsychism. It is also quite tempting to revert to logical positivism and discard the whole mind-brain issue as meaningless, despite Feigl's fairly compelling arguments that it is not (Feigl, 1960). If so, I would not be the first one in recent years to do so. Smart believes there is "no conceivable experiment which could decide between materialism and epiphenomenalism".

(Smart, 1959, p. 65). I am very tempted to add cluster dualism and panpsychism to the theories. He continues on to say that only considerations of parsimony and simplicity really favor the identity theory (see note 17); it is just not a scientific hypothesis. But if so the same can be said for panpsychism; I see no scientific standing for it except its evident parsimony and simplicity. For a revised, panpsychicalistic version of the identity theory might assert that every physical state is contingently identical to some mental state (my version of 'panpsychism'); rather than that every mental state is identical to some physical (brain) state (materialistic identity). This new position is equally simple and parsimonious. And it has the distinct advantage of circumventing the problem of psychic emergence, if that concerns you, and of unwanted discontinuities in our theories of the of the universe.[19] Instead of the problem of emergent mind you would have one of mordant mind (matter) with less strain perhaps on one's entropical intuitions. Of course it has the disadvantage of running counter to our quite generally held convictions that the physical has some ontological primacy. However, this is no real philosophical objection. The main objection is positivist, and we might not do better than to toss it out with the other philosophies and simply accept the separate reality of mental occurrents and their empirical correlations with bodily events wherever neuroscientists establish them, and rest with a pluralistic philosophy. I must confess, however, that in the end some kind of identity theory does recommend itself as a complement to mechanism to yield a full logic of mind.

An identity theory combines nicely with a mechanist logic of mind. Mental states as contingently identical to certain physical states would in some cases realize automaton states. In the interests of vocabulary revision, here where it seems it is genuinely needed in philosophy, one might restrict 'mental state', then, not just to experienced mental events ranging from pains to higher thoughts but to just those identified with physical states that realize an automata sufficiently complex to merit the epithet 'intentional'. As I meant to convey in Chapter I to term pain 'mental' is really the modern philosopher's very own special abuse of the usual conception of things. It has been used over and over again to attempt to get across sentience, the real thing, to those who might have trouble distinguishing between computer sensing and *our* sensing and between tacit belief and belief accompanied by blushing, a rapid heart beat, neurasthenic palms and the raw feel of heat and generalized misery. But there can be pain suffered, possibly, in any living thing, even the ones lacking any intentional traits whatever. Now that we have an idea of how the intentional might plausibly be understood there is no need to confuse intelligence with backaches although they otherwise might go together in the combined scheme of mechanism with materialism.

It seems plausible to speak of mental states as having causal efficacy, attributable not just to their being identical to physical states in causal state to state to output sequences, but also and equally to their being psychological conditions for the very existence of such causal sequences. In some automata, to be more precise, a physical complex a might produce along with a stimulus input b efferent output via some appropriate transducing means only if a is identical to an experienced mental event. Still more carefully, the pair (a, b) might in many cases be fit as interpretation of an automaton pair (q, s) yielding output *only if a be consciously experienced*. Of course this feature of certain organisms would be pretty mysterious from the point of view of contemporary science, but no more so than the contingent identity phenomenon itself. It might be a fact of the universe that only human organisms or similar beings within a natural kind have higher mental and moral functions that do enter causally into physical affairs under the kind of conditions mentioned. Computers might embody extremely intricate computational networks and programs, for instance, but not the right ones for these functions as they lack sentience. I explore this in my (1988a).

As long as I am indulging myself in this excessive fashion I might add that my intuitions say the *materialist* version of the identity thesis serves better here than the panpsychist: only 'higher' organic structures such as cortex are susceptible to occurrent mentality; (analogy for panpsychism: only X type mental states are susceptible to physicality). Typically mental phenomena are, in virtue of this identity, felt or experienced; a perceptual expectation, for instance, would be an *experience* owing to its realizing a logic mechanism in which some states, the winners and the perceptual, were contingently mental.

Saul Kripke has stirred up some trouble for the identity theory and hence for a theory that combines it with mechanism as just proposed. In a nutshell, Kripke's argument is that if mind and brain are identical the identity is necessary, not contingent; and while this is true of other well-known identities in physical science, there is a way of explaining our intuitions that these identities, as they are discovered *a posteriori*, are contingent. However there is no way of explaining our intuitions that mind and brain could be distinct if the mind-brain identity thesis is true. This is an extremely sophisticated argument, and there simply is not space left in an already overly long book to do it complete justice, even if I knew how. However I shall run through his argument sketchily (I hope faithfully) and then tender a few points that I believe might figure against it.

In Chapter X we saw, also very briefly, that in Kripke's philosophy of language proper names are 'rigid designators' meaning that they refer to the same things in all possible worlds. Reference thus is not fixed, for Kripke, by association of some sort of proper names to codesignative definite descriptions, a theory attributable to Frege, Russell and Quine (but in different ways.). Reference is fixed by a causal link with the object *in situ* and then is transmitted to other users of the language via various possible devices including perhaps a wide variety of descriptions none of which essentially fix the reference of the name. On this view empirical identity statements such as 'Hesperus = Phosphorus' are necessary, if true, and not contingent.

Now Kripke's theory of names extends to ordinary common names, i.e., in particular to natural kind or species terms (Kripke, 1972, pp. 322 ff). Not only proper names such as 'Peter' but predicate expressions such as 'man' or 'toothache' have direct reference; their objects, properties or whatever are not represented in virtue of meanings or intensions in the head that select reference, but by direct causal links. Hence, by the same reasoning as obtains for proper names, identity statements about kinds using common names rather than descriptions (whatever these latter might be like) are *necessary a posteriori*. They hold in all possible worlds, if true. Therefore such typical statements of science as 'water is H_2O' or 'heat is average kinetic energy' are necessary identities even though synthetic a posteriori. 'Water' and 'H_2O' are rigidly designating names, and they designate the same in all possible worlds — independently of describable contingencies — , and hence the equation statement is necessarily true.

Kripke is not one to skip over the likely complaint that empirical identities of the kind we have mentioned do seem to be contingent in many cases. It would seem to be quite possible, for instance, that what we call 'gold' designates an element with the atomic weight w, not 197.2; or that heat, if the world were arranged differently, be median kinetic energy not average kinetic energy. Neither one of these alternatives seems to be impossible. Kripke has to protect his theory against such intuitions under the general principle, which we must surely agree with, that a theory of naming like any other philosophical proposal satisfy reasonable preanalytic intuitions. Intuition does say that the evening star could have been other than Venus and that gold could have a different atomic weight. Kripke must show how these views about empirical identities can be explained away.

First, such cases as 'the evening star is Venus' or 'Franklin was the discoverer of bifocals' *are* contingent identities as it is entirely possible that in some other world the discoverer of bifocals be some one else or that they be not discovered at all. 'The discoverer of bifocals' is not a rigid designator as it could denote different individuals in different worlds. Bifocals might have been discovered by Johnny Carson in another severer, more demanding world. Of course this does not answer the question about respect for intuitions but just clears the air. We are worrying about explaining away contrary feelings about *necessary* identities.

The real answer, says Kripke, is that under some circumstances this very thing I call 'gold' might have had an atomic weight w while yet this gold itself could not possibly be any different that it is. One could be in the *"qualitatively same epistemic situation"* and have at hand the very same observational evidence he might have for 'gold' while the thing is not gold (Kripke, 1972, p. 332). Some of the describable qualities, possibly accidental ones, by which we fix the reference of names are merely contingent. You learn 'Loon' by way of 'the boat Nelson owns' thereby establishing a link in a causal chain from the naming of the Loon that might very well have been established some other way. Maybe the boat Nelson owns isn't the Loon but the Loon is still the Loon; 'Loon' fixedly designates Loon. Similarly in the gold story, the seen properties could be the same as those of a substance having a different atomic weight. Generally stated, our intuitions can be accounted for in terms of the possibility that our learning of a rigid name could take place under contingent circumstances that might, on other occasions, lead us to apply the name to something other than the fixed referent. There is always a kind of epistemic slack in our phenomenal identification of objects.[20]

Now let us shift over to the standpoint of the mind-body identity theory, considering certain attacks on it and the rejoinders thereto as if we were unaware of Kripke's theory of rigid designation. The former theory says that certain nerve fiber excitations are the same as salient thoughts, images, or pains. The stock example is "C-fiber stimulation is contingently identical to experience of a pain". Some of the stock criticisms of this theory run like this: You can know you have a toothache and not know anything about C-fibers; moreover, 'toothache' does not mean the same as 'C-fiber stimulation'. In brief, the criticism goes, the identity can not hold because you are not talking about or understanding the same. If you know or say something about x and $x = y$ is true then you know or say something about y. If you understand a statement about one and not the other, or refer to x and y with terms having different meaning, then x can not be the same as y.

The by now traditional materialist reply to this type of criticism is that

science contains numerous identity statements of the contingent sort; moreover these statements are true quite independently of our understanding of
codesignating terms or of their lack of synonymy. 'Heat is average kinetic
energy' is such a statement of contingent identity. Heat could be otherwise
in some possible world, and so forth. The statement is *aposteriori* while all
necessary statements are *apriori*. The naive might know a body is hot and
know nothing about the molecular theory of heat; and 'heat' and 'average
kinetic energy' are not synonymous terms. So there are true statements in
physics, an abundance of them, that express contingent identities. Why not
in psychology?

Kripke's analysis of naming undermines such materialist arguments from
the pervasive contingence of identities in science, if he is right, as the subject
statements are all necessarily true though experiential. 'Heat' and the other
illustrative terms are rigid designators. Hence the connection between heat
and molecular motion is necessary, and the putative support for the identity
theory offered by the examples is illusory.

If the mind-body connection is an identity, it is *necessary* since 'mind' and
'body' and 'C-fiber' or whatever are rigid, species terms. So the contingent
identity theory can not be true.

One bent on identity might have recourse to the old adage, "if you can't
beat 'em, join 'em": mind-body is a necessary identity. However in order
to justify a theory of a necessary connection one must be prepared to explain
in analogy to the account of our intuitions about the contigency of necessary
statements in physics how it is that one can believe that mental states and
brain states are distinct.[21] Kripke, however, denies that these intuitions can
be explained away. Suppose that you attempt to account for your believing
pain is contingently identical to nerve stimulation by arguing that phenomenal
pain — a pain sensation — such as might have provided the epistemic context
in which 'pain' was learned by you is merely contingent. But, says Kripke,
any such a proposal is doomed. You would have to say that *being a sensation*
is a contingent property of the reference of 'pain', much as being the inventor
of bifocals is a contingent feature of the reference of 'Franklin'. But this
is unintelligible. "Can any case of essence be more obvious than the fact
that being a pain is a necessary property of each pain?" (Kripke, 1972, p.
335).

Kripke's argument casts a shadow on the very theory we would like to
join with mechanism. It appears to do so on two counts: (a) if there is a
state-to-state identity it is necessary, not contingent as our adopted theory
would like to have it; and (b) if necessary, one must go on to explain one's

intuitions that they could be distinct. (b) is not likely for reasons Kripke has given: "This task might not be impossible . . . . The task, however, is obviously not child's play . . . ." (Kripke, 1972, pp. 331–337).

There are several ways of saving the theory, even in the face of Kripke's bold argument and his pessimism about Cartesian intuitions being explained away, without retreating (as I am sometimes prone) to the pluralistic correlation view suggested by the old logical empiricist criterion of meaningfulness. Of course the 'saving' is not going to be a knock-down argument. I will only show that Kripke's argument itself is doubtful. One can at best blunt the attack, and if *that* succeeds, the identity theory remains where it was before, neat and attractive but without much of anything in the way of scientific credentials.

One reply is the obvious one of challenging the concept of possible world on which the idea of rigid designator depends. Like Quine and others I do not care much for possible worlds, except for the parent concept of *model* in formal semantics. The notion of essence (as in 'x' necessarily refers to x) or of *de re* necessity is relative to context (Quine, 1977, p. 10; 1976), or as I would prefer to say, relative to a formalizable theory. A closely related point is that Kripke's position entails a kind of realism. Gold is really gold. Natural kinds have objectivity standing outside of our everyday understanding of things as experienced in contingent contexts. Now I, too, hold to a realist position and would be the first to argue, as I have in several chapters above, for it. But the real is relative to theory and in the realm of features of the mind is that which guides. The real is literally a realization, for me, in the semantic sense, of an algorithmic theory (cf. pp. 84–86). I know of no other concept of the real that has any standing at all in a naturalistic philosophy.

Even if possible worlds could be made more tolerable, thereby in part securing the concept of rigid designator, I would have serious doubts about 'pain' or other such mental state terms. For there could be contexts of experience in which there might be a toothache-like pain that was not a toothache (I mean of course a tooth*a*che, not a *tooth*ache). I know this runs counter to that popular dogma of philosophy, *viz.*, that there is no mistaking our having of mental occurrent states. I agree – regarding my own awareness content within the *specious present* (within, i.e., a small neighborhood of *now*), but not outside of that. I have had doubts, on occasion, as to whether I felt a twinge just a fraction of a second ago; and I settle the matter, sometimes, with various kinds of collateral data. Perhaps I can't or in fact don't doubt that I doubt while doubting, but I certainly can and do doubt that I doubted a moment ago (cf. Russell, 1927, p. 174). Furthermore there is all the difference in the world between pain and attended pain, as lately discussed, and between having a pain and unmistakeably designating it. There do seem to be contexts, heavy with supplementary information, for correctly designating an anginal pain as such and not as alimentary pain. Couple this observation with the primary one that there are mistaken *havings* or awarenesses outside of the specious present and you have at least the beginnings of a refutation of the argument that you can not account for belief in a contingent relation in the area of the mental as readily as you can in physics or chemistry.[22]

Concerning (b), Christopher Hill has presented a very elegant argument to the effect that we can explain away Cartesian intuitions that the mind and the brain could be distinct (Hill, 1981). His argument attempts to show that if there is a theory that satisfies the following conditions one could satisfactorily explain these intuitions.

(i)   The theory implies that the belief that mind and brain are distinct is false;

(ii)   apart from the fact that it seems to be the case that the mind and brain are distinct, there is every reason to believe that the theory is true; and

(iii)   either the theory itself affords an adequate basis for explaining *why* it seems to be the case that the mind and brain are distinct, or the theory is compatible with another that does provide such a basis (Hill, 1978, p. 3).

It is clearly correct, I think, that any such theory would suffice to explain our intuitions that sensations could exist without being accompanied by brain processes either that actually exist or could be. Indeed his paper argues that a certain strong version of the *necessary identity* thesis (argued essentially within Kripke's own ground rules) does provide such a theory.

There still is, then, ample reason for entertaining the simple, conceptually appealing philosophy that sentient events and brain states are one within a mechanist logic of mind.

TABLE OF FIGURES, FORMULAS AND TABLES

Figures

II.1	32
II.2	33
II.3	38
II.4	46
II.5	48
II.6	56
III.1	66
III.2	73
III.3	79
VI.1	167
VI.2	169
VI.3	170
VI.4	170
VI.5	174
VIII.1	225

Formulas

II(1a)	19
II(1b)	19
II(2a)	39
II(2b)	39
II(2c)	39
II(3)	44
II(3a)	49
II(3b)	49
II(3c)	49
II(3d)	51
II(3e)	51
II(4)	52
III(1a)	61
III(1b)	61
III(1c)	61
III(2)	61

III(3a)	63
III(3b)	64
III(3c)	64
III(3d)	64
V(1)	134
V(2)	136
V(2a)	136
V(3)	136
V(4)	136
V(5)	137
V(6)	139
V(7)	154
V(8)	154
VI(1)	171
VI(2)	171
VI(3)	183
VI(4)	183
VI(5)	184
VI(6)	187
VI(6a)	187
VI(7)	188
VI(8)	188
VI(9)	188
VI(10)	192
VI(10a)	192
VI(11)	192
VI(12)	192
VI(13)	192
VI(14)	193
VI(15)	193
VII(1)	200
VII(1a)	201
VII(2)	201
VII(3)	203
VII(4)	203
VII(5)	206
VII(6)	206

VII(7)   206
VII(8)   206
VII(9)   206
VII(10)   206
VII(11)   207
VII(12)   207
VII(13)   207

VIII(1)   214
VIII(2)   214
VIII(3)   215
VIII(4)   222
VIII(5)   223
VIII(6a)   223
VIII(6b)   223
VIII(7a)   224
VIII(7b)   224
VIII(8)   228
VIII(9)   228
VIII(10)   228
VIII(11)   229
VIII(12)   229
VIII(13)   229
VIII(14)   230
VIII(14a)   230
VIII(15)   230
VIII(16)   230
VIII(17)   235
VIII(18)   235
VIII(19)   237
VIII(19a)   237
VIII(20)   240

IX(1)   255
IX(2)   255
IX(3)   255
IX(4)   255
IX(5)   255
IX(6)   256
IX(7)   258
IX(8)   258
IX(9)   258
IX(10)   260
IX(11)   266
IX(12)   266
IX(13)   268
IX(14)   272
IX(15)   272

IX(16)   272
IX(17)   272
IX(18)   273

X(1)   283
X(1a)   283
X(2)   284
X(3)   384
X(4)   293
X(5)   294
X(6)   295
XI(1)   309
XI(2)   309
XI(3)   309

Tables

II.I   20
II.II   30
II.III   41
II.IIIa   43
II.IV   42
II.V   49
II.Va   50
II.VI   52

III.I   62
III.II   62
III.IIIa   71
III.IIIb   71
III.IV   72
III.V   78

IV.I   114
IV.II   115

V.I   138
V.II   140
V.III   140

VI.I   172
VI.II   175

VIII.I   217

XI.I   315
XI.II   325

NOTES

CHAPTER I

[1] Rules of this sort are not always (or hardly ever) consciously followed, nor are they normative or prescriptive in character. It is tempting to use 'laws' instead of 'rules' except that I want to avoid confusion with the common meaning of 'law' in a deterministic sense or any suggestion that the laws are laws of physics or reducible thereto. Rules of the logic of mind, as we shall see, are more like (in fact include) rules of grammar, and strictly speaking are simply recursive relations, as explained in Chapter II. *Among* them I later distinguish goal-directed or intentional rules, and the like, and *from* them habits and dispositions.

[2] That is to say, the theory is realistic in the epistemic sense that the rules the mind follows are independent of our thinking them to be such and such and in the ontological sense that they are formally distinguishable from the organic material, hardware, or other, that they inform.

[3] For instance, Burks (1972/73, p. 55) seems to feel that we can get along with the more restricted concept, which is that of a *deterministic* finite automaton.

[4] A detailed argument concerning the implications of Hilbert's programme and Gödel's incompleteness results for philosophy of mind has been presented in Webb (1980).

[5] I prefer 'naturalism' over 'physicalism' for although there is nothing not in space-time, physics is not the only science at bottom; psychology, for example is not fully reducible to physics, as I shall argue. If 'physicalism' means simply 'pertaining to what exists in space and time' then it is equivalent to 'naturalism' but lacks the color, the intimations of antisupernaturalism, and the stress on the bio-social.

[6] Quine (1966) eliminates the problematic entities only in the sense that he favors a canonical scheme that makes do with material states.

[7] For Peirce, cf. 5.103 for example. As I read Peirce, there is no essential distinction between mental occurrents (seconds) and other (physical) events since the material quality or firstness of an actual thing is of one category. There is no mind-body problem (mental vs physical firsts) for Peirce. Dewey contrasts mind as 'contextual and persistent' with perceptive consciousness as 'focal': "a series of flashes of varying intensities" (Dewey, 1925, p. 301). Ryle, whose concept of mind is marred by failure consistently to observe the distinction, on occasion marks it quite sharply: "motive words [for example, 'laziness'] . . . signify tendencies of propensities, and therefore cannot signify the occurrence of feelings" (Ryle, 1949, p. 85). Also see Nagel (1972, p. 223); J. C. C. Smart (1963, pp. 89 ff.); U. T. Place (1956); a similar distinction is Keith Gunderson's 'programmed receptive' and 'programmed-resistant' features of mentality (Gunderson, 1971, p. 73); finally, Field (1978, p. 9).

[8] Unless one takes impressions as coming under a controlling law. See Hume (1739, p. 73).

CHAPTER II

[1] I first heard this from Jan Mycelski and later obtained confirmation from my former colleage, the late Zdzislaw Kochanski. Kolmogoroff lectured on the topic in Moscow in 1956. I understand that notes in Polish and Russian exist but I have never been able to obtain copies.

[2] The idea of what is now called a 'Turing machine' first appeared in Turing (1936).

[3] Recall that this is not to say there is a decision procedure for identifying the theorems and nontheorems. One could generate proofs during a lifetime (any bounded time) and never hit one with a given designated formula as the last in a proof, even though it be a theorem.

[4] The set of recursive functions of nonnegative integers of one variable is defined roughly as follows: there are three *basis* functions $f(x) = x + 1$, $g(x) = x$ and $h(x) = 0$ which may be thought of as axioms; there are three schemes of combination, using the axioms as premises, that generate all of the recursive functions. A familiar schema is that of primitive recursion: $\phi(0) = k$; $\phi(x + 1) = \psi(x, (x))$, k a constant and ψ a given total function. The other two are functional composition and minimalization (see Nelson, 1968). Turing's Thesis was propounded in Turing (1936) and Church's in Church (1936), each in complete independence of the other.

[5] The distinction between free and embodied rules is observed only implicitly in the literature of logic (as it is so obvious), but unfortunately not at all in philosophy or cognitive science. Pylyshyn's notion (1984 p. 98) of evaluating versus emulating rules is not the same. Both of these are free rules in my sense. Pylyshyn unfortunately tends to identify FA as systems of embodied rules. But they can be described either way. See pp. 45–6, 68–9 below.

[6] Universal machines operate on the encodements of the machines they simulate. For an excellent history of the development of stored program digital computers see Herman Goldstein (1972). For the von Neumann contribution see especially pp. 253–270. Also see Arthur W. Burks (1978b).

[7] Actually his classic paper (Turing, 1936) on the decision problem dealt with computable real numbers.

[8] Post, who was virtually unknown except to a few logicians but at the time unsung by all, anticipated Gödel's incompleteness work by a decade; he was also more than anyone else the founder of modern recursive function theory (Post, 1944); he also formulated a concept of an idealized machine not unlike Turing's, but quite independently (Post, 1936).

[9] This remarkable statement occurs in an unpublished paper in 1941 which includes material he had presented in his doctoral dissertation 20 years earlier. The paper is "Absolutely Unsolvable Problems and Relatively Undecidable Propositions, Account of an Anticipation" printed in (Davis, 1965, p. 423).

[10] Chomsky has presented his ideas in numerous paper and books. In my opinion the best introduction to that part of his theories which is most closely related to logic appears in his (Chomsky, 1963).

[11] These are mnemonics for noun phrase (NP), verb phrase (VP), conjunctive (C), pronoun (Pr), Adjective (Adj), Adverb (Adv), Article (Art), Noun (N), and Verb (V).

[12] Incidentally, Shannon was one of the first to make a clear distinction between signal and energy inputs to a system. His theory of communication is concerned with idealized signals independent of other physical realizations; thus a careful history should ultimately

credit Shannon at least in part with the concept of signal and control systems which are formally distinct in any particular material embodiment.

[13] To aid the reader's understanding, we give a very simple example of a finite state grammar. The initial symbol is S, and the nonterminals are capital letters. Rewriting rules are those in the following list

$$S \rightarrow he\ V$$
$$S \rightarrow she\ V$$
$$V \rightarrow ran$$
$$V \rightarrow loves$$
$$V \rightarrow ran\ C$$
$$V \rightarrow loves\ D$$
$$C \rightarrow and\ S$$
$$D \rightarrow her.$$

[14] If $x(t) \equiv T$, then $\sim x(t) \equiv F$.

[15] As a *structural* characterization of real nerve networks in the brain the Pitts-McCulloch theory is not very adequate. Although axons do fire or not (T or F), inputs may *sum* temporally across synapses so that the lag time cannot be fixed for all cells; the threshold of cell-firing — roughly the potential level sufficient to cause firing — may change over time; memory states are not all represented by neuronal feedback; input summing may be a function of continuous, not discrete, signals; etc. Also this idealized model does not include the interaction with nonneuronal cells such as the glial cells which may play an important part in memory and anticipatory phenomena.

[16] John von Neumann, who made more extensive contributions to the development of automata both actual (digital computers) and abstract than anyone else, must be given joint credit. His main theoretical interests were in analogies between hardware and brains, problems of reliable automaton operation and in an abstract theory of automaton self-reproduction. The latter idea led to that of self-description, which is used in this book to analyze intentional mental attitudes. In his work of the time, however, he defined 'finite automaton' in a way that does not make explicit use of internal states, but only time delays, although his examples for discussion are strictly full automata in Kleene's sense. See "Probabilistic Logics and the Synthesis of Reliable Organisms from Unreliable Components" (von Neumann, 1951). The published paper is based on notes of the lecture series taken by R. S. Pierce in 1951 at the California Institute of Technology. Also see von Neumann (1966), esp. Arthur Burks' Introduction, and Part One.

[17] Nerve networks apparently do not have axons with such characteristics, although no one knows for certain. Inputs might well have levels of values as remarked in note 15. In this present generalization the numbers (e.g., 0, 1, 2, 3, etc.) designating values do not have ordinary arithmetic significance, but rather that of multiple-valued logics.

[18] This way of defining finite automata using outputs is not quite standard, but is equivalent to the usual formulation, and moreover leads naturally to the next part of the history of computer circuits.

[19] This was proved by Ranan Banerji and myself in 1960. We later found that we had been scooped by Y. Bar-Hillel and E. Shamir (1960).

[20] Languages such as English are by no means finite state, however, and it is extremely doubtful that human perceptual capabilities, linguistic or otherwise, can be accounted for by any theory at the level of even more complex grammars than the finite state

or their associated automata. However, all mechanism will need to argue for is that the logic of mind, including the logic of grammar, consists of recursive rules of some kind.

[21] The main contributors to the developments were D. A. Huffman (1954); G. H. Mealy (1955); and E. F. Moore (1956).

[22] The differences are quite subtle. A finite automaton in the sense just described can be thought of as computing simple functions or as transforming information using finite memory means only (i.e., the output strings may be entirely different entities than the inputs – technically they come from different 'alphabets'). An example is an electronic binary adder, whose input consists of *pairs* of bits, whose two internal states (the states of a 'flip-flop') represent a carry or not from one bit position to another, and whose output is the sum. By contrast, a recognizing automaton à la Kleene can be constructed which recognizes *triples* of strings of 0's and 1's such that the rightmost string of the triple is the binary sum of those on the left.

[23] Program schemes also lend themselves in principle to reduction to sets of production rules (Nelson, 1968, p. 82).

[24] It is of passing interest to note that Hebb's theories were among the first to be investigated by computer simulation. See (Rochester *et al.*, 1956). At one time I had the impression that E. C. Tolman's form of behaviorism entailed mechanism in the specific form that an organism is a finite automaton. He explicitly represents the behavior of an organism as depending on the environment, heredity, drives, etc. together with certain 'mental processes' or 'intervening variables', which have a character of 'intermediating function processes' (the last phrase is William James'). However on closer examination it turns out that these intervening entities are not autonomous (in roughly Hebb's meaning), but are all functions of stimuli and hence are essentially eliminable from psychological theory except for a kind of economizing of thought. Thus Tolman, in this respect, is a strict behaviorist, and had not caught the mechanist or functionalist idea of the internal state. See (Tolman, 1936). The issues involved will be discussed in considerable detail in a later chapter.

[25] I am indebted to Rick Herder for calling my attention to Craik's work.

[26] Recall that negative feedback systems are ones in which the performance is constantly measured in time against a desired value, and is then adjusted so as to keep the difference between the two as small as possible.

[27] It is rather easy to see that many automatic control systems including our opening illustration of the heating system can be described as finite automata in which, in addition to the transition and output functions, there is a function that maps output entities into inputs. A furnace, for example, is either on or off (two states) and the output of the signal-control system indirectly, by way of the operation of the furnace, generates the input signal which is the absolute value of the difference between the setting and the temperature in the room. See below, p. 16.

[28] I included grammars in the family of automata in Nelson (1968) for the same reason.

CHAPTER III

[1] As a matter of fact the very same question might be asked about computers, which it is widely claimed, are able to perform symbolic and mathematical operations that simulate our higher intellectual processes.

[2] This appears to be as good a place as any to introduce probabilistic automata, if only to familiarize the reader with something he is going to miss until Chapter XI. Some writers investigate the possibility that a human being is a *probabilistic automaton* (Block and Fodor, 1972). Such a system is an NFA to which is associated – or more precisely to the transition relation M of which is associated – a transition *probability* $P_{q,s}$ so that if $M(q, s) = \{q_{i_0}, q_{i_1}, \ldots, q_{i_m}\}$ (where $\{q_{i_0}, q_{i_1}, \ldots, q_{i_m}\}$ is the set of states the system can go to from (q, s)), then $P_{q,s}(q_{ij}) = r_j$ is a real number in the interval 0 to 1 and the sum of the r_j's is equal to 1, $j = 0, \ldots, m$. In less formal terms, such an automaton in a state q given input s goes to some one of a number of possible states with a fixed probability, just as a coin when tossed lands either heads or tails with a probability of 1/2 each. We do not use this concept for three reasons: (1) it's too complex for what we need; (2) a plain NFA does for most philosophical purposes; (3) at the present time it is very hard to make any sense at all out of the concept of probability that is required. The position of the logic of mind that men are NFA is of course true even if it turns out that they are probabilistic automata or fruitfully so studied; every probabilistic automaton is an NFA.

[3] From the formula in the text we first get (omitting P subscripts)

$$o_3 N(S, s_3 s_1) N(S, s_3 s_1 s_2) N(S, s_3 s_1 s_2 s_0).$$

Then by (1b) we get

$$o_3 N(M(S, s_3), s_1) N(S, s_3 s_1 s_2) N(S, s_3 s_1 s_2 s_0).$$

By the table (M part),

$$o_3 N(S, s_1) N(S, s_3 s_1 s_2) N(S, s_3 s_1 s_2 s_0).$$

Again by the table (N part)

$$o_3 o_3 N(S, s_3 s_1 s_2) N(S, s_3 s_1 s_2 s_0).$$

Again using (1b)

$$o_3 o_3 N(M(S, s_3 s_1), s_2) N(S, s_3 s_1 s_2 s_0).$$

By (1a)

$$M(S, s_3 s_1) = M(M(S, s_3), s_1) = M(S, s_1) \quad \text{[by the Table II] = S.}$$

So we have by the N part of the table, $N(S, s_2) = o_2$, whence,

$$o_3 o_3 o_2 N(S, s_3 s_1 s_2 s_0).$$

And by similar computations, finally,

$$o_3 o_3 o_2 o_0.$$

[4] Please note that in the Peter example there are such things as null stimuli and null

responses relative to the description of tables I and II. One might therefore interpret s_3 as absence of relevant input and o_3 likewise absence of relevant output. Hence a little thought shows that an input (either positive or not) might have positive output that appears at some time much later than input. For one can deliver input to a computer and get relevant output an hour or day or days later. This does not seem to be possible of representation in stimulus-response models (without introducing delays via chains of intervening variables) owing to lack of a genuine memory (state) space.

5 The isomorphism relation is of course secured simply by rewriting the Table II with primes. But for complex finite (or infinite) cases this cannot be done in practice and the equations (3) are needed to establish the relation.

6 Actually Peter's alarm-jab stimuli at different times all differ, so that properly speaking his stimulus s_0, say, is a *type* or *equivalence class*. In mathematical automata theory it is already conventional to consider symbols of alphabets, states, etcs., as designating their own types, and we do the same for interpretations of automata. Peter's and Paul's stimuli differ even more widely but correspond one-one in our new, more realistic model.

7 Thus we have not defined 'same structure' for networks; but it will suffice for all our purposes to identify net structure with that of the associated logical formula, although even a superficial comparison of Figures II.5 and III.1 reveals the differences clearly enough. The expression corresponding to the output of the delay element y_1 Figure 1 is

$$y_1(t + 1) \equiv ((x_1(t) \wedge x_2(t)) \vee (y_1(t) \wedge (x_1(t) \vee x_2(t))))$$

and the expression for the output z_1 is

$$z_1(t) \equiv [y_1(t) \wedge (\sim(x_1(t) \vee x_2(t)) \vee (x_1(t) \wedge x_2(t)))] \vee$$
$$[\sim y_1(t) \wedge \sim(x_1(t) \wedge x_2(t)) \wedge (x_1(t) \vee x_2(t))]$$

Comparison of these formulas with II.(3b) and II.(3c) respectively shows they are syntactically non-identical (their derivations via inductive definition are different), and this is sufficient to individuate net structures. Owing to certain trivial differences that we wish to exclude here the criterion has to be qualified in certain ways – e.g., formulas and the corresponding nets that differ only with respect to commutativity of *and* and *or* are ordinarily considered to be the same; but we may safely skip the refinements (cf. Burks and Wang, 1957a).

8 One family of automata (e.g., the full Turing machine) has greater capability than another (e.g., an FA) if its class of behaviors includes that of the other. Obviously there are incomparable behaviors, behaviors the same up to isomorphism, etc.

9 The same is perhaps true of other rules of mind. This is a question for future psychology. Arthur Burks speaks 'analogically' of man as an adaptive algorithm. "In interaction with his environment, a man's genetic program has guided the development of the specific programs . . . by which he processes the information he receives from the environment and by which he responds" (Burks, 1978).

10 If we were to conceive of a human being as a Turing machine (Nelson, 1969, p. 433 fn) and of her environment as her tape, then of course her memory would be practically boundless, and the only thing that would prevent her from being equivalent to a universal Turing machine would be her finite life span.

11 I leave it to the reader to discover whether there is any combined alarm clock-roommate strategy that can succeed in getting Peter out of bed.

[12] Subtraction is achieved in binary notation by adding the one's complement of the subtrahend to the minuend. Our combined circuit does not indicate an end-around-carry, which is also needed and which constitutes another net part.

[13] Recall (footnote 7) that nets are individuated by associated logical formulas; so a proper part of a network is essentially the same thing as a proper part of a truth functional formula, by its recursive construction (See Nelson, 1968, p. 242).

[14] Of course I do not mean to rule out *a priori* the possibility that memory is not seated in a nerve structure *qua* nerve net at all; it may be an intraneuronal, glial, or molecular phenomenon. On the other hand, a mechanistic explanation does not rule out the possibility that human memory is associative or holographic.

[15] Besides subroutines (like grammatical rules in an FA), feedback, and product systems, there are cascade and parallel systems (at the abstract automaton level), coding complexity (at that level), coding complexity (at the level of networks), complexity of programming and computation (in computer FA) that have been studied to some extent. Complexity is not well understood in any discrete state system in general and less so in the mind.

[16] The early Carnap is expressed in (Carnap, 1936), the later in Carnap, (1956b).

[17] I do not reject the analytic-synthetic distinction *in toto* but only its use to separate off mathematics from material science.

[18] I borrow 'realize' with variations from semantical theory. When I write of an interpretation of an automaton I mean of course interpretation of an automaton theory of mind or mental features formalized in some appropriate language. The variations are two: (1) all interpretation maps are one-one from constants and relations to the domain; (2) the true interpretation *is* the realization, whereas in model theory given a collection of formulas F in a language and D an interpretation, "D realizes F" is approximately synonymous with "F is satisfiable in D" (cf. Chang and Keisler, 1973, p. 74). Thus for my purposes the FA table (c) of Figure 3 below does not realize (a) because there is no onto map from (a) to (c). Intuitively, the M and N functions of (b) and (c) compute differently, even though there is an onto homomorphism from (c) to (b). Of course the differences between (b) and (c) in terms of *guiding* are quite trivial. In the instance of non-FA rules (like phrase structure or perhaps transformational rules) the differences between the rule structures of two equivalent grammars can be radical. Figure 3 and the attending discussion is only meant to illustrate a principle.

[19] I borrow the felicitous expressions 'guide' and 'fit' from Quine (1972, pp. 442–54). Whether Quine thinks of rules as I do or as dispositions is a question for discussion in Chapter V. The idea of effective rules that tacitly guide speakers of a language is Chomsky's and pervades all of his thought. An old but clear statement of guiding (or as he calls it, 'knowing') is in Chomsky (1965, p. 8). Michael Root (1975) argues that behavior-guiding rules are in general rules involving 'nesting' and 'hierarchies' in ways analogous to phrase structure rules in linguistic behavior. I agree with him. His rules are, so far as I can tell, just our recursive rules.

[20] The nature of explanation in a mechanistically oriented psychology is taken up in Chapter XI, while a precise characterization of 'description' follows here a few paragraphs on.

[21] (ii) and (iii) together assume a generalized form of CT as follows: (ii) effective structures are those whose behaviors are effective, and thus are systems of recursive rules in the generalized interpretation of Section II.6; (iii) says these systems are

equivalent to some automaton T, which might be any machine up to a full Turing machine. As explained in the text, $\mathcal{S}$ itself is an NFA.

[22] 'Represents' thus is a relation between the strictly automaton parts of a theory and the recursive rules embodied in $\mathcal{S}$. The expression 'represents' in 'mental representations,' of which more later, is something else. The issue concerns, among other things whether beliefs or other propositional attitudes involve representations of what is believed. See below, Section VIII.4.

[23] Professor Estes finds many differences including time (human) versus space (computer) orientation; graded versus all-or-none retention; low versus high transfer rates; dependence on experience versus total interdependence; dependence on context versus independence (Estes, 1980).

[24] As elsewhere in science and philosophy my use of 'model' inverts that of mathematical logic. There a model is a true interpretation of a formal language; here a model is a set of sentences which are not true but 'approximate' in some sense which I suppose could be made clear, and are used 'heuristically'. Actually, on an informal level, the two concepts collapse into one. I could just as well have said that a model is a surrogate or analogue of the subject of study, a feature of the mind, and then set out to examine that domain. The idea of a model here includes that of formulas in a way reminiscent of Mary Hesse's treatment of models in physics, with the exception, I take it, that her conception of model is one of *true* formulas (Hesse, 1953). The extent to which models are predictive will be approached in Chapter XI.

[25] Fodor (1966) does not specifically use machine models, however. Also see his more thoroughing development of the Phase I, Phase II distinction in Fodor (1968).

[26] This formal system goes back to Thoralf Skolem (1923). Recursive arithmetic was first explicitly used for logic nets by Arthur W. Burks and Jesse B. Wright in (Burks and Wright, 1955).

[27] Although I frequently have referred to physical geometry as a kind of 'model' for the conception of the science of mind including interpreted formalisms, realistic conclusions similar to mine do not apply to physics. Physics is perhaps empirically real, but the guiding-fitting distinction can be secured, so far as I can see, only if expressibility in the strong sense of recursive processes can be plausibly argued. If this is right the classical form-matter distinction which I think shows up in mental philosophy does not apply, at least on similar grounds, to physical science.

[28] Classical realism in this empirical version is related somewhat to Putnam's internal realism, although he is pushing a theory of knowledge – realism explains how language users succeed – while I'm after real rules of the mind. In both the real is relative to a theory formulated in a language. However his 'real' is nearly my 'true', (p. 80 above), while my 'strongly real' and 'weakly real' (which is meant to capture the classical anti-nominalist not just the epistemological concept) has no counterpart in his theory (Putnam, 1976, 1977).

CHAPTER IV

[1] A philosophical acquaintance of mine once advanced the following argument against mechanism: Men could not possibly be machines, because if you were to cut open a human skull you wouldn't find a computer in it. He meant by 'computer' 'electronic calculating device,' and he was serious.

[2] Turing felt that there was nothing in principle to prevent building a robot that would like strawberries, be conscious, etc. I prefer to remain neutral on such an issue here because even if one could not construct such a thing that fact would cut no ice against mechanism. If asked, however, I should say that machines[2] are not conscious because they are not alive (I am unimpressed by the kind of argument which purports to show life by way of such analogies as electricity to food, energy expenditure to metabolism, etc.). Cf. Michael Scriven (1964). For an opposite view see Scriven (1960). In the last chapter I consider relationships among our concepts of life, consciousness and mental occurrents as already roughly sketched in the Introduction.

[3] As I understand Smart physicalism is the doctrine that the only true science is physics and that biology, psychology, etc. are 'empirical generalizations' lacking any underlying theory, i.e., body of laws, except physics and chemistry applied to natural history. This is a version of physicalism which says essentially that all scientific terms (for Smart 'theoretical' terms) are *terms of physics*. Physicalism in a broader sense is the position that everything science studies is in space-time, which of course does not imply any kind of reducibility of a discipline to physics. This general position is what I prefer to call 'naturalism.'

[4] This kind of functionalist solution to the mind-body problem is considered and rejected in Chapter XI below.

[5] We will refine the example in Section 5 and in V.2.

[6] See Burks (1972/73, pp. 39–57). More precisely, the response and stimulus sets are families of equivalence classes of events or, alternatively, event-types.

This concept of natural function with its terminology of 'response' and 'stimulus' may suggest to some a view in which the organism is a box having inputs and outputs. For some reason, unclear to me, there are philosophers who find this repugnant, thinking perhaps that such 'models' also used by engineers, degrade, oversimplify, mechanize, etc. the organism. But in reality all that is at stake is whether we believe it to be possible to have any empirical science about animal behavior at all. If we do, then the name of the game is discovering laws describing that behavior. *Some* of these laws correlate events which have impact or influence on the organism, ranging from pin pricks and light beams to chess situations and phonemic sequences generated by poem readers, to animal reactions, some overt, some not. When a law-like or strong statistical correlation has been found, it is convenient to have at hand terms such as 'stimulus' and 'response' or 'input' and 'output.' This does not presuppose that every overt act (speech acts, for example) has a correlative outer stimulus nor that every external impact has an overt response.

[7] Cf. Turing's comment (1936, p. 250): "If we admitted an infinity of states of mind [of the human computer], some of them will be 'arbitrarily' close and will be confused."

[8] Note that I say 'physical', not 'physicalist'. We are using scientific data in support of the discreteness hypothesis, plus some speculation; but this does not imply a commitment to strict physicalism but only to naturalism.

[9] My former colleague, Lewis Creary, once suggested to me that a view that cognitive processes are *not* effective, i.e., decomposable into computation-like sub-processes may not even be empirically meaningful. This would appear to be almost immediately evident in the case of speech and speech understanding.

[10] I choose these examples of programming languages because they are used so prevalently in artificial intelligence. An understandable introduction is given in (Winograd, 1972, pp. 76 ff., also see Boden, 1977).

11 Dennett does not draw this conclusion.

12 This is the heart of J. R. Lucas' (1961) form of the argument from the incompleteness theorem.

13 " – although it is established that there are limitations to the powers of any particular machine, it has only been stated, without any sort of proof that no such limitations apply to the human intellect" (Turing, 1950, p. 16). An excellent critical discussion of attempts to use incompleteness results against mechanism is presented by Charles S. Chihara (1972). Also see my (1987a) for a detailed refutation of Lucas.

14 Lady Lovelace (Augusta Ada Byron, daughter of Lord Byron) was a friend of Charles Babbage and an expositer of his work. See Herman H. Goldstein (1972, pp. 25–26).

15 A heuristic procedure can be partially characterized as one which is directed toward the solution of a problem and which is nonalgorithmic. Many philosophers and practitioners of artificial intelligence believe that all such procedures boil down to generate-and-test routines. A generator (a part of a program, perhaps) spawns possible solutions or parts of solutions of problems, either at random or by a subroutine with pseudo-random elements, and the testor selects those of the generated set according to given criteria, which may have been learned, and are themselves subject to revision.

16 A practical algorithm is an algorithm that can produce a result in a time and at a cost that a user is willing to tolerate. If chess is a finite game (by the usual rules it is), a nonpractical algorithm exists that tries all possible moves.

17 My allusion is to the hall (where according to Maestro Kondrashin one always gets two concerts for the price of one), not to the listeners.

18 A considerable amount of work has been done on the computer formation of hypotheses (see, for example, Hajek, Havranek, 1978).

19 Mr. Robert W. Nealy, a former Connecticut checkers champion, quoted in Appendix D in Samuel's paper cited in the text. This is printed in (Feigenbaum and Feldman, 1963, p. 104).

20 MACHACK, developed by R. D. Greenblatt, is good enough to attract Bobby Fischer's interest as reported in *New York Times*, Sunday, July 30, 1978. For the really curious expert, see (R. D. Greenblatt *et al.*, 1967). I understand that of this writing (1980) still more powerful programs are coming on the chess scene. A very fine introduction to the whole field of game-playing programs and more generally to artificial intelligence and heuristic programming methods is Margaret Boden's (1977).

21 See (Lee, 1963). This result is a fairly direct corollary of the recursion theorem proved by Kleene in 1938.

22 In general however computers or Turing machines cannot determine whether an alleged program for a given problem is indeed such a program. This phenomenon is directly related to the Gödel incompleteness results for arithmetical logics.

23 This statement appears to contradict the putative fact that we can learn by introspection. However there is growing experimental evidence that we are more aware of the products of cognitive processes than of the processes themselves. What you see is the 'end result' of an extremely complicated neurophysiological process of which you are entirely unaware.

24 In other words Tolman's idea of behavior cannot be taken as evidence against a theory of machines₁.

25 An alternative would be to explain actions, intentions, and other features appearing in behavior by *imputations*. The suggestion here is to extend Melden's treatment of actions to all mental features. We observe a human being within the context of practices in which "rules are obeyed, criteria employed, policies observed. . . . " (Melden, 1956, p. 43). In these contexts we observe *actions*, where otherwise we would observe only bodily movements in a physical causal nexus. If 'action' does not include other mental features supposedly manifest in behavior, let us so extend its designation. This yields a behavioral type theory of features.

This strategy does not get around the objection registered above because our perfect robot could operate in sufficiently rich contexts to invite imputation of mental features. Besides this treatment will not apply to non-social animals to which we would still attribute purposes. Our theory should have a continuity parallel to that of the natural world.

26 The implicit criticism here of a philosophical method that does not allow for a suitable analysis (whatever that turns out to mean) is not meant to be extended to psychologists such as Tolman. He could always properly claim that his doctrine of the emergent properties of molar behavior holds for psychology, leaving the possibility of analysis open to the physiologist. I do not think, however, that this tolerant attitude is possible for a consistent Wittgensteinian or Rylean behaviorist.

27 The sense in which this constitutes a theoretical explanation will be considered at some length in a later chapter. One of the conclusions we shall draw is that possession of an explanation in the form of a complete table − assuming that is possible − that guides an organism's behavior is not, in general, enough to *predict* that behavior even for strictly deterministic organisms.

28 Checking through the table: If the ancestor is in q_0 with input s_4 she goes to state q_1; and then if there is input s_1 she wriggles, by the output part of the table.

29 I suspect that annelida are too simple for this kind of complexity to occur. But I hope the example still serves to make the point.

CHAPTER V

1 Throughout this discussion I will assume that not only the human organism as a whole but its parts as well are NFA, contrary to the weaker hypothesis developed in Chapter III. For the most part FA's will be used here as models − to render certain expressions such as 'state', 'same state', 'disposition', and the like precise enough to formulate meaningful philosophical discussion.

2 Grice, in his own theory, goes on to argue that beliefs, etc. are implicitly defined by some set of laws. The computationalist view I am criticizing makes them explicitly automaton-type laws (rules). Also see (Dennett, 1978, pp. 3−22).

3 This paragraph is adapted from Nelson (1976a, pp. 368−369).

4 In all fairness I must say that neither Fodor nor Putnam seem to hold quite these views any longer. Indeed, for Fodor having propositional attitudes such as belief is contingently identical to being in a computational relation to a certain formula. See Fodor (1975, p. 77). This does *not* identify belief with a state and hence does not necessarily restrict definition to the implicit. Similarly, in later papers (e.g., Putnam, 1970, p. 244) Putnam takes a functional state to be a (property of being) a finite automaton, which is a far cry from being just an automaton state. In his (Putnam, 1973b, p. 298) Putnam argues that his earlier espousal of mechanism in the form that (1) a man is a Turing

machine and (2) psychological states are machine states was essentially wrong. I think he is *now* wrong on (1) and right on (2). Psychological states are not machine states, as I myself am about to argue. Part of the trouble in the earlier identification was·inevitable: trying to account for an extremely slippery idea in terms of a precise one, here the idea of a psychological state in terms of the mathematical idea of a state space. Nevertheless functionalism is consistently identified, and perhaps rightly so, as ascribing intentionality to functional systems and as not providing for explicit definitions of intentional terms (Margolis, 1980, p. 244 *passim*).

[5] A type is a universal. We want to say that two materially different things might be of the same type, which is motivated by (a) above. Then they would be instances or tokens of the same type even if they were to have no material, singulary properties in common.

[6] This definition assumes realism or what Block and Fodor, following Putnam, call a 'best description' (Block and Fodor, 1972, p. 170).

[7] An 'automorphism' is an isomorphism of an automaton with itself; i.e., the 1−1 mapping is from the set of states Q back onto Q.

[8] Of course for inputs or outputs to be the same they must still relate to other inputs, outputs and states the same according to some standard or other like (i)−(iii) above. Cf. Quine's handling of essentially the same problem in his (Quine, 1969a, p. 157).

[9] If an organism could be in but one state at a time, then the interanimation of attitudes like belief and desire in Grice's implicit characterization would not be possible either.

[10] Block and Fodor remark that complex (parallel) automata are equivalent to single automata (i.e., take $(R_0, 8, S)$, lump it or decode it into one abstract symbol, say q, and do likewise with inputs and outputs, if they are n-tuples of some sort); but that the two can't both have *best descriptions*, i.e., be *real* (see footnote 6 and reference there). But who says such a single automaton has to be constructed? To preserve the one-state-at-a-time idea? I think the idea of one state *relative* to a taken whole is simpler; and there is only one best description of the whole including the parts. If that is not the way the organism is arranged, then the theory is not real.

[11] Parallel adders have been around for a long time. I myself have a discovered an n-input sorting network that sorts n items (such as payroll records) by comparing n bytes *at once*, and if each item is m bytes in length sorts in m bit times − these days in about m nanoseconds. This is truly parallel. Also see above, p. 98 f.

[12] There is a literature going back at least as far as 1968. See (Gilmore, 1968).

[13] Hoy (1979) points out that one can have a disposition for a short time and then lose it. However 'event' may be analyzed, it still seems to me that a short term type disposition could be exercised or not and that exercising is an event.

[14] The place-holder idea says that dispositions are really specific structures underlying behavior and that disposition terms like 'belief', 'want', 'perceive', etc. are kinds of conceptual crutches we use in theoretical science until such time as we are able to grasp the anatomy of those structures (cf. Levi and Morgenbesser, 1964, pp. 1−12; also Quine, 1973, pp. 12 ff.).

[15] The basis or *ground* of a disposition in Tuomela's sense (Tuomela, 1976, p. 458) is an automaton in my theory. For Armstrong (1972) the bases of dispositions are states; I think that what Armstrong means by 'state' is some kind of a structure rather than a formal automaton state.

[16] The distinction between mathematical and historical is exactly that between abstract descriptions of a system of axioms or rules, and real-time proofs or computations applying the axioms or rules.

17 "If Jones were to see Steve, her toes would curl, etc." means Jones has an automaton of a certain description in her.

18 Chomsky's devastating attack (Chomsky, 1959a) should be required reading for psychology students even today. My own article (Nelson, 1969) is an attack from the point of view of mechanism. Chomsky's is directed specifically against behaviorist theories of language while mine is directed at behaviorism as a general methodology in psychology. For a comprehensive review see Zuriff (1985).

19 The concept of central state in D. M. Armstrong's philosophy is "the concept of that, whatever it may turn out to be, which is brought about in man by certain stimuli and which in turn brings about certain responses" (Armstrong, 1968, p. 79). This makes out a mental state to be an intervening variable. However in a later passage he says that this mediator is in fact a central nervous system, which I guess puts Armstrong closer to my version of mechanism or at any rate to some version of functionalism.

20 If Rylean dispositions (p. 7–8 above) are understood to entail (5) – see (Nelson, 1988c) – our ensuing argument applies: there are automaton states that are not Rylean dispositions.

21 For a discussion of the relation of semantics to the question of tacit knowledge see Nelson (1978, pp. 337–381). Hilary Putnam has expressed skepticism towards semantics in a fairly extreme but in the end just way. " . . . it [current semantics] does not concern the meaning of words . . . the dimension of language associated with the word 'meaning' is, in spite of the usual spate of heroic if misguided attempts, as much in the dark as it ever was" (Putnam, 1975, p. 131).

22 The concept of *competence* corresponds roughly to De Saussure's *langue, performance* corresponds to *parole*. See Nelson (1978, pp. 339–343).

23 Consider the following two sentences.

(A)   The book the man the dog the girl loves bit bought is on his lap.
(B)   The book the man bought is on his lap.

(A), though grammatical, is hard to understand and probably would not be spoken by anyone outside of a classroom, while this is not so for (B). The reason is that (A) takes more short-term memory to keep straight than (B) does: the nesting of sentences within sentences has more levels. In this case both exemplify the competence of the speaker of English, but only (B), for reasons indicated, his performance. The reader is no doubt able to make up examples of other types of departure of performance from competence mentioned in the text. See Chomsky (1965, p. 4 ff.).

24 See for example (Terrace, 1979, pp. 891–900). Terrace himself, who has done extensive experimental work with chimpanzes, reluctantly concludes that apes cannot create sentences. "Apes can learn many isolated symbols (as can dogs, horses, and other non-human species), but they show no unequivocal evidence of mastering the conversational, semantic, or syntactic organization of language." An excellent survey of the status of the evidence for true linguistic behavior in apes is in (Savage-Rumbaugh *et al.*, 1980, pp. 49–61).

25 The Introduction from which this is cited was written in 1973.

26 A good introduction to the field of psychology of language is (Fodor *et al.*, 1974).

27 There are more if we include the semantical rules and other nonlinguistic cognitive phenomena. But my contention is that too little is known of the semantical to support blanket arguments one way or the other.

28 The pioneering work on a mathematical theory of self reproduction was initiated

by John von Neumann (see von Neumann, 1966). The theory of self-describing automata, which rests on the same mathematical principles as that of self-reproduction, is due to C. Y. Lee (1963).

[29] A sublanguage of a language might place higher in Chomsky's hierarchy than the language itself, just as recursive sets in logic can have non-recursive subsets. For example, the *theorems of the propositional calculus* under one of the appropriate axiomatizations is *context sensitive*, while the language as a whole is context-free.

[30] The suggestion is Fodor's (1984, p. 5). His interpretation follows below.

[31] This is by way of contrast with notions of information in philosophy of mind and epistemology that view it as a species of causal correlation (Cf. Dretske, 1981). Drawing out the explicit entailment of *content* by *display* is my gloss on Fodor; but I have no idea what else he could mean.

[32] The computer-semantics connection is closer than is intimated in the last paragraph. Zenon Pylyshyn (1984), a cognitivist who writes in very much the same spirit as Fodor (1981), claims the very idea of a computation entails semantics commitments. Addition, for instance, which is a Turing computable function, is a relation on natural numbers; not on formal Turing symbols, but on semantically interpreted symbols. A digital computer, strictly speaking, does not do arithmetic but merely pushes meaningless physical objects around. It does arithmetic only as interpreted by us.

Note that on this view, doing arithmetic is on all fours with believing something or other. Both are computable relations to semantically interpreted symbols, numerals (which in thought are surely MR's) in the one case and sentences in Mentalese in the other.

If I get this right, Pylyshyn would not accept the idea of a neutral language of recursive functions used in the arguments for mechanism in Chapter IV. Despite my disclaimers there, the computer-mind analogies presuppose meaningful function operands. One answer (there's more to come) is that we third-person theorists tacitly ascribe content to arithmetical operations of both machines and men, so the analogies are firm. (Cf. Dennett, 1978).

Whether or not and whence semantical ascriptions or predications can be made, the notion that there is no such thing as syntactical computation is a mistake. See Davis (1958, Chap. I) and Nelson (1987a, 1987b). Of course mechanism as I am characterizing it depends on the idea of syntactical computations. (See above, p. 58).

[33] This work came to my attention too late for me to pretend to understand it very well. I will allude only to the direct, dyadic notion of cause he employs and to his express statements about the interrelationships of causal semantics as he sees it and the theory of intentionality. I don't see how to square the causal theory with everything Fodor says in earlier essays (1981, pp. 257–316), or in particular, to nativism. In an earlier discussion of mine (1988c, in press) I attributed the latter views to him as an example of rationalism.

[34] The stress on 'input' is no quibble. MR's for Fodor are always like Lockean ideas or Humean impressions. The primitive ones are foundational, the originals of all cognition; they are not *products* of cognition. Likewise *interpreted* inputs are the arguments of computable functions, as I have stressed about RTM many times over.

[35] I believe this puts the logic of mind in the same circle of ideas as Brian Loar's *Mind and Meaning* (1986) as regards the relationships between theories of intentionality and semantics.

CHAPTER VI

1 See above Section I.3, and the references there to Quine. H. H. Price (1932, p. 2) puts the typical empiricist position that I reject as follows. How do we justify perceptual belief? The physiologist might in part answer by pointing out that when a man sees something, e.g., a tomato, "light rays emanating from the object impinge upon his retina and this stimulates the optic nerve, which in turn causes a change in the optic centers in his brain. . . . " But all the psychologist has done is "to put forward certain other beliefs concerning a retina and a brain. Those other beliefs have themselves to be justified in exactly the same way as the first [perceptual] belief, and we are as far as ever from knowing what way that is. Instead of answering our question we have found another instance of it."

2 It is well to be careful about one's usage of 'stimulus'. According to some authorities a stimulus is an "object that elicits an action" or in "(physiology) any outer or inner factors that cause the organism to act" (Wolman, 1973, p. 35). I reject the reading 'object' because I shall later want to make some epistemically relevant observations on the basis of the theory — namely, organisms have beliefs or disbeliefs about objects, not stimulus patterns; and perceived objects, whatever they are, are not 'inner factors'. So 'stimulus' refers to a result of reception as now to be discussed.

3 I'm not suggesting that the constitution of stimuli can not be understood as a kind of computation, although it might be. The justification for skipping quickly over reception and stimulus constitution is that it contains no *intentional* elements, and our interest is mainly in the properly *mental* (cf. Dretske, 1969). See especially his chapter on Non-Epistemic Seeing, where he gives a number of interesting arguments for what is essentially the same distinction. His approach, however, is entirely different depending essentially on folk intuitions and linguistic analysis.

According to Pylyshyn the contemporary study of visual processing confirms this very distinction between the receptual and the perceptual.

I would argue that from a computational point of view it is appropriate to treat this early semi-autonomous phase of vision as a special purpose transducer, which takes physical magnitudes as inputs and produces symbol structures as outputs. Regardless of the precise details of this phase . . . there is reason to believe that: (a) there is a semi-autonomous, pre-attentive phase in visual perception, (b) this phase is initiated by energy arriving at the sense organs, (c) only the output of this phase, and not intermediate steps, are available for further perceptual analysis, and (d) such processes as "noticing" and the assimilation of sensory patterns into cognitive structures take place after this phase (Pylyshyn, 1978, p. 21).

4 For a lively and readable account of reception of frogs and cats see (Arbib, 1972, pp. 39–54).

5 Selfridge and Neisser's discussion of preprocessing is especially revealing as it shows by contrast with computers the remarkable capabilities it takes for a human being just to read Morse Code (Selfridge and Neisser, 1963, pp. 238 ff.).

6 The enquiring psychologist's puzzle about when the subject's responses (or, as a matter of fact, stimuli) like 'damn' vs 'darn' counts as the *same* does not arise in the same way for the subject itself. The organism's discriminations, we are saying, are there; they are built in. His nervous system decides for him.

[7] A detailed neural network model of perception using automata-theoretic ideas applied to D. O. Hebb's (see Section II.6) cell assembly theory has been constructed in (Whitehead, 1978).

[8] Following Ryle and after him Kenneth M. Sayre, perception is a completed act or attainment (Sayre, 1965, pp. 29–31).

[9] This engaging piece is the creation of the rather cloudy figure Luis D'Antin van Rooten (van Rooten, 1967).

[10] This scheme is used in Nilsson (1965).

[11] The notion of many functional structures collapsed to one by, in effect, biasing initial and final state parameters might be an alternative to population selection theories of how the brain gets organized. (Edelman, 1987, see Note VIII.21).

[12] Every mathematics student knows there are usually several distinct algorithms for computing function values. So why not choose 'same algorithm' for 'compute in the same way' instead of 'same function'? But this proposal misses the leading idea; what is wanted and what we got is identification of *same type* with *same response*, even though the response be virtual.

[13] Postulating qualitatively different sets involves no gratuitous dependence on the concept *same property*, a direct analysis of which we have eschewed. Here A and A' are made up of qualitatively different elements if people generally regard them as different (Bach in C vs Bach in E). The concept is a given, not the analysandum in the question.

[14] Let f be a partial function of nonnegative integers A to nonnegative integers B, which is computed by T_k. This implies that there are codings $\theta: A \to \mathcal{U}_T$ and $\psi: \mathcal{R} \to B$ such that

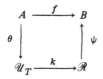

commutes. From this diagram we have that $f = \psi k \theta$ and since from (5) $\phi'k = k'\phi$ and ϕ' is bijective, $k = \phi'^{-1}k'\phi$, whence $f = \psi\phi'^{-1}k'\phi\theta$. It is easy to show that $\psi\phi'^{-1}$ and $\phi\theta$ are codings, and hence k' represents f and $T_{k'}$ computes the same function. So T' hears $\mathcal{K}$ in a different key, $\mathcal{K}'$.

[15] For a discussion of acceptance of sentences see (Fodor *et al.*, 1974, Chapter 6) and also (Nelson, 1968, Section 8.3).

[16] Thus I am assuming throughout that all FSA are *quasi-connected*: for every final state q of any FSA there is a string x such that $M(q_0, x) = q$.

[17] See Note II.16. See also (Thatcher, 1963). These works were suggested by von Neumann's ideas on self-reproducing automata which have been edited by Arthur Burks in (von Neumann, 1966). The idea of self-coding, which has the partial history indicated, ultimately derives from the work of Gödel who introduced the formal concept of languages that express syntactical facts about themselves in his epoch-making work on incompleteness of arithmetic (Gödel, 1931). The idea of using self-coding in recognition of vague objects was introduced in my (Nelson, 1971). The take relation, K, introduced below, was so labelled when I saw the similarity to Chisholm's concept of taking in his theory of perception (Chisholm, 1957, p. 56 passim). The overall approach to expecta-

tion is from my attempt to show that machines can have expectations (Nelson, 1975b).
[18] The idea of a random selection does not imply that our system is nondeterministic, but only that it computes random numbers or has access to a random number table. This assumption is avoided by a somewhat involved device discussed in Nelson (1976b, p. 44).
[19] Edelman (1987) would put it, from his standpoint as a neurobiologist, that the perceptual world is not prelabelled. However absence of labelling is no bar to a mechanist theory of perception, contrary to what he argues, so far as I can see.
[20] There is a trivial way of refuting Dreyfus' claim, that appeals to finiteness. According to him, one recognizes similarities by use of paradigm cases: if one is given x and has to decide whether it is in family F, since the members have no 'exactly similar traits' in common, one proceeds on the basis of *resemblances* of x with known items of F. This is done by comparing x with a paradigm, perhaps via intermediate cases; there might be, in other words, a kind of chain of comparisons leading, in favorable cases, to a chain of resemblances sufficiently strong to entitle one to say x is in F. Now I maintain on neurological grounds that there can be only a finite number of paradigms to be compared with. Further, if there were unbounded chains, there would be necessarily an unbounded number of comparisons called for, which is obviously impossible as comparisons of intermediate cases with ideals are discrete cognitive acts. Therefore, all chains are bounded whence F is finite. But every finite set is accepted by some Turing acceptor.
[21] Goodman would disagree. His 'resemblance' is symmetrical; and what I call 're-semblance' is closer to his 'representation.' But I want 'represents' later for a relation between stimulus and perceptual object. Actually his 'representation' for my 'resem-blance' is not right either since the former, on his reckoning, has denotation at its core (Goodman, 1968, p. 4, 5).

CHAPTER VII

[1] This is essentially Chisholm's 'perceive x' in the meaning that x appears in some way (Chisholm, 1957, p. 115, 149).
[2] Taking need not be construed as yielding a y from x in $K(x, y, t)$ from some t in the sense of T' overprinting y for x in the computation. The theory can be rigged so that if a symbol b of x is degraded T goes to a winning state without symbol replacement. See pp. 190–191. This might actually be closer to what humans do. Christopher Hill has pointed out that in many cases one does not literally replace phenomenal experiences in taking. One hears a flatted E and takes it to be true in a play of a piece without hearing it as true. It seems to me that in other cases there is some sort of rectification.
[3] We are still using τ vaguely and ambiguously as a property of the real object x as well as of the type of strings accepted by T.
[4] I.e., schematically, 'x fulfills' implies 'x fulfills if and only if x occurs or x does not occur and x is taken to occur'; and 'x disrupts' implies 'x disrupts if and only if x does not occur or x occurs and x is not taken to occur'. Then use VI(13) to obtain (2).
[5] This is not an out-and-out contradiction any more than intransitive preference order-ings are. On the other hand, if there are no simon pure stimuli, then all acceptance involves taking; but then there is no issue, for we know there will be occurrences now and then of incompatible fulfillments.
[6] Despite the emphasis I wish to place on the *plausibility* rather than on the hopelessly premature completion of a logic of mind, the question of the origins of mental capabil-

ities does continue to surface. The obvious suggestion from evolutionism is that realized accepting automata are the result of natural selection in part, and in part the product of perceptual learning. I have no ideas whatever about where the phyllogenetic contribution ends and the ontogenetic begins. A theory of acquisition of perceptual dispositions clearly belongs to psychology and neuroscience.

[7] There is an automaton that is the union of paradigmatic families, all elements of which are degraded (see above, pp. 196 f.).

[8] For example Wallace Matson says in his book (Matson, 1976, p. 78) that man is not a machine; then later, on pp. 120–121, that he "must be a mechanism", unless we were "to sink back into a morass of mystification". Part of the trouble here may stem from his thinking that digital computers *qua* digital machines contain servos, and that 'discrete state' means 'jerky transitions'. They don't; and the definiteness of pulses (bit representations) is achieved by clocking and gating in electronic digital machines. A perfectly discrete square wave is a fiction.

[9] Some professional psychologists without necessarily opposing the mechanist hypothesis are tending to drop the atomistic hypothesis, namely, that perception requires atomic elements, which is "formally similar to the decompositional approach of transformational grammar" (Kolers and Perkins, 1975, p. 229).

[10] Condition IV – which calls for taking of degraded, illformed items – has been successfully simulated on a Univac 1108 using my T' and relation K construction by my former students Steven Epstein and Paul Schack.

[11] At the very moment of this writing (1982) I have been told that a large U.S. computer manufacturer has designed a working recognizer that 'listens' to ordinary speech and correctly prints what it has heard. I trust that in 1988, what with the widespread sophistication about the principles and uses of computers, no philosopher will feel moved to say that Edison did it a century ago.

CHAPTER VIII

[1] To the Freudian any human belief is expressible, presumably, but you might require the services of a psychoanalyst to get it all out into the conscious and expressed.

[2] There is an ambiguity in 'believes that x is τ at t'. To see it consider 'Jones believes her maple was green last summer on November 10th'. This means the same as 'Jones believes on November 10th that her maple tree was green last summer'. The dependent clause means 'her maple tree was green last summer' is true, not 'her maple tree was green' was true last summer. 'Her maple tree, etc. . . . ' is not a perceptual sentence, and for this reason one must be explicit in applying 'November 10th to Jones' belief and 'last summer' to green-maple-tree. But in the case of perceptual sentences and belief we may write simply 'believes that x is τ at t', as the ambiguity is self-resolving in perception. But to play safe, one might write 'believes at t that x is τ'.

[3] Historically the doctrine that knowledge is true opinion goes back to Plato, especially *Theatetus* 201–202.

[4] The example is Gettier's updated and adjusted for inflation and the pressures of the women's movement.

[5] I owe this example to my wife, Hendrieka.

[6] The following passages are based on my (Nelson, 1978, pp. 122 ff).

[7] It is at this point that the theory diverges from a straight evolutionist account of perception. We did argue above that evolutionism would cull out wild takes; but this

is not a sufficient ground for a theory of evidence. It is just possible that it would be a sufficient ground for organisms all of whose stimuli fall into 'well-defined' receptual classes. See also Fred Dretske's discussion of this point in his (Dretske, 1971).

[8] In VIII(14 and 15) we'll see that acts do depend on beliefs but that more than one act could depend on the same belief. Variation stems from differing belief states and what is desired. Christopher Peacock thinks denial of the necessity of a belief producing a distinguished act is a mark of *holism* (Peacock, 1979). So that makes my theory holistic. Of course I think there's more to it than that.

[9] In *Word and Object* intentional talk, which Quine agrees with Brentano is self-contained, is to be dropped from the 'canonical scheme' of scientific vocabulary altogether when "limning the true and ultimate structure of reality" (Quine, 1960, p. 221).

[10] We have already mentioned some functionalists: Block, Fodor, Grice, and Putnam among many others. The relationists relate persons to either sentences or propositions. For the sentence version see (Scheffler, 1963); Scheffler's view goes back to a suggestion of Quine's in his (Quine, 1956, pp. 177—187). For the propositional version see (Lewis, 1969). As we have seen, some cognitivists (Fodor, 1981) think of the objects as interpreted mental representations (MR's having propositional content); others as mental sentences of some sort (Field, 1978).

[11] Intentional terms such as 'want' and 'belief' are to be implicitly defined by the laws in which they figure (Grice, 1974—75, pp. 25 ff).

[12] A similar position can be found in Davidson (Davidson, 1963, p. 687), although he writes of *reasons* underlying actions. A reason for an agent's action A consists of a pro-attitude of the agent towards actions with a "certain property of a belief of the agent that A . . . has that property." I think this is easily renderable in terms of our technical concepts of act, etc., and if so, support for my statement of an adequacy condition goes up to five.

[13] The standard idea of a serial machine is this. Suppose that $T^1 = \langle S^1, Q^1, O^1, M^1, N^1 \rangle$ and $T^2 = \langle S^2, Q^2, O^2, M^2, N^2 \rangle$ are two general finite state automata with outputs O^1, O^2 (i.e., they are finite state transducers without initial states); then the *serial* automaton $T = T_1 \otimes T_2 = \langle S^1, Q^1 \times Q^2, O^2, M, N \rangle$ is the machine such that $S^2 = O^1$ and the M and N functions are given by

$$M((q^1, q^2), x) = (M^1(q^1, x), M^2(q^2, N^1(q^1, x))), \quad \text{and}$$
$$N((q^1, q^2), x) = N^2(q^2, N^1(q^1, x)), \quad \text{where } x \in (S^1)^*.$$

The next state is a pair consisting of the next state of T^1 under input x and the next state of T^2 under an input that is the output of T^1. Similarly the output of T from a state pair (q^1, q^2) is just the output of T^2 from its present state and the output of T^1 from q^1 under input x. See (Hartmanis and Stearns, 1966, pp. 42—43). Our own version differs in four ways: N_T is defined on states alone; both component automata have initial states; both have sets of final states that are subsets of the state sets; we ignore the output of $N_{T'}$ of the serial machine but not of T_T. In addition the output of our T_T goes through the A-box to generate input strings for $T_{T'}$ with some unformalized delay. This construction is elaborated in later sections where difference in ways of computing are used to explicate differences in intension for a simple language.

[14] Moore machines are behaviorially equivalent to our standard FA. See (Moore, 1956).

[15] Strictly speaking the 'N' on the left is a new function, but custom dictates we take the same symbol.

[16] Inasmuch as the acceptor of T_T is incorporated in a superautomaton T' (not shown) shown) that allows taking, the computation of N can not really be so simple as is represented in (11). Some of the elementary symbols of x might be vague, in which case the take induces a replacement that might or might not lead to a winner. But nothing hinges on a completely detailed treatment of N, and we shall just assume that if T' takes, then x is the result thereof.

[17] Perhaps the best known discussion of purpose and control systems is (Rosenbluth *et al.*, 1943) which has been thoroughly worked over in the past four decades. The thesis of that paper is that active, negative feedback, extrapolative control systems of high order are purposive, independent of questions of the material embodiment of the system. There is no doubt in my mind but what the approach of that paper already enounced a 'functionalist' approach to questions of mind even though it was quite possibly inadequate for reasons discussed in the text. As recently as 1979, however, a very authoritative AI figure could say that thermostats *believe* (McCarthy, 1979)! This doesn't make the task of supporting any kind of mechanism any easier.

[18] It is tempting to say the distinction I am trying to make is just that of Peirce between icon and symbol. But on reflection it is less a matter of the way a sign connects with its object than a matter of the manner of interpretation. In Peirce's terminology representations in the referential sense are dicent symbols or arguments (Peirce, 1932, II. 243–264).

[19] If there is anything in the literature on this question about belief I am not aware of it. Hintikka's important work is concerned with *rational* belief, not the psychology of belief, and in particular not with belief structures in the subject or with the distribution of operators (Hintikka, 1962). Some relevant observations however occur in Dretske (1970).

[20] In the special case that T_T and $T_{T'}$ are finite automata the intersection is the product

$$\langle S, Q_T \times Q_{T'}, M_T \times M_{T'}, (q_{0_T}, q_{0_{T'}}), Q_{F_T} \times Q_{F_{T'}} \rangle = T_T \times T_{T'}$$

where $M_T \times M_{T'}$ is defined as in the discussion of Condition I in VI.2. This is again an FSA (Nelson, 1968, p. 294). Similarly

$$\bar{T}_T = \langle S, Q_T, M_T, q_0, \bar{Q}_{F_T} \rangle.$$

For the union,

$$T_T \cup T_{T'} = \langle S, Q_T \times Q_{T'}, M_T \times M_{T'}, (q_{0_T}, q_{0_{T'}}), \overline{\bar{Q}_{F_T} \times \bar{Q}_{F_{T'}}} \rangle$$

which is like the system for the intersection excepting that the set of final states is the relation $\overline{\bar{Q}_{F_T} \times \bar{Q}_{F_{T'}}}$. These are again FSA. The n-fold union is precisely the product machine required in our discussion of Condition I for adequacy of accepting automata, pp. 174–175 above.

[21] An example is the adder-subtractor of Section III.1. Another: it is well known that all sixteen truth functions can be realized in a single, primitive logic organ (*not* a multi-fold of Sheffer – 'nand' – gates) which only need to be biased to realize each of the several functions on command of biasing signals. By 'learned' biasing patterns I meant some re-enforcement or habituation regime that has established signal patterns for actuating brain functions according to external circumstances and desired ends or

purposes. In addition to the addition-subtraction example of Figure III.2, please also see the discussion above, pp. 176–177.

[22] I borrow the expression but not quite the sense from (Dennett, 1978, p. 45).

[23] Suppose we are given that $a < b$, a strict ordering, and $T_L = \langle S \times S, Q, q_0, M, Q_F \rangle$ where $S = \{a, b\}$, $Q = \{q_0, q_1\}$ and $Q_F = \{q_0\}$. The elements of the input set $S \times S$ are (a, a), (a, b), (b, a), (b, b) which are ordered pairs. In analogy to the operation of concatenation of symbols into strings in the usual way we concatenate pairs thus: $(a, b)\,(b, b)\,(a, a)\ldots$ and adopt the convention

$$(aba, bba)\ldots = (a, b)\,(b, b)\,(a, a)\ldots$$

and so on in general. $(S \times S)^*$ is the set of pairs of equal length strings $\{(a, a), (a, b), (b, b), (aa, aa), (aa, ab), (aa, ba), (aa, bb), (ab, aa),$ etc.$\}$ The M-function of T is given by

q	(a, a)	(a, b)	(b, a)	(b, b)
0	0	0	1	0
1	1	1	1	1

This automaton accepts just those strings $(s_1 s_2 s_3 \ldots s_n, t_1 t_2 t_3 \ldots t_n)$ such that $s_i \leq t_i$ for all $i = 1, \ldots, n$ where s, t range over a, b. Thus T accepts $(abaa, abbb)$ but not $(aaba, aaaa)$, for instance.

[24] In more recent writing Fodor takes a dim view of the possibility of basing semantics on psychology, because psychological "mental states" are not referential (Fodor, 1980). But they are (at least mental features, attitudes are) *intentional*, and the relation of this aspect of semantics to the referential is no simple matter. The *structure* of reference, it seems to me, is a matter of psychology, whereas the *content* is not. This is the tack I will take up in the next chapter.

[25] Robert Schwartz, speaking of language rules, objects to the view that the infiniteness of language (and presumably the infiniteness of any processable domain as per our Condition I) entails the use of rules without adding some additional empirical premises. For the argument from infinity to rules, he says, leads to a regress.

If rules are construed as internalized instructions, formulas, or principles that specify membership conditions or describe the members of a given infinite set, use of such rules would require the ability to apply the concepts or criteria employed in the rule specification. But the skills needed to apply the rule to a theoretically unlimited number of cases would themselves be unbounded and thus require the use of additional rules, and so on ad infinitum (Schwartz, 1978, p. 188).

Schwartz has missed one of the key attractions of the computer paradigm which had already emerged full blown in Turing's (1936). Turing's version of the Church-Turing thesis is supported by an argument that one of his machines can do anything a human computist can. As noted in Section II.2 and II.4, Turing quadruples themselves (or net structures) specify the design of autonomous machines – they *inform* embodied algorithms and need no little clerk-homunculi to govern the application of rules. Similarly for executive-driven free programs. See Dennett's (1978, pp. 101–2) engaging discussion of Hume's problem: how can there be impressions or ideas, except for other ideas *ad infinitum* or for a knower?

CHAPTER IX

[1] There is in fact an ambiguity in 'pragmatical theory', assuming I am right in attributing promotion of such to Dummett: (a) a theory of meaning in terms of understanding and underlying acceptance and/or belief structures; (b) in terms of use in social and institutional contexts. I am inclined to think that a complete theory would have to include (b); but here I am focusing just on (a) and the Davidson-Dummett opposition. A 'full-blooded' theory is one embracing (b). Katz has argued quite forcefully for a 'modest theory' of meaning independent of contexts of use and possibly of what I take to be the psychology of acceptance and belief. In particular he believes that a theory of the speech act would be extragrammatical and should be radically distinguished from a purely linguistic type of semantics (Katz, 1977). He also regards Davidson's proposals as totally inadequate and not really representative of a 'modest theory' (Katz, 1975). On the other hand it could be argued that Katz' 'intensionalist' approach is a species of psycholinguistics, hence is pragmatic in sense (a) above, but of course along entirely different lines from my own nonlinguistic treatment of intentions and from my aim to understand intensionality in terms of intentionality (see note 4 below).

Davidson's semantical and Dummett's pragmatical (in sense (a)) proposals reflect a distinction that was emerging quite strongly in Carnap's later writings (Carnap, 1956, Supplement, pp. 233–250). In his earlier purely semantical stage (Carnap, 1942; 1956, Sections I–V), pragmatics (Carnap's 'Wastebasket') was a tangle of natural language odds and ends – emotive, exhortatory, etc. expressions and usages – beyond the circle of pure or formal semantics. But in (Carnap, 1956, Supplement) intensions of natural language predicates he suggests be characterized in terms of the language user. " . . . the intension of a predicate 'Q' for a speaker X is the general condition which an object y must fulfill in order for X to be willing to ascribe the predicate 'Q' to y." More explicitly, "that X is able to use a language L means that X has a certain system of interconnected dispositions for certain linguistic responses. That a predicate 'Q' in a language L has the property F as its intension for X, means that among the dispositions of X constituting the language L there is the disposition of ascribing the predicate 'Q' to any object y if and only if y has the property F. (F is here always assumed to be an observable property, i.e., either directly observable or explicitly definable in terms of directly observable properties)" (Carnap, 1956, p. 242). Dispositions, in turn, were to be understood either behavioristically or in terms of 'structure analysis' (Carnap, 1956, p. 243). Carnap thought that a fairly complete theory of intensionality might be found in studying robots, and that states and dispositions to respond could be calculated from a robot's blueprint. If one reads 'automaton structure' for 'blueprints' and takes the further step of setting up robots as models in the sense of this book, then clearly Carnap was on the track of a mechanist logic of mind. This tentative approach, on the other hand, was quite aside from his 'modest' theory of intensions and modality for formal languages; the latter has had the greatest influence on current possible world semantics and pragmatics.

[2] Although I think it desirable and possible eventually to develop a theory of meaning that includes the use of language in institutional, ritualistic, etc. settings and one that includes communication of information, the present sketch is just of the relationships among sentences, intentional attitudes expressed therein and meanings. That is to say the remarks will be confined to what Harman calls level one – "the use of language in thinking" (Harman, 1968).

3 This section draws heavily on my (Nelson, 1978b).

4 'Intentional' is a term that applies to mental features such as 'believing' and 'seeking' and to acts that are goal directed; some writers including myself in the last paragraph also use it for sentences that express intentional attitudes. 'Intension' and 'extension' are semantical terms that apply to linguistic entities as in 'the set of red things is the *extension* of the word "red"', and in 'the *intension* of "horse" is large equine mammal' or ' "horse" and "cheval" are *synonymous*'. According to Davidson in the passages discussed earlier 'intention' would perhaps apply only to creatures that talk (or at least 'intentional attitude' would).

5 Modal sentences also satisfy these conditions and are thus often termed 'intentional' but I have no such application in mind; in my opinion a satisfactory disposition of modality is an entirely separate matter from an analysis of belief.

6 It is left as an exercise for the reader to show that any totally degraded, vague string as instanced by y in the Scrooge scenario will be taken to lead to a final state, i.e., $M_M(q_0, y) = q_F$. This shows, I think, that hallucination can be plausibly explained in a mechanistic way and might even suggest the etiology of it. Of course a bank of other acceptors are on deck also; but the Marley acceptance can reasonably be accounted for in terms of context and attention cf. p. 194 and 231 f.

7 The notion of intension as a function from certain entities to extensions (Lewis, 1972, p. 174) appears to capture this meaning of 'sense' in Frege, although it strikes me that the extension ought to be the domain, not the range. Also, Lewis, and others, tend to reify abstract functions into the objects of Frege's 'sense' in the secondary meaning, roughly the indirect object. I will later on suggest that intensions or meanings in this sense of 'sense' are objective properties à la Carnap (1956), or more recently Putnam (1973).

8 Having absolved myself in advance (like the savage who blocks his own path into alien, forbidden territory and then climbs over the block) I must briefly explain that FSA do not retain the computational structure of their base machines except in a trivial way. The reason for this is as follows. A minimal FSA is one that is quasi-connected (note VI.16) and such that if q is equivalent to q', then $q = q'$ for any q, q' in the state set Q. Now any two FSA which are minimal and equivalent are also *isomorphic* (Nelson, 1968, p. 167). To say they are equivalent is just to say they accept the same set $\mathcal{U}$. And if they are isomorphic they certainly can't compute differently. So the only sense in which two FSA accepting the same set could compute differently would be in the sense that one or both had superfluous states, that is, that one or both be nonminimal. But this seems to me, on intuitive grounds, to be hardly sufficient to pin the idea of 'same way' or 'same sense' on.

9 This view of pragmatics is entirely different from Montague's. Following Bar-Hillel, Montague thought of pragmatics as concerned with pragmatic *languages*, where a pragmatic language is one whose semantical interpretations are relative to a set of 'point references' or 'indexes' that might include language users. Roughly, the idea is that reference cannot be determined without 'knowledge of the context of use'. For example the truth of 'I see a dog' can not be determined without knowledge of who the indexical 'I' is. On Montague's terms our simple core C is not pragmatic as it contains only the indexical 'this' and proper names. From my side, Montague had nothing to do with pragmatics as his semantics is not based on nonlinguistic intentions of speakers of a language (Bar-Hillel, 1954; Montague, 1968, pp. 96 ff.).

10 That is, she realizes all complements, unions, etc. of acceptors that underly truth

functional compounds of sentences, is capable of all inferences drawn to ascriptions to individuals and has at least sufficient memory required for knowing quantified sentences (cf. pp. 238–243).

[11] So-called model-theoretic semantics and Fregean type semantics are indifferent to users; but there always lurks an ideal user (for Frege and also for Gödel) who grasps abstract objects in a way shared by all rational speakers and mathematicians. All my exemplar needs is veridical perception of instances of types (the right biology).

[12] In effect, that is, adopting Quine's treatment of time could be extended, conceivably, throughout the core at least in a theory of reference. Quine's way in contrast to operator logics that transform neutral sentences into tensed sentences is essentially to construe individuals as scattered chunks of space-time manifolds. Thus proper names such as 'Steve' can be thought of as replaceable by names such as 'Steve-now'; and the tensed sentences of ordinary language are all phrased in a neutral way as regards tense with all temporal reference vested in names (see esp. Quines, 1960a, pp. 170 ff.).

[13] Russell's theory of logically proper names, which mine turns out to resemble in certain obvious respects, was closely tied-in with his doctrine of knowledge by acquaintance. Logically proper names directly denote "sense-data." For Russell, apparently, the vagueness I am mildly worried about is avoided by his logical atomism; logically proper names signify ultimate, simple particulars in the field of sense data, and if they don't signify the right one they have no meaning (Russell, 1918, p. 201 and 1914, *passim*). Even if atomism does the trick (which is far from clear to me) it won't help here as there are no ultimate parts to the world of my perceivers and believers. A sensible property or relation is just what the empirical psychologist says it is that subjects accept things as, i.e., *expect.*

[14] Tyler Burge has argued, for very similar reasons but without the accompanying theory of acceptance and belief, that proper names are not abbreviated descriptions (as advocated by Frege and Russell) but *predicates.* Among other reasons this can be argued linguistically from the fact that proper names can be pluralized and have definite and indefinite articles attached to them (Burge, 1973). cf. Quine (1960, p. 95f)

[15] In still more detail, I am asserting a psychological proposition about exemplar $\mathscr{S}$ which says that if $Rep\,(a, x)$ and $x = \tau$ and $Rep\,(a, x)$ and x is τ', then $\mathscr{S}$ (nonperceptually) believes τ is τ'. I have no complete analysis of nonperceptual belief to draw on; but however such an analysis might go, it would presumably include the clause $x \in \mathscr{U}_\tau$ and perhaps some 'representation' of the identity.

[16] No doubt the reader has noticed that whereas $\mathscr{U}_\tau$ is a *unit set* in the foregoing in our discussion of item (3) in the context of substitutional matters in Section IX.1, $\mathscr{U}_\tau$ is a possibly infinite domain of a partial function! But as explained there, that domain is an equivalence class modulo τ, τ an individual. It might be comforting to read, for the parenthetical remark immediately above, "$x = [\tau]$ when $[\tau]$ is the class of individuals equivalent to τ if and only if $x \in \mathscr{U}_\tau$," and then in our theories of reference make correspond 'this' to a where $Rep\,(a, x)$ and $x = [\tau]$. In a naturalistic theory the individual object a, not only the stimulus pattern, is an equivalence class also; cf. Quine's conception of individual things as momentary objects (Quine, 1976, p. 859). My objective equivalence class is the same as a set of his momentary stages; it is the projection of a space-time manifold onto the spatial components chunked according to continuous time slabs.

[17] I.e., 'P' in our metalanguage is a translation of p in C (cf. Field, 1972, p. 355).

[18] Departing even more radically from anything like decent English: There is an x such that acceptability to $\mathscr{S}$ applies to x is τ if and only if acceptability to $\mathscr{S}$ applies to there exists an x, x is τ.

[19] For the reader who is not quite familiar with Tarski's theory and some of the motivations for these definitions, there is a short, very appealing discussion in (Haack, 1978, pp. 104–108).

[20] Field's programme to get a satisfactory definition of truth for mental representations in the head would surely rest on some such material assumptions (Field, 1978, pp. 44 ff.). However there is a gap between the sort of thing he seems to recommend and the present theory. Truth, for me, does depend on acceptance by an ideal speaker, but not on the truth of 'mentalese' sentences as my theory is not one about a mental language (except for the strings x, which are just surrogates for individuals).

[21] The exposition above actually follows the treatment of Tarski's theory by Quine and Mendelson most closely (Mendelson, 1964; Quine, 1970).

[22] I am assuming that all of the compound property types in the core are built-up step-by-step from perceptual types by compositions of the underlying automata.

[23] Since in the next chapter I am going to assign the *meanings* of various kinds of linguistic entity to underlying automata and computations, the present observation suggests the part of semantics that deals with intensions and meanings will necessarily be finitary, not infinitary. An adequate grammatical theory, according to Chomsky, must account for an infinity of sentences considered *syntactically*. A consequence of my approach is that there are only *finitely* many synonymy classes of terms, predicates, sentences or whatever. This topic is discussed a little bit more in my (Nelson, 1978a). Davidson has argued that a language is not learnable unless it have only a finite number of primitives (Davidson, 1967, p. 304 and 1965, pp. 383–394).

[24] Putnam, who adopts Dummett's point of view in his theory of science at one stage, does, however, takes intuitionistic logic as a logic of sentences, and proposes that truth valuations be recast in terms of intuitionist provability. In sentential logic, 'asserting p' becomes 'asserting p is constructively provable'; $\overline{p} \wedge \overline{q}\rceil$ means p is provable and q is provable (Putnam, 1976, p. 184). I suppose Putnam's assertability of p might be something like my acceptability of P plus expressive delivery of p.

[25] Speaking strictly if 'effectively decidable' means 'intuitionistically decidable' then it is *not quite the same as* 'acceptable'. The latter *does* mean 'recursively decidable' and whether *that* means 'intuitionistically decidable' is moot. But this is a fine point of only questionable relevance here. Cf. my (1987a).

CHAPTER X

[1] This section is based on ideas I first formulated in (Nelson, 1975, 1976b, and 1977b).

[2] A possible world is a state of affairs, if that helps (Plantinga, 1974, p. 44); on the other hand a state of affairs is a *class* of possible worlds (Quine, 1969a, p. 147). This is all quite foggy. Intuitively the idea, which is Leibniz', is that things could be other than they actually are, and as they actually are is the best. Contemporary thinkers drop the value considerations and think of possible worlds as just the alternative possibilities we carry in our heads when we plan and consider. A possible world is then just the possible outcome or consequence that figures in decision theory and ethics. Even more

simply, the world-of-my-desk has a phone to my right. It could be to my left; and if so the world-of-my-desk would be a different though possible one. There are two main ways of making the idea precise for formal languages. Consider a very simple language that has just two names, 'cube$_1$' and 'cube$_2$' and two monadic predicates, 'blue', and 'large' with the usual interpretations. The atomic sentences are such as 'cube$_1$ is blue'; a *basic pair* is a couple consisting of an atomic sentence and its negation. Thus a basic pair is ⟨cube$_1$ is blue, cube$_1$ is not blue⟩. A possible world is a conjunction in which exactly one sentence from each basic pair of the language occurs. The idea is Carnap's (Carnap, 1950, p. 72); he calls these conjunctions 'state descriptions'. For example, 'cube$_1$ is blue and cube$_1$ is large, and cube$_2$ is blue and cube$_2$ is not large' is one of sixteen possible worlds or state descriptions. Just one (given a couple of cubes on your desk that either have or don't have the properties) is actual.

The other way is in terms of *interpretations* of language. 'Possible world' according to this approach, refers not to sentences, but to domains of interpretation so that a possible world of the example would be one in which cube$_1$ is blue and large, etc. The difference between these ways principally concern questions of cardinality and the fact that in the first way each individual of the world needs a name. Such questions are far from our preoccupations in this book.

[3] Recall that word functions are the same if they are the same set of pairs – if they are the same *extensionally*.

[4] Somewhat similarly, for Davidson the meaning of a sentence is its truth conditions (Davidson, 1967), although for him these are not to be found in pragmatic terms, i.e., they are not embodied in built-in (acquired or native) mental features, even for perceptual truth, presumably.

[5] That is to say, by identifying the intensional object of the sentence with the intentional object of the intention. This is very much the sort of thing that some functionalists propose. Field prefers to speak of internal representations, sentences of a sort, as the (intentional) objects of attitudes (Field, 1978, p. 40).

[6] The following paragraphs are an adaptation of Quine's notion of 'Democritean world' and of 'propositional object' (Quine, 1969a, pp. 147 ff.).

[7] Quine remarks that the representation can be beefed up still more in order to accommodate units of measurement, nonEuclidean spaces, the presence of fields, non-homogeneous matter, and so forth. All of this would be mathematically routine.

[8] Georgette: *D'où vient qu'à tout le monde il veut tant la cacher, et qu'it ne saurait voir personne en approcher?*
Alain: *C'est que cette action le met en jalousie.*
Georgette: *Mais d'où vient qu'il est pris de cette fantaisie?*
Alain: *Cela vient . . . cela vient de ce qu'il est jaloux.*

Moliere, *L'École des Femmes*, Acte II. Scene III. This delightful fragment of Moliere was called to my attention by Emilie Kadish.

[9] If 'Steve' is held to *apply* to a unit set as extension, then 'Steve is blond' can be rendered in the usual manner of formal logic as 'for any x, if x is Steve, then x is blond': if it is held to *denote* Steve, then in the rendition in the usual notation B$_{Steve}$, where 'B' is an abbreviation for 'blond', 'Steve' counts as a proper name.

[10] I must confess that I am slightly bothered myself about making individuals properties, which is of course a pretty piece of Platonism. On the other hand there is a complementary Platonism in making so-called proper names *logically* proper names on all fours with indexicals like 'this'. It seems to me that the widely and tacitly held attitude that an

individual is an entity transcending individual *events* is as Platonistic as anything can be. Of course to say that an individual is a *type* as in our example of the Morley acceptor may not appear to avoid Platonism either – until we remind ourselves that a type is individuated by a mathematical function. That, too is abstract, but it's as far as we need to go in our ontology for the mind (cf. note IX.14).

11 The extension must not be confused with the propositional object U. In hallucination there are elements of U that correspond to *no* element of the extension (cf. IX(6)); and besides, U is a set of stimulus patterns.

12 I am inclined to take the following definition seriously, although I am not otherwise presuming to delve into the ontology of natural kinds: A *kind* (*kind predicate*) is a recursive or computable property (predicate) over the domain of physical objects. Earlier in this volume I have used expressions such as 'blond' and 'red' in examples of core beliefs and sentences. As they were held to be examples of the acceptable in my technical sense, this makes them kinds. But 'blond' is not a kind word. To set things right we might replace 'blond' by 'blond thing' in these examples and similarly for like expressions.

13 My purpose is not exegesis of Putnam, but exposition of the logic of mind. I hope my spotty approach to the references does not do serious injustice to his thoughts.

14 The example is from (Putnam, 1975, p. 704).

15 Putnam argues that the doctrine that meanings are psychological states or concepts is really no different than Platonism and that the "whole psychologism/platonism issue appears somewhat as a tempest in a tea pot. . . . " (Putnam, 1975, p. 138). The reference is to Frege's antagonism toward conceptualism or psychologism and various rejoinders thereto. If Platonism is true, then the psychological states we assume when we grasp meaning are the same for everyone, and there is no issue. If Platonism is not true, however, there's no telling how far apart our meanings might range. In fact in the elm-tree example the key idea is *subjectivity* of concepts.

16 This affords yet another reason for arguing that it is a theoretical error to identify beliefs with states. If meanings are concepts in the head and if beliefs are distinguished one from the other by meanings, then one could have two distinct beliefs fulfilling the same expectation!

17 My theory, such as it is, seeking as it does to shine light on meaning in terms of underlying nonlinguistic, intentional features of mind, is bound to run counter to semantical theories that have grown in the soil of contemporary psycholinguistics. Any theory, it seems to me, that hunts for meaning in terms of linguistic structures or lexical structures in the mind, is probably stuck with lists or enumerations of some sort. For one criticism along the line I am rather hinting at see Putnam's critique of Katz (Putman, 1970). On deeper philosophical grounds I find myself in agreement with Katz except possibly for the rationalism. His semantical theories are presented in (Katz, 1972) and more lately in Katz (1981) in a radical move to platonistic semantics.

CHAPTER XI

1 One might argue that there are far more significant differences than resemblances between the Scotist and myself. For the Scotist, forms, formalities, haecceities, and so forth, are metaphysical ultimates and absolute whereas for me or any other empirical realist foundationalism or any doctrine of ultimate principles is moot, and the real is real relative to formalizable languages – for Peirce, relative to representation (5.312). Also, assuming that mental rules correspond roughly to the common natures of Scotus,

there may be important differences. For Scotus common natures are neither singular not universal, but are universals *as abstracted by the mind*; and I surely would not know how to take a stand on such an issue. Finally, although I did use 'haecceity' in several earlier passages, all I meant was that an individual is recognized by an acceptor in terms of uniquely distinguishing traits (not definite descriptions). This is no metaphysical formality but just a further determination of a species, as a medievalist might say. Finally the underlying structures might not be isomorphic (universal) from individual to individual. But I contend that they are enough alike for science at some level.

[2] Scotus would not have made such an application because the body and soul were really distinct for him. According to a Quinean point of view my position on automaton rules realized in things is a species of Platonism inasmuch as I quantify over automata, in fact over n-tuples of sets. However since the sets are all finite (except for the set of unbounded sequences of symbols, S*) this is not much of a committment − no more than to Quinean Democritean worlds. The quantificational criterion of ontological committment does not seem to be able to capture the difference between moderate or aristotelian realism, which is interpreted in Scotus in the manner just discussed, and Platonic realism. I hope that my similar idea of real rules and guiding *versus* fitting shows that there is something to capture.

[3] This is not new by any means. It is possible to axiomatize relevant portions of automata theory in such a manner as to satisfy Craig's idea of a replacement program (Craig, 1956). Then it is also possible to obtain all of the theorems containing only behavioral predicates from a subtheory of the original without using theoretical, that is , state, terms at all.

Every FA can be represented as in II.(3a, b, c) with equivalences for each output z and each internal state y. Then each expression can be interpreted in ring arithmetic as defining primitive recursive functions of time relative to the input functions x; and all these are replaceable by explicit definitions (which effectively eliminates internal state expressions) by the well-known Dedekind-Frege method (cf. Bealer, 1978).

The behavior (III(2)) of any FA is a regular set in the sense of Kleene (Kleene, 1956; Elgot, 1961), and all such sets are definable in terms of set-theoretic operations on input and output symbols only; given an FA, there is an algorithm for producing the regular set.

All FA are representable in a second-order arithmetic. The result is a Platonistic language, but it contains no internal state predicates (Büchi, 1960). In fact for the class of primitive recursive functions as alluded to above, not only internal state predicates but *all* automaton predicates are eliminable in favor of purely arithmetic expressions.

For noninitial state FA one can apply other procedures roughly equivalent to explicit definition of recursively defined predicates, but for automata in abstract, not coded, form (Thomas, 1978).

In each case one starts from an initially given automaton formulation and proceeds to the reductive analysis; and the mother analogy applies: the respective exercises are interesting, but they do not eliminate states (they do eliminate 'states'), if mechanism is true.

[4] To attempt to reduce anything as complex as VIII(16), which defines 'desire', involves a lot more than the relatively simple-minded approaches alluded to in Note 3. I certainly agree with Goodman that the evidence for reducibility is negligible, not just to physics but more so to S-R psychology, where very little in the way of solid theory has been established at all (Goodman, 1978).

5 This passage borrows almost word-for-word from my (Nelson, 1977, pp. 536–537).

6 In a probabilistic automaton each state goes into another state of a *set* of states under the transition function M with a certain probability such that the probabilities associated to the states of the set sum to 1. Then another probability function is defined on input sequences which gives the probability $p(x)$ of x carrying the automaton from an initial state into a final or perceptual state. Next a fiducial point λ is chosen, and we say that x is *accepted* by the automaton if and only if $\lambda < p(x)$ (Rabin, 1964). A *winner q* is a state such that there exists a sequence x such that $\lambda < p(x)$, starting from state q. Using this new idea of winner one could then proceed to 'expectation' 'fulfills', and so on in a relatively straightforward way. I attempt this in the Appendix to my (1984).

7 I have already indicated briefly in Section VIII.3 why control theory is not an adequate means for explaining purposive behavior as it lacks the feature of expectation and in particular of self-description. So the 'cybernetic hypothesis' if that means negative feedback is not adequate either. One might argue, however, that control theory would suffice for biological functions short of the psychological level (whatever *that* means!)

8 Knowing the table for an attitude or feature is a case of pure science fiction, just as complete knowledge of a physical disposition of some material object is. Very likely, as we have stressed often, very few organisms of the same species have exactly the same structures underlying a feature; and if the rule systems are probabilistic, not even identical behaviors. But as elsewhere, one 'idealizes'; and so the example is still instructive. We are not contrasting psychological explanation with the deductive model in point of the possible uncertainty attributable to incomplete knowledge of conditions. The point lies elsewhere, as we shall see. Any explanation fulfilling the Hempelian model is ideal too. The contrast we want comes out when we assume perfect circumstances for both.

9 As already mentioned twice this is a kind of irreducibility thesis in that it denies the explicit definability of 'belief' but affirms that the microprocesses are elementary mechanical believers. Margaret Boden, too, in her excellent book on AI and psychology asserts that intentional terms are applicable to computer programs as 'thinking', 'believing', and 'talking', and hence that if human mental features are like computer programs questions of the intentional vanish. So "[the] basic insight that psychological truths cannot be expressed in nonpsychological terms must be acknowledged" while at the same time AI saves us from Brentano and his thesis (Boden, 1977, p. 397). She also equates 'intentionality' with 'subjectivity' (Boden, p. 185), which means that anything that 'internalizes' its world has purposes. For further discussion of this and similar points see my (Nelson, 1980) and for a more complete treatment of the necessity of meeting adequacy conditions in AI programs that are not just engineering enterprises but meant to illuminate or explain the mental, see Nelson (1981a).

10 Fodor stands in a middle position. He, too, denies with me that semantics in AI has anything much to do with *reference*; on the other hand he shares the programming model with AI and presumably would not go along with the idea that meaning arises in perception, but rather that perception presupposes semantically laden input. See Section V.4.

11 I mean only that it naturalizes special psychological entities such as Reid's moral sense or, perhaps, Kant's practical reason, not that the doctrine that some acts are right only if they produce ethically good consequences is mistaken.

12 Smart distinguishes between events such as after-images and the experience of after-images (Smart, 1959, p. 61). For, if one embraces the identity of mental and

physical events as he does it is hard to see how a yellow-orange after-image could be a physical property; but *the experience of it could be*. I am going to assume that there are no unexperienced instantiated qualia and that *qua* experienced they are *mental states*. This decision holds only for occurrents, not for features. Many, if not most, features are below the threshold of consciousness, and certainly the recursive mechanisms are.

[13] I hope to make 'attended by experience of . . .' clearer in the discussion to follow of mechanism combined with some version of the identity theory, which says that states of sentience are the same as brain states.

[14] I have often wondered whether the distinction between mental events *qua* suffered and *qua* intentional might not account for the Cartesian claim that animals do not have feelings. Descartes must have meant, when he took speech as a sign of mind, that *ideas are intentional*. Indeed, he is explicit. "Now as far as ideas are concerned, if we consider them only in themselves and do not relate them to something else, they cannot, properly speaking, be false. . . . " (Descartes, 1614, p. 94). Quite possibly animals have pain (not for all Cartesians!) but relate them to nothing else, at least via linguistic expression, and hence do not have fully attentive or intentional pain. In my mechanism, of course, there can be, and undoubtedly is in the animal world, intentionality without speech, and therefore full pain.

[15] The following discussion is based on my (Nelson, 1976a, pp. 372–379). William Lycan has advanced a similar argument (Lycan, 1974) earlier than myself and independently.

[16] The analogy between minds and machines, and in later papers the doctrine that human beings are probabilistic automata; the distinction between purely logical descriptions and physical descriptions; the observation that the *same* logical descriptions can be given for physically different systems; the conclusion, that these points apply to human psychology as well as to machines in virtue of the analogy or of the out-and-out espousal of mechanism (Putnam, 1960, 1964, 1967).

[17] The identity theory says that mental events are contingently identical to some physical brain events or other ('token-token' identity); or, that mental quala are identical to physical properties ('type-type' identity). If mental states are machine states, this popular materialist position is liable to be vague and confusing (see discussion of psychological types in Section V.1).

[18] Block has written a thoroughgoing study of troubles with functionalism, including the difficulties in accounting for occurrents (Block, 1978).

[19] In a lecture delivered at Cleveland State University and in private conversation, Arthur Burks has suggested an argument of evolutionary continuity as support for panpsychism.

[20] The type of epistemic situation here is certainly one of the most familiar in all of philosophy, and in perceptual acceptance is analyzed in terms of my concept of taking.

[21] We have already argued that features are formally distinct from nerve firing patterns. Kripke speaks of 'Cartesian conclusions' about *mind* and *body*. But for reasons set forth in this book this could entail serious confusions. The present topic of discussion is Kripke adapted to occurrents alone, not to substances or to features. The mind, in this book, is a system of features some conscious – accompanied by awareness – and others not.

[22] An interesting discussion of a similar point appears in (Levin, 1975, pp. 154 ff.).

BIBLIOGRAPHY

Anscombe, G. E. M.: 1974, 'Comments on Professor Gregory's Paper', in S. C. Brown (ed.), *Philosophy of Psychology*, Barnes and Noble, New York.

Arbib, Michael, A.: 1972, *The Metaphorical Brain*, John Wiley and Sons, New York.

Armstrong, D. M.: 1968, *A Materialist Theory of Mind*, Routledge and Kegan Paul, London.

Armstrong, D. M.: 1972, *Belief, Truth, and Knowledge*, Cambridge University Press, Cambridge.

Bar-Hillel, Y.: 1954, 'Indexical Expressions', *Mind* 63, 359–379.

Bar-Hillel, Y. and E. Shamir: 1960, 'Finite State Languages: Formal Representations and Adequacy Problems', *The Bulletin of the Research Council* of Israel 8F, 155–166.

Bealer, George: 1978, 'An Inconsistency in Functionalism', *Synthese* 38, 333–372.

Block, N.: 1978, 'Troubles with Functionalism', in C. Wade Savage, (ed.), *Minnesota Studies in the Philosophy of Science* Vol. IX, *Perception and Cognition: Issues in the Foundations of Psychology*, University of Minnesota Press, Minneapolis.

Block, N. and J. A. Fodor: 1972, 'What Psychological States are not', *Philosophical Review* 81, 159–181.

Boden, Margaret: 1977, *Artificial Intelligence and Natural Man*, The Harvester Press, Hassock, England.

Brentano, Franz: 1924, *Psychologie vom Empirische Standpunkte*, third edition, Leipzig.

Büchi, J. R.: 1960, 'Weak Second Order Arithmetic and Finite Automata', *Zeitschrift für Mathematisch Logic und Grundlagen der Mathematik*, VI, pp. 66–92.

Burge, Tyler: 1973, 'Reference and Proper Names', *The Journal of Philosophy* LXX, pp. 425–438.

Burks, A. W.: 1972/73, 'Logic, Computers, and Men', *Proceedings and Addresses of the American Philosophical Association* XLVI, 39–57.

Burks, A. W.: 1978a, 'Man: Sign or Algorithm? A Rhetorical Analysis of Peirce's Semiotic', Semiotic and Art Conference, University of Michigan.

Burks, A. W.: 1978b, 'From Eniac to the Stored Program Computer: Two Revolutions in Computers', Logic of Computers Technical Report No, 210, the University of Michigan.

Burks, A. W. and I. M. Copi: 1957b, 'The Logical Design of an Idealized General Purpose Computer', *Journal of the Franklin Institute* 261, 297–314, 421–436.

Burks, A. W. and H. Wang: 1957a, 'The Logic of Automata', *Journal of the Association for Computing Machinery* 4, 193–218, 279–297.

Burks, A. W. and J. B. Wright: 1955, 'Theory of Logical Nets', *Proceedings of the IRE* 78, 1357–1365.

Carnap, Rudolf: 1936, 'Testability and Meaning', *Philosophy of Science* 3, 4; reprinted by Graduate Philosophy Club, Yale University.

Carnap, Rudolf: 1942, *Introduction to Semantics*, University of Chicago Press, Chicago.

Carnap, Rudolf: 1950, *Logical Foundations of Probability*, University of Chicago Press, Chicago.

Carnap, Rudolf: 1956a, *Meaning and Necessity*, second edition (first edition, 1947), University of Chicago Press, Chicago.

Carnap, Rudolf: 1956b, 'The Methodological Character of Theoretical Concepts', *Minnesota Studies in the Philosophy of Science*, Vol. 1, *The Foundations of Science and the Concepts of Psychology and Psychoanalysis*, H. Feigl and M. Scriven (eds.), University of Minnesota Press, Minneapolis.

Chang, C. C. and H. J. Keisler: 1973, *Model Theory*, North Holland Publishing Co., Amsterdam.

Chihara, Charles S.: 1972, 'On Alleged Refutations of Mechanism using Gödel's Incompleteness Results', *The Journal of Philosophy* LXIX, 507–526.

Chisholm, Roderick: 1957, Perceiving: A Philosophical Study, Cornell University Press, Ithaca, N.Y.

Chomsky, Noam: 1959a, 'Review of Skinner's *Verbal Behavior*', *Language* 35, 26–58.

Chomsky, Noam: 1959b, 'On Certain Formal Properties of Grammars', *Information and Control* 2, 137–167.

Chomsky, Noam: 1963, 'Formal Properties of Grammars', in R. D. Luce, R. R. Bush, and E. Galanter (eds.), *Handbook of Mathematical Psychology* Vol. 2, John Wiley and Sons, Inc. New York.

Chomsky, Noam: 1965, Aspects of the Theory of Syntax, MIT Press, Cambridge, Mass.

Chomsky, Noam: 1966, *Cartesian Linguistics*, Harper and Row, New York.

Chomsky, Noam: 1969, 'Comments on Harman's Reply', in Sidney Hook (ed.), *Language and Philosophy*, New York University Press New York.

Chomsky, Noam: 1972, *Language and Mind*, enlarged edition, Harcourt, Brace, Jovanovich, New York.

Chomsky, Noam: 1975a, 'Knowledge of Language', in Keith Gunderson (ed.), *Minnesota Studies in Philosophy of Science* Vol. VII, 'Language, Mind, and Knowledge', University of Minnesota Press, Minneapolis.

Chomsky, Noam: 1975b, *Reflections on Language*, Pantheon Books, New York.

Chomsky, Noam: 1977, *The Logical Structure of Linguistic Theory*, Plenum Press, New York.

Chomsky, Noam: 1980, *Rules and Representations,* Blackwell, Oxford.

Chomsky, Noam: 1981, *Lectures on Government and Binding,* Foris, Dordrecht.

Chomsky, Noam: 1986, 'Perspectives on use of Language' in Miles Brand and Robert M. Harnish (eds.), *The Representation of Knowledge and Belief,* University of Arizona Press, Tucson.

Chomsky, Noam and Jerrold Katz: 1974. 'What the Linguist is Talking about', *The Journal of Philosophy* LXXI, 347–366.

Church, Alonzo: 1936, 'An Unsolvable Problem of Elementary Number Theory', *American Journal of Mathematics* 58, 345–363.

Couturat, Louis: 1903, *Opuscules et Fragments Inedits de Leibniz*, Paris.

Craig, William: 1956, 'Replacement of Auxiliary Expressions', *Philosophical Review* 65, 38–55.

Craik, K. J. W.: 1943, *The Nature of Explanation,* Cambridge University Press, Cambridge.

Culbertson, James T.: 1963, *The Minds of Robots*, University of Illinois Press, Urbana.

Davidson, Donald: 1963, 'Actions, Reasons, and Causes', *The Journal of Philosophy* LX, 685–699.

Davidson, Donald: 1965, 'Theories of Meaning and Learnable Languages', in *Proceedings of the 1964 International Congress for Logic, Methodology and Philosophy of Science*, North-Holland Publishing Co., Amsterdam.

Davidson, Donald: 1967, 'Truth and Meaning', *Synthese* 17, 304–323.

Davidson, Donald: 1975, 'Thought and Talk', in Samuel Gutenplan (ed.), *Mind and Language*, Clarendon Press, Oxford.

Davis, Martin: 1958, *Computability and Unsolvability*, McGraw-Hill Book Co., New York.

Davis, Martin (ed.): 1965, *The Undecidable: Basic Papers on Undecidable Propositions, Unsolvable Problems and Computable Functions*, Raven Press, Hewlett, New York.

Dennett, D. C.: 1976, 'Why the Law of Effect Will Not Go Away', *Journal of the Theory of Social Behavior* 5, 169–187.

Dennett, D. C.: 1978, *Brainstorms: Philosophical Essays on Mind and Psychology*, Bradford Books Publishers, Inc. Montgomery, Vt.

Descartes, Rene: 1641, *Meditations Concerning First Philosophy*, Laurence J. Lafleur (trans.), Bobbs Merrill Publisher, Inc. Indianapolis, 1960.

Dewey, John: 1916, *Essays in Experimental Logic*, University of Chicago Press, Chicago.

Dewey, John: 1925, *Experience and Nature*, Open Court Publishing Co. LaSalle, Ill.

Dretske, Fred: 1969, *Seeing and Knowing*, University of Chicago Press, Chicago.

Dretske, Fred: 1970, 'Epistemic Operators', *The Journal of Philosophy* LXII, 1007–1023.

Dretske, Fred: 1971, 'Perception from an Epistemological Point of View', *The Journal of Philosophy* LXVIII, 584–590.

Dretske, Fred: 1981, *Knowledge and the Flow of Information*, The MIT Press, Cambridge.

Dreyfus, Hubert L.: 1967, 'Why Computers must have Bodies to be Intelligent', *Review of Metaphysics* 21, 13–32.

Dreyfus, Hubert L.: 1972, *What Computers Can't do: a Critique of Artificial Intelligence*, Harper and Row Publishers, New York.

Dummett, Michael: 1958–59, 'Truth', *Proceedings of the Aristotelian Society*, Vol. 59, reprinted in P. F. Strawson (ed.), *Philosophical Logic*, Oxford University Press, Oxford.

Dummett, Michael: 1975, 'What is a Theory of Meaning?' in Samuel Gutenplan (ed.), *Mind and Language*, Clarendon Press, Oxford.

Edelman, Gerald M.: 1987, *Neural Darwinism*, Basic Books, Inc., New York.

Elgot, Calvin C.: 1961, 'Decision Problems of Finite Automata and Related Arithmetics', *Transactions of the American Mathematical Society* 98, 21–51.

Estes, W. K.: 1980, 'Is Human Memory Obsolete?' *American Scientist* 68, 62–69.

Feigl, Herbert: 1958, 'The "Mental" and the "Physical"', *Minnesota Studies in the Philosophy of Science*, Vol. 2, in H. Feigl, M. Scriven, and G. Maxwell (eds.), *Concepts, Theories, and the Mind-Body Problem*, University of Minnesota Press, Minneapolis.

Feigl, Herbert: 1960, 'Mind-Body, *not* a Pseudo Problem', in Sidney Hook (ed.), *Dimensions of Mind*, New York University Press, New York.

Feigenbaum, Edward A. and Feldman Julian, (eds.): 1963, *Computers and Thought*, McGraw-Hill Book Co. New York.

Feyerabend, Paul: 1963, 'Materialism and the Mind-Body Problem', *The Review of Metaphysics* XVII, 49–66.

Field, Hartry: 1972, 'Tarski's Theory of Truth', *The Journal of Philosophy* LXIX, 347–374.

Field, Hartry: 1978, 'Mental Representation', *Erkenntnis* 13, 9–61.

Fodor, Jerry A.: 1966, 'Explanations in Psychology', in Max Black (ed.), *Philosophy in America*, Cornell University Press, Ithaca, New York.

Fodor, Jerry A.: 1968, *Psychological Explanation: An Introduction to the Philosophy of Psychology*, MIT Press, Cambridge, Mass.

Fodor, Jerry A.: 1975, *The Language of Thought*, Thomas Crowell Co., New York.

Fodor, Jerry A.: 1981, *Representations*, The MIT Press, Cambridge, Mass.

Fodor, Jerry A.: 1984, *The Modularity of Mind*, The MIT Press, Cambridge.

Fodor, Jerry A.: 1986, 'Information and Association' in Miles Brand and Robert M. Harnish (eds.), *Representation of Knowledge and Belief*, University of Arizona Press, Tucson.

Fodor, Jerry A.: 1987, *Psychosemantics*, The MIT Press, Cambridge.

Fodor, Jerry A., T. G. Bever and M. F. Garrett: 1974, *The Psychology of Language*, McGraw-Hill Book Co., New York.

Frege, Gottlob: 1892, 'On Sense and Reference', in Peter Geach and Max Black (eds. and trans.), *Philosophical Writings of Gottlob Frege*, Basil Blackwell, Oxford, 1966.

Gettier, Edmund: 1963, 'Is Justified True Belief Knowledge?' *Analysis* 23, 121–123.

Gilmore, P. A.: 1968, 'Structuring of Parallel Algorithms', *Journal of the Association for Computing Machinery* 15, 176–192.

Gödel, Kurt: 1931, 'Über Formal Unentscheidbare Sätze der Principia Mathematica und Verwandter Systeme I', *Monatsheft für Mathematik und Physik* 38, 173–198.

Goldstein, Herman H.: 1972, *The Computer from Pascal to von Neumann*, Princeton University Press, Princeton.

Goodman, Nelson: 1968, *Languages of Art*, The Bobbs Merrill Co. Inc., Indianapolis.

Goodman, Nelson: 1978, *Ways of World Making*, Hackett Publishing Co. Indianapolis.

Graves, C., Katz, J. J., Nishiyama, Y., Soames, S., Stecker, R., and Tovey, P.: 1973, 'Tacit Knowledge', *The Journal of Philosophy* LXX, 318–330.

Greenblatt, R. D., Eastlake, D. E., and Crocker, S. T.: 1967, 'The Greenblatt Chess Program', *American Federation of Information Processing Society Conference Proceedings* 31, 801–810.

Grice, Paul: 1974–75, 'Method in Philosophical Psychology', *Proceedings and Addresses of the American Philosophical Association* XLVIII, 23–53.

Gunderson, Keith: 1971, *Mentality and Machines*, Doubleday, Anchor New York.

Haack, Susan: 1978, *Philosophy of Logics*, Cambridge University Press, Cambridge.

Hajek, P. and Havranek, T.: 1978, *Mechanizing Hypothesis Formation: Mathematical Foundations for a General Theory*, Springer Verlag, New York.

Harman, Gilbert: 1963, 'Generative Grammars without Transformation Rules', *Language* 39, 597–616.

Harman, Gilbert: 1967, 'Psychological Aspects of the Theory of Syntax', *The Journal of Philosophy* LXIV, 75–87.

Harman, Gilbert: 1968, 'Three Levels of Meaning', *The Journal of Philosophy* LXV, 590–601.

Harman, Gilbert: 1969, 'Linguistic Competence and Empiricism', in Sidney Hook (ed.), *Language and Philosophy*, New York University Press, New York.

Harman, Gilbert: 1973, *Thought*, Princeton University Press, Princeton.

Harman, Gilbert: 1978, 'Is there Mental Representation?' in C. Wade Savage (ed.), *Minnesota Studies in the Philosophy of Science* Vol. IX, *Perception and Cognition: Issues in the Foundations of Psychology*, University of Minnesota Press, Minneapolis.

Hartmanis, J. and Stearns, R. E.: 1966, *Algebraic Structure of Sequential Machines*, Prentice Hall, Inc., New York.

Hebb, H. O.: 1949, *Organization of Behavior*, John Wiley and Sons, Inc., New York.

Hempel, Carl G. and Oppenheim, Paul: 1948, 'The Logic of Explanation', *Philosophy of Science* 15, 135–178.

Hesse, Mary: 1953, 'Models in Physics', *The British Journal for the Philosophy of Science* 4, 198–214.

Hill, Christopher S.: 1981, 'Why Cartesian Intuitions are Compatible with the Identity Thesis', *Philosophy and Phenomenological Research* 42, 254–265.

Hill, Christopher S.: 1988, 'Intentionality, Folk Psychology and Reduction' in Herbert Otto and James A. Tuedio (eds.), *Perspectives on Mind*, D. Reidel Publishing Co., Dordrecht.

Hintikka, Jaakko: 1962, *Knowledge and Belief*, Cornell University Press, Ithaca, N.Y.

Hintikka, Jaakko: 1969, 'Semantics for Propositional Attitudes', reprinted in Leonard Linsky (ed.), *Reference and Modality*, Oxford University Press, London, 1971.

Hollander, John: 1974, 'Coiled Alizadrine', reprinted in Gilbert Harman (ed.), *On Noam Chomsky: Critical Essays*, Anchor Books, Garden City, N.Y.

Hook, Sidney (ed.): 1969, *Language and Philosophy*, New York University Press, New York.

Hoy, Ronald: 1979, 'Dispositions, Logical States, and Occurents', *Synthese* 44, 207–246.

Huffman, David: 1954, 'The Synthesis of Sequential Switching Circuits', *Journal of the Franklin Institute* 257, 275–303.

Hume David: 1739, *A Treatise of Human Nature*, Selby Bigge (ed.) Oxford University Press, Oxford, 1896.

James, William: 1909, *The Meaning of Truth*, printed in *Pragmatism: A New Name for some Old Ways of Thinking*, Longman, Green and Co., New York.

Kalke, William: 1969, 'What is Wrong with Fodor and Putnam's Functionalism', *Nous* III, 83–94.

Katz, Jerrold: 1965, 'The Relevance of Linguistics to Philosophy', *The Journal of Philosophy* LXVII, 590–601.

Katz, Jerrold: 1972, *Semantic Theory*, Harper and Row, New York.

Katz, Jerrold: 1975, 'Logic and Language: an Examination of Recent Criticisms of Intensionalism', in Keith Gunderson (ed.), *Minnesota Studies in the Philosophy of Science* Vol. VII, *Language, Mind and Knowledge*, University of Minnesota Press, Minneapolis.

Katz, Jerrold: 1977, *Propositional Structure and Illocutionary Force*, Crowell, Harper and Row, New York.

Katz, Jerrold J.: 1981, *Language and other Objects,* Rowman and Little field, Totowa, N.J.

Kleene, S. C.: 1951, 'Representation of Events in Nerve Nets and Finite Automata', Project RAND Research Memorandum RM 704, 1951; published in C. E. Shannon and J. McCarthy (eds.) *Automata Studies*, Princeton University Press, Princeton, 1956.

Kleene, S. C.: 1952, *Introduction to Metamathematics*, D. Van Norstrand Co., New York.

Kolers, A., Paul: 1974, 'Two Kinds of Recognition', *Canadian Journal of Psychology* 28, 51–61.

Kolers, A., Paul and Perkins, David N.: 1975, Spatial and Ordinal Components of Form and Perception Literacy', *Cognitive Psychology* 7, 228–267.

Kripke, A., Saul: 1972, 'Naming and Necessity', in Donald Davidson and Gilbert Harman (eds.), *Semantics of Natural Language*, D. Reidel Publishing Co., Dordrecht, Holland.

Lee, C. Y.: 1960, 'Automata and Finite Automata', *Bell System Technical Journal* 39, 1267–1295.

Lee, C. Y.: 1963, 'A Turing Machine which Prints its own Code Script', in *Proceedings of the Symposium on Mathematical Theory of Automata*, Polytechnic Press, Brooklyn.

Levi, Isaac and Morgenbesser, Sidney: 1964, 'Belief and Disposition', *American Philosophical Quarterly* I, 1–12.

Levin, Michael E.: 1975, 'Kripke's Argument against the Identity Theory', *The Journal of Philosophy* LXXII, 149–167.

Lettvin, J. Y., Maturana, H., McCulloch, W. S., and Pitts, W. H.: 1959, 'What the Frog's Eye tells the Frog's Brain', *Proceedings of the IRE* 47, 1940–1951.

Lewis, David: 1969, *Convention*, Harvard University Press, Cambridge, Mass.

Lewis, David: 1972, 'General Semantics', in Donald Davidson and Gilbert Harman (eds.), *Semantics of Natural Language*, D. Reidel Publishing Co., Dordrecht.

Lewis, David: 1973, *Counterfactuals*, Harvard University Press, Cambridge, Mass.

Loar, Brian: 1986, *Mind and Meaning*, Cambridge University Press, Cambridge, Great Britain. 3.

Locke, John: 1690, *An Essay Concerning Human Understanding*, Vol. I fifteenth edition, London, 1790.

Lucas, J. R.: 1961, 'Minds, Machines, and Gödel', in Alan Ross Anderson (ed.), *Minds and Machines*, Prentice-Hall, Inc. Englewood Cliffs, N.J.

Lycan, William G.: 1974, 'Mental States and Putnam's Functionalist Hypothesis', *Australasian Journal of Philosophy* 52, 48–62.

Margolis, Joseph: 1980, 'The Trouble with Homunculus Theories', *Philosophy of Science* 47, 244–259.

Matson, Wallace I.: 1976, *Sentience*, University of California Press, Berkeley.

McCarthy, John: 1979, 'Ascribing Mental Qualities to Machines', in Martin Ringle (ed.) *Philosophical Perspectives on Artificial Intelligence,* Humanties Press, Atlantic Highland, N.J.

McCulloch, Warren S. and Walter H. Pitts: 1943, 'A Logical Calculus of the Ideas Immanent in Nervous Activity', *Bulletin of Mathematical Biophysics* 5, 115–133.

McKeon, Richard P. (ed.): 1941, *The Basic Works of Aristotle*, Random House, New York.

Mead, George H.: 1934, in Charles Morris (ed.), *Mind, Self, and Society*, The University of Chicago Press, Chicago.

Mead, George H.: 1938, in Charles Morris (ed.), *Philosophy of the Act*, The University of Chicago Press, Chicago.

Mealy G. H.: 1955, 'A Method of Synthesizing Sequential Circuits', *Bell System Technical Journal* 34, 1045–1079.

Melden, A. I.: 1956, 'Action', reprinted in Norman S. Care and Charles Landesman (eds.), *Readings in the Theory of Action*, Indiana University Press, Bloomington.

Mendelson, Elliott: 1964, *Introduction to Mathematical Logic*, D. Van Nostrand Co., Inc., Princeton, N.J.

Miller, George A.: 1964, *The Psychology of Communication*, Penguin Books, Inc., Baltimore.

Miller, George A.: Eugene Galanter and Pribram, Karl H.: 1960, *Plans and the Structure of Behavior*, Holt, Rinehard, and Winston, New York.

Minsky, Marvin: 1965, 'Matter, Mind, and Models', in Marvin Minsky (ed.), *Semantic Information Processing*, The MIT Press, Cambridge, Mass, 1968.

Minsky, Marvin and Papert, Seymour: 1969, *Perceptrons: An Introduction to Computational Geometry*, The MIT Press, Cambridge, Mass.

Moore, E. F.: 1956, 'Gedanken Experiments on Sequential Machines', in C. E. Shannon and J. McCarthy (eds.), *Automata Studies*, Princeton University Press, Princeton, N.J.

Montague, Richard: 1970, 'Pragmatics and Intensional Logic', reprinted in Richmond H. Thomason, (ed.), *Formal Philosophy: Selected Papers of Richard Montague*, Yale University Press, New Haven, 1974.

Nagel, Ernest: 1961, *The Structure of Science*, Harcourt, Brace, and World, New York.

Nagel, Ernest and James R. Newman: 1956, *Goedel's Proof*, reprinted in James R. Newman (ed.), *The World of Mathematics*, Simon and Schuster, New York.

Nagel, Thomas: 1972, Review of D. C. Dennett, *Content and Consciousness, The Journal of Philosophy* LXIX, 220–224.

Nelson, R. J.: 1968, *Introduction to Automata*, John Wily and Sons, Inc., New York.

Nelson, R. J.: 1969, 'Behaviorism is False', *The Journal of Philosophy* LXVI, 417–451.

Nelson, R. J.: 1971, 'Are Humanly Recognizable Patterns Effective?' in Jerome Fox (ed.), *Computers and Automata*, Polytechnic Press, Brooklyn.

Nelson, R. J.: 1975a, 'Behaviorism, Finite Automata, and Stimulus Response Theory', *Theory and Decision* 6, 249–267.

Nelson, R. J.: 1975b, 'On Machine Expectation', *Synthese* 39, 129–139.

Nelson, R. J.: 1976a, 'Mechanism, Functionalism, and the Identity Theory, *The Journal of Philosophy* LXXIII, 365–585.

Nelson, R. J.: 1976b, 'On Mechanical Recognition', *Philosophy of Science* 43, 24–52.

Nelson, R. J.: 1977, 'Structure of Complex Systems', in F. Suppe and P. D. Asquith (eds.), *PSA 1976* 2, Philosophy of Science Association.

Nelson, R. J.: 1978a, 'The Competence Performance Distinction in Mental Philosophy', *Synthese* 39, 337–381.

Nelson, R. J.: 1978b, 'Objects of Occasion Beliefs', *Synthese* 39, 105–139.

Nelson, R. J.: 1980, Review of Margaret Boden, *Artificial Intelligence and Natural Man*, *Synthese* 43, 433–451.

Nelson, R. J': 1982, 'Artificial Intelligence, Philosophy, and Existence Proofs', in Donald Michie (ed.), *Machine Intelligence* 10, (to appear).

Nelson, R. J.: 1984, 'Naturalizing Intentions' *Synthese* 61, 174–203.

Nelson, R. J.: 1987a, 'Church's Thesis and Cognitive Science' *Notre Dame Journal of Formal Logic* 28, 581–614.

Nelson, R. J': 1987b, 'Models for Cognitive Science', *Philosophy of Science* 54, 391–408.

Nelson, R. J.: 1988a, 'Mechanism and Intentionality: the New World Knot' in Herbert R. Otto and James A. Tuedio (eds.), *Perspectives on Mind*, D. Reidel Publishing Co., Dordrecht.

Nelson, R. J.: 1988b, 'Connections among Connections' *Behavioral and Brain Sciences* 11, 45–46.

Nelson, R. J.: 1988c, 'The Mind-Machine Connection' in Ephraim Nissan (ed.), *Advances in Humanities and Computing* (to appear).

Nilsson, Nils: 1965, *Learning Machines*, McGraw-Hill Book Co. New York.

Pao, Tsyh-Won Lee: 1969, 'A Solution of the Induction Problem for Context-Free Languages', Doctoral Dissertation, The Moore School of Electrical Engineering, University of Pennsylvania.

Peacocke, C.: 1979, *Holistic Explanation*, Clarendon Press, Oxford.

Peirce, C. S.: 1932, 1934, in Charles Hartshorne and Paul Weiss (eds.), *Collected Papers* Vol. II and V, Harvard University Press, Cambridge, Mass.

Piaget, Jean and W. May: 1957, *Logic and Psychology*, Basic Books, Inc., New York.

Place, U. T.: 1956, 'Is Consciousness a Brain Process?' *British Journal of the Philosophy of Science* XLVII, 44–51.

Plantinga, Alvin: 1974, *The Nature of Necessity*, The Clarendon Press, Oxford.

Popper, Karl and Eccles, John C.: 1977, *The Self and its Brain*, Springer International, New York.

Post, Emil: 1936, 'Finite Combinatory Processes, Formulation I', *Journal of Symbolic Logic* I, 103–105.

Post, Emil: 1941, 'Absolutely Unsolvable Problems and Relatively Undecidable Propositions – Account of an Anticipation', printed in (Davis, 1965).

Post, Emil: 1944, 'Recursively Enumerable Sets of Positive Integers and their Decision Problems', *Bulletin of the American Mathematical Society* 52, 284–316.

Post, Emil: 1947, 'Recursive Unsolvability of a Problem of Thue', *Journal of Symbolic Logic* 12, 1–11.

Price, H. H.: 1932, *Perception*, Methuen and Co., London.

Putnam, Hilary: 1960, 'Minds and Machines', in Sidney Hook (ed.), *Dimensions of Mind*, New York University Press, New York.

Putnam, Hilary: 1964, 'Robots: Machines or Artificially Created Life?' *The Journal of Philosophy* LXI, 668–691.

Putnam, Hilary: 1967, 'Psychological Predicates', in Captain and Merrill (eds.), *Art Mind and Religion*, University of Pittsburgh Press, Pittsburgh.

Putnam, Hilary: 1970, 'Is Semantics Possible?' reprinted in *Mind, Language, and Reality*, Cambridge University Press, Cambridge, 1975.

Putnam, Hilary: 1969, 'On Properties', in N. Rescher (ed.), *Essays in Honor of Carl G. Hempel*, D. Reidel Publishing Co., Dordrecht, Holland, pp. 235–255.

Putnam, Hilary: 1973a, 'Meaning and Reference', *The Journal of Philosophy* LXX, 699–711.

Putnam, Hilary: 1973b, 'Philosophy and our Mental Life', reprinted in *Mind, Language, and Reality*, Cambridge University Press, Cambridge, 1975.

Putnam, Hilary: 1975, 'The Meaning of "Meaning"', in Keith Gunderson (ed.), *Minnesota Studies in the Philosophy of Science* Vol. VII, *Language, Mind, and Knowledge*, University of Minnesota Press, Minneapolis.

Putnam, Hilary: 1976, 'What is Realism?' *Proceedings of the Aristotelian Society 1975–76*, 177–194.

Putnam, Hilary: 1977, 'Realism and Reason', *Proceedings and Addresses of the American Philosophical Association* 50, 483–497.

Pylyshyn, Zenon: 1978, 'Imagery and Artifical Intelligence', in C. Wade Savage (ed.),

Minnesota Studies in the Philosophy of Science Vol. IX, *Perception and Cognition: Issues in the Foundations of Psychology*, University of Minnesota Press, Minneapolis.

Pylyshyn, Zenon W.: 1984, *Computers and Cognition*, The MIT Press, Cambridge.

Quine, W. V.: 1956, 'Quantification and Propositional Attitudes', *The Journal of Philosophy* LIII, 177—187.

Quine, W. V.: 1960, *Word and Object*, John Wiley and Sons, Inc., New York.

Quine, W. V.: 1966, 'Mental Entities', in *The Ways of Paradox and other Essays*, Random House, New York.

Quine, W. V.: 1969a, *Ontological Relativity and other Essays*, Columbia University Press, New York.

Quine, W. V.: 1969b, 'Linguistics and Philosophy', in Sidney Hook (ed.), *Language and Philosophy*, New York University Press, New York.

Quine, W. V.: 1970, *Philosophy of Logic*, Prentice Hall, Inc., Englewood Cliffs, N.J.

Quine, W. V.: 1972, 'Methodological Reflections on Current Linguistics', in Donald Davidson and Gilbert Harman (eds.), *Semantics of Natural Language*, D. Reidel Publishing Co., Dordrecht, Holland.

Quine, W. V.: 1973, *The Roots of Reference*, Open Court, La Salle, Ill.

Quine, W. V.: 1976, 'Worlds Away', *The Journal of Philosophy* LXXIII, 859—863.

Quine, W. V.: 1977, 'Intensions Revisited', *Midwest Studies in Philosophy* II, 5—11.

Rabin, M. O.: 1964, 'Probabilistic Automata', in E. F. Moore (ed.), *Sequential Machines*, Addison-Wesley Publishing Co. Reading, Mass.

Rabin, M. O. and Dana Scott: 1959, 'Finite Automata and their Decision Problems', *IBM Journal of Research and Development* 3, 114—125.

Reed, Stephen K. and Friedman, Morton P.: 1973, 'Perceptual vs Conceptual Categorization', *Memory and Cognition* 1, 157—163.

Reid, Thomas: 1788, *Essays on the Active Powers of the Human Mind*, reproduced from Vols. III and IV, *The Works of Thomas Reid*, The MIT Press, Cambridge, Mass., 1969.

Rochester, N., Holland, J. H., Haibt, L. H., and Duda, W. L.: 1956, Test on a Cell Assembly Theory on the Action of the Brain using a Large Digital Computer', *IRE Transactions on Information Theory* IT-2, 80—93.

Root, Michael: 1975, 'Language, Rules, and Complex Behavior', in Keith Gunderson (ed.), *Minnesota Studies in the Philosophy of Science* Vol. VII, *Language, Mind, and Knowledge*, University of Minnesota Press, Minneapolis.

Rorty, Richard: 1970, 'Incorrigibility as the Mark of the Mental', *The Journal of Philosophy* LXXVII, 399—424.

Rosenbluth, Arturo, Weiner, Norbert, and Bigelow, Julian: 1943, 'Behavior, Purpose, and Teleology', *Philosophy of Science* X, 18—24.

Rounds, William C.: 1970, 'Mappings and Grammars on Trees', *Mathematical Systems Theory* 4, 257—297.

Rumelhart, David E. and McClelland, James L.: 1987, *Parallel Distributed Processing; Explorations in the Microstructure of Cognition, Vol. 1: Foundations*, The MIT Press, Cambridge, Mass.

Russell, Bertrand: 1914, 'On the Nature of Acquaintance', reprinted in Robert C. Marsh (ed.), *Logic and Knowledge*, Allen and Unwin, London, 1956.

Russell, Bertrand: 1918, 'Philosophy of Logical Atomism', reprinted in Robert C. Marsh (ed.), *Logic and Knowledge*, Allen and Unwin, London, 1956.

Russell, Bertrand: 1927, *An Outline of Philosophy*, Allen and Unwin, London.

Russell, Bertrand: 1948, *Human Knowledge, its Scope and its Limits*, Simon and Schuster, New York.

Ryle, Gilbert: 1949, *The Concept of Mind*, Barnes and Noble, New York.

Samuel, A. L.: 1959, 'Some Studies in Machine Learning using the Game of Checkers', *IBM Journal of Research and Development* 3, 211–229.

Savage-Rumbaugh, Sue, Rumbaugh, Duane M. and Roysen, Sarah: 1980, 'Do Apes Use Language?' *American Scientist* 68, 49–61.

Sayre, Kenneth: 1963, 'Human and Mechanical Recognition', in Kenneth Sayre and Frederick Crosson (eds.), *The Modelling of Mind: Computers and Intelligence*, University of Notre Dame Press, Notre Dame, Indiana.

Sayre, Kenneth: 1965, *Recognition: A study in the Philosophy of Artifical Intelligence*, University of Notre Dame Press, Notre Dame, Indiana.

Scheffler, Israel: 1963, *The Anatomy of Inquiry*, Alfred S. Knopf, New York.

Schneider, R. E.: 1974, 'The Neuron as a Sequential Machine', Proceedings of Conference on Biologically Motivated Automata Theory, 1974.

Schwartz, Robert: 1978, 'Infinite Sets, Unbound Competences, and Models of Mind', in C. Wade Savage (ed.), *Minnesota Studies in the Philosophy of Science* Vol. IX, *Perception and Cognition: Issues in the Foundations of Psychology*, University of Minnesota Press, Minneapolis.

Scriven, Michael: 1960, 'The Compleat Robot: A Prolegomena to Androidology', in Sidney Hook (ed.), *Dimensions of Mind*, New York University Press, New York.

Scriven, Michael: 1964, 'The Mechanical Concept of Mind', in Alan Ross Anderson (ed.), *Minds and Machines*, Prentice-Hall, Inc. Englewood Cliffs, New Jersey.

Searle, John: 1972, 'Chomsky's Revolution in Linguistics', *The New York Review of Books*, reprinted in Gilbert Harman (ed.), *On Noam Chomsky: Critical Essays*, Anchor Books, New York.

Searle, John: 1980, 'Minds, Brains, and Programs' *Behavioral and Brain Sciences* 3, 417–57.

Selfridge, Oliver G. and Neisser, Ulric: 1963, 'Pattern Recognition by Machines', in Edward A. Feigenbaum and Julian Feldman (eds.), *Computers and Thought*, John Wiley and Sons, Inc., New York.

Shannon, Claude E.: 1956, 'A Universal Turing Machine with Two Internal States', in C. E. Shannon and J. McCarthy (eds.), *Automata Studies*, Princeton University Press, Princeton.

Shannon, Claude E. and Weaver, Warren: 1949, *The Mathematical Theory of Communication*, The University of Illinois Press, Urbana, Illinois.

Shimony, Abner: 1971, 'Perception from an Evolutionary Point of View', *The Journal of Philosophy* LXVIII, 571–583.

Simon, Herbert: 1977, 'How Complex are Complex Systems?' in F. Suppe and P. D. Asquith (eds.), *PSA 1976* 2, Philosophy of Science Association.

Simon, H. A. and Newell, Allen: 1963, 'GPS, A Program that Simulates Human Thought', in Edward Feigenbaum and Julian Feldman (eds.), *Computers and Thought*, McGraw Hill Book Co., N.Y.

Skinner, B. F.: 1953, *Science and Human Behavior*, The Macmillan Co., New York.

Skinner, B. F.: 1963, 'The Flight from the Laboratory', in N. H. Marx (ed.), *Theories in Contemporary Psychology*, The Macmillan Co., New York.

Skolem, Thoralf: 1923, 'Foundations of Recursive Arithmetic Established by Means of Recursive Modes of Thought without the Use of Apparent Variables Ranging over Infinite Domains', reprinted in Jan van Heijenoort (ed.), *From Frege to Gödel*, Harvard University Press, Cambridge Mass., 1967.

Sloman, Aaron: 1978, *The Computer Revolution in Philosophy*, Humanities Press, Atlantic Highlands, New Jersey.

Smart, J. C. C.: 1959, 'Sensations and Brain Processes', *Philosophical Review* LXVIII, reprinted in C. V. Borst (ed.), *The Mind-Brain Identity Theory*, Macmillan and Co. Ltd., London, 1962.

Smart, J. C. C.: 1963, *Philosophy and Scientific Realism*, Routledge and Kegan Paul, London.

Smolensky, Paul: 1988, 'On the Proper Treatment of Connectionism' *Behavioral and Brain Sciences* 11, 1–23.

Spence, Kenneth W.: 1948, 'The Postulates and Methods of Behaviorism', *Psychological Review* LV, 67–78.

Stevens, Charles F.: 1966, *Neurophysiology: A Primer*, John Wiley and Sons, Inc., New York.

Suppes, Patrick: 1969, 'Stimulus Response Theory of Finite Automata', *Journal of Mathematical Psychology* 6, 327–355.

Suppes, Patrick: 1975, 'From Behaviorism to Neobehaviorism', *Theory and Decision* 6, 269–286.

Tarski, Alfred: 1936, 'The Concept of Truth in Formalized Languages', in J. H. Woodger (trans.) *Logic, Semantics and Metamathematics*, The Clarendon Press, Oxford, 1956.

Terrace, Herbert S.: 1979, 'Can an Ape Create a Sentence?' *Science* 206, 891–900.

Thatcher, James W.: 1963, 'The Construction of a Self-Describing Turing Machine', in *Mathematical Theory of Automata*, Polytechnic Press, Brooklyn.

Thomas, Stephen N.: 1978, *The Formal Mechanics of Mind*, Cornell University Press, Ithaca, New York.

Tolman, E. C.: 1932, 'Behavior, a Molar Phenomenon', Chapter I of *Purposive Behavior in Animals and Men*, reprinted in Norman S. Care and Charles Landesman (eds.), *Readings in the Theory of Action*, Indiana University Press, Bloomington, Indiana, 1968.

Tolman, E. C.: 1936, 'Operational Behaviorism and Current Trends in Psychology', *Proceedings of the 25th Anniversary of the Inauguration of Graduate Studies*, University of Southern California Press, Los Angeles.

Tuomela, Raimo: 1976, 'Disposition, Realism, and Explanation', *Synthese* 34, 457–478.

Turing, A. M.: 1936, 'On Computable Numbers with Applications to the Entscheidunsproblem', *Proceedings of the London Mathematical Society* 42, 230–265.

Turing, A. M.: 1950, 'Computing Machinery and Intelligence', *Mind* LIX, 433–460.

van Rooten, L.: 1967, *Mot d'Heures: Gousses, Rames*, The Viking Press, New York.

von Neumann, J.: 1951, 'Probabilistic Logics and the Synthesis of Reliable Organisms from Unreliable Components', in C. E. Shannon and J. McCarthy (eds.), *Automata Studies*, Princeton University Press, Princeton, 1956.

von Neumann, J.: 1966, in Arthur W. Burks (ed.), *Theory of Self-Reproducing Automata*, University of Illinois Press, Urbana, Ill.

Webb, Judson: 1980, *Mechanism, Mentalism, and Metamathematics,* D. Reidel Publishing Co., Dordrecht, Holland.

Wertheimer, M.: 1944, 'Gestalt Theory', *Social Research* 2, 78–99.

Whitehead, Bruce A.: 1978, 'A Neural Model of Human Pattern Recognition', Ph. D. Dissertation, The University of Michigan.

Wiener, Norbert: 1948, *Cybernetics, or Control and Communication in the Animal and Machine*, The MIT Press, Cambridge, Mass.

Williams, B. A. O.: 1951, 'The Hypothesis of Cybernetics', *The British Journal for the Philosophy of Science* II, 1–24.

Winograd, Terry: 1972, *Understanding Natural Language*, Academic Press, New York.

Wiggenstein, Ludwig: 1953, *Philosophical Investigations*, Trans. G. E. M. Anscombe, The Macmillan Co., New York.

Wolman, Benjamin R. (ed.): 1973, *Dictionary of Behavioral Science*, Van Nostrand Reinhold Co., New York.

Wolter, Allan B.: 1967, 'John Duns Scotus', in Paul Edwards (ed. in chief), *The Encyclopedia of Philosophy* Vol. 2, Macmillan Publishing Co., New York.

Zadeh, L. A.: 1964, 'The Concept of State in Systems Theory', in Mihajlo D. Mesarovich (ed.), *Views on General Systems Theory*, John Wiley and Sons, Inc., New York.

Zuriff, G. E.: 1985, *Behaviorism: a Conceptual Reconstruction*, Columbia University Press, N.Y.

INDEX

abstract automaton, *see* automaton

abduction 232

acceptability 193, 266; and effective decidability 263, 277; for fixed believer

acceptance 43, 45, 163, 171, 228, 294, 322; contextual 194; in extended sense 193; of relations 241–243, virtual 190, 193, 206–207; and semantics 253

acceptor 43, 45, 342; *see also* automaton

accepted set 171–172

act 226, 229f

action relation (A) 225, 227, 229

action potential 67

adequacy condition 82; for belief-desire model 218, 221–224, 357; for analysys of intentional sentences 253–254; for perception model 166–171, 200–201, 209, 355; for truth definition 274–275

adder 47–51; *see also* serial adder

Albert Hall 105, 348

Albert the Great 15, 18

algorithm 25, 27, 55, 85; free and embodied 27, 48, 119, 157, 160, 319, 340; practical 348

analytic 76, 345

and-gate, *see* logic, component

annelid 10, 114–116, 134; nondeterministic 116; *also see* automaton

anomalous monism 310

Anscombe, G. E. M. 211

Aquinas, T. 15, 306

argument from analogy (for mechanism) 89, 93–99, 116–118

Aristotle xiv, 3, 14, 167

Armstrong, D. M. 350, 351

Aronson, Jerry xvi

artificial intelligence (AI) 2, 82, 249,

317; *see also* model, simulation

ascription to individuals 240, 262, 266, 268; and naming 301

atomic act 100–101

atomistic hypothesis (perception) 356

atomic sentence 278

attention 54, 166, 222, 237, 323; and truth definition 274

automaton 8, 23, 34, 56; abstract 39–42; annelid as 97, 114–116, 135; autonomous 16–17; backward indeterministic 140, 316; behavior 60–63, 139; Cartesian 15, 17; complex 176–177; deterministic finite state (FA) 41, 43–44, 45, 60, 65, 68–81, 94, 98, 120–131, 133–136, 342, 349, 366; finite state acceptor (FSA) 171–173; initial state FA 133–134, 177, 225; general FA 133, 135; finite transducer (sequential machine) 45; minimal 361; nondeterministic finite automaton (NFA) 4, 35, 36, 40, 45, 58, 60, 69, 81, 114–116; nondeterministic finite state acceptor 171; parallel 174–175; part-whole 177; probabilistic 311, 342–343; quasi-connected 354; reduced 139; self-describing 189–192; serial 225, 227–229, 357; super (T') 189–190, 225; *see also* Turing machine

automorphism 350

awareness 14

axiom 24

axon 37–38, 67, 341

Babbage, Charles 348

Bach, J. S. 3, 105, 168–169, 184, 185, 186, 196, 225, 226, 227, 231, 235, 237, 323, 346, 354

backward indeterministic automaton, *see* automaton
Banerji, Ranan 341
Bar-Hillel, Y. 341, 361
base Turing machine 181, 214, 260–261, 294; *see also* Turing machine
Bealer, George 366
Beethoven, Ludwig van 222
Bever, T. G. 244
behavior 59, 84, 101, 179; externalized 111–112; shared 108–109; *see also* automaton behavior
behavioral equivalence 61, 65, 80, 86, 123, 325
behavioral similarity (human and computer) 93–95
behaviorism 1, 7, 110, 117, 119, 131–142, 153, 220, 342; logical 76, 132, 307–308, 366; metaphysical 132; methodological 132, 133
belief 160; as disposition 218–219, 221; as relational 220; as a state 130, 131, 365; and computational structures 249; and verbalization 247–249; core 256–257, 262; de dicto 257–258; de re 255–257, 262; expression of 243, 252, 356; kinds of 218–219; objects of 212; occurrent vs. dispositional 130; of abstract relations 241–242, 358–359; perceptual 130, 131, 199, 213–215, 219, 232, 318; of logical relations vs. relations of belief 235–238; psychology of 212; standing 233, 242, 247–250; tensed 356; weak de re 255–258
bio-social matrix 6, 10
black box 347
Block, N. 342, 123–131, 350, 357, 368
Boden, Margaret 317, 348, 367
bodily movement 110; contrasted to action 229
Boolean algebra of accepted sets 177; of acceptors (FSA) 238, 358
boundaries and levels of description 80, 83–85
brain 37
brain state 54–55, 70, 74

Brentano, Franz 5, 81, 142, 219–220, 235, 246, 252, 253, 357, 367
Brentano's Thesis xv, 81, 219–221, 252–253, 357; and computationalism 367
Büchi, J. R. 366
Burge, Tyler 362
Burks, A. W. 3, 45, 46, 52, 95, 97, 99, 101, 111, 184, 340, 341, 344, 347, 368

CP30 111
calculus ratiocinator 27
Carnap, Rudolf xv, 76, 82, 136–137, 179, 233, 249, 275, 282, 345, 351, 360, 369
Carson, Johnny 333
Cartesian intuition 334–336, 368
Cartesian rationalism 154
catatonic 315, 321
categorical imperative 322
categorical structure 68
categories (Kant) 87
category mistake 11
causal theory of reference, *see* reference, *see also* naming
causal theory of perception 202–205
cell assemblies 54
cell body 37
central state materialism 351
Chang, C. C. 345
characteristic function 261
chauvinism 125
checkers 91, 101–107, 110
chess 106–107
Chihara, Charles S. 348
chinese translator 112f, 318f
Chisholm, Roderick 200–202, 208, 220, 253–255, 345, 355
Chopin, Frederic 248
Chomsky, Noam xiv, xvi, 6, 29, 32, 34, 37, 44, 55, 69, 86, 87, 119, 142–157, 159, 184, 219, 249, 265, 276, 290, 313, 340, 351, 352
Church, Alonzo 57, 340
Church's Thesis 26, 27, 68, 100–101, 340, 345
Churchland, Paul 309-310

Churchland, Patricia 309
Classical mechanics 304
Clemens, Samuel 306
clocks 16
coding 40, 49-51
cognition 55
cognitivism 5, 55, 119, 157–61, 244
communication 243
commutative diagram 183–184, 354
commutatively 51
competence 34, 69, 75, 145, 147-148, 155–156; performance distinction 310
complete theory 31
complex system 70, 81
complexity 69–73, 79, 126–127, 358; see also automaton complexity
composite function 98
computer 2, 10, 27, 45–46, 51, 81, 89, 101–108; and intentionality 318–319; hypothesis formation 348; learning 105–107; mistakes 108–110; networks 45–53; sensing 10, 11
computer program 100; as deductions 104; machine language 100; heuristic 104–105, 348
computation 21, 25–26, 57, 58; human 100–101; syntactical 112, 319, 352
concept 295; and extension 298
connectionism 98f, 131
computationalism 317
concept 295; and extension 298
consciousness 10, 322; continuum of 322; of self 323; selective 323; stream of states of 322; machine₂ 347
consistent theory 103
context-free grammar, see grammar
context-free language, see language
contingent identity 96, 109, 331–336; see also identity, mind-body identity
continuity 96, 109; continuous geometry 96f
control theory, see cybernetics
Copi, I. M. 45, 46, 52, 95
core belief 241–242, 247, 249, 252, 283, 358
core language (C) 263–264, 270, 362;

semantics 271–273; syntax 270
core sentence 254, 284
correspondence theory, see truth
Couturat, Louis 340
Craig, William 366
Craik, K. J. W. 55, 119, 158, 342
Creary, Lewis 347
creativity (machine 103–107)
Culbertson, James T. 128, 130
cybernetics 16, 55–56, 93, 231, 358, 367

Darwin, Charles 34
Davidson, Donald 251, 252, 276, 357, 360, 361, 363, 364
Davis, Martin 239, 240, 352
decision procedure 340
decoding, see coding
decomposition 70
de dicto belief, see belief
Dedekind, Richard 366
deep structure 30, 151
definite description 299, 332, 333; and names 300
definition: explicit 142, 218, 219–220, 221; implicit 221–222; eliminative 138
degraded stimulus 169, 190, 193, 202, 203, 205
degree of dilation 96
deictic 241; see also name
Deism 328
Democritean world 285–287, 364
Democritus 3
Dennett, D. C. 100–101, 112, 121, 221–224, 245, 305, 317, 332, 348, 349, 357, 359
denotation 263–270; or demonstratives 266–267; of proper names 268; of logically proper names 362; and intentionality 269
de re belief, see belief
derivation tree 31–33
De Saussure, Ferdinand 351
Descartes, Rene 9, 12, 14, 15, 17, 87, 112, 220, 368
description: automaton 80, 97; explicit 134–139; historical 227; mathemati-

cal 192, 227; mathematical vs historical 129–130
descriptive adequacy 147–148
design stance 121
desire 193, 212, 230–231; to communicate 243–244, 252; to understand
243–244
deterministic finite state automaton, *see*
automaton
determinism 4, 113–118; physical necessity 320; *see* automaton
Dewey, John xv, 6, 7, 11, 278, 339
Dickens, Charles 254, 256
differential response 114
discrete state system 35–36, 73, 95–99,
347; mental 99, 100
disposition 7, 109, 112; to act 128–129;
to act conditionally 236; and relational belief 236; and states 128–129
disruption 188, 192, 202, 231
dominant hemisphere 82
doxastic operator (B) 235–237, 358
Dretske, Fred 352f, 357, 358
Dreyfus, Hubert L. 91, 107, 195, 209,
355
dualism 3, 146, 304, 328–330
Dummett, Michael xv, 251, 252, 276,
277, 360, 363
Duns Scotus, John 3, 87, 305–307,
365–366

Eccles, John C. 328
Edelman, Gerald 205, 354f
Edison, Thomas 356
effectively calculable function 25, 28,
57; *see also* Church's Thesis
effectiveness 25, 57, 347; see also
Church's Thesis
Elgot, Calvin 366
eliminative materialism 11, 161, 339
embodied algorithm, *see* algorithm
embodiment 67, 74, 85–86
emergence 11, 349
empiricism 75, 76, 87, 158–161
epiphenomenalism 208, 304, 329
epistemic situation (in learning names)
333

epistemology 9, 87, 96, 112, 199, 215–
218
Epstein, Steven 356
equivalence class 344, 347
essence 306
Estes, W. K. 346
evidence and taking 215–218; *see also*
taking
evolutionism 205–206, 215, 232, 356;
and truth definition 275
excusive or, *see* subtraction
exemplar 283; *see also* ideal language
user
existence 306
expectation 109, 111, 163, 187–194,
202, 206, 213, 226, 232; simultaneous 194; and meaning 288
explanatory adequacy 147–148
explanation, rational 5; covering law
model of 312–313; mechanistic
313–317; probabilistic 317; purposive 313
explication 82; and explanation 317
extension 281, 293
extension$_1$ 293; and propositional object
365
extension$_2$ 294; and taking 296
external world 8
external control 16

failure theory 310
family resemblance 170–171, 195–198,
207–209; as taking 196–197; *see
also* resemblance
feedback 158, 352; negative 231–232,
342
feedback link 87
feeling 10
Feigenbaum, Edward A. 348
Feigl, Herbert 13, 14, 329
Feldman, Julian 348
Feyerabend, Paul 11
Field, Hartry xv, 212, 246, 251, 252,
269, 339, 357, 362, 364
finite state acceptor, *see* automaton
finite automaton, *see* automaton
finite state grammar, *see* grammar

finite state identity theory (FSIT) 123–131, 158
finite state language, *see* language
finite transducer (sequential machine), *see* automaton
first, firstness 339
first order logic 238, 270
Fischer, Bobby 348
fitting 77, 141, 148, 350; and functionalism 305; *see also* guiding
fixed believer 283, 293, 294
Fodor, Jerry A. xiii, 84, 112, 121, 123–131, 156, 158, 185, 210, 243, 245, 249, 285, 309, 342, 346, 349, 350, 351, 354, 357, 359, 367
form 4
formal distinction 3, 87, 305, 363
formal system 24, 28, 68, 101–103
formula: truth functional 50–51; network 46–49
formalism (ethical) 321
formalized automaton 325
framework hypothesis 162
Franklin, Benjamin 332, 334
freedom 112, 320
free algorithm; *see* algorithm
Frege, Gottlob 249, 259–260, 284, 288, 296, 299, 332, 361, 362, 366
Freund, Sigmund 321, 356
Friedman, Morton P. 209
frustration 231
fulfillment 188, 192, 200, 203, 231, 232
functional state 324, 349; and belief 220; *see also* state
functionalism 5, 7, 11, 83, 87, 119, 120–131, 147, 157, 304–305, 358, 368

game configuration 105–106
Garrett, M. F. 244
gating 223, 226, 237
generals 12, 13–14
generative grammar, *see* grammar
generative rules, *see* rule, rewriting; *see also* Post production
Gettier, Edmund 163, 213, 215–218, 255, 265, 256

Gettier counterexamples 163, 213, 215–218
gestalt pattern 54, 107, 128
gestalt theory 54, 186
ghost in the machine 110
Gilmore, P. A. 350
goal 231
goal directedness 110–111
Gödel, Kurt xv, xvi, 5, 28–29, 102, 103, 107, 110, 232, 307, 354, 362
Gödel theorems 28, 102–103, 339, 340; formula 103; argument against mechanism 102–103, 105, 107, 348
Goldberg, Rube 72
Goldstein, Herman 27, 340, 348
Goodman, Nelson 169, 187, 190, 306, 350, 355, 366
grammar 30, 35, 43; context-free phrase structure 30–33; equivalent 155; finite state 36, 43, 58, 340–341; transformational 34; universal 145–146, 147, 149, 156f
grammatical complexity and meaning 248
grammatical rule, *see* rule
grammatical transformation 68
Graves, C. 154–155
Greenblatt, R. D. 348
Grice, Paul 121, 221–226, 280, 281, 283, 350, 357
guiding 4, 148, 305, 316, 354, 361; and music perception 194; strong and weak 77–80, 86, 91
Gunderson, Keith 339

Haack, Susan 363
habit 86
haecceity 365–366
Hajek, P. 348
hallucination 254–256
halting problem, *see* recursive unsolvability
Harman, Gilbert 113, 149, 153, 158, 247, 249, 252, 280, 360
Harmon, Leon xvi
Hartmanis, J. 357
Havranek, T. 348

Hebb, H. O.
Helman, David xvi
Hempel, Carl G. 112, 312, 314
Herder, Rick xvi, 342
Hesse, Mary 346
heuristics, *see* computer program
Hilbert, David 5, 328
Hilbert programme 339
Hill, Christopher xiv, xvi, 336, 355
Hintikka, Jaakko 282, 288, 289, 358
Hobbes, Thomas 3
Hollander, John 357
holism 221, 232, 357
homomorphism 63
homunculus 100
Hoy, Ronald 350
Huffman, David 45, 341
Hume, David 76, 113, 219, 339
humanoid, *see* robot
hypothesis formation and perception, *see* perception
hypothetical construct 158

icon 358
idea 246
idealism 3, 93
idealized language user (exemplar) 264–265; and truth definition 275–276
identity: of acceptance 182, 183; of algorithms 292, 345; of belief 214, 260, 283–284; of computation 181, 182, 260, 262; of intension 295; of programs 185; of property type 179–182, 200, 207, 289, 354; of propositions 215, 284; of response 124–125, 254; of states 122–124, 325–329; of structures 291; of strings 63; substitutivity of 254, 258, 294; in extended sense 184, 195; *see also* synonymy
identity theory illusion 8, 254, 256
immediately demonstrative term 241; *see also* name
indeterminism 116; see also automaton, backward indeterministic and probabilistic
individuation of networks 51, 67, 79, 344, 345; *see also* identity of states

inductive construction 103; *see also* learning
inexistence 142, 156, 163, 220
infinitary character of language 30–31, 143, 148
infinite regress of rules 359
information 159
information source 35–36
initial symbol 30
initial value 39
initial state 43
innate ideas 6, 63; *see also* innate structure
innate structure 68, 145, 147, 151
input 16, 18, 37, 60, 65, 70, 114; element 39, 62, 114, 126; energy 16–17, 340; external 38; excitatory 38, 98; inhibitory 38, 98; internal 38; receptors 38; signal 16–17, 23, 340; symbol 19, 30, 164; synaptic 37–38; *see also* stimulus
input free 17, 143
instantaneous description 21, 28, 63
instrumentalism 75
intellectus agens 173
intelligible species 173
intension 7, 246, 258, 281, 285, 295, 361; as fixing denotation 296–298
intention 361
intentional act 109–113; as emergent 110, 112; intentional object 285, 298; *see also* act
intentional term 109–112, 192; sentence 253
intentionality 5, 81, 109–112, 120–122, 142, 159, 208, 210f, 213, 282, 318f, 341
internal control 16, 23
internal state, *see* state
internalization 69, 74, 76–77
interpretation 98, 346
intervening variable 133, 135–141, 158, 308
intuitionism 263, 277
isomorphism 63–64, 324

James, William 92, 241, 242, 342
just noticeable difference 97, 287

Kadish, Emilie 364
Kadish, Mortimer xvi
Kalke, William 83, 324–325
Kaminsky, Jack xvi
Kant, Immanuel 87, 320, 322, 367
Katz, Jerrold 143–144, 154,
    360, 365
Keisler, H. J. 345
kind predicate 394
Kleene, Stephen 39, 42, 45, 55, 100,
    101, 128, 245, 341, 342, 366
know 215
knowledge: how 165; of 153–154; that
    153; tacit 144, 153–156; communal
    159–160; of language C 264; of
    sentences 241
knowledge and belief 163
Kochanski, Zdislaw 340
Kolers, Paul 209, 356
Kolmogoroff, A. N. 15, 54, 340
Kondrashin, Maestro 348
Kripke, Saul xv, 269, 297, 300–301,
    331–336, 368

Lady Lovelace (Augusta Ada Byron)
    104, 105, 110, 118, 348
lag time 37, 46
lambda conversion 57
LaMettrie, Julien 3, 15, 90, 328
language: context-free 30–34, 103, 151,
    152, 190, 243, 269; core (C) 264–
    272; external, internal 156; finite
    state 44, 105, 341; first order 264,
    362; generation 264; hierarchy 152,
    325; tenseless 264–266, 362; and
    belief 214; and representation 245;
    and winner solvability problem 190
language generation, see language
language learning, see learning
lapse in representation 202–203
learning: abductive 150, 158; biased
    patterns 358; human 106; language
    144–145, 150; machine 103–107;
    names 333
Lee, C. Y. xiv, 52, 189, 348, 352
Leibniz, Gottfried 3, 27, 55, 93, 340
Lettvin, J. Y. 164
level of understanding 248

Levi, Isaac 350
Levin, Michael 368
Lewis, C. I. 218, 219
Lewis, David 282, 286, 288, 296, 357,
    361
liking 226
linearity of doxastic operator 237; re-
    vised 272
linguistic creativity 143
listener 242–243
Loar, Brian 221, 352
Locke, John 241
Lockean idea 166
logic, formal 5, 24, 26, 75, 76, 340;
    components 46–47, 77; connective
    270; multi-valued 67, 341; net 48–
    49, 65, 78–80
logic of belief 237–240
logic of mind 2–4, 6–9, 76, 81, 87, 93,
    112, 142, 304, 339; and semantics
    243
logical distinction 305
logical reconstruction 133
logical state: as abstract entity 327–328;
    as described 329; as class of physical
    states 329; as symbol type 327
logical truth 281, 292
logically proper name see name
look-up process 95
Lucas, J. R. 102, 105, 151, 348
Lucretius 3, 15
luminous intensity 96, 98
Lycan, William 368

Machack 348
Machian theory 75
machine: thinking 89–92; nondeter-
    ministic 113–118; recognition 208–
    209; see also automaton
machine$_1$ 91, 95, 102–108, 348
machine$_2$ 91, 94, 106, 108, 111, 208–
    211, 347, 356
Margolis, Joseph 350
Martin, Joyce xvi
Markov algorithm 57
Markov process 35–36
material structure 67
materialism 3, 330–336

mathematical theorem 76
Matson, Wallace 94, 208, 217, 356
matter 3
McCarthy, John 137, 358
McClelland, James C. 98
McCulloch, Warren 16, 37, 43, 97, 128
Mead, G. H. 11, 323
Mealy, George 45, 341
meaning 7, as list 298, 362; as computation 7; and empirical realism 307; and intentionality 282; finiteness of 362; in communication contexts 280; psychology vs. logic of 281; reduction to reference 281; theories of 1, 251, 252, 262, 280; see also semantics
mechanism 3–5, 8, 10, 29, 54–56, 58, 81, 93, 95, 102–103, 116, 120, 160, 162, 304, 308–310, 320, 323, 324; and neorationalism 146–157; as basis for semantics 273–274; see also mind as rules
medieval realism 307
Melden, A. I. 348–349
memory 47, 73, 81, 239; boundless 344, 345; and finite quantification 239–240; content addressable 98
memory state, see state
Mendelson, Elliot 363
mental features 12–14, 57, 69, 75, 80, 109–112, 124, 246, 304; as states 260
mental occurrents 12–14, 93, 119, 322–327, 347; as logical states 324–329; as intentional 323; causal efficacy of 331; functional theory of 304, ·368; same as experience of 367–368
mental representation MR, see representation
mental set 54
Mentalese 158–160, 245
mentalism 119; see also neorationalism
metalanguage 103, 263; pragmatic 263
metaphysical theory 320, 321; logic of mind as 4, 9, 83–86
Mill, J. S. 300
Miller, George 55–56, 248
mind: as intentional 5, 6–7, 10; substantial 3; as system of rules 24, 304, 307

mind-body identity 209, 246, 325, 329, 333–336, 368; and logic of mind 330, 336
mind-body problem 11–14, 68, 304–305, 339
minimal deductive capability 241, 268
Minsky, Marvin 128, 320
modal sentence 361
model 75, 82, 162, 346; computer model of the world contrasted with self-description 319
molar 110, 349
molecular 110
Moliere, Jean 364
monads 93
Montague, Richard 282, 361
Moore, E. F. 45, 140, 228, 341, 357
Moore machine 228, 357
moral conduct 321; as internalized expectation 321–322
moral sense 321–322, 367
Morgenbesser 350
morse code 353
Mozart, Wolfgang 105
Mycelski, Jan 340

Nagel, Ernest 102, 103, 313
Nagel, Thomas 11, 339
name; proper 240; logically proper 241; as predicate 362
n-ary predicate 270, 294
natural kind 365
natural language programming 249
natural selection 356
naturalism 3, 6–9, 11, 204, 321, 339, 347
Nearly, R. 348
necessary identity aposteriori 332–334; see also mind-body identity
Necker cube 167, 207
negative feedback, see feedback
Neisser Ulric 353
Nelson, Hendrieka xvi, 356
neorationalism (NR) 142–157
nerve network 37–41, 67
network formula, see formula
neuron 37
next state 23; see also state

Newell, Allen 317
Newman, James 102, 103
Nilsson, Nils 354
nominalism 88, 305, 307, 346
nonalgorithmic skill 104; see also heuristic computer program
nondeterminism 113–118, 314; see also automaton
nondeterministic finite automaton (NFA), see automaton
nonpropositional perception 199
nonterminal symbol 30
not, see logic component
noumenal self 320
nucleotide 98
null stimulus, response 343
null string 60

object 200–201; as equivalence class 362; see also perceptual object, propositional object
observation sentence 233
observation term 131–132
occasion sentence 233
Occam's Razor 304
one-token-many-type condition 167–168, 178
one-type-many-token condition 168–169, 183–186
ontology 3
ontological commitment 257, 282
ontological primacy 330
Oppenheim, Paul 312, 314
or gate, see logic component
output 37, 45, 49, 60, 61, 70, 114; element 62; see also response
output function 41, 45, 49, 54

pain 11, 12; intentional 330, 368
panpsychism 305, 329–330, 368
Papert, Seymour 128, 370
parallel computation 175
parallelism 76, 81, 127, 128, 350
Pao, Tsyh-Won Lee 150
partial recursive function 180, 214, 260, 291
partial word function 242
particular 12

pattern recognition 91; see also machine recognition, perception
pattern type 163; see also identity type
Peacocke, Christopher 357
Peirce, C. S. xv, 80, 83, 102, 121, 190, 339, 346, 349, 351, 357, 365
Peirce stroke 46
perceivable 207
perceiving 206–207
perception 9, 45, 69, 91, 162–163, 166–171; analytic 187, 194; as inferential 232; as matching 234; of music 184; of sentences 184; of relations 241–242, 358–359; gestalt 167, 176, 195; propositional 194; and hypothesis formation 210; and truth 278–279
perceptual belief, see belief
perceptual object 163, 199–208; kinds of 246; and representation 288
perceptual state 322, 323; and imagery 246; see also state, final
performance 34, 69, 75, 144, 147–148, 351; and functionalism 310–311; see also competence
Perkins, David 209
Peterson, Oscar 248
Phenomenal certainty 333–336
phonological rules 144
phrase structure language 30, 303, 345; see also language
physical geometry 76, 346
physical states 11, 77, 78, 325–326, 339; see also state
physicalism 10, 93, 339, 347
Piaget, Jean 177
Pierce, R. S. 341
Pitts, Walter 16, 37, 43, 97, 129
Pitts-McCulloch nerve nets 37–39, 341
Place, U.T. 339
place-holder 8, 226–227, 316; see also disposition, subjunctive conditional
Plantinga, Alvin 363
Plato 163, 213, 306, 356
Platonism 7, 306, 328, 364–365, 366
polygenic rules 36, 113; see also rule
Popper, Karl 328
positivism 1, 75–76, 329

possible world 285, 289, 290, 332, 335; as alternative to actual 286, 288; and logical truth 292; and state description 364; semantics 281–282, 296

Post, Emil xvi, 15, 18, 28–29, 57, 101, 340

Post production 29, 32, 104; *see also* rule, rewriting

practical reason 367

pragmatics 212, 360; contrasted with Montague 361

prediction 75, 314

present state 23; *see also* state

probabilistic automaton; *see* automaton

production rule; *see* rule, rewriting

program, *see* computer program

program scheme 324; *see* computer program

proof 24, 340

property type 179–182, 189; *see also* identity

proposition 282–290; as set of possible worlds 282

propositional attitude 255

propositional function of time 37, 96

propositional object 156; 284–285; as a pair; communality of 290; subjectivity of 288; and expectation 287; *see also* Democritean world

propositional knowledge 154–7 ception 213

psychological state, *see* state, finite state identity theory

psycholinguistics 77

psychological explanation 84

psychology 9, 53, 75–84, 305; of perception 213

psychosemantics 160

pulse divider 77–79

purpose 120–122, 231, 358

purposive explanation, *see* explanation

Putnam, Hilary xvi, 3, 80, 83, 103, 121, 190, 277, 282, 297–299, 300, 302, 307, 323–329, 346, 349, 351, 357, 363, 365, 368

Pythagorean diagram 184

Pylyshyn, Zenon 357, 383

quadruple (Turing machine) 19, 52

quale 322

quality space and reception 165

qualitative dissimilarity 151–152

quanta 96, 97

quantification 239–240, 270

quantifiers, order of 83

quantum mechanics 140

Quine, Willard V. xiv, xv, xvi, 6, 7, 9, 11, 12, 76, 132, 164, 165, 220, 233, 242, 257–258, 266, 282, 284f, 286–288, 291, 299, 306, 332, 339, 345, 350, 353, 357

Rabin, M. O. 44, 367

random choice 191, 353

random number table 106

rationalism 5, 6, 119, 157; *see also* neorationalism

Reagan, Ronald 283, 306

real: strongly 80, weakly 80; rules 305

real distinction 305

realism 3; classical 4, 160, 305–307, 346; empirical 68, 84–88, 305, 316, 320, 335, 365

realization 67, 74, 77–81, 345

recursive 4, 57; arithmetic 85, 346; function 25–26, 340; set 172, 340; unsolvability 190

recursive function, *see* recursive; *see also* partial recursive function, partial word function

Reed, Stephen 209

reception 63, 164–166, 210

recognition, *see* acceptance, perception

receptual class 357

reducibility 113, 128, 147, 339, 347; of intentional terms 308, 366; of mental rules 307; of theories 305, 307–308, 366; of purposive to mechanical explanation 314; to computer programs 317, 367; to neuroscience 308–311

reduction sentences 137–141

reference 259, 293, 332; as dispositional 266; as triadic 263; causal theory of 300–303; vague 277

Reid, Thomas 321, 367

rejection 163, 171, 353
relational type 241–243
relational theory of belief, *see* belief as relation
represent 8, 346
representation: referential 156–60, 234; mental 5, 212, 233–234, 244–246, 278, 363; surrogative 156, 203, 210, 234; Rep relation 202–208, 213, 216–218, 265, stimulus pattern as 233
representation theory of mind (RTM) 158-160
resemblance 170–171, 195–198, 192; paradigm 195–196, 355; typal 196 355; *see also* family resemblance
response 59, 62; element 62, 65; *see also* output
rest potential 67
rigid designator 300–303, 322
robot 110–111, 112
Rochester, N. 342
role-playing states 5, 6, 120–122
Root, Michael 345
Rorty, Richard 12, 13, 14, 120
Rosenblueth, Arturo 358
Rounds, William 149
Rowland, Vernon xvi
rule: of inference 24, 26; of mind 69, 75, 77, 142–143; automaton 2, 339; grammatical 30, 144, 339, 345; recursive 26, 28, 35, 42, 85, 87, 159, 193, 345; rewriting 29, 30–34, 56, 63, 68; structures 30, 149; Turing machine 19; computers as structures of 52–53; functional state as 43; nerve network as 39–41; transformation 30, 146, 149
Rumelhart, David E. 98
Russell, Bertrand 225, 241, 249, 278, 284, 332, 336, 362
Ryle, Gilbert 8, 109, 111, 131f, 157, 162, 328, 339, 349, 354, 357
Rynasiewicz, Robert xvi

Sagan, Carl 254
Samuel, Arthur, 105, 107, 348

satisfaction 231
satisfies 217–272
Saussure, F. de 350
Sayre, Kenneth 209, 354
scene analysis 166
Schack, Paul 356
Scheffler, Israel 223–224, 357
Schneider, R. E. 67, 70
Schopenhauer, Arthur 11
Schwartz, Robert 359
Scott, Dana 44
Scriven, Michael 347
Searle, John xv, 34, 112f, 159, 317–19
second, secondness 322, 339
second order arithmetic 366
self-reference 28
self-description 107, 150, 189–192, 232, 342, 354, 355; *see also* automaton
self-reproduction 341
Selfridge, Oliver 353
semantics 212, 241, 246, 351f; and communication 243, and belief 252; pragmatical 267, 269, 360, 361; reductive 282
semantics of belief 212; *see also* belief, psychology of
semantical content 158f
semantical rule 144
semi-algorithm 104–105
sense 259; as mode of presentation 259, 266–263; as object 259
sense data 246
sense modality 178
sensible predicate 207, 238, 240
sentience 11; and intentionality 208–209
sequential machine, *see* automaton
serial 81
serial adder 47–49, 65–66
set theory 85, 292
Shamir, E. 341
Shanker, S. G. xvi
Shannon, Claude 35, 37, 340
Sheffer, Henry 358
Shimony, Abner 205
signals and control 15–18, 340
significance and social institutions 284

Simon, Herbert 70
simulation 356, 367; *see also* model
Skinner, B. F. 1, 132, 136
Skolem, Thoralf 346
Sloman, Aaron 317
Smart, J. C. C. 92–93, 102–103, 329–330, 339, 347, 367
solipsism 8
Smolensky, Paul 98
space-time quantum 97
speaker 241–243
speech in apes 146, 351
speech recognition 356
specious present 335
Spence, Kenneth 135–136
stability principle 223
standing sentence 233
state 19, 54, 295, 319; automaton 120, 123, 126–127; elements 39, 51, 126–127; external 141; internal 93, 95, 98, 113, 114–117, 122–131; perceptual (or final) 43, 163, 171, 173, 214, 229, 322, 323; logical 324–329; physical 324; space 122 291
Sterns, R. E. 357
step function 97
Stevens, C. F. 67
S-R theory 54, 95
stimulus 54, 62, 97–98, 165, 353; element 40; equivalence class of 165; free 143, 321; level 97; type 344; *see also* input
stimulus free, *see* stimulus, *also* automaton, autonomous
stimulus pattern 163, 165, 213; and automaton strings 164; and memory
string 18, 20, 35
string reverser 18–23
string identity, *see* identity
stored program, *see* computer program
structure 63–68, 123, 175
subjunctive conditional 8, 62, 227; and mathematical description 316; and recursive rule 129
subroutine 68, 233
substitutivity of identity, *see* identity

subtraction 73–74, 345
subsystem 70, 73
superautomaton (T') 189–190
Suppes, Patrick 150
surface structure 29
symbol 338
synonymy 7, 215; of sentences 215, 284, 291
synthetic 76

taking 165, 169–170, 188, 195, 198, 200–202, 213, 222, 355; computation 191–192; and desire 232; and template matchine 246; and idealized language user 265; and truth 265; simulation of 246
Tarski, Alfred 82, 246, 269, 271, 273–277, 363
template matching 209, 234, 246
terminal symbol 30
Terrace, Herbert 351
Thatcher, James 354
theorem 24
theorem proving 110
theoretical term 76, 132
theories 75–81; strong 80, 85; weak 86
thirds, thirdness 12, 322
Thomas, Stephen 366
Thomistic philosophy 306
Tolman, E. C. 110–111, 342, 348, 349
topic neutral term 94, 109
tote unit 55–56
transformation rule 30, 146, 149
transformational grammar 34; *see also* grammar
transition function 40, 45, 54; extended 61
transition probability 35, 343
truth 75–77, 80, 102–103; correspondence theory 277; definition 273, 274; full-blooded theory 276–278; modest theory 252; and effective decidability 276–277; *see also* perception
truth function 37
Tuomela, Raimo 350

Turing, A. M. 15, 18–20, 27, 28, 35, 39, 43, 89–92, 94, 100, 101, 104, 107, 108, 142, 152, 328, 340, 347, 348, 349, 359
Turing machine 5, 18–24, 57, 61, 81–86, 99–101, 104, 105, 172, 178, 182, 185, 190, 238; as abstract automaton 42; as formal system 28, 34; as production rule system 42; universal 27, 99
Turing computable function 26, 100
Turing machine tape 19, 42
Turing's Thesis 26

unexplained intelligence 100, 112
unit set (of individual) 261
universals 205, 365
universal Turing machine, see Turing machine
universal grammar, see grammar
universality and discrimination condition 167, 171, 178–182, 185

vague input, see degraded stimulus
van Gogh, Vincent 168
van Rooten, L. 354
verifiability 75
virtual acceptance, see acceptance
virtual set 189, 193
vocabulary 30
Voltaire, Francois 306
von Neumann, John xiv, 5, 15, 27, 189, 232, 340, 341, 352, 354

von Neumann machine 99

Wang, Hao 344
wave theory 96, 97
Weaver, Warren 35
Webb, Judson 339
Whitehead, Bruce 354
Whorf, Benjamin 178, 354
Whorfian theory 178
Wiener, Norbert 16, 232
Wiener, Phillip 340
will 319–320
Williams, B. A. O. 16
winner 187, 201–202, 213; see also state
winner problem, see recursive unsolvability
Winograd, Terry 347
Wittgenstein, Ludwig xiv, 132, 170, 195–197, 209, 349
Wittgensteinian behaviorist 349
Wolman, Benjamin 353
Wolter, Allan 305
world knot 11, 12
worm, see annelid
Wright, Jesse 346

Yagasawa, Takashi xvi

Zadeh, Lofti 313
Zuriff, G. E. 351